PEDIGREES OF SOME

OF THE

EMPEROR CHARLEMAGNE'S DESCENDANTS

Compiled by

MARCELLUS DONALD ALEXANDER R. von REDLICH

With a Foreword by

PROFESSOR ARTHUR ADAMS, Ph.D.

Volume I

Southern Historical Press, Inc.
Greenville, South Carolina

Please direct all correspondence and book orders to:
SOUTHERN HISTORICAL PRESS, Inc.
PO Box 1267
Greenville, SC   29602-1267

Originally published 1941
        by: Order of Crown of Charlemagne
ISBN #978-1-63914-233-0
Printed in the United States of America

PEDIGREES OF SOME OF THE
EMPEROR CHARLEMAGNE'S DESCENDANTS

PEDIGREES OF SOME OF THE EMPEROR CHARLEMAGNE'S DESCENDANTS

Compiled By

MARCELLUS DONALD R. von REDLICH, LL.B., LL.D., Ph.D.

Fellow of the Royal Society of Literature of the United Kingdom; Honorary Member of the British Association of Descendants of the Knights of the Garter, Institut Grand-Ducal de Luxembourg, &c. Membre-Adhérer de l'Académie Diplomatique Internationale. Member of Order of the Crown of Charlemagne (Delegate General), P.E.N. (London Centre), Society of the Sons of the Revolution, Military Order of Foreign Wars, Military Order of the World War, New England Historic Genealogical Society, National Genealogical Society, Hungarian Heraldic Genealogical Society, &c.

With A Foreword By

PROFESSOR ARTHUR ADAMS, Ph.D.

Fellow of Society of Genealogists of London, Society of Antiquaries of London, Royal Society of Literature of the United Kingdom; Registrar General and one of the Priors of the Order of the Crown of Charlemagne; Registrar General of the Order of the Founders and Patriots of America; Registrar General of General Society of Colonial Wars; Member of Committee on Heraldry, New England Historic Genealogical Society. Member of: Society of the Sons of the Revolution, Order of Three Crusades, Saint Nicholas Society, American Historical Society, Modern Language Association of America, Connecticut Historical Society, &c.

VOLUME I

Publishers:

ORDER OF THE CROWN OF CHARLEMAGNE

1941

PREFACE

This book, which I have called PEDIGREES OF SOME OF THE EMPEROR CHARLEMAGNE'S DESCENDANTS, is not a superficial collection of elaborate pedigrees; it contains the true facts in regard to names known to history and of many families who have contributed in some way, great or small, to the development of our culture, progress, and government. Furthermore, in these pages may be found corrections of a multitude of errors hitherto accepted without challenge in other genealogical works, and some of the more distant historic and domestic alliances are brought to light, where previously they were either ignored or misstated.

Genealogy is a component part of history and biography, to which it is a help or a hindrance in proportion as the historical evidence is followed or ignored. For we must understand that the science of genealogy is not simply the tracing of a line of descent; it points the direction of our heredity. Just as a name or title is transmitted, so also are most of the physical and mental characteristics capable of being transmitted, handed down. These also must fall into the province of the genealogist who must weigh every factor in the searching out of a family tree.

While the remark that "he who careth not whence he come careth not whither he goeth," is a bit too caustic, utter insensibility to family origin is felt by few. Those who have no knowledge whatsoever of their ancestry affect an attitude of contempt to screen their innate jealousy of others who possess pride of ancestry.

Pride of ancestry is not to be confused with pride of birth. The former is an unselfish emotion, while the possessor of the latter is probably a snob. Nor is one's interest in one's fore-fathers restricted to those who reflect honor on their descendants, but rather it is a longing to know the history of those whose blood flows in our veins, to preserve humbly our links with the past in hopes that our children may perform the same act of filial love for us. Rarely does man build for himself alone. He struggles in the short span of years allotted to him to set up and/or preserve a code of honor, and perhaps to provide material comfort for those of his flesh and blood who are to follow him; he is a link in a chain uniting the past and the future. As a man lives in the persons of his ancestors, so does he wish to live in his children and his children's children.

The boastful and false pedigree-maker has brought pride in long descent into ridicule, and genealogy has similarly suffered discredit. From such as these, the satirist finds unlimited material for his hollow barbs. The more deprecating the satirist becomes, the more one may suspect that he 'protesteth too much.' As Sir Egerton Brydges wrote, (AUTOBIO-GRAPHY, p. 153): "There is no subject more difficult to be dwelt on than that of honourable descent; none on which the world are greater sceptics, none more offensive to them; and yet there is no quality to which every one in his heart pays so great a respect." But as long as genealogical studies are honestly employed in the search after the truth only, liberation from the petty present, improvement of the living and esteem of the dead, the satirist may beat his drum of echoing envy and only the ignorant will heed him.

History tells us that Armorial Bearings originated about the time of the First Crusade. About that period, when a family began to gain prominence, it chose an emblem by which it was known. In like manner the soldier suited his fancy in Armorial Bearings. And as the family and the soldier became famous so did their respective Arms. The head of a family inherited his late father's Arms as well as his sword, and his son inherited from him, until Armorial Bearings became a matter of inheritance and therefore something to be treated with respect and esteem.

Anything that commands respect is soon copied, and prolific copying brought abuse. There were those who had no Armorial Bearings and wished to have them. The demand made the supply, and merchants soon sprang up who could "draw" Armorial Bearings from the imagination. Centuries ago the official heralds did what they could to suppress the illegal use of Arms, but the general public did not know of the official standing and authority of the Officers of Arms of Great Britain and Ireland. It was, and is, ignorant of heraldic knowledge and law. So the quacks flourished—and flourish. Then, as now, the practice is the same. There are two methods generally used. First, the coat-of-arms is drawn entirely from imagination and is spurious from start to finish, and secondly, absolutely legitimate Arms belonging to old and distinguished families, extant or extinct, are assigned to people bearing a similar name without a shadow of connection, or even a remote chance of being able to establish a descent from the ancient family. In comparison with this heraldic folly, others, and many there are, seem mere triflings.

The laws of the United States provide no penalties for these fraudulent practices, yet they must not be tolerated if these honorable emblems are ever to regain their significance and splendor. The only way by which the innocent public may be enlightened is by advertising, insofar as the law permits, the evil these imitators are perpetrating. Thus, those who have been unconscious victims may right their mistakes, and the unwary will be preserved from falling into the same trap. As for those who are aware of the laws of Arms and disregard them—they are soon found out when an experienced eye falls upon the description of "their" Arms.

It will be difficult indeed to maintain the ancient significance of these signs and tokens of honor when they can be secured so cheaply now at second-hand stores or drawn by "creative" artists. Nor is it to be wondered at that those families possessing their own Arms do not particularly care to display them. If the shining light of chivalry and honor be waning, then let their signs and tokens go with them; it is monstrous to consider that the former may be dead, and their signs degenerating into a senseless farce, into disgraceful abuse. But perhaps the pendulum, having swung so far in one direction, will return equally in the opposite, and honor and its emblems will once more hold the place they occupied "when knighthood was in flower."

After the illegal use of coats-of-arms, comes the illegal use of titles. I put Arms first because they are the more difficult to trace.

Each European nation has its own laws and rules governing the inheritance of a title. The rule in England and the *general* rule in Germany and other countries is that only the oldest or the oldest surviving son has the right to the title his father held in the nobility; rarely can a second, third, or fourth son legally use his father's rank. But when the younger sons come to America! Often they are aided and abetted by their American wives who seek to bask in the distinction of a title despite law or family regulations. Examples of this abound in these United States. The American public, however, is becoming more blasé, less impressed, and accordingly such deceptions will disappear.

Swamped under the wholesale "trade in blazon," a few groups are struggling to help and safeguard those who are entitled to Armorial Bearings and titles. In England, Ireland, and Scotland the Officers of Arms can act to suppress the illegal use of Arms and like bogus practices. But in America we have no official and legal means of curbing such activities. However, the New England Historic Genealogical Society has organized an able Committee on Heraldry. Armorial

Bearings may be registered with this Committee. If the coat-of-arms is found in order and to belong to the person or family submitting it, it will be formally enrolled. On the other hand, if the Arms do not belong to the person or family submitting them, the eminent and sincere experts serving on this Committee, solely for the love of truth and opposition to the abuse of hereditary rights, will quickly discover and point out to the applicant the impropriety of the use of such Arms.

The only proper method of legally securing a coat-of-arms is to make formal petition to the official authorities concerned with such matters in England, Ireland, or Scotland for a grant of Arms. If the petitioner is deemed a proper person to bear Arms and possesses the required ancestry, &c., a grant of Arms by Letters Patent will be made.

Here let me say that many so-called heraldic Colleges and Societies exist in America, Canada, France, and in other European countries, pretending to possess official status and the right to register, assign, or grant Armorial Bearings and perhaps even titles. These pretenses are ridiculous and without any official or governmental status. Such Colleges and Societies are purely private organizations. The only exceptions to this, in addition to England, Ireland, and Scotland, are the Kings of Arms of Spain, who are governmental officials, and the governmental bureaus or departments specially established for such purposes in Belgium, Germany, Hungary, Italy, Luxemburg, and the Vatican. Similar governmental departments existed in Austria and Portugal during the monarchies as well as in the various Grand Duchies, Duchies, and Principalities that existed in Europe prior to the first World War.

While the above paragraphs are in the nature of a digression from my main subject, they are perforce related to genealogy just as branches are to the tree. In dealing with genealogical matters, their abuses are not to be ignored or suffered in silence.

Probably most families that possess a pedigree of more than eight generations in the paternal line, have a royal line; that is, a descent from the Kings of England and France, although they may be quite unaware of it. The difficulty is to trace and prove their descent.

It is vastly more interesting to work out a royal descent than to trace the pedigree of one's paternal ancestor. The excitement of seeking links to the British and French Royalty is entirely lacking when plodding on to an unknown goal. In the paternal line one is confronted with generations of names practically unknown. The most one may hope for is to be able to find the facts of birth, baptism, places of abode, marriage, death—that is, if one can find the names—and often their Wills. This is generally the sum total of a paternal search, and while these estimable ancestors were no doubt good and solid citizens in their times, history rarely, if ever, extols their memory. Very few of us can claim in our paternal ancestry an Adams, an Allyn, a Bacon, a Batte, a Bruen, a Bulkeley, a Bulloch, a Byrd, a Calvert, a Carleton, a Deighton, a De La Warr, a Dudley, a Fairfax, a Hamilton, a Hancock, a Haynes, a Patrick Henry, a Jefferson, a John Paul Jones, a Lewis, a Ludlow, a Marbury, a Morris, a Pelham, a Penn, a Reade, a Saltonstall, a Warner, a Washington, a West, or a Wyllys, and those of us who can, have a reason for pride.

Royal descent implies the possession of distinguished historical personages as ancestors—men and women whose achievements are recorded in the pages of history—not only emperors and kings, but statesmen and warriors who have made history. It is true that the quantity of these ancestors' blood that flows in any descendant's veins must be infinitesimally small, but so is the blood of that distant paternal ancestor. We can work out the fraction for ourselves! Though we may have but little of their blood coursing in our veins, yet we are proud of being descended from them, for they are our lineal ancestors. Furthermore, probably we have as much of their blood as any other person now living.

Now as to the facts of a royal descent. First, the descent from royalty can be traced only through a succession of female lines; secondly, King Henry VII is the *last* English King from whom anyone, outside royalty, can trace a legitimate descent.

The younger sons and daughters of the Plantagenet Kings frequently intermarried with nobles and knights, and it is mostly through the issue of these marriages that English and American families may trace their royal descents. Descent from King John is derived through the marriage of his daughter, Eleanor, with Simon de Montfort, Earl of Leicester. The last English Sovereign from whom commoners may trace descent, as stated above, is King Henry VII, whose daughter, Mary Tudor, Dowager Queen of France, married Charles Brandon, Duke of Suffolk. Since the year 1515, English princesses have intermarried only with the royalty of other European countries; thus no descent can be traced from the Blood Royal, with the exception of morganatic marriages, during the reigns of the Guelphs and the Stuarts.[1] In the last few decades, however, we find this ancient practice reverted to by the marriages of the Princess Royal Louise to the Duke of Argyll, the Princess Royal Louise Victoria Alexandra to the Duke of Fife, the Princess Royal Mary to the Earl of Harewood, and the Duke of Windsor to Mrs. Wallis Warfield Simpson.

The following twelve royal princes and princesses, children of Kings John, Henry III, Edward I, Edward III, and Henry VII, are the ones from whom royal descent can most frequently be traced.

King John father of:

    (1)   Princess Eleanor, wife of Simon de Montfort.

King Henry III father of:

    (2)   Prince Edmund, "Crouchback," Earl of Lancaster and Leicester.

King Edward I father of:

    (3)   Princess Eleanor, wife of Henry, Count of Bar in France;

---

1.   All reference to the illegitimate children of English Kings is omitted. However, Nell Gwynn's 311 living descendants are listed in the January, 1901, issue of THE GENEALOGICAL MAGAZINE. Other issues of that magazine contain many royal lines.

     (4)   Princess Joan of Acre, wife of Gilbert de Clare, Earl of Gloucester and Hertford;

     (5)   Princess Elizabeth, wife of Humphrey de Bohun, Earl of Hereford and Essex;

     (6)   Prince Thomas, of Brotherton, Earl of Norfolk and Marshal of England;

     (7)   Prince Edmund, of Woodstock, Earl of Kent.

King Edward III father of:

     (8)   Prince Lionel, of Antwerp, Duke of Clarence;

     (9)   Prince John, of Gaunt, Duke of Lancaster;

    (10)   Prince Edmund, of Langley, Duke of York;

    (11)   Prince Thomas, of Woodstock, Duke of Gloucester.

King Henry VII father of:

    (12)   Princess Mary, Queen-Dowager of France, wife of Charles Brandon, Duke of Suffolk.

A descent from any one of these implies a descent from the Emperor Charlemagne, King Alfred the Great, William the Conqueror, St. Louis IX, King of France, Frederick I (of Hohenstauffen), surnamed Barbarossa, Rudolph of Habsburg, King of the Romans, founder of the Imperial House of Habsburg, and from several Scottish Kings. Descent from Edward III, Eleanor de Bar, Joan of Acre, or from Elizabeth de Bohun carries descent from the canonized St. Ferdinand III, King of Castile.[2] Furthermore, from Edward III, Thomas of Brotherton, and Edmund of Woodstock, one can establish descent from St. Louis of France.[3] Descent from Hugh Capet and a long line of French Kings is also opened up.

Descent from the Emperor Charlemagne and the French Kings is also made possible through the Vermandois Family, Isabel de Vermandois, daughter of Hugh the Great, son of Henry I, King of France, and through her mother Adelaide (Adelheid) de Vermandois; through Alice de Courtenay, wife of Aymer de Taillefer, Count d'Angouleme, and their daughter Isabel de Taillefer, wife of King John. Alice de Courtenay

---

[2] King Edward II and the three Princesses mentioned were his grandchildren.

[3] The second Queen of Edward I was a granddaughter of King St. Louis, Edward II's Queen was the French King's great-granddaughter.

was the daughter of Pierre de Courtenay, son of Louis VI, surnamed *Le Gros*, King of France, a descendant of the Emperor Charlemagne. Mathilda of Flanders, wife of William the Conqueror, was also a direct descendant of the Emperor Charlemagne.

Knowing the Royal sons and daughters through whom we can trace a line, the next question is how to make the necessary search.

A careful study of what one knows of one's own pedigree is the first important task. List the wives of all your paternal ancestors and note the male and female ancestry of each one in turn. Where dates of births, baptisms, marriages, and deaths are available note them by all means. Now in your chart you have your mother, both your grandmothers, four great-grandmothers, eight great-great-grandmothers, and so on *ad infinitum*, so far back as it is possible to trace them. It is very likely that after a few generations you will find an ancestor intermarrying into a family of royal descent. Watch the female lines in this family and try to trace them to some peer or baronet, or to some family whose pedigree is well known. Our next endeavor is to connect this family with one of those families undoubtedly descended from royalty: Vermandois, Beaumont, Berkeley, Neville, Seymour, Percy, Howard, FitzWilliam, Tyrwhit of Kettleby, Dymoke, Despenser, Courtenay, Burgh of Mawddy, Talbot, Manners, Ferrers, Grey, Russell, Flanders, Vane, Corbet, Mortimer, St. Leger, Bourchier, Devereux, Beauchamp, Stapleton, Clifford, Savage, Brudenell, Bohun, Blount, Cecil, Stanley, Egerton, Brydges, Greville, Pole, FitzAlan, De La Warr, Pelham, or some of the numerous other historic houses of the European nations, and having accomplished this, the connecting link with royalty will easily be found.

There is royal blood in people of all ranks of life. A Computation has it that there are about a hundred thousand descendants of Edward III, the difficulty, of course, is to trace the line back to him. The task of making such a search is amply rewarded in proving one's connection with all the traditions of a magnificent past. It is well stated that, "while a word from the King can put one into 'the Peerage,' or a successful financial speculation into the 'Landed Gentry,' birth alone entitles one to a place in the Plantagenet Roll, for on one side at least there must be a strain of gentle blood, through which it is possible to trace ancestry to the feudal and crusading days."[4]

Contrary to the methods used by some American and European genealogists, only such pedigrees as can be proved beyond any doubt, with absolutely unquestionable evidence, have been included in this volume. Fables, unsubstantiated traditions, family beliefs, and lines lacking sufficient proof are disregarded entirely. Each pedigree contained in this volume has been scrutinized generation by generation; in many cases this is the first time they have been set out in detail; that is, in a book of this kind published in the United States. The most careful search has been made and the most authoritative works have been consulted to assure accuracy. Every detail of every pedigree has been carefully checked. Every effort has been strained to render the book as authoritative as possible. However, I am aware that some imperfections are unavoidable in a first attempt of this character, and I ask for the leniency of my readers. I shall be appreciative to those who will call my attention to errors or omissions.

I am also glad to receive copies of all royal descents. They will be carefully studied and verified, and those found to be correct will be included in the volumes to be printed in the future, however, I reserve the unconditional right to use or reject such lines in the forthcoming volumes, without being required to give reasons for not inserting them.

Not a single pedigree appearing in this book has been paid for. No person whose name appears in this volume has been solicited for any fee or donation whatsoever, and no person gave any financial help.

Experimentation has proved it impossible to cite authorities habitually as such a course would have enlarged this volume intolerably. The majority of the works I have consulted appear in the Bibliography. Other works are listed also with the aim of affording readers some assistance in their own endeavors. Of course, not *all* of the books appearing in the Bibliography are *entirely* authoritative.

This is but the first volume of a series of books I intend to prepare for publication under the same title, therefore, I have marked this Volume I.

---

4 Ruvigny: THE PLANTAGENET ROLL OF THE BLOOD ROYAL, Exeter Volume, Preface, p. x.

This First Volume of this Work, as well as all future volumes, is published under the auspices and with the financial aid of the ORDER OF THE CROWN OF CHARLEMAGNE, a few of the lines herein contained are of the members of this distinguished Order which is composed of those who can unquestionably trace their descent back to the Emperor Charlemagne; however, the Order and its officers are in no way responsible for any of the statements herein contained, I alone am responsible for the statements, especially those contained in this Preface.

My profound appreciation is expressed to that outstanding, sincere authority on genealogy, Professor Arthur Adams, Ph.D., whose time and research have contributed so largely to the correction of many facts, and who has so graciously and carefully scrutinized the entire manuscript. Though it would be unfair to settle any responsibility for this work on Professor Adams, yet if no errors are found in the lines herein contained, the credit is largely due to his great knowledge and supervision. I also wish to express my thanks to Professor Adams for writing the Foreword.

My sincere thanks are also due and wholeheartedly conveyed to the Honorable Robert Munro Boyd, Jr., Judge Advocate General of the Order of the Crown of Charlemagne, for pertinent advice, and to Mrs. Harry Clark Boden, one of the Priors of the Order of the Crown of Charlemagne, for valuable services rendered.

I acknowledge, too, my indebtedness to my wife, Fredricka Adelaide Jeter Doll von Redlich, for assistance in reading and correcting proofs.

Marcellus Donald R. von Redlich

Post Office Box 53,
Old Post Office Annex,
Chicago, Illinois.

November 5, 1941.

FOREWORD

Somebody has said that a proved line of descent from Charlemagne is the supreme achievement in genealogy. If this be so, it is so not because of any inherent superiority such blood may give the descendant, though perhaps something might be said as to that, but because of the difficulty of finding records to give an unbroken line of descent for some twelve hundred years. Doubtless thousands, even millions, of people are descended from the great Emperor, though we should not be misled by computations in geomatrical progression to the belief that everybody on the earth *must* be. But not many thousands, probably, can prove the descent. So the search after a proved descent from Charlemagne has the interest of an historical quest and demands the use of all we know of the history of Western Europe through the centuries, all we can learn of sources and methods of historical research. The working out of a descent from the great progenitor of European royalty, for practically all the royalty at least of Europe descend from him, gives one a cross section of the whole scope and sweep of mediaeval and modern history to be gained hardly in any other way.

As to the value of such a descent when established: first, one can't go so far back into history with his ancestry without finding that he descends not only from Charlemagne but from any number of other men and women who have played their parts on the stage of human affairs. One gains a sense of an actual relationship with men and events that makes them real to him, not people and things merely read of in books.

Then they realize that their descent from Charlemagne and from other great figures of history is as real and as near as anybody else's. They come to a new realization of their obligation to their fellow men—a sense of *noblesse oblige* comes to them. However, the chief benefit, perhaps, is the gratification of what Aristotle regards as one of the chief characteristics of the human race. He says "all men by nature desire to know." So we all have a desire to know about our origins, even our remote origins, and we can't know our remote origins without learning of all the intervening generations. So, probably the gratification of the primary human desire to *know* is the chief satisfaction of our successful effort to trace our own origins to the greatest figure in mediaeval history.

Furthermore, in almost all cases the knowledge of such a descent has to be acquired by painful effort. Sometimes, of course, we are fortunate enough—if it be good fortune to miss the fun of the hunt—to find that some member of our family has done the work for us.

Still, this happens only occasionally. One is astonished to find how many people there are who can not name their eight great-grandparents, or even their four grandparents!

Let us suppose that a person's curiosity, his desire to know, about his ancestry is aroused. This may well come about, indeed frequently does come about, through an invitation to become a member of one of the hereditary-patriotic societies, which are so distinctive a feature of American social life, such as the D.A.R., the Colonial Dames, the D.A.C., the S.R., the S.A.R., or the Society of Colonial Wars.

Probably this first ambition is easily realized. One discovers that he has Revolutionary ancestry; then that he has Colonial ancestry. Then, if he is really "bitten," he wants to know who and what manner of people the ancestors of these Colonial ancestors were.

Here, again, he may be fortunate, for in the last one hundred years or so, much has been learned as to the origins of our Colonial immigrant ancestors. We have learned that most of them came from the middle classes; that there were relatively few of the "gentry," though there was probably a larger proportion of them among our immigrants than in the population of contemporary England. In some cases, one may trace back to a large number of Colonial immigrant ancestors and not find one whose English origin and ancestry are known, though more often one will find, perhaps, that the origin of one in ten of his immigrant ancestors is known. He is fortunate if he finds two or three families that belonged even to the minor gentry, and fortunate indeed if he finds even one ancestor with a known descent from a great family. Of course, this is only a rough generalization. Society was more or less stratified, and one may find that almost all the connections of a prominent ancestor belonged to the same stratum as that to which he himself belonged.

If the writer may be pardoned the personal element, he may illustrate his meaning and give an example of the procedure to be followed in working out a Magna Charta, a royal, and a Charlemagne descent.

He had traced back to, say, thirty immigrant ancestors; of these the English place of origin is known in about fifteen instances. That is an unusually high proportion; it is explained by the fact that he descends from a number of New Jersey Quaker families, the progenitors of which had purchased their land before leaving England.

However, there was not one family in this ancestry, the English origin of which had been traced. Yet, having been badly "bitten," he became very desirous of tracing his origin in England.

Naturally, he began with his first Adams ancestor in America, one Jeremy, who came to Cambridge, Massachusetts, with the Reverend Thomas Hooker's company in 1632. Knowing this much, one would think it should be possible without great difficulty to determine his parentage and then to work out his ancestry, for probably most of Hooker's company came from within a radius of ten or fifteen miles of Braintree and Chelmsford, Essex. Repeated efforts, nevertheless, failed to prove Jeremy's parentage. A rather surprising number of Jeremys of the period were found within the area of Hooker's influence, but all seemed to be accounted for or left as bare possibilities, the identity with my Jeremy unestablished.

In general, where one has only a clue of this general nature, one must do as I did. Fortunately, the search is often better rewarded.

Having failed with the Adams family, the next step was to study the families whose places of origin were definitely known from record evidence. One or two came from London; they were left till the last, for London with her myriad churches is a hard place in which to try to trace an ancestor.

Were the family names the names of well-known families? Did families of the names appear in the Visitations and the county histories? Of course, the commonness of the particular name must be taken into account. A name such as the proverbial Smith, Jones, or Brown gives no clues to the immigrant's place of origin.

Among the list of names of immigrant ancestors, appeared the name of Denne or Denn, a somewhat uncommon name. John Denne was one of the early Quaker settlers of Salem County, New Jersey.

A search through the indexes of Besse's "SUFFERINGS," an account of the persecutions to which the early Friends in England were subjected, brought to light the fact that John Denne was one of the "sufferers" in Canterbury, Kent. A glance at the Visitations of Kent and at Berry's "KENTISH GENEALOGIES" showed that the Denne family was one of the most ancient and best known families in that county.

Now the problem resolved itself into finding the place in the Visitation pedigree where my John Denne belonged.

At first, it seemed that this would be easy. My ancestor was a turner by occupation. I found a John Denne, turner, son of a Thomas Denne, sometimes Recorder of the city, but, alas, investigation established the fact that he lived and died in Canterbury. However, research led to the discovery of the records of birth of several of the children who accompanied my ancestor to New Jersey.

To make a long story short, long continued effort was necessary to establish the connection of my John Denne with the Visitation family. We had to go back five generations before we came to an ancestor appearing in the Visitation pedigree. Though the family is distinctively Kentish, yet naturally in the course of centuries, the bearers of the name had become numerous and were found in all walks of life.

Not finding a royal or Magna Charta line in any of the recorded marriages of the Denne family, the next step was to trace out the families brought into the Denne connection by marriage.

Again to make a long story short, it was found that our New Jersey Denne married in Canterbury 17 May 1662 Margaret Halsnode; that she was the daughter of John Halsnode and Margaret Ladd; and that John Halsnode was a son of another John Halsnode, who married 6 November 1608 Martha Harfleet.

Now the Harfleets are another ancient and distinguished family of Kent, appearing in the Visitations and the county histories.

Margaret's place in the family was soon found, by the aid of Planché's "A CORNER OF KENT." From this point on it was not difficult to work out by the aid of the Visitations, etc., the descent from Charlemagne that appears elsewhere in this book. Indeed, there was only one "snag"; the books had made Margery Peche, who married Sir Nicholas de Criol, the daughter of the wrong man. This was corrected by the then recently published "Knights of Edward I" (Harleian Society). One must constantly be on his guard against such errors and check so far as possible visitations and other printed pedigrees by reference to printed original sources.

Now I was the proud possessor of a well-established line of descent from Charlemagne, but I had no Magna Charta ancestor. It was a close "miss," having a descent from Alice, sister of Robert Fitz Walter, "leader of the armies of God and of Holy Church" in the struggle with King John that lead to the granting of the Great Charter. Indeed, many of the books made her a daughter of Robert Fitz Walter instead of his sister, but a study of original documents showed conclusively that she was really his sister.

Having so far as possible worked out all the ancestry of John Denne, and a most interesting study it proved, without finding the desired Magna Charta baron, there was nothing to do but turn to another family and repeat the process. (Every ancestor for five generations was found and of course many others going back to a very remote past).

Among my New Jersey Quaker ancestors was one George Elkington. This is an unusual name and his place of origin was known. So, though the Elkington's of Mollington, Oxfordshire, are not a Visitation family, since the place of origin and the name of his father were known, I thought it would at least be interesting to learn more about George Elkington's ancestry, even if it did not prove to be noble or distinguished —and there was nothing to suggest that it would prove to be either.

George Elkington was a blacksmith and came over to Burlington County, New Jersey, about 1677 with Dr. Daniel Wills, of Northampton, England, who secured vast tracts of land in New Jersey.

About 1740, the heirs of George Elkington sent one John Gill, as their attorney, to England to recover an estate claimed by them. In support of their claim, a number of affidavits were taken in New Jersey by persons who had known George Elkington in England. These affidavits are of record in the Office of the Secretary of State, Trenton, New Jersey. They show that George Elkington came from Mollington in Oxfordshire and that his father's name was Joseph, and give much information concerning the family in New Jersey. This part of the story has an unusual ending, for the American claimants actually proved their descent and received the property. However, as in most such cases, probably John Gill, the lawyer, profited more than any of the heirs, not that his bill for services rendered was unreasonable. Trips to England and long-drawn-out litigation was necessarily expensive.

With so good a point of departure, a very satisfactory pedigree of the Elkington family was worked out. George was baptised at Mollington 7 December 1650, a son of Joseph and Ann Elkington. Joseph was the son of William of Mollington and a grandson of Richard of the neighboring parish of Cropredy. They were good yeomen, with nothing in particular of note connected with them. But what at once excited my interest and my hope was the fact that William Elkington married, as his second wife, Alice Woodhull, at Mollington 16 May 1588.

I knew the Woodhull family of this region was ancient and that much concerning it was in print. It was, for example, one of the families from which the distinguished Bulkeley family of New England is descended. So it became of the first importance, genealogically, to trace the ancestry of Alice Woodhull.

Fortunately this did not prove difficult.

The Mollington parish register showed that she was baptised at Mollington in 1570, a daughter of Thomas and Margaret Woodhull of Thenford, and later of Mollington. Thomas Woodhull's will was proved in the Prerogative Court of Canterbury 6 May 1594. He was a son of Fulke Woodhull, whose will was proved in the same Court, 16 May 1575, and whose wife was Alice, daughter of Henry Wickliffe, of Addington.

Northamptonshire. Fulke was a son of Lawrence Woodhull, of Thenford, whose wife was a daughter and co-heir of Edmund Hall, of Swerford, Oxfordshire.

The more remote generations are most correctly—and conveniently—given in Donald Lines Jacobus's "BULKELEY GENEALOGY," pp. 60-61. They are:

Fulke and Ann Newenham;
John and Joan, daughter of Henry Etwell, LL.D.;
Thomas and Isabel, daughter of Sir William Trussell;
Thomas and Elizabeth Chetwode;
Nicholas and Margaret Foxcote;
John and————————;
Thomas and————————;
John and————————;
Walter and Heloise, daughter of Hugh de Vivonia;
Saher and Alice;
Walter and Albreda Tallebois;
Walter and Roheise;
Simon and Sibil;
Walter the Fleming; and
Saher, who takes us back to the Conquest and to Domesday Book.

Here we have the clue to the long-desired Magna Charta baron, for Hugh de Vivonia married Mabel, daughter and one of the two co-heirs of William Mallet, one of the twenty-five Sureties for Magna Charta.

John Woodhull, son of Walter and Heloise de Vivonia, married Agnes, daughter of Henry de Pinkeny and Alicia, daughter of John Lindesay. John de Lindesay was a son of another John de Lindesay, whose wife was Marjorie, daughter of Earl Henry, Prince of Scotland.

Earl Henry was a son of David I of Scotland, who married Matilda, daughter and heir of Waltheof, Earl of Huntingdon, widow of Simon de St. Lis, Earl of Northumberland, through whom there is a descent from Charlemagne. King David I was a son of Malcolm III, King of Scotland, who married, secondly, St. Margaret, daughter of Eadward the Aetheling, and his wife Agatha of Hungary.

This pedigree offers much of interest and suggests numerous lines of investigation.

Who, for example, was Edmund Hall, whose daughter and co-heir, Alice, was wife of Lawrence Woodhull, of Thenford, Northamptonshire? It was found that he was a son of Richard Hall, of Swerford, Oxfordshire, whose wife was Elizabeth, daughter of Sir Edmund Rede, of Boarstall, co. Bucks, Knight. Much of interest in regard to this family appears in the Boarstall Cartulary, published by the Oxford Historical Society. A chart pedigree of the Fitz-Nigel, Haudlo, de la Pole, Bruyn, Rede, Dynham, Banastre, and Lewis connection appears in Lipscomb's "HISTORY AND ANTIQUITIES OF THE COUNTY OF BUCKINGHAM." This, however, is not accurate in all details. Interesting as this group of families is, it however yielded no Magna Charta or Charlemagne ancestry.

What, then, about the ancestry of Sir William Trussell?

In Ormerod's "HISTORY OF CHESHIRE," the descent is traced back: Lawrence, Sir Warin, to Sir William, who married Matilda, daughter and heiress of Sir Warin Mainwaring. Sir Warin Mainwaring married Agnes, daughter of Sir Peter Arderne, of a family going back to Anglo-Saxon, pre-Norman times. The Mainwaring line runs through Sir Thomas, Sir Roger, to Sir Ralph, who married Amicia, daughter of Hugh Kevelioc, Earl of Chester.

Hugh, Earl of Chester, was a son of Ranulph de Gernon, Earl of Chester, whose wife was Maud, daughter of Robert of Gloucester, an illegitimate son of Henry I, King of England, of course a descendant of Charlemagne. Robert, Duke of Gloucester, married Mabel, daughter of Robert Fitz Hamon and Sibyl de Montgomery. She was a daughter of Roger de Montgomery, Earl of Shrewsbury, and Mabel d'Alencon. Through the d'Alencon family there is a direct descent from Charlemagne, and also a descent from him through Hugh Capet and Robert I, King of France.

Sir Peter de Arderne, whose daughter Agnes married Sir Warin Mainwaring, was a son of Sir Walkelyn de Arderne who married Agnes, daughter and heir of Philip de Orreby. Philip de Orreby, who was a son of Philip de Orreby, Justiciary of Cheshire, married Leuca, daughter and heir of Roger de Montault. Roger de Montault married Cicely, daughter and ultimately one of the co-heiresses of William de Albini, third Earl of Arundel. William de Albini married Mabel, daughter of Hugh Kevelioc, Earl of Chester, and sister of Ranulph de Blundeville, Earl of Chester. William was son of

William, second Earl of Arundel, and grandson of William, the first Earl, who married Queen Adeliza, widow of Henry I, King of England. She was a daughter of Godefroy, the bearded, Duke of Lower Lorraine, by his first wife, Ide, daughter of Albert III, Count of Namur. From both Godefroy of Lorraine and Albert III, there are ascending lines to Charlemagne.

One would think this should suffice, but one's curiosity and desire to know carry him on.

Sir William Trussell married Margery Ludlow. A pedigree of the Ludlow family is given in the 1623 Visitation of Shropshire. Margery appears as a daughter of John Ludlow and Isabel, daughter of Sir Ralph Lingen. Blakerway in his "SHERIFFS OF SHROPSHIRE" and in an article in the Publication of the Shropshire Archaeological and Agricultural Society, tells us that Sir Ralph Lingen married a daughter of Fulke Pembridge and sister of Sir Robert Pembridge. The Pembridge line runs Fulke, Fulke, and Henry, who married Orabella, daughter of Sir William de Harcourt and Alice la Zouche. Sir William was a son of Sir Richard de Harcourt, who married Orabella, a daughter of Saher de Quincy, Earl of Winchester, a Surety for Magna Charta, whose wife was Margaret, daughter of Robert de Beaumont, or Bellomont, Earl of Leicester. Robert de Beaumont was a son of Robert, the second Earl of Leicester, and a grandson of Robert the first Earl, whose wife was Isabel de Vermandois, through whom there is another descent from Charlemagne.

Another illustration or two will, perhaps, suffice.

Sir Edmund Rede whose daughter Elizabeth married Richard Hall, of Swerford, Oxfordshire, married Christiana, daughter and heir of Robert James, of Wallingford, co. Berks. Robert James married Catharine, daughter and co-heir of Sir Edmund de la Pole, a brother of Michael de la Pole, Earl of Suffolk. Sir Edmund de la Pole married Elizabeth, daughter of Sir Richard de Haudlo. Sir Richard de Haudlo married Isabel, daughter of John de St. Amand, Lord St. Amand.

Burke's "EXTINCT PEERAGE" says that John de St. Amand married Margery, daughter of Hugh Despenser the Elder, Earl of Winchester. This was a "find" indeed. However, G. E. C.'s "COMPLETE PEERAGE" said it was doubtful if Hugh Despenser had such a daughter. The new "COMPLETE PEERAGE" did not mention the alleged marriage at all in its account of the Despenser family. So, with great regret and reluctance, I dismissed the matter from my mind.

I happened later to be looking through the printed volumes of "Ancient Deeds" issued by the Public Record Office of the British Government for an entirely different reason. By chance my eye fell on a document in which the names Despenser and St. Amand caught my eye. The document proved to be the marriage settlement of John de St. Amand and Margaret, daughter of Hugh Despenser.

So Burke, whose works one must always use with caution, was vindicated and the new "COMPLETE PEERAGE" had missed a trick! I understand the omission will be supplied when "St. Amand" is reached in the course of the work.

This discovery opened up a large field of most distinguished ancestry, for the wife of Hugh Despenser was Isabel, daughter of William de Beauchamp, Earl of Warwick. The wife of William de Beauchamp was Maud Fitz John, daughter of Sir John Fitz Geoffrey and his wife Isabel le Bigot. Isabel le Bigot was a daughter of Hugh le Bigot, Earl of Norfolk, Hugh was a Surety for Magna Charta, as was also his father Roger le Bigot, Earl of Norfolk. Hugh le Bigot, the Magna Charta Surety, married Maud, eldest daughter of William Marshall, Earl of Pembroke. William Marshall's wife was Isabel, daughter of Richard de Clare, Earl of Pembroke, the renowned Strongbow.

William de Beauchamp, father of William de Beauchamp who married Maud Fitz John, married Isabel Mauduit, daughter of William Mauduit, Earl of Warwick. Walter de Beauchamp, father of William who married Isabel Mauduit, married Isabel, daughter of Roger Mortimer, who was descended from William the Conqueror, and so from Charlemagne.

Gilbert de Clare, father of Richard de Clare, Strongbow, married Isabel de Beaumont, daughter of Robert, Earl of Leicester, whose wife Isabel de Vermandois, descends from Charlemagne.

William Mauduit, father of Isabel who married William de Beauchamp, married Alice de Newburgh, daughter of Waleran de Newburgh, Earl of Warwick. He was a son of Roger de Newburgh, Earl of Warwick, whose wife was Gundred de

Warren, a daughter of William de Warren, Earl of Surrey, whose wife was Isabel de Vermandois, descended from Charlemagne.

To sum up what may be learned from this narrative of one person's search for a descent from Charlemagne, we may say that, first, one should work out as completely as possible his ancestry in America. He should then note those ancestors whose English origin is known. He should ascertain whether the pedigrees of these families appear in the Herald's "VISITATIONS" or the county histories, using Marshall's "GUIDE." If so, having ascertained his American ancestor's place in the pedigree, he should consider the marriages carefully, carrying on the process till he finds a marriage leading to one of the great baronial families of the Middle Ages. He will then be on firm ground and can use with confidence the great works on the Peerage, such as G. E. C.'s "COMPLETE PEERAGE" and the new edition of this begun under the editorship of Vicery Gibbs and now perhaps two-thirds completed.

He will need to check the Visitation pedigrees with printed original sources, such as the Inquisitions Post Mortem, the Patent Rolls, the Close Rolls, the Liberate Rolls, Ancient Deeds, etc., brought out by the Public Record Office of the British Government. As he works, he will of course gain confidence and will come to know and use other source material.

Having once traced his ancestry to one of the great mediaeval baronial families, new vistas and new fields to conquer keep presenting themselves to one's eyes. The possibilities are endless. Some new goal is ever presenting itself to one's ambition. For example, the present writer has not yet found a Knight of the Garter in his ancestry. He wants to, and so a new quest is before him.

When the Baron von Redlich kindly asked me to work with him in the preparation of a volume of pedigrees traced back to Charlemagne, in spite of my misgivings as to my qualifications for the task, I gladly accepted his invitation.

I did so for two reasons: first, because of my interest in mediaeval genealogy, and secondly, because I knew that no effort would be spared to ensure the accuracy of the pedigrees included.

There are a number of volumes of royal pedigrees already in print. Whatever may have been the wish of the compilers in the matter of accuracy, there is not one of these books that is not disfigured by pedigrees the incorrectness of which is known to any competent worker in the field. Largely because of these hoary errors, the pedigree books of our societies based on roval descent are full of pedigrees the glaring inaccuracy of which any competent genealogist could demonstrate in half an hour.

It is doubtless too much to expect that no errors will be found in this book; we have to depend, especially for the Continental part of the pedigrees, on secondary works and cannot verify all the statements from original sources. However, only the most authoritative of these secondary sources have been used; it is believed that they are generally reliable, especially when their statements can be checked by reference to other works of high quality.

Whatever errors may be found are due not to any lack of will to secure accuracy or to any effort to achieve it, but to such mistakes as must be charged to our sources or to that fatal tendency to make mistakes that seems to inhere in human nature.

We assure our readers that every effort has been made to avoid mistakes and we express the fervent hope that we have fallen into but few.

Arthur Adams

September 7, 1941.

ABBREVIATIONS

A.B.—Bachelor of Arts
A.M.—Master of Arts
Apr.—April
Assn.—Association
Atty.—Attorney
Aug.—August

B.—Order of the
          Bath of England
b.—Born
B.A.—Bachelor of Arts
B.C.E.—Bachelor of
          Civil Engineering
B.C.L.—Bachelor of Civil Laws
B.D.—Bachelor of Divinity
B.E.—Bachelor of Engineering
B.Sc.—Bachelor of Science
Bt.—Baronet

C.—Companion
c.—*circa*
ca.—*circa*
Calif.—California
Can.—Canada
Capt.—Captain
Cav.—Cavalry
C.B.—Companion of the
          Bath of England
C.I.—Lady of the Imperial Order
          of the Crown of India
C.I.E.—Companion of the
          Indian Empire
C.M.G.—Companion of
          St. Michael and St. George
          of England
co.—County
Col.—Colonel
Coll.—College
Colo.—Colorado
Conn.—Connecticut
cr.—Created
C.S.I.—Companion of the
          Star of India
C.V.O.—Commander of the
          Royal Victorian Order

d.—Died
dau.—Daughter
D.A.C.—Daughters of the
          American Colonists

D.A.R.—Daughters of the
          American Revolution
D.C.—District of Columbia
D.C.L.—Doctor of Civil Laws
D.D.—Doctor of Divinity
dec.—Deceased
Dec.—December
Del.—Delaware
div.—Divorced
D.L.—Deputy Lieutenant
D.Sc.—Doctor of Science
D.S.O.—Distinguished
          Service Order
d.s.p.—Died without issue

E.e.et m.pl.—Envoy
          Extraordinary and Minister
          Plenipotentiary
E.E.—Electrical Engineer
etc.—et cetera
Exc.—Excellency

Feb.—February
Fla.—Florida
FM.—Field Marshal
F.R.S.L.—Fellow of the
          Royal Society of Literature
F.S.A.—Fellow of the
          Society of Antiquaries
F.S.G.—Fellow of the Society of
          Genealogists

G.—Order of the Garter
          of England
Ga.—Georgia
G.C.—Grand Cross
G.C.B.—Grand Cross of the
          Bath of England
G.C.H.—Grand Cross
          of Hanover
G.C.I.E.—Grand Commander
          of the Order of the
          Indian Empire
G.C.M.G.—Grand Cross of
          St. Michael and St. George
          of England
G.C.S.I.—Grand Commander
          of the Order of the
          Star of India

G.C.V.O.—Grand Cross of the
    Royal Victorian Order
        of England
G.F.a.—Order of the
    Golden Fleece of Austria
G.F.s.—Order of the
    Golden Fleece of Spain
G.O.—Grand Officer

h.—Heir - Heiress
H.G.—Order of the Holy Ghost
        of France
H.H.—His (Her) Highness
H.I.—Hawaiian Islands
H.I.H.—His (Her)
    Imperial Highness
H.I. & R.H.—His (Her)
  Imperial and Royal Highness
H.I.M.—His (Her)
    Imperial Majesty
H.M.—His (Her) Majesty
Hon.—Honorable
Honry.—Honorary
Ho. of Rep.—House of
    Representatives
H.R.H.—His (Her)
    Royal Highness
H.S.—Order of the
  Holy Sepulchre of Jerusalem
H.S.H.—His (Her)
    Serene Highness

I.C.—Order of Isabella
    the Catholic of Spain
I.E.—Order of the
    Indian Empire
Ill.—Illinois
Ind.—Indiana
I.S.O.—Companion of the
    Imperial Service Order

Jan.—January
J.P.—Justice of the Peace,
    or Magistrate
Jr.—Junior

K.—Knight
Kans.—Kansas
K.C.—Knight Commander
    or King's Counsel
K.C.B.—Knight Commander
    of the Bath of England
K.C.I.E.—Knight Commander
    of the Indian Empire
K.C.M.G.—Knight Commander
  of St. Michael and St. George
    of England

K.C.S.I.—Knight Commander
    of the Star of India
K.C.V.O.—Knight Commander
    of the Royal Victorian Order
K.G.—Knight of the Order of the
    Garter of England
K.P.—Knight of the Order of
    St. Patrick
K.T.—Knight of the Order of the
    Thistle

Ky.—Kentucky

La.—Louisiana
L.H.—Order of Legion of
    Honor of France
L.I.—Long Island
LL.B.—Bachelor of Laws
LL.D.—Doctor of Laws
LL.M.—Master of Laws
Lt.—Lieutenant
Lt. Col.—Lieutenant Colonel
Lt. Gen.—Lieutenant General

M.—Sovereign Order of Malta
    (Order of St. John
      of Jerusalem)
m.—Married
M.A.—Master of Arts
Maj.—Major
Maj. Gen.—Major General
Mar.—March
Mass.—Massachusetts
M.B.—Bachelor of Medicine
Md.—Maryland
M.D.—Doctor of Medicine
Me.—Maine
M.E.—Mechanical Engineer
M.G.—Order of St. Michael and
    St. George of England
Mich.—Michigan
Mo.—Missouri
M.O.F.W.—Military Order of
    Foreign Wars
M.O.W.W.—Military Order
    of the World War
M.P.—Member of Parliament
M.V.O.—Member of the
    Royal Victorian Order

N.C.—North Carolina
N.D.—North Dakota
Nebr.—Nebraska
Nev.—Nevada
N.H.—New Hampshire
N.J.—New Jersey

Nov.—November
N.Y.—New York

O.—Officer
Oct.—October
Okla.—Oklahoma
Or.—Order
O.R.C.—Officers' Reserve Corps
Oreg.—Oregon

P.—Order of St. Patrick
                        of Ireland
Pa.—Pennsylvania
P.C.—Privy Councillor
Penn.—Pennsylvania
Ph.D.—Doctor of Philosophy
P.I.—Philippine Islands
Prof.—Professor

ret.—Retired
R.N.—Royal Navy
Rt. Hon.—Right Honorable

s.—Son
S.A.—South America
S.A.R.—Society of the Sons of
        the American Revolution
S.C.—South Carolina
S. Dak.—South Dakota
Sept.—September
s.p.—(sine prole)
                        without issue
s.p.l. (sine prole legitimâ)—
        without legitimate issue
s.p.m. (sine prole masculâ)—
                without male issue
s.p.m.s. (sine prole masculâ
  superstite)—without surviving
                        male issue

s.p.s. (sine prole superstite)—
        without surviving issue
S.R.—Society of the Sons
                of the Revolution
Sr.—Senior

T.—Order of the Thistle
                of Scotland
Tenn.—Tennessee
T.R.H.—Their Royal Highnesses

U.D.C.—United Daughters
                of the Confederacy
U.S.A.—United States Army
U.S.M.C.—United States
                Marine Corps
U.S.N.—United States Navy

Va.—Virginia
V.A.—Lady of the Royal Order
        of Victoria and Albert
V.C.—Victoria Cross
v.m. (vita matris)—during
                mother's life
V.O.—Victorian Order of
                Great Britain
v.p. (vita patris)—during
                father's life
Vt.—Vermont

Wash.—Washington (State)
Wis.—Wisconsin
W.Va.—West Virginia
Wyo.—Wyoming

yrs.—Years.

PEDIGREES OF SOME OF THE
EMPEROR CHARLEMAGNE'S DESCENDANTS

AUSTRIA

CHARLEMAGNE

See Page 65

JAMES I, King of England (and VI of Scotland), m. Anne, dau. of Frederick II, King of Denmark and Norway,

PRINCESS ELIZABETH, m. Frederick V, Duke of Bavaria, Elector Palatine of the Rhine, and King of Bohemia,

PRINCE CHARLES LOUIS, Elector Palatine of the Rhine, b. 1617/8; d. Aug. 28, 1680; m., Feb. 1650, Charlotte, b. Nov. 1627; d. March 1686; dau. of William V, Landgrave of Hesse-Cassel, and his wife, Amelia Elizabeth, dau. of Philip Louis, Count of Hanau,

PRINCESS ELIZABETH CHARLOTTE, only dau., b. May 27, 1652; d. Dec. 8, 1722; m., (his second wife), Prince Philippe, Duke of Orleans, b. Sept. 21, 1640; d. June 9, 1701; 2nd and youngest son of Louis XIII, King of France,

PRINCESS ELIZABETH CHARLOTTE, b. Sept. 13, 1676; d. Dec. 23, 1744; m., Oct. 1698, Leopold Joseph Charles, Duke of Lorraine, b. Sept. 11, 1679; d. March 27, 1729; son and heir of Charles Leopold, Duke of Lorraine, and his wife, Marie, dau. of Emperor Ferdinand III, and widow of Michael, King of Poland,

FRANCIS I (STEPHEN), Emperor of Germany in 1745; Duke of Lorraine, March 27, 1729; Grand Duke of Tuscany, 1737; b. Dec. 8, 1708; d. Aug. 18, 1765; m., Feb. 12, 1736, Maria Theresa of Austria, b. May 13, 1717; d. Nov. 29, 1780; eldest dau. of Charles VI, Emperor of Germany, and his wife, Elizabeth Christinia, eldest dau. of Louis Rudolph, Duke of Blankenburg, afterwards Duke of Brunswick-Wolfenbuttel,

PETER LEOPOLD JOSEPH, 3rd son, b. May 5, 1747; d. March 1, 1792; succeeded his father as Grand Duke of Tuscany in 1765, and became Emperor of Germany on the death of his brother, Joseph II, in 1790; m. Feb. 16, 1765, Marie Louise, Infanta of Spain, b. Nov. 24, 1745; d. May 15, 1792; dau. of Charles III, King of Spain, and his wife, Princess Marie

34

Amelia, eldest dau. of Augustus III, Elector of Saxony, King of Poland,

FRANCIS II (JOSEPH CHARLES JOHN), Archduke of Austria, King of Hungary and of Bohemia, King of the Romans and Emperor of Germany, 1792-1806; Emperor of Austria, 1804; King of Illyria, Grand Duke of Cracow, &c., b. Feb. 12, 1768; d. March 2, 1835; m. 2ndly, Sept. 19, 1790, Maria Theresa, b. June 6, 1772; d. April 13, 1807; eldest dau. of Ferdinand I, King of the Two Sicilies, and his wife, Archduchess Marie Caroline, 10th dau. of Emperor Francis I and the Empress Maria Theresa,

FRANCIS CHARLES JOSEPH, Archduke of Austria, &c., 3rd son, b. Dec. 7, 1802; renounced his right to succession, Dec. 2, 1848; d. March 8, 1878; m. Nov. 4, 1824, Princess Sophia Frederica Dorothy Wilhelmina, b. Jan. 27, 1805; d. May 28, 1872; 6th dau. of Maximilian I, King of Bavaria, and his wife, Princess Carolina, 2nd dau. of Charles Louis, Hereditary Prince of Baden,

FRANCIS JOSEPH I, eldest son and heir, Emperor of Austria, King of Hungary and of Bohemia, Galicia, Lodomeria, Dalmatia, Illyria, of Jerusalem, &c., b. Aug. 18, 1830; succeeded his uncle, Ferdinand I, Dec. 2, 1848; d. Nov. 21, 1916; m., April 24, 1854, Duchess Elizabeth Amelia Eugenia, b. Dec. 24, 1837; assassinated at Geneva, Sept. 10, 1898; dau. of Maximilian, Duke in Bavaria. Issue:

1.) ARCHDUCHESS GISELA LOUISE MARIE of Austria, b. July 12, 1856; d. at Munchen, July 27, 1932; m. at Vienna, April 20, 1873, Prince Leopold Maximilian Joseph Maria Arnolph of Bavaria, b. at Munchen, Feb. 9, 1846; d. there Sept. 28, 1930. Issue:

a) PRINCESS ELIZABETH MARIE of Bavaria, b. at Munchen, Jan. 8, 1874; m., Dec. 2, 1893, Otto, Baron, after Jan. 10, 1904, Count of Seefried auf Buttenheim, Baron zu Hagenbach, 5th Baron von Seefried auf Buttenheim, &c., b. Sept. 26, 1870. Issue:

i COUNTESS ELIZABETH, b. June 10, 1897;

ii COUNTESS AUGUSTA, b. June 20, 1899;

iii COUNTESS VALERIE, b. Aug. 20, 1901;

iv COUNT FRANCIS JOSEPH, b. July 29, 1904.

b) PRINCESS AUGUSTA MARIE LOUISE of Bavaria, b.
at Munchen, April 28, 1875; m. at Munchen,
Nov. 15, 1893, Archduke Joseph of Austria, b.
at Alcsut, Hungary, Aug. 9, 1872; D.Sc., Honorary President of the Royal Hungarian
Academy of Sciences, Knight of the Golden
Fleece (Austria), &c., and have issue, among
others:

  i ARCHDUKE JOSEPH FRANCIS of Austria, b.
  March 28, 1895; m., Oct. 4, 1924, Anne,
  Princess of Saxony, b. at Lindau, Baden,
  May 4, 1903. Issue:

    1. ARCHDUCHESS MARGUERITE of Austria,
    b. at Budapest, Aug. 17, 1925;

    2. ARCHDUCHESS ILONA of Austria, b. at
    Budapest, April 20, 1927;

    3. ARCHDUCHESS ANNE THERESA of Aus-
    tria, b. at Budapest, April 19, 1928;

    4. ARCHDUKE JOSEPH ARPAD of Austria,
    b. at Budapest, Feb. 8, 1933;

    5. ARCHDUKE ISTVAN DOMOKOS of Aus-
    tria, b. at Budapest, July 1, 1934.

c) PRINCE CONRAD of Bavaria, b. at Munchen, Nov.
22, 1883; m., Jan. 8, 1921, Bonna Marguerite,
Princess of Savoy-Genoa, b. Aug. 1, 1896, dau.
of Prince Thomas of Savoy-Genoa, 2nd Duke of
Genoa, and his wife, Princess Isabella, dau.
of Prince Adalbert of Bavaria. Issue:

  i PRINCESS AMELIA ISABELLA of Bavaria, b.
  Dec. 15, 1921;

  ii PRINCE EUGENE LEOPOLD of Bavaria, b. July
  16, 1925.

2.) ARCHDUKE RUDOLPH of Austria, Crown Prince of Aus-
tria and Hungary, b. Aug. 21, 1858; d. at Mayerling,
Jan. 30, 1889; m. at Vienna, May 10, 1881, Princess
Stephanie Clotilda, b. May 21, 1864, dau. of Leopold
II, King of the Belgians. Issue:

a) ARCHDUCHESS ELIZABETH MARIE, b. Sept. 2, 1883;
   m. at Vienna, Jan. 23, 1902, Otto, Prince of
   Windisch-Graetz (marriage was dissolved by
   divorce, March 26, 1924), b. at Graz, Austria,
   Oct. 7, 1873. Issue:

   i PRINCE FRANCIS JOSEPH of Windisch-Graetz,
   b. at Prague, March 22, 1904; m. at Brussels, Jan. 3, 1934, Ghislaine, Countess
   d'Arschot Schoonhoven, b. at Brussels,
   March 10, 1912;

   ii PRINCE ERNEST DE WINDISCH-GRAETZ, b. at
   Prague, April 21, 1905; m. at Vienna, Oct.
   17, 1927, Ellen Skinner, b. at Scheibbs,
   Lower Austria, April 6, 1906. Issue:

     1. PRINCE OTHO ERNEST, b. at Vienna,
   Dec. 5, 1928;

     2. PRINCESS STEPHANIE MARIE, b. at
   Vienna, Jan. 21, 1933.

   iii PRINCE RUDOLPH JOHN DE WINDISCH-
   GRAETZ, b. Feb. 4, 1907;

   iv PRINCESS STEPHANIE ELEONORE DE WIN-
   DISCH-GRAETZ, b. July 9, 1909; m. at Brussels, July 22, 1933, Pierre, Count d'Alcantara de Querrieu.

3.) ARCHDUCHESS MARIE VALERIA of Austria, b. at Ofen,
   April 22, 1868; d. Sept. 6, 1924; m. at Ischl, July 31,
   1890, Archduke Francis Salvator of Austria, Knight
   of the Golden Fleece (Austria), &c., General of Cavalry, retired &c., b. Aug. 21, 1866; 2nd son of Archduke Charles Salvator of Austria, and his wife, Marie,
   Princess of Bourbon-Sicily, and have had issue:

   a) HUBERT SALVATOR, Archduke of Austria, b. April
   30, 1894; m., Nov. 25, 1926, Rosemary, Princess
   of Salm-Salm, b. at Potsdam, April 13, 1904.
   Issue:

     i FREDERICK SALVATOR, Archduke of Austria,
   b. at Vienna, Nov. 27, 1927;

     ii ARCHDUCHESS AGNES CHRISTINA, b. Dec. 14,
   1928;

iii Archduchess Marie Marguerite, b. Jan. 29, 1930;

iv Archduchess Marie Ludowika, b. Jan. 31, 1931;

v Archduchess Marie Adelaide, b. July 28, 1933;

vi Archduke Andrew Salvator, b. April 28, 1936.

b) Archduchess Hedwiga Marie of Austria, b. Sept. 24, 1896; m., April 24, 1918, Bernard, Count of Stolberg-Stolberg;

c) Archduke Theodore Salvator of Austria, b. Oct. Oct. 9, 1899; m., July 28, 1926, Marie Theresa, Countess of Waldburg-Zeil-Trauchburg, b. Oct. 18, 1901, dau. of Georges, 5th Prince of Waldburg, of Zeil and Trauchburg, 10th Count of Waldburg-Zeil, and have issue:

i Archduke Francis Salvator, b. Sept. 10, 1927;

ii Archduchess Theresa Monica, b. Jan. 9, 1931;

iii Archduchess Marie, b. Dec. 7, 1933;

iv Archduke Charles Salvator, b. June 23, 1936.

d) Archduchess Gertrude Marie of Austria, b. Nov. 19, 1900; m., Dec. 29, 1931, George, Count of Waldburg-Zeil;

e) Archduchess Marie Elizabeth of Austria, b. Nov. 19, 1901; d. Dec. 29, 1936;

f) Archduke Clement Salvator of Austria, b. Oct. 6, 1904; renounced his rights and titles as a member of the Imperial Family and with the consent of the Head of the Imperial Family assumed the name and title of Count of Altenburg, April 2, 1931, for him and his family; m. at Vienna, Feb. 20, 1930, Elizabeth, Countess Ressegnier de Miremont, b. Oct. 28, 1906. Issue:

i Countess Marie Valerie, b. Jan. 16, 1931;

ii Count Clement, b. Feb. 8, 1932;

iii Count George Adam, b. Sept. 23, 1933;
iv Count Peter Frederick, b. Sept. 18, 1935.

g) Archduchess Mathilda Marie of Austria, b. Aug. 9, 1906.

CHARLEMAGNE

See Page 35

Francis Charles Joseph, Archduke of Austria, 3rd son, b. Dec. 7, 1802; d. March 8, 1878; m., Nov. 4, 1824; Princess Sophia Frederica Dorothy Wilhelmina, b. Jan. 27, 1805; d. May 28, 1872; 6th dau. of Maximilian I, King of Bavaria,

Charles Ludwig, Archduke of Austria, Prince of Hungary and Bohemia, b. July 30, 1833; d. May 19, 1896; m., 2ndly, Oct. 21, 1862, Annunciata, Princess of Bourbon-Sicily, b. March 24, 1843; d. May 4, 1871; and had, among others,

Otto Francis Joseph Charles Ludwig Maria, Archduke of Austria, Prince of Hungary and Bohemia, b. at Graz, Austria, April 21, 1865; d. Nov. 1, 1906; m. at Dresden, Oct. 2, 1886; Marie Josepha Louise Philippina Elizabeth Pia Angelica Margarete, Princess of Saxony, b. at Dresden, May 31, 1867; dau. of Prince Frederick August George of Saxony, and his wife, Maria Anna, Infanta of Portugal

Charles (Karl) I (Francis Joseph Louis Hubert George Otto Maria), Archduke of Austria, Prince of Hungary and Bohemia, &c., b. at Persenbeug, Aug. 17, 1887; succeeded his grand uncle, Emperor Francis Joseph I, Nov. 21, 1916, and ascended the throne as Emperor of Austria and Apostolic King of Hungary and Bohemia, &c., King of Jerusalem, Dalmatia, Croatia, Galicia, Illyria, &c., Grand Duke of Tuscany, Cracow, Transylvania, &c., d. at Funchal, Madeira, April 1, 1922; m. at Schwarzau am Steinfelde, Oct. 21, 1911, Zita Marie des Graces Adelgonda Michelle Raphaelle Gabriella Josephine Antonia Louise Agnes, Princess de Bourbon de Parma, (a descendant from Emperor Charlemagne), b. in Villa Pianore, May 9, 1892, dau. of Robert, Duke of Parma, and have had issue:

1. FRANCIS JOSEPH OTTO (FRANZ JOSEF OTTO) (ROBERT MARIA ANTHONY CHARLES MAXIMILIAN HENRY SIXTE XAVIER FELIX RENATUS LOUIS GAETAN PIUS IGNACE), Archduke of Austria, Crown Prince of Austria and Hungary, &c., Imperial and Royal Highness, Princely Count von Habsburg, Grand Duke of Tuscany, Cracow and of Transylvania, Duke of Lorraine, Salzburg, Modena, Parma, Plaisance et Guastalla, &c., Prince of Trente et Brixen, &c., rightful heir to the Imperial Throne of Austria and to the Throne of Hungary, Bohemia, &c., b. in Villa Wartholz, near Reichenau, Austria, Nov. 20, 1912; Doctor of Political and Social Science, University of Louvain, Belgium; Sovereign and Chief of the Austrian Imperial Order of the Golden Fleece, Grand Master of the Military Order of Marie Theresa, &c.;

2.) ADELAIDE MARIE (JOSEPHINE SIXTA ANTONIA ROBERTA OTTONIA ZITA CHARLOTTE LOUISE IMMACULATA PIA THERESA BEATRIX FRANCES ISABELLA HENRIETTA), Archduchess of Austria, Princess of Hungary, Bohemia, &c., b. Jan. 3, 1914; Doctor of Political Science;

3.) ROBERT CHARLES (LOUIS MAXIMILIAN MICHAEL), Archduke of Austria-Este, Prince of Hungary and Bohemia, b. Feb. 8, 1915;

4.) FELIX FREDERICK AUGUSTUS, Archduke of Austria, Prince of Hungary and of Bohemia, b. May 31, 1916;

5.) CHARLES LOUIS (MARIA FRANCIS), Archduke of Austria, Prince of Hungary and Bohemia, b. March 10, 1918;

6.) RUDOLPH (SYRINGUS PETER CHARLES), Archduke of Austria, Prince of Hungary and Bohemia, b. Sept. 5, 1919;

7.) CHARLOTTE HEDWIGE (FRANCES JOSEPHINE), Archduchess of Austria, Princess of Hungary and Bohemia, b. March 1, 1921;

8.) ELIZABETH CHARLOTTE (ALPHONSIA CHRISTINA), Archduchess of Austria, Princess of Hungary and Bohemia, b. May 31, 1922.

See Page 35

FRANCIS CHARLES JOSEPH, Archduke of Austria, 3rd son, b. Dec. 7, 1802; d. Mar. 8, 1876; m. Princess Sophia Frederica Dorothy Wilhelmina, dau. of Maximilian I, King of Bavaria. Issue:

1.) FERDINAND MAXIMILIAN JOSEPH, Archduke of Austria, b. July 6, 1832; Emperor of Mexico as Maximilian I, April 10, 1864, to June 19, 1867, on which day he was assassinated in Mexico; m. July 27, 1857, Maria Charlotte Amelia Augusta, Princess of Belgium, only dau. of Leopold I, King of the Belgians;

2.) CHARLES LOUIS, Archduke of Austria, &c., b. July 30, 1833; d. May 19, 1896; m., 2ndly, Oct. 21, 1862, Maria Annunciata, b. March 24, 1843; d. May 4, 1871; dau. of Ferdinand II, King of the Two Sicilies, and had, among others:

a) FRANCIS FERDINAND CHARLES LOUIS JOSEPH MARIA, Archduke of Austria-Este, &c., b. Dec. 18, 1863; assassinated at Sarajevo, June 28, 1914; m., July 1, 1900, Sophie, cr. Princess of Hohenberg, July 1, 1900; cr. Duchess of Hohenberg, Oct. 4, 1909; b. March 1, 1868; assassinated at Sarajevo, June 28, 1914; dau. of Bohuslaw, Count Chotek of Chotkowa and Wognin. Issue:

i PRINCESS SOPHIE VON HOHENBERG, b. July 24, 1901;

ii PRINCE MAXIMILIAN CHARLES VON HOHENBERG, b. Sept. 29, 1902;

iii PRINCE ERNEST VON HOHENBERG, b. May 27, 1904.

BADEN

JAMES I, King of England, France and Ireland, (and VI of Scotland); m. Anne, dau. of Frederick II, King of Denmark and Norway,

PRINCESS ELIZABETH, m. Frederick V, Elector Palatine of the Rhine, Duke of Bavaria, King of Bohemia,

PRINCESS SOPHIA, m. 1658, Ernest Augustus I, Elector of Hanover, Duke of Brunswick, d. 1698,

GEORGE I, King of Great Britain, France and Ireland, Elector of Hanover, d. 1727; m. 1681, Sophia Dorothy of Zell, d. 1726,

GEORGE II, King of Great Britain, France, and Ireland, Elector of Hanover, d. 1760; m. 1705, Wilhelmina Carolina, dau. of John Frederick, Markgrave of Brandenburg-Anspach, and his second wife Eleanor, dau. of John George, Duke of Saxe-Eisenach,

PRINCESS LOUISA, b. 1724; d. 1751; m. 1743, Frederick V, King of Denmark and Norway, d. 1766,

PRINCESS SOPHIA MAGDALENE, b. 1746; d. 1813; m. 1766, Gustavus III, King of Sweden, d. 1792,

GUSTAVUS IV, King of Sweden, d. 1837; m. 1797, Frederica of Baden, d. 1826,

PRINCESS SOPHIA, b. May 21, 1801; d. July 6, 1865; m. July 25, 1819, Leopold, Grand Duke of Baden, b. Aug. 29, 1790; d. April 24, 1852,

PRINCE WILLIAM, b. Dec. 18, 1829; d. April 27, 1897; m. at St. Petersburg, Russia, Feb. 11, 1863, Maria Marinilianowna, Princess Romanowsky, Duchess of Leuchtenberg, b. Oct. 4/16, 1841,

PRINCE MAXIMILIAN ALEXANDER FREDERICK WILLIAM, b. at Baden, July 10, 1867; d. Nov. 6, 1929; m. at Gmunden, Austria, July 10, 1900, Marie Louise, Princess of Great Britain, Ireland, and Hanover, Duchess of Brunswick-Luneburg, b. at Gmunden, Oct. 11, 1879,

BERTHOLD FREDERICK WILLIAM ERNEST AUGUST HENRY CHARLES, Prince and Markgrave of Baden, Duke of Zahringen, b. at Carlsruhe, Feb. 24, 1906; Hereditary Grand Duke of Baden; m. at Baden-Baden, Aug. 17, 1931, Theodora, Princess of Denmark and of Greece, b. at Athens, May 30, 1906, and have issue:

1.) PRINCESS MARGUERITE ALICE THYRA VICTORIA MARIE LOUISE SCOLASTIQUE, b. at the Palace of Salem, July 14, 1932;

2.) PRINCE MAXIMILIAN ANDREW FREDERICK GUSTAV ERNEST AUGUST BERNARD, b. at the Palace of Salem, July 3, 1933;

3.) PRINCE LOUIS WILLIAM GEORGE ERNEST CHRISTOPHE, b. at Carlsruhe, Baden, Mar. 16, 1937.

BERTHOLD FREDERICK WILLIAM ERNEST AUGUST HENRY CHARLES, Prince and Markgrave of Baden, Duke of Zahringen, b. at Carlsruhe, Feb. 24, 1906; Hereditary Grand Duke of Baden; m. at Baden-Baden, Aug. 17, 1931, Theodora, Princess of Denmark and of Greece, b. at Athens, May 30, 1906, and have issue:

1.) PRINCESS MARGUERITE ALICE THYRA VICTORIA MARIE LOUISE SCOLASTIQUE, b. at the Palace of Salem, July 14, 1932;

2.) PRINCE MAXIMILIAN ANDREW FREDERICK GUSTAV ERNEST AUGUST BERNARD, b. at the Palace of Salem, July 3, 1933;

3.) PRINCE LOUIS WILLIAM GEORGE ERNEST CHRISTOPHE, b. at Carlsruhe, Baden, Mar. 16, 1937.

Maria Theresa Henrietta Dorothea, Archduchess of Austria-Este, Princess of Hungary and of Bohemia, b. July 2, 1849; d. Feb. 3, 1919; m., Feb. 20, 1868, Ludwig III, King of Bavaria, b. Jan. 7, 1845; d. Oct. 18, 1921,

Prince Rupert (Rupprecht) Maria Leopold Ferdinand, Crown Prince of Bavaria, Duke of Bavaria, Franconia and of Swabia, Count Palatine of the Rhine, etc., b. at Munchen, May 18, 1869; m., first, July 10, 1900, Maria Gabriella, Duchess in Bavaria, b. Oct. 9, 1878; d. Oct. 24, 1912; m., secondly, Apr. 7, 1921. Princess Antoinette Roberta Sophia Wilhelmina of Luxemburg and Nassau, dau. of William, Grand Duke of Luxemburg, Duke of Nassau, and his wife Maria Anna, Grand Duchess of Luxemburg, Infanta of Portugal.

Issue by first wife:

Prince Albert (Albrecht) Leopold Ferdinand Michael, Hereditary Prince of Bavaria, b. at Munchen, May 3, 1905; m., Sept. 3, 1930, Maria (Marita), Countess Draskovich de Trakostjan, b. at Vienna, Mar. 8, 1904, and have issue two sons and two daughters.

Issue by second wife:

1.) Prince Henry Francis William, b. Mar. 28, 1922;

2.) Princess Irmgard Marie Josephine, b. May 29, 1923;

3.) Princess Edith Marie Gabriella Anna, b. Sept. 16, 1924;

4.) Princess Hilda Hildegarde Marie Gabriella, b. Mar. 24, 1926;

5.) Princess Gabriella Aldegonda Marie Theresia Antoinette, b. May 10, 1927;

6.) Princess Sophia Marie Theresa, b. June 20, 1935.

Ludwig III, King of Bavaria, b. January 7, 1845; d. Oct. 18, 1921; m., Feb. 20, 1868, Maria Theresa Dorothea, Archduchess of Austria-Este, Princess of Hungary and of Bohemia, b. July 2, 1849; d. Feb. 3, 1919; dau. of Ferdinand Charles Victor, Archduke of Austria-Este. Issue:

A. Princess Marie Ludwiga Theresa of Bavaria, b. near Lindau, July 6, 1872; m. at Munchen, May 31, 1897, Ferdinand Pius Maria, Prince of Bourbon-Sicily, Duke of Calabra, b. at Rome, July 25, 1869, son of Prince Alphonso de Bourbon-Sicily, Count of Caserta, and have issue:

　1.) Princess Maria Antoinette Leonia, b. at Madrid, Apr. 16, 1898;

　2.) Princess Maria Christinia, b. at Madrid, May 4, 1899;

　3.) Princess Lucia Maria Reniere, b. at Munchen, July 9, 1908;

　4.) Princess Urraca Maria Isabella Carolina Adelgonda Carmela, b. at Munchen, July 14, 1913.

B. Prince Francis Maria Luitpold of Bavaria, b. Oct. 10, 1875; m. July 8, 1912, Isabella, Princess de Croy, b. Oct. 7, 1890, and have issue:

　1.) Prince Louis Charles Maria Anthony Joseph, b. at Munchen, June 22, 1913;

　2.) Princess Marie Elizabeth Frances Josephine Theresa, b. at Munchen, Sept, 9, 1914; m. Aug. 19, 1937, Pierre Henry, Prince d'Orleans et de Braganza;

　3.) Princess Aldegonda Marie Antoinette Elizabeth Josephine, b. at Munchen, June 9, 1917;

　4.) Princess Eleonore Theresia Marie Josephine Gabriella, b. at Munchen, Sept. 11, 1918;

　5.) Princess Dorothy Theresa Marie Frances, b. May 25, 1920;

　6.) Prince Rasso Maximilian Rupert (Rupprecht), b. May 24, 1926.

Belgium

James I, King of England (VI of Scotland) and Queen Anne,

Princess Elizabeth m. Frederick V, Duke of Bavaria, Elector Palatine of the Rhine, King of Bohemia,

Princess Charles Louis, Elector Palatine of the Rhine, m. Charlotte, dau. of William V, Landgrave of Hesse-Cassel,

Princess Elizabeth Charlotte, only dau., m., (his second wife), Prince Philippe, Duke of Orleans, 2nd and youngest son of Louis XIII, King of France,

Philippe II, Duke of Chartres, Duke of Orleans, Regent of France during the minority of King Louis XV, b. Aug. 2, 1674; d. Dec. 2, 1723; m., 1692/3, Frances Marie, Mademoiselle de Blois, b. May 4, 1677; d. Feb. 1, 1748/9, natural dau. of Louis XIV and Madame de Montespan,

Prince Louis, Duke of Orleans, only son, b. Aug. 4, 1703; d. Feb. 4, 1752; m., July 13, 1724, Augusta Marie Joan, b. Nov. 10, 1704; d. Aug. 8, 1726; only dau. of Louis William, Marggrave of Baden,

Prince Louis Philippe, Duke of Orleans, only son, b. May 12, 1725; d. Nov. 15, 1785; m., Dec. 17, 1743, Louise Henrietta, b. Jan. 20, 1726; d. Feb. 9, 1759; only dau. of Louis Armand de Bourbon, Prince of Conti, and his wife, Louise Elizabeth, 2nd dau. of Louis III, Prince of Condé and Duke of Bourbon,

Prince Louis Philippe Joseph, surnamed Egalité, Duke of Orleans, only son and heir, b. April 13, 1747; guillotined Nov. 6, 1793; m., April 5, 1769, Louise Marie Adelaide, b. March 3/13, 1753; d. June 23, 1821; dau. of Louis John, Duke of Penthièvre, and his wife, Princess Maria Theresa Felicita d'Este, dau. of Francis III, Duke of Modena.

Louis Philippe, Duke of Orleans, afterwards King of the French, eldest son and heir, b. at Paris, Oct. 6, 1773; d. at Claremont, co. Surrey, England, Aug. 26, 1850; m., Nov. 25, 1809, Princess Marie Amelia, dau. of Ferdinand IV, King of the Two Sicilies, and his wife, Archduchess Marie Caroline,

10th dau. of Emperor Francis I and the Empress Maria Theresa,

PRINCESS LOUISE MARIA THERESA CHARLOTTE ISABELLA, b. at Palermo, April 3, 1812; d. Oct. 11, 1850; m., Aug. 9, 1832, Prince Leopold of Saxe-Coburg and Gotha, Duke of Saxony, King of the Belgians, b. Dec. 16, 1790; d. Dec. 10, 1865; son of Francis, Duke of Saxe-Coburg-Saalfeld, and had Leopold Louis Philippe Maria Victor, Duke of Brabant, who succeeded his father as King of the Belgians under the name of Leopold II, and,

PHILIPPE EUGENE FERDINAND MARIA CLEMENT BALDWIN LEOPOLD GEORGE, Prince of Belgium, Count of Flanders, b. March 24, 1837; d. Nov. 17, 1905; m., April 26, 1867, Princess Marie Louise Alexandrina Carolina of Hohenzollern-Sigmaringen, b. Nov. 17, 1845; d. Nov. 26, 1912; 2nd and youngest dau. of Charles Anthony, Prince of Hohenzollern-Sigmaringen, and his wife, Josephine Friederike Louise, Princess of Baden.

Issue, among others:

1.) PRINCESS HENRIETTA MARIE CHARLOTTE of Belgium, b. Nov. 30, 1870; m., Feb. 12, 1896, Philippe Emmanuel, Prince of Orleans, Duke of Vendome and of Alencon, b. Jan. 18, 1872; d. Feb. 1, 1931; son of Prince Ferdinand Philippe Maria, Duke of Alencon, and his wife, Sophie Charlotte Augusta, Duchess of Bavaria, dau. of Duke Maximilian of Bavaria. Issue:

    a) PRINCESS MARIE LOUISE FERDINANDE CHARLOTTE HENRIETTA, b. Dec. 31, 1896; m., first, Jan. 12, 1916, Philippe, Prince de Bourbon-Sicily, (marriage annulled May 31, 1926, and she m., 2ndly, at Chichester, England, Dec. 12, 1928, Walter Kingsland). Issue:

        i PRINCE GAETAN DE BOURBON-SICILY, b. April 16, 1917.

    b) PRINCESS GENEVIEVE MARIE JOANNA FRANCES, b. Sept. 21, 1901; m., July 2, 1923, Anthony, Count de Chaponay;

    c) PRINCE CHARLES PHILIPPE EMMANUEL FERDINAND, Duke of Nemours, b. April 4, 1905; m., Sept. 24, 1928, Marguerite Watson, b. at Richmond, Feb. 12, 1899.

2.) PRINCESS JOSEPHINE CAROLA MARIE ALBERTINA of Belgium, b. Oct. 18, 1872; (now a nun at the Monastery of Coquelet at Namur); m., May 28, 1894, Charles Anthony, Prince of Hohenzollern-Sigmaringen, b. Sept. 1, 1868; d. Feb. 21, 1919. Issue:

    a) PRINCESS STEPHANIE JOSEPHINE of Hohenzollern-Sigmaringen, b. April 8, 1895; m., May 18, 1920, Joseph Ernest, Hereditary Count of Fugger de Gloett, b. Oct. 26, 1895;

    b) PRINCESS MARIE ANTOINETTE WILHELMINA of Hohenzollern-Sigmaringen, b. Oct. 23, 1896; m., Nov. 27, 1924, Egon, Baron Eyrl de Waldgries et Liebenaich;

    c) PRINCE ALBERT (ALBRECHT) LOUIS LEOPOLD TASSILLON of Hohenzollern-Sigmaringen, b. Sept. 28, 1898; m., May 19, 1921, Ilse Margot Claire Helena Willy de Friedeburg, b. June 28, 1901. Issue:

        i PRINCESS JOSEPHINE WILHELMA, b. Feb. 15, 1922;

        ii PRINCESS LOUISE DOROTHEA, b. Feb. 9, 1924;

        iii PRINCESS ROSE MARGUERITE, b. Feb. 19, 1930.

3.) PRINCE ALBERT, ascended the throne as Albert I, King of the Belgians, b. April 8, 1875; d. by accident Feb. 17, 1934; m., Oct. 2, 1900, Elizabeth Valeria Gabriella Marie, Duchess in Bavaria, b. July 25, 1876, dau. of Charles Theodore, Duke of Bavaria, and his wife, Marie Josephine (Jose), Infanta of Portugal. Issue:

    a) LEOPOLD III (PHILIPPE CHARLES ALBERT MEINRAD HUBERT MARIA MIGUEL), King of the Belgians, Prince of Belgium, b. Nov. 3, 1901; m., Nov. 4/10, 1926, Astrid, Princess of Sweden, b. at Stockholm, Nov. 17, 1905; d. in an automobile accident in Switzerland, Aug. 29, 1935. Issue:

        i PRINCESS JOSEPHINE CHARLOTTE of Belgium, b. Oct. 11, 1927;

        ii PRINCE BALDWIN ALBERT CHARLES of Belgium, Duke of Brabant, b. Sept. 7, 1930;

        iii PRINCE ALBERT FELIX HUMBERT of Belgium, Prince de Liège, b. June 6, 1934.

b) PRINCE CHARLES THEODORE of Belgium, Count of Flanders, b. Oct. 10, 1903;

c) PRINCESS MARIE José CHARLOTTE of Belgium, b. Aug. 4, 1906; m. at Rome, Jan. 8, 1930, Humbert (Umberto), Prince de Piedmont, Crown Prince of Italy, &c., b. Sept. 15, 1904; son of Victor Emmanuel III, King of Italy. Issue:

    i PRINCESS MARIA PIA ELIZABETH of Italy, b. Sept. 24, 1934.

PRINCESS LOUISE MARIA THERESA CHARLOTTE ISABELLA of Orleans, m. Leopold I, King of the Belgians, Prince of Saxe-Coburg and Gotha, Duke of Saxony, b. Dec. 1790; d. Dec. 10, 1865,

LEOPOLD II, King of Belgians, b. April 9, 1835; d. Dec. 17, 1909; m., Aug. 10/22, 1853, Marie Henrietta, Archduchess of Austria, b. Aug. 23, 1836; d. Sept. 19, 1902. Issue:

1.) PRINCESS STEPHANIE CLOTILDE LOUISE HERMINA MARIE CHARLOTTE of Belgium, b. May 21, 1864; widow of Archduke Rudolph, Crown Prince of Austria and Hungary, who d. at Mayerling, Jan. 30, 1889; m., 2ndly, at Miramar, March 22, 1900, Elemer, Count of Lonyay of Nagy-Lonya and Vasaros-Nameny, Lord of Bodrog-Olaszi, Botragy and Csonka-Papi, Imperial and Royal Chamberlain, Hereditary Member of the Hungarian House of Lords; cr. Prince de Lonyay de Nagy-Lonya, Feb. 9, 1917; b. Aug. 24, 1863;

2.) PRINCESS CLEMENTINA ALBERTINA MARIE LEOPOLDINA of Belgium, b. July 30, 1872; m., Nov. 14, 1910, Prince Napoleon Victor, Head of the ex-Imperial House of France, b. July 18, 1862; d. May 3, 1926. Issue:

a) PRINCESS MARIE CLOTILDA EUGENIE, b. March 20, 1912;

b) PRINCE NAPOLEON LOUIS JEROME, b. Jan. 23, 1914.

BOURBON

CHARLES I, King of England, &c.,

PRINCESS HENRIETTA MARIA ANNE, b. June 10/16, 1644; d. June 30, 1670; m., Mar. 31, 1661, (his first wife), Prince Philippe, Duke of Orleans, b. Sept. 21, 1640; d. June 9, 1701; youngest son of Louis XIII, King of France, and only brother of Louis XIV, King of France,

PRINCESS ANNE MARIE, Mademoiselle de Valois, b. Aug. 27, 1669; d. Aug. 26, 1728; m. by proxy, Apr. 10, 1684, Victor Amadeus, Duke of Savoy, afterwards King of Sardinia, b. May 14, 1666; d. Oct. 31, 1732,

CHARLES EMMANUEL III, King of Sardinia, b. Apr. 27, 1701; d. at Turin, Jan. or Feb. 20/21, 1773; m., 2ndly, July 2, 1724, Polyxena Christina Jane, b. Sept. 21, 1706; d. Jan. 13, 1735; dau. of Ernest Leopold, Landgrave of Hesse-Rheinfels, and his wife, Eleanore Maria Anne, dau. of Maximilian Charles, Count of Loewenstein,

VICTOR AMADEUS III, King of Sardinia, b. June 26, 1726; d. Oct. 16, 1796; m., Mar. 31, 1750, Princess Marie Antoinette Ferdinanda, b. Nov. 17, 1729; d. Sept. 19, 1785; youngest dau. of Philip V, King of Spain, by Princess Elizabeth Farnese, only child and h. of Odoardo, Hereditary Prince of Parma, and his wife Dorothea Sophia, dau. of Philip William of Neuburg, Elector Palatine, by Isabella (or Elizabeth) Amelia, dau. of George II, Duke of Hesse Darmstadt,

VICTOR EMMANUEL I, King of Sardinia, Duke d'Aosta, b. July 24, 1759; d. Jan. 10, 1824; m., Apr. 21, 1789, Maria Theresa, b. Nov. 1, 1773; d. Mar. 29, 1832; dau. of Ferdinand, Duke of Modena, and his wife, Princess Maria Beatrice Richarda of Este, only dau. and h. of Hercules III, Duke of Modena and Brisgau,

PRINCESS MARIE BEATRICE VICTORIA JOSEPHINE, b. Dec. 6, 1792; d. Sept. 15, 1840; m., June 20, 1812, her uncle, Francis IV, Duke of Modena, Prince of Massa and Carrara, b. Oct. 6, 1779; d. Jan. 21, 1846, eldest son of Ferdinand, Duke of Modena and Brisgau,

Princess Marie Beatrice Anne Frances, Archduchess of Austria-Este, b. Feb. 13, 1824; d. at Gratz, Austria, Mar. 18, 1906; m., Feb. 6, 1847, Don Juan (Charles Marie Isidore), Infant of Spain, b. May 15, 1822; d. Nov. 21, 1887; 2nd son of Don Carlos (Charles V), Infant of Spain, (by his wife, Infanta Theresa, eldest dau. of John VI, King of Portugal), and brother and h. of Don Carlos (Charles VI), Count of Montemolino,

Don Carlos, Prince de Bourbon, Duke of Madrid, b. Mar. 30, 1848; d. July 18, 1909; m., first, Feb. 4, 1867, Margaret, Princess de Bourbon de Parma, b. Jan. 1, 1847; d. Jan. 29, 1893; eldest dau. of Charles III, Duke of Parma, and his wife, Louise Marie Therese, dau. of Charles Ferdinand, Duke of Berry, (son of Charles X, King of France), and his wife Marie Caroline Ferdinanda Louise, eldest dau. of Francis I, King of the Two Sicilies, by Archduchess Marie Clementine, dau. of Leopold II, Emperor of Germany. Issue:

1.) Blanche de Castile Marie de la Conception, Princess de Bourbon, b. at Graz, Austria, Sept. 7, 1868; m., Oct. 24, 1889, Leopold Salvator, Archduke of Austria, &c., b. Oct. 15, 1863; d. Sept. 4, 1931; son of Archduke Charles Salvator. Issue, among others:

   a) Archduke Leopold Marie Alphonso of Austria, b. at Zagreb, Jan. 30, 1897; m. at Vienna, Apr. 12, 1919, Dagmar, Baroness Nicolics-Podrinska, b. July 15, 1898, (marriage dissolved by divorce in 1931), and have issue;

   b) Archduchess Marie Antoine Roberta of Austria, b. at Zagreb, July 13, 1899; m. at Barcelona, July 16, 1924, Don Ramon de Orlandis y Villalonga;

   c) Archduke Anthony Marie Francis of Austria, b. at Vienna, Mar. 20, 1901; m., July 26, 1931, Ileana, Princess of Rumania, b. Dec. 23, 1908/Jan. 5, 1909, and have issue;

   d) Archduke Francis Joseph Charles of Austria, b. at Vienna, Feb. 4, 1905;

   e) Archduke Charles Pia of Austria, b. at Vienna, Dec. 4, 1909.

2.) MARIE BEATRICE THERESA, Princess de Bourbon, b. Mar. 21, 1874; m. at Venice, Feb. 27, 1897, Fabrizio, Principe Massino, Principe di Roviano, Duca di Anticoli Corrado, b. at Rome, Nov. 23, 1868, and had issue, among others:

    a) MARGHERITA MARIA BEATRICE, b. July 31, 1898; m., Sept. 28, 1922, Count Emilio Pagliano, Ambassador of Italy, b. at Rome, Mar. 30, 1881;

    b) FABIOLA MARIA CAROLINA, b. July 27, 1900; m., Sept. 2, 1922, Baron Enzo Galli Zugaro;

    c) MARIA DELLA NEVE FRANCISCA JACOBA, b. Jan. 18, 1902; m., 1926, Carlo Piercy;

    d) BIANCA MARIA ALFONSA, b. Apr. 16, 1906.

3.) MARIE ALICE ILDEPHONSA MARGUERITE, Princess de Bourbon, b. June 29, 1876; m., first, Apr. 26, 1897, (his first wife), Victor Frederick Ernest, Prince von Schoenburg-Waldenburg, b. Oct. 20, 1872; d. Oct. 27, 1910; (marriage dissolved by divorce at Dresden, Dec. 23, 1903, and annulled by the Holy See on May 26, 1906). Issue:

    a) PRINCE MARIE CHARLES LEOPOLD SALVATOR VON SCHOENBURG-WALDENBURG, b. June 2, 1902; m. at Rome, June 6, 1928, Ornella Alagia Catherine, b. June 16, 1904, dau. of Vincenzo Ravaschieri-Fieschi, Duca di Roccapiemonte, and his wife, Donna Maria Beatrice, sister of Principe Lodovico Spada-Veralli-Potenziani, Principe di Castelviscardo, &c.

BOURBON—ORLEANS

CHARLEMAGNE

See Page 47

LOUIS PHILIPPE, Duke of Orleans, afterwards King of the French, eldest son and heir, b. at Paris, Oct. 6, 1773; d. at Claremont, co. Surrey, England, Aug. 26, 1850; m., Nov. 25, 1809, Princess Marie Amelia, dau. of Ferdinand IV, King of the Two Sicilies,

FERDINAND PHILIPPE LOUIS CHARLES HENRY, Duke de Chartres, Duke of Orleans, eldest son and heir-apparent, b. Sept. 3, 1810; d. July 13, 1842; m., May 30, 1837, Helena Louisa Elizabeth, b. Jan. 24, 1814; d. May 18, 1858; dau. of Frederick Louis, Hereditary Grand Duke of Mecklemburg-Schwerin,

LOUIS PHILIPPE ALBERT, Count of Paris, eldest son and heir, b. Aug. 24, 1838, d. Sept. 8, 1894; m., May 30, 1864, Marie Isabelle, Princess of Orleans, b. Sept. 21, 1848; d. April 23, 1919; dau. of Prince Anthony of Orleans, Duke of Montpensier. Issue, among others:

> 1.) PRINCESS ISABELLE MARIE LAURA, b. May 7, 1878; m., Oct. 30, 1899, Prince John Peter (Jean Pierre) Clement Maria of Orleans, Duke of Guise, Head of the Royal House of France, b. at Paris, Sept. 4, 1874, son of Prince Robert of Orleans, Duke de Chartres, by Princess Frances, dau. of Prince Francis of Orleans, Prince of Joinville. Issue elsewhere given in this book. (See below).

LOUIS PHILIPPE, Duke of Orleans, afterwards King of the French, (above mentioned), m., Nov. 25, 1809, Princess Marie Amelia, dau. of Ferdinand IV, King of the Two Sicilies,

FRANCIS FERDINAND PHILIPPE LOUIS, Prince de Joinville, b. Aug. 14, 1818; d. June 16, 1900; m., May 1, 1843, Infanta Frances Carolina Joanna, b. Aug. 2, 1824; d. March 27, 1898;

dau. of Pedro I (Peter), Emperor of Brazil and King of Portugal,

PRINCESS FRANCES MARIE AMELIA of Orleans, b. Aug. 14, 1844; d. Oct. 25, 1925; m., June 11, 1863, her cousin, Prince Robert Philippe Louis Eugene Ferdinand of Orleans, Duke of Chartres, b. Nov. 9, 1840; d. Dec. 5, 1910; son of Prince Ferdinand, Duke of Orleans,

PRINCE JOHN PETER (JEAN PIERRE) CLEMENT MARIA of Orleans, Duke of Guise, Head of the Royal House of France, b. at Paris, Sept. 4, 1874; m., Oct. 30, 1899, Princess Isabelle Marie Laura, b. May 7, 1878, dau. of Louis Philippe Albert, Count of Paris, by Marie Isabelle, Princess of Orleans, Infanta of Spain. Issue:

1.) PRINCESS ISABELLE FRANCES HELEN MARIE, b. at Paris, Nov. 27, 1900; m., first, Sept. 15, 1923, Bruno, Count d'Harcourt, who d. Apr. 19, 1930; m., 2ndly, July 12, 1934, Pierre, Prince Murat, b. at Paris, Apr. 6, 1900, son of Prince Eugene Louis Michael Joachim Napoleon Murat, by Violet Ney, dau. of Michael Ney, 3rd Duke of Elchingen;

2.) PRINCESS FRANCES ISABELLE LOUISE MARIE, b. at Paris, Dec. 25, 1902; m., Feb. 11, 1929, (his second wife), Prince Christophe of Greece, b. July 29, 1888;

3.) PRINCESS ANNE HELEN MARIE, b. Aug. 5, 1906; m. at Naples, Nov. 5, 1927, Prince Amadeus (Amedeo) Humbert of Savoy-Aosta, Duke d'Aosta, b. Oct. 21, 1898. Issue:

a) PRINCESS MARGHERITA ISABELLA, b. Apr. 7, 1930;

b) PRINCESS MARIA CHRISTINA, b. Sept. 12, 1933.

4.) PRINCE HENRY ROBERT FERDINAND MARIE LOUIS PHILIPPE, Count of Paris, Prince of France, &c., b. July 5, 1908; m., Apr. 8, 1931, Isabelle, Princess of Orleans and of Braganza, b. Aug. 13, 1911, and have issue elsewhere listed in this book. (See Braganza.)

BOURBON—PARMA

MATHILDA OF FLANDERS, dau. of Baldwin V, the Pious, and his wife Adele, dau. of Robert, King of France; m. William, Duke of Normandy, Conqueror of England, King of England,

PRINCESS ADELA, b. about 1062; d. in 1137; m., 1080, Stephen, Count of Blois and Chartres, d. 1101; son of Eudes (or Theobald III.), Count of Blois, Chartres, Tourain, Brie, and Champaigne,

STEPHEN OF BLOIS, b. c. 1095/6; d. Oct. 25, 1154; crowned King of England, Dec. 26, 1135, m., c. 1123, Mathilda (or Maud), Countess of Boulogne, b. c. 1105; d. May 3, 1151, dau. and h. of Eustace, Count of Boulogne,

PRINCESS MARY, Countess of Boulogne, b. 1136; was Abbess of Romsey in Hampshire until 1160, when she was forcibly abducted from the convent and m. by Matthew of Alsace, son of Dietrich, Count of Flanders, and his 2nd wife Sybil, dau. of Fulke V, Count d'Anjou and King of Jerusalem, and a sister of Geoffrey Plantagenet, Count d'Anjou. She separated from her husband and resumed a conventual life in 1169 at St. Austrebert, near Montreuil, France, where she once more took the veil as a nun, she d. in 1182. Two daughters were the issue of Matthew and the Princess Mary, the youngest was,

MATHILDA, b. 1162; d. c. 1211; m., 1179, (his first wife), Henry I, Duke of Brabant, b. c. 1158; d. Sept. 5, 1235, son of Godfrey III, Count of Louvaine, and his wife Margaret, dau. of Henry, Count of Limburg,

HENRY II, Duke of Brabant, eldest son and heir, b. 1189; d. Feb. 1, 1247/8; m., first, Feb. 9, 1207, Mary of Hohenstauffen, d. 1240, dau. of Philip, Emperor of Germany, and his wife Irene, Queen of Sicily, dau. of Isaac, Emperor of Constantinople,

HENRY III, Duke of Brabant, eldest son and heir, d. Feb. 28, 1260/61; m. Alice, d. Oct. 23, 1273, dau. of Hugh IV, Duke of Burgundy, and his wife Yolanda, dau. of Robert, Count of Dreux,

JOHN I, Duke of Brabant, 2nd son, b. 1251; d. May 4, 1294; m., secondly, 1273, Margaret of Flanders, d. *c.* July 3, 1285, dau. of Guy, Count of Flanders, and his wife Matilda, dau. of Robert, Count of Bethune,

JOHN II, Duke of Brabant, only surviving son and heir, d. Oct. 27, 1312; m., July 9, 1290, Princess Margaret, b. at Windsor, Sept. 11, 1275; d. 1318, dau. of Edward I, King of England, and his wife, Queen Eleanor,

JOHN III, Duke of Brabant, only son and heir, b. 1296/9; d. Dec. 5, 1355; m., 1314, Mary, d. Oct. 30, 1335, dau. of Louis, Count of Evreux, and his wife Margaret, dau. of Philip d'Artois, great-grandson of Louis VIII, King of France,

MARGARET, d. 1368; m., July 1, 1347, Louis de Mâle, Count of Flanders, b. Nov. 25, 1330; d. 1384; son of Louis I, Count of Flanders, and his wife Princess Margaret, dau. of Philip V, King of France,

MARGARET OF FLANDERS, only dau. and h., b. Apr. 1350; d. March 16, 1405; m., secondly, June 19, 1369, Philip the Bold, Duke of Burgundy, b. Jan. 15, 1341/2; d. Apr. 27, 1404; son of John, King of France, and his wife Bona, dau. of John, King of Bohemia,

JOHN, Duke of Burgundy, eldest son and h., b. May 28, 1371; d. Sept. 10, 1419; m., at Cambrai, Apr. 9, 1385, Margaret of Holand and Hainault, d. Jan. 23, 1423, dau. of Albert, Count of Holand and Hainault, and his wife Margaret, dau. of Louis I, Duke of Brieg,

PHILIP THE GOOD, Duke of Burgundy, only son and h., b. June 30, 1396; d. June 15, 1467; Founder of the Order of the Golden Fleece; m., thirdly, Jan. 10, 1429/30, Isabel of Portugal, b. Feb. 21, 1397; d. Dec. 17, 1472; only surviving dau. of John I, King of Portugal, and his wife Princess Philippa Plantagenet, eldest dau. of John, Duke of Lancaster, and sister of Henry IV, King of England,

CHARLES THE BOLD, Duke of Burgundy, only surviving son and h., b. Nov. 10, 1433; d. Jan. 5, 1477; m., secondly, Oct. 30, 1454, Isabella, d. Sept. 25, 1465, dau. of Charles, Duke of Bourbon, and his wife Agnes, seventh and youngest dau. of

John, Duke of Burgundy, and his wife Margaret of Holand and Hainault (see above),

MARY, only dau. and h., b. Feb. 12, 1457; d. Mar. 27, 1483; m. at Ghent, Aug. 20, 1477, (his first wife) Maximilian I, Emperor of Germany, b. Mar. 22/3, 1459; d. Jan. 12, 1519; only son of Emperor Frederick III, and his wife Eleanor, dau. of Edward I, King of Portugal,

PHILIP I, King of Castile, eldest son and heir-apparent, b. July 22, 1478; d. Sept. 25, 1506; m., Oct. 21, 1496, Joanna, b. at Toledo, Nov. 6, 1479; d. Apr. 4, 1555; 2nd dau. of Ferdinand and Isabella, King and Queen of Spain,

CHARLES V, Emperor of Germany (and I, King of Spain), b. at Ghent, Feb. 24/5, 1500; d. Sep. 21, 1558; m., March 11, 1526, Isabel of Portugal, b. Oct. 4, 1503; d. May 1, 1539; dau. of Emanuel, King of Portugal, and his wife Mary, 3rd dau. of Ferdinand and Isabella, King and Queen of Spain,

PHILIP II, King of Spain, only son and heir, b. at Valladolid, May 21, 1527; d. Sept. 13, 1598; m., fourthly, Nov. 12, 1570, Anne Mary, b. Nov. 1/11, 1549; d. Oct. 26, 1580; dau. of Maximilian II, Emperor of Germany, and his wife Mary, eldest dau. of the Emperor Charles V,

PHILIP III, King of Spain, only surviving son and heir, b. at Madrid, Apr. 14, 1578; d. at Madrid, Mar. 31, 1621; m., Apr. 18, 1599, Margaret of Austria, b. Dec. 25, 1584; d. Oct. 3, 1611; dau. of Archduke Charles of Austria, and his wife Mary, dau. of Albert V, Duke of Bavaria,

PHILIP IV, King of Spain, eldest son and heir, b. at Valladolid, Apr. 8, 1605; d. at Madrid, Sept. 17, 1665; m., first, Oct. 8, 1615, Elizabeth of France, born at Fontainebleau, Nov. 22, 1602; d. Oct. 6, 1644; eldest dau. of Henry IV, King of France, and his wife Mary de Medici, dau. of Francis, Grand Duke of Tuscany,

MARIE THERESE, eldest dau., b. Sept. 20, 1638; d. July 30, 1683; m., June 9, 1660, Louis XIV, King of France, b. at St. Germain-en-Laye, Sept. 5, 1638; d. at Versailles, Sept. 1, 1715,

LOUIS, Dauphin of Viennois, eldest son and heir-apparent, surnamed the Great Dauphin, b. at Fontainebleau, Nov. 1, 1661; d. Apr. 14, 1711; m., Mar. 7, 1680, Marie Anne of Bavaria, b. Nov. 7, 1660; d. Apr. 20/29, 1690; eldest dau. of Ferdinand,

Elector of Bavaria, and his wife Adelaide, dau. of Victor Amadeus I, Duke of Savoy,

LOUIS, Duke of Burgundy, afterwards Dauphin of France, eldest son and heir, b. at Versailles, Aug. 6, 1682; d. Feb. 18, 1712; m. Dec. 7, 1697, Marie Adelaide of Savoy, b. Dec. 16, 1685; d. Feb. 12, 1712; eldest dau. of Victor Amadeus II, Duke of Savoy, afterwards King of Sardinia, and his wife Princess Anne Marie, granddau. of Charles I, King of England,

LOUIS XV, King of France, second and youngest surviving son, succeeded his great-grandfather as King of France, b. at Versailles, Feb. 15, 1710; d. May 10, 1774; m., Sept. 5, 1725, Marie Charlotte Sophia Felicita Leczinska, b. at Breslau, June 23, 1703; d. June 14/24, 1768; dau. of Stanislas, King of Poland, and his wife Catherine, Countess Opolinski,

LOUIS, Dauphin of France, eldest son and heir-apparent, b. at Versailles, Sept. 4, 1729; d. Dec. 20, 1765; m., secondly, Feb. 9, 1747, Marie Josephine of Saxony, b. Nov. 4, 1731; d. Mar. 13, 1767; 4th dau. of Frederick Augustus, Elector of Saxony and King of Poland, and his wife Archduchess Marie Josephine, dau. of Joseph I, Emperor of Germany,

CHARLES X, King of France, 3rd surviving and youngest son, b. at Versailles, Oct. 9, 1757; d. at Goritz, Austria, Nov. 4, 1836; m., Nov. 16, 1773, Marie Therese, Countess d'Artois, b. Jan. 31, 1756; d. June 2, 1805; dau. of Victor Amadeus III, King of Sardinia, and his wife Infanta Marie Antoinette, 3rd and youngest dau. of Philip V, King of Spain,

CHARLES FERDINAND, Duke of Berry, 2nd and youngest son, b. at Versailles, Jan. 24, 1778; d. at Paris, Feb. 14, 1820; m., June 17, 1816, Marie Caroline Ferdinanda Louise, b. at Naples, Nov. 5, 1798; d. Apr. 16, 1870, eldest dau. of Francis I, King of the Two Sicilies, and his wife Archduchess Marie Clementine, 3rd dau. of Leopold II, Emperor of Germany,

LOUISE MARIE THERESE, only surviving dau., b. in the Palace of the Elysée Bourbon, Paris, Sept. 21, 1819; d. Feb. 1, 1864; m. Nov. 10, 1845, Charles III, Duke of Parma, b. Jan. 14, 1823; d. Mar. 27, 1854; only son of Charles (Louis) II, Duke of Parma, and his wife Princess Marie Therese, 4th dau. of Victor Emmanuel I, King of Sardinia,

Robert, Duke of Parma, eldest son and heir, b. at the Villa of Montui (Montughi), near Florence in Tuscany, July 9, 1848; d. at Pianore, Tuscany, Nov. 17, 1907; m., first, Apr. 5, 1869, Princess Maria Pia des Graces, b. Aug. 2, 1849; d, Sept. 29, 1882; 3rd dau. of Ferdinand II, King of the Two Sicilies, and his wife Archduchess Theresa, eldest dau. of the Archduke Charles of Austria, and had issue; he m., secondly, at the Palace of Fischhorn, near Zell-am-See, Oct. 15, 1884, Princess Maria Antonia, Infanta of Portugal, b. at Bronnbach, Nov. 28, 1862, 6th and youngest dau. of Don Miguel of Portugal, and had, among others,

1.) Prince Sixte Ferdinand Maria Ignace Pierre Alphonse de Bourbon de Parma, b. Aug. 1, 1886; d. at Paris, Mar. 14, 1934; m. at Paris, Nov. 12, 1919, Hedwige de La Rochefoucauld, des Ducs de Doudeauville, b. at Paris, Feb. 15, 1896. Issue:

    a) Princess Isabelle Marie Antoinette Louise Hedwige, b. at Paris, Mar. 14, 1922.

2.) Prince Francis Xavier Charles Maria Anne Joseph de Bourbon de Parma, b. May 25, 1889; m., Nov. 12, 1927, Marie Madeleine Yvonne, Countess de Bourbon (of the Bourbon-Busset branch), b. at Paris, Mar. 23, 1898. Issue:

    a) Princess Marie Frances, b. at Paris, Aug. 19, 1928;

    b) Prince Hugues, b. at Paris, Apr. 8, 1930;

    c) Princess Marie Therese, b. at Paris, July 28, 1933;

    d) Princess Cecile, b. at Paris, Apr. 12, 1935;

    e) Princess Marie des Neiges, b. at Paris, Apr. 29, 1937.

3.) Princess Zita Marie des Grâces Adelgonde Michelle Raphaelle Gabriella Josephine Antonia Louise Agnes de Bourbon de Parma, b. at Villa Pianore, May 9, 1892; m. at Schwarzau am Steinfelde, Oct. 21, 1911, His Imperial and Royal Highness Charles (Karl) Francis Joseph Louis Hubert George Otho Maria, Archduke of Austria, who succeeded his great

uncle, Emperor Francis Joseph I, 1916, as Emperor
of Austria, Apostolic King of Hungary, King of Bohemia, Dalmatia, Croatia, Jerusalem, etc., Grand Duke
of Tuscany, Lorraine, Transylvania, etc., b. at Persenbeug, Aug. 17, 1887; d. at Funchal, Madeira, Apr. 1,
1922; son of Archduke Otho Francis Joseph of
Austria, and have issue as listed elsewhere in this
book. (See Austria.)

4.) PRINCE FELIX MARIA VINCENT DE BOURBON DE PARMA,
Prince of Luxemburg, b. at Schwarzau am Steinfelde,
Sept. 28, 1893; m. at Luxemburg, Nov. 6, 1919, Charlotte Aldegonda Elise Marie Wilhelmina, Grand
Duchess of Luxemburg, Duchess de Nassau, Princess
de Bourbon de Parma, Countess Palatine of the
Rhine, Countess of Sayn, Konigstein, Katzenelnbogen
and Dietz, Burggravine of Hammerstein, etc., Sovereign Ruler of Luxemburg, b. at the Palace of Berg,
Jan. 23, 1896, dau. of William, Grand Duke of Luxemburg, and his wife Marie Anne, Infanta of
Portugal, Grand Duchess of Luxemburg, and have
issue elsewhere listed in this book. (See Luxemburg.)

5.) PRINCE RENÉ CHARLES MARIA JOSEPH DE BOURBON DE
PARMA, b. at Schwarzau, Oct. 17, 1894; m. at Copen-
hagen, June 9, 1921, Marguerite, Princess of Denmark,
b. Sept. 17, 1895. Issue:

a) PRINCE JACQUES MARIA ANTOINE ROBERT VALDE-
MAR CHARLES FELIX SIXTE ANSGAR DE BOURBON
DE PARMA, b. June 9, 1922;

b) PRINCESS ANNE ANTOINETTE FRANCES CHARLOTTE
DE BOURBON DE PARMA, b. Sept. 18, 1923;

c) PRINCE MICHAEL MARIA XAVIER VALDEMAR
GEORGE ROBERT CHARLES AYMARD DE BOURBON
DE PARMA, b. Mar. 4, 1926;

d) PRINCE ANDREW (ANDRÉ) DE BOURBON DE PARMA,
b. Mar. 5, 1928.

6.) PRINCE GAETAN MARIA JOSEPH PIUS DE BOURBON DE
PARMA, b. at Pianore, June 3, 1905; m. at Paris, Apr.
29, 1931, Marguerite Marie Therese Elizabeth Fred-
erique Alexandrina Louise, Princess de Thurn-et-

Taxis, b. at Beloeil, Belgium, Nov. 8, 1909, dau. of Prince Alexander Charles Egon Theobald Lamoral John Baptist Maria de Thurn-et-Taxis, 1st Duke di Castel Duino, and his 1st wife Marie Susanne Marguerite Louise, Princess de Ligne. Issue:

   a) PRINCESS DIANE MARGUERITE DE BOURBON DE PARMA, b. at Paris, May 22, 1932.

GREAT BRITAIN

CHARLEMAGNE, King of the Franks and Emperor of the West, m. the Swabian Princess Hildegard,

LOUIS I, the Pious, surnamed *le Debonnaire*, King of the Franks and Emperor of the West; m., 2ndly, 819, Judith, d. Apr. 19, 843, dau. of Guelph I, Count of Altdorf and Duke of Bavaria,

PRINCESS GISELE, b. about 820; d. about 874; m., 836/40, Eberhard, Markgraf (or Duke) of Frioul, d. 864/6,

HATWIGE, m. Ludolph the Great, Count and afterwards Duke of Saxony, d. Sept. 6, 864,

OTHO, the Illustrious, Duke of Saxony, d. Nov. 12/3, 912; m. Hedwige (or Edith), a dau. of Emperor Arnoul (Arnulph),

HENRY I, the Fowler, (l'Oiseleur), Emperor of Germany, Duke of Saxony, Brunswick and Zelle, b. about 876; d. July 2, 936; m., 2ndly, about 911, Mathilda, dau. of Dietrich, Count of Ringelheim, and a sister of Siegfried, 1st Count (Markgraf) of Brandenburg,

PRINCESS HATWIDE (or Hatwin, or Hawise, or Hatwige), m., (his 3rd wife), Prince Hugh the Great, surnamed "the White," Duke of France and Burgundy, &c., d. about June 17 - July 1, 956, son of Robert, Duke of France, who was crowned King of France about June 29, 922, (killed in battle about June 15, 923), and grandson of Robert, surnamed "the Strong," Duke of France and Count of Anjou, who was killed about 866/7,

HUGH CAPET, King of France, d. Oct. 24, 996; m. Adelaide,

ROBERT II, the Pious, King of France, b. about 970/1; d. July 20, 1031; m., 2ndly, Constance, dau. of William de Taillefer, Count of Toulouse,

HENRY I, King of France, d. Aug. 4/24, 1060; m., about Jan. 29, 1044, Anne, dau. of Yaroslav I, Grand Prince of Kiev,

PHILIPPE I, King of France, b. about 1053; d. July 29, 1108; m., first, 1071/2, Bertha, d. 1093, dau. of Florent I, Count of Holland (or Holand),

LOUIS VI, surnamed *le Gros,,* King of France, b. 1077/8; d. Aug. 1, 1137; m., about 1120, Adelaide (or Alix), dau. of Humbert III, Count of Maurienne (or of Savoy), and his wife Gisele de Bourgogne,

LOUIS VII, surnamed *le Jeune,* King of France, b. about 1120; d. Sept. 18, 1180; m., 3rdly, Nov. 13, 1160, Alix (or Alice), d. June 24, 1206, dau. of Theobald the Great, Count of Champagne,

PHILIPPE II, King of France, b. Aug. 21, 1165; d. July 14, 1223; m., first, Apr. 28, 1180, Isabelle, b. about 1170; d. Mar. 15/27, 1188/90, presumably a dau. of Baldwin V, Count of Hainault and Hennegau,

LOUIS VIII, surnamed *the Lion,* King of France, b. Sept. 4/5, 1187; d. Nov. 8, 1226; m., May 23, 1200, Blanche, dau. of Alphonso IX (or X?), King of Castile,

LOUIS IX, the Saint, (Saint Louis), King of France, b. Apr. 25, 1215; d. Aug. 25, 1270; m. Marguerite, dau. of Raymond Berenger, Count of Provence,

PHILIPPE III, surnamed *le Hardi* and *Coeur de Lion,* King of France, b. about 1245; d. Oct. 5, 1285; m., first, May 28, 1262, Isabelle, d. Jan. 28, 1271, dau. of James I, King of Aragon,

PHILIPPE IV, surnamed *le Bel,* King of France and Navarre, b. about 1268, d. Nov. 29, 1314; m., Aug. 16,`1284, Jeanne (Joanna), Queen of Navarre, d. Apr. 2, 1305, dau of Henry I, King of Navarre,

PRINCESS ISABELLE, d. Aug. 22, 1358; m., Jan. 25, 1307/8, Edward II, King of England, d. Sept. 21, 1327,

EDWARD III, King of England, b. Nov. 13, 1312; d. June 21, 1377; m., Jan. 24, 1327, Philippa of Hainault, b. about 1312; d. Aug. 14/5, 1369; dau. of William III, *Le Bon,* Count of Hainault and Holland (or Holand), and his wife Joanna (or Jane), dau. of Charles, Count of Valois, and granddau. of Philippe III, *le Hardi,* King of France,

PRINCE EDMUND, "of Langley," Earl of Cambridge, Duke of York, K.G., b. June 5, 1341; d. Aug. 1, 1402; m., first, Isabel, b. about 1355; d. 1392/3; dau. and co-heiress of Peter (Pedro) the Cruel, King of Castile and Leon,

PRINCE RICHARD, "of Conisburgh," or "of York," Earl of Cambridge, Almoner of England, &c., b. about 1376; beheaded Aug. 5/6, 1415; m., first, about 1406, Anne de Mortimer, b. Dec. 27, 1390; d. about 1411; dau. of Roger de Mortimer, 4th Earl of March, Earl of Ulster, &c.,

PRINCE RICHARD, Earl of Cambridge, Duke of York, sometime Regent of France, K. G., b. Sept. 20, 1410/11/12; slain at Wakefield, Dec. 31, 1460; m. Cecily, b. May 3, 1415; d. May 31, 1495; dau. of Ralph de Neville, 1st Earl of Westmorland, K. G.,

EDWARD IV, King of England, b. April 28, 1442; d. April 9, 1483; m., May 4, 1464, (her second husband), Elizabeth Wydeville (Woodville), b. about 1437; d. June 7, 1492; widow of John, Lord Ferrers of Groby, and dau. of Sir Richard Wydeville (Woodville), Earl of Rivers, K.G.,

PRINCESS ELIZABETH, m. Henry VII, King of England,

PRINCESS MARGARET TUDOR, d. Oct. 18, 1541; m., first, James IV, King of Scots, b. March 17, 1472/3; killed at the battle of Flodden, Sept. 9, 1513; son of James III, King of Scots, and his wife Princess Margaret, dau. of Christian I, King of Denmark,

JAMES V, King of Scots, b. April 10, 1512; d. Dec. 14, 1542; m., 2ndly, 1538, Marie de Lorraine, Duchess of Longueville, d. June 10, 1560, eldest dau. of Charles (or Claude) of Lorraine) Duke of Guise, and widow of Louis d'Orleans, Duke de Longueville,

MARY, Queen of Scots, b. Dec. 7/8, 1542; beheaded Feb. 8, 1586/7; widow of Francis II, King of France; m., 2ndly, July 29, 1565, her cousin, Henry Stewart, Lord Darnley, murdered at Edinburgh, Feb. 10, 1566/7,

JAMES I, King of England (and VI of Scotland), b. June 19, 1566; d. March 27, 1625; m., Nov. 24, 1589, Princess Anne, d. March 2, 1618/9, dau. of Frederick II, King of Denmark and Norway, and his wife Sophia, dau. of Ulric, Duke of Mecklenburg,

PRINCESS ELIZABETH, b. Aug. 19, 1596; d. Feb. 13, 1661/2; m., Feb. 14, 1612/3, Frederick V, Duke of Bavaria, Elector Palatine of the Rhine, and King of Bohemia, d. Nov. 9/19, 1632,

PRINCESS SOPHIA, b. Oct. 13, 1630, d. June 8, 1714; m., Sept. 30, 1658, Ernest Augustus, Duke of Brunswick-Luneburg, Elector of Hanover, d. Jan. 13/23, 1698,

GEORGE I, (GEORGE LOUIS), Elector of Hanover, King of Great Britain, France, and Ireland in 1714; b. May 28, 1660; d. June 11, 1727; m., about 1682, Sophia Dorothy, d. Nov. 13, 1726, only dau. and heiress of George William, Duke of Brunswick-Luneburg and of Zelle,

GEORGE II, (GEORGE AUGUSTUS), Prince of Wales, King of Great Britain, France, and Ireland, crowned Oct. 11, 1727; b. Oct. 30, 1683; d. Oct. 25, 1760; m., 1705, Wilhelmina Carolina, dau. of John Frederick, Marggrave of Brandenburg-Anspach, and his second wife Eleanor, dau. of John George, Duke of Saxe-Eisenach,

FREDERICK LOUIS, Prince of Wales, b. Jan. 20, 1707; d. March 20, 1751; m., April 27, 1736, Augusta, youngest dau. of Frederdick II, Duke of Saxe-Gotha,

GEORGE III, (WILLIAM FREDERICK), King of Great Britain, France, and Ireland, Oct. 25, 1760; b. May 24, 1738; m. Sept. 8, 1761, Princess Sophia Charlotte, b. May 19, 1744; d. Nov. 17, 1818; dau. of Charles Louis Frederick, reigning Duke of Mecklenburg-Strelitz, and his wife Albertina Elizabeth, dau. of Ernest Frederick, Duke of Saxe-Hildburghausen,

EDWARD, Prince of Great Britain and Ireland, Duke of Brunswick-Luneburg, Duke of Kent and of Strathearn, Earl of Dublin, K. G., &c., b. Nov. 2, 1767; d. Jan. 23, 1820; m., May 29, 1818, Maria Louisa Victoria, b. Aug. 17, 1786; d. March 16, 1861; widow of Emich Charles, reigning Prince of Leiningen, and dau. of Francis I (Frederick Anthony), reigning Duke of Saxe-Coburg-Saalfield, and his second wife, Augusta Caroline Sophia, dau. of Henry XXIV, Count of Reuss-Ebersdorf,

VICTORIA (ALEXANDRINA), Queen of Great Britain, Ireland, &c., Empress of India; succeeded to the throne June 20, 1837; b. May 24, 1819; d. Jan. 22, 1901; m., Feb. 10, 1840, Prince Francis Albert Augustus Charles Emanuel of Saxe-Coburg-Gotha, Duke of Saxony, Prince Consort of Great Britain,

b. Aug. 26, 1819; d. Dec. 14, 1861; naturalized in Great Britain, Jan. 24, 1840; son of Ernest, Duke of Saxe-Coburg-Gotha,

EDWARD VII (ALBERT EDWARD), Prince of Wales, Duke of Saxony, Prince of Coburg-Gotha, Duke of Cornwall, Duke of Rothsay, Earl of Chester, Carrick and of Dublin, &c.; King of Great Britain and Ireland, Emperor of India; b. Nov. 9, 1841; d. May 6, 1910; m., March 10, 1863, Princess Alexandra (Caroline Mary Charlotte Louisa Julia), b. Dec. 1, 1844; d. Jan. 28, 1906; dau. of Christian IX, King of Denmark, and his wife Louisa, Princess of Hesse-Cassel,

GEORGE V (GEORGE FREDERICK ERNEST ALBERT), King of the United Kingdom of Great Britain and Ireland, Emperor of India, &c., b. June 3, 1865; d. Jan. 20, 1936; m. July 6, 1893, Princess Victoria Mary Augusta Louisa Olga Pauline Claudine Agnes of Teck, b. at Kensington Palace, May 26, 1867, only dau. of Francis Paul Charles Louis Alexander, Prince and Duke of Teck, and his wife, Princess Mary Adelaide Wilhelmina Elizabeth, dau. of Adolphus Frederick, Prince of Great Britain, Duke of Cambridge, Duke of Brunswick and Luneburg, &c., 7th and youngest surviving son of George III, King of Great Britain, France, and Ireland,

GEORGE VI (ALBERT FREDERICK ARTHUR GEORGE), King of the United Kingdom of Great Britain and Ireland, and of the British Dominions Beyond the Seas, King Defender of the Faith, Emperor of India, Imperial and Royal Majesty, &c., b. at York Cottage, Sandringham, Dec. 14, 1895; succeeded to the Throne on the abdication of his brother, Edward VIII, Dec. 12, 1936, crowned May 12, 1937; m. at London, April 26, 1923, Lady Elizabeth Angela Marguerite Bowes-Lyon, b. at London, Aug. 4, 1900, dau. of Claude George Bowes-Lyon, 14th Earl of Strathmore and Kinghorne, 22nd Lord Glammis, Lord Tannadyce, Sidlaw, and Stradichtie, Viscount Lyon, Baron Bowes of Streatlam Castle, co. Durham, and of Lunedale, co. York, K.G., K.T., G.C.V.O., Lord-Lieutenant of the co. of Forfar, Deputy Lieutenant of the co. of the city of Dundee, J.P. for Herts, &c., and his wife, Nina Cecilia, d. 1938, dau. of the late Rev. Charles William Frederick Cavendish-Bentinck, grandson of William Henry, 3rd Duke of Portland. Issue:

1.) PRINCESS ELIZABETH ALEXANDRA MARY, b. at London, April 21, 1926;

2.) PRINCESS MARGARET ROSE, b. in the Palace of Glammis, Scotland, Aug. 21, 1930.

VICTORIA (ALEXANDRINA), Queen of Great Britain, Ireland, &c., Empress of India, m. Prince Francis Albert Augustus Charles Emanuel of Saxe-Coburg-Gotha, &c. Issue:

1.) EDWARD VII, King of Great Britain and of Ireland, Emperor of India, &c., m. Princess Alexandra, dau. of Christian IX, King of Denmark, by his wife Louisa, Princess of Hesse-Cassel. Issue:

    a) GEORGE V, King of Great Britain and of Ireland, Emperor of India, m., his cousin, Princess Victoria Mary Augusta Louisa Olga Pauline Claudine Agnes of Teck. Issue, among others:

        i EDWARD ALBERT CHRISTIAN GEORGE ANDREW PATRICK DAVID, Prince of Great Britain and of Ireland, Duke of Windsor, K. G., &c., ascended the throne upon the death of his father as Edward VIII, abdicated in favor of his brother, George VI, Dec. 11/2, 1936; b. at White Lodge, Richmond Park, Surrey, June 23, 1894; m., June 3, 1937, Bessie Wallis Warfield, b. at Monterey, Va., June 19, 1896;

        ii PRINCESS VICTORIA ALEXANDRA ALICE MARY, b. at Sandringham, April 25, 1897; m. at London, Feb. 28, 1922, Henry George Charles, Viscount Lascelles, Earl of Harewood, &c. Issue:

            a) GEORGE HENRY HUBERT, Viscount Lascelles, b. Feb. 7, 1923;

            b) GERALD DAVID, b. Aug. 22, 1924.

        iii PRINCE HENRY WILLIAM FREDERICK ALBERT, Duke of Gloucester, Prince of Great Britain and Ireland, Count of Ulster, Baron Culloden, &c., b. at Sandringham, March 31, 1900; m. at London, Nov. 6, 1935, Alice Montagu Douglas Scott, b. at London, Dec. 25, 1901, 3rd dau. of John Charles Montagu Douglas Scott, 7th Duke of Buccleuch and 9th Duke of Queensberry, by his wife, Margaret Alice Bridgeman, dau. of George Cecil Orlando, 4th Earl of Bradford;

iv PRINCE GEORGE EDWARD ALEXANDER EDMOND of Great Britain and Ireland, Duke of Kent, Count of St. Andrews, Baron Downpatrick, &c., b. at Sandringham, Dec. 20, 1902; m. at London, Nov. 29, 1934, Marina, Princess of Greece and of Denmark, b. at Athens, Dec. 13, 1906, dau. of the late Prince Nicholas of Greece. Issue:

a) PRINCE EDWARD GEORGE NICHOLAS PAUL PATRICK, b. at London, Oct. 9, 1935;

b) PRINCESS ALEXANDRA HELEN ELIZABETH OLGA CHRISTABEL, b. at London, Dec. 25, 1936.

b) PRINCESS LOUISE VICTORIA ALEXANDRA DAGMAR of Great Britain and Ireland, b. at Marlborough House, Feb. 20, 1867; d. Jan. 4, 1931; m., July 27, 1889, Alexander William George, Earl of Fife, 1st Duke of Fife, K.G., K.T., G.C. V.O., P.C., &c., b. Nov. 10, 1849; d. Jan. 29, 1912; only son of James Duff, 5th Earl of Fife, and his wife Agnes Georgiana Elizabeth Hay, 2nd dau. of William George, 7th Earl of Erroll. Issue:

i PRINCESS ALEXANDRIA VICTORIA ALBERTA EDWINA LOUISE, Duchess of Fife, Countess of Macduff, b. at East Sheen Lodge, May 17, 1891; m. at London, Oct. 15, 1913, Arthur Frederick Patrick Albert, Prince of Great Britain and Ireland, Prince of Connaught, b. at Windsor Castle, Jan. 13, 1883; d. Sept. 12, 1938. Issue:

a) ALASTAIR ARTHUR DUFF, Earl of Macduff, b. Aug. 9, 1914.

ii PRINCESS MAUD ALEXANDRA VICTORIA GEORGINA BERTHA of Great Britain and

Ireland, b. at East Sheen Lodge, April 3, 1893; m. at London, Nov. 12, 1923, Lord Charles Alexander Carnegie, b. Sept. 23, 1893; K.C.V.O.; eldest son of Charles Noel Carnegie, 10th Earl of Southesk, Baron Carnegie, Baron Balinhard, Baronet of Nova Scotia, and his wife Ethel, dau. of Sir Alexander Bannerman, 9th Baronet of Elsick. Issue:

> a) James Alexander Bannerman Carnegie, Master of Carnegie, b. Sept. 23, 1929.

2.) Prince Arthur William Patrick Albert of Great Britain and of Ireland, Duke of Connaught and Strathearn, Count of Sussex, b. at Buckingham Palace, May 1, 1850; renounced for himself and his sons the right to succession to the Dukedom of Saxe-Coburg and Gotha, June 30, 1899; formerly Governor General of the Dominion of Canada; K.G., K.T., K.P., G.C.B., G.C.S.I., G.C.M.G., G.C.I.E., G.C.V.O., P.C., &c.; m., March 13, 1879, Princess Louise Margaret of Prussia, b July 25, 1860; d. at London, March 14, 1917; dau. of Prince Frederick Charles of Prussia. Issue:

> a) Princess Margaret Victoria Augusta Charlotte Norah of Great Britain and of Ireland, b. Jan. 15, 1882; d. at Stockholm, May 1, 1920; m. at Windsor Castle, June 5, 1905, (his first wife), Prince Oscar Frederick William Olaf Gustave Adolphe of Sweden, Duke of Scania, b. at Stockholm, Nov. 11, 1882, Crown Prince of Sweden, eldest son of Gustaf V (Oscar Gustave Adolphe), King of Sweden, and his wife, Queen Victoria, Princess of Baden. Issue:

>> i Prince Gustave Adolphe Oscar Frederick Arthur Edmund, Duke of Vasterbotten, b. at Stockholm, April 22, 1906; m. at Coburg, Oct. 20, 1932, Sibylle, Princess of Saxe-Coburg and Gotha, Duchess of Saxony, b. at Gotha, Jan. 18, 1908. Issue:

>>> a) Princess Margaretha Désirée Victoria, b. Oct. 31, 1934;

b) PRINCESS BIRGITTA INGEBORG ALICE, b. Jan. 19, 1937.

ii PRINCE SIGVARD OSCAR FREDERICK, Duke of Upland, b. June 7, 1907; by reason of his marriage he lost his rights to succession to the throne and his titles and privileges of a Prince of Sweden. He now bears the name of the family Bernadotte;

iii PRINCESS INGRID VICTORIA SOPHIA LOUISE MARGARETHA, b. at Stockholm, March 28, 1910; m. at Stockholm, May 24, 1935, Christian Frederick, Prince of Denmark and of Iceland, Crown Prince of Denmark and of Iceland, b. March 11, 1899, son of Christian X, King of Denmark and of Iceland;

iv PRINCE BERTIL GUSTAVE OSCAR CHARLES EUGENE, Duke of Holland, b. at Stockholm, Feb. 28, 1912;

v PRINCE CHARLES JOHN ARTHUR, Duke of Dalécarlie, b. at Stockholm, Oct. 31, 1916.

b) PRINCE ARTHUR FREDERICK PATRICK ALBERT of Connaught, Prince of Great Britain and of Ireland, K.G., K.T., G.C.M.G., G.C.V.O., C.B., Governor General and Commander-in-Chief of the Union of South Africa and High Commissioner for South Africa, 1920-23; b. Jan. 13, 1883; d. Sept. 12, 1938; m. Princess Alexandra Victoria Alberta Edwina Louise Duff, Duchess of Fife, Countess of Macduff, who is mentioned elsewhere in this book.

c) PRINCESS VICTORIA PATRICIA HELEN ELIZABETH of Great Britain and of Ireland, b. at Buckingham Palace, London, March 17, 1886, (abandoned her rank and princely title with royal authorization and bears the name of Lady Patricia Ramsay); m. at London, Feb. 27, 1919, Vice-Admiral Sir Alexander R. M. Ramsay, G.C.V.O., K.C.B., C.B., D.S.O., b. May 29, 1881, son of the 13th Earl of Dalhousie and his wife

Ida, dau. of the 6th Earl of Tankerville, and have issue.

3.) PRINCESS ALICE MAUD MARY of Great Britain and of Ireland, b. April 25, 1843; d. Dec. 14, 1878; m., July 1, 1862, Frederick William Louise Charles, Prince of Hesse, afterwards Louis IV, Grand Duke of Hesse and of the Rhine, b. Sept. 12, 1837; d. March 13, 1892. Issue:

a) ERNEST LUDWIG CHARLES ALBERT WILLIAM, Grand Duke of Hesse and the Rhine, &c., b. at Darmstadt, Nov. 25, 1868; d. Oct. 9, 1937; m., 2ndly, Feb. 2, 1905, Eleonore, Princess of Solms-Hohensolms-Lich, b. at Lich, Sept. 17, 1871; d. in an accident Nov. 16, 1937. Issue living:

i PRINCE LOUIS HERMANN ALEXANDER CLOVIS of Hesse and the Rhine, heir to the Grand Duchy of Hesse and the Rhine, b. at Darmstadt, Nov. 20, 1908; m. at London, Nov. 17, 1937, Margaret Campbell Geddes, b. at Dublin, March 18, 1913, dau. of Sir Auckland Campbell Geddes.

b) PRINCESS VICTORIA ELIZABETH MATHILDE ALBERTA MARIE, b. at Windsor Castle, April 5, 1863; m. at Darmstadt, April 30, 1884, Louis Alexander, Prince of Battenberg, Count of Battenberg, Marquess of Milford Haven, G.C.B., G.C.V.O., &c., b, at Graz, Austria, May 24, 1854; naturalized as a British subject, Sept. 30, 1868; d. at London, Sept. 11, 1921; eldest son of Prince Alexander of Hesse and the Rhine, and his wife Julia Theresa, Princess of Battenberg, dau. of Maurice, Count de Houcke. Issue:

i PRINCESS VICTORIA ALICE ELIZABETH JULIA MARIE, b. at Windsor Castle, Feb. 28, 1885; m. at Darmstadt, Sept. 24/Oct. 7, 1903, Prince Andrew of Greece, b. at Athens, Jan. 20/Feb. 1, 1882, and have issue;

ii PRINCESS LOUISE ALEXANDRA MARIE IRENE, b. July 13, 1889;

iii PRINCE LUDWIG VICTOR GEORGE HENRY SERGIUS, b. Nov. 6, 1892;

iv PRINCE LOUIS FRANCIS, b. June 25, 1900.

c) PRINCESS IRENE LOUISE MARIE ANNA, b. at Darmstadt, July 11, 1866; m., May 24, 1888, her cousin, Prince Henry of Prussia, b. Aug. 14, 1862, and had issue;

d) PRINCESS VICTORIA ALICE HELENA LOUISE BEATRICE, b. at Darmstadt, June 6, 1872; m., Nov. 14/26, 1894, her cousin, Nicholas II, Emperor of all the Russias, b. at St. Petersburg, May 6/18, 1868; assassinated with his family at Ekaterinburg, July 16/7, 1918.

4.) PRINCESS HELENA AUGUSTA VICTORIA of Great Britain and of Ireland, b. May 25, 1846; d. June 9, 1923; m., July 5, 1866, Prince Frederick Christian of Schleswig-Holstein, K.G., G.C.V.O., &c., b. Jan. 22, 1831; d. Oct. 28, 1917; son of Christian, Duke of Schleswig-Holstein-Sonderburg-Augustenburg, and his wife Louisa Sophia, dau. of Christian Conrad, Count of Danneskjold-Samsoe. Issue:

a) PRINCE ALBERT JOHN CHARLES FREDERICK ALFRED GEORGE, Duke of Schleswig-Holstein, Stormarn, Dithmarses and of Oldenburg, b. Feb. 26, 1869; d. at Berlin, April 27, 1931;

b) PRINCESS HELENA VICTORIA LOUISE SOPHIA AUGUSTINA AMELIA, b. May 3, 1870;

c) PRINCESS FRANCES JOSEPHINE LOUISE AUGUSTINE MARIE CHRISTINA HELENA, b. Aug. 12, 1872; m. July 6, 1891, Aribert Joseph Alexander, Prince of Anhalt, b. June 18, 1864; d. Dec. 24, 1933; (marriage was dissolved by divorce, Dec. 13, 1900); 4th son of Frederick, then reigning Duke of Anhalt, and his wife Princess Antoinette of Saxe-Altenburg.

5.) PRINCESS BEATRICE MARIE VICTORIA FEODORA of Great Britain and of Ireland, b. at Buckingham Palace, April 14, 1857; m., July 23, 1885, Henry Maurice, Prince of Battenberg, K.G., P.C., Captain General and

Governor of the Isle of Wight, Governor of Carisbrooke Castle, b. Oct. 5, 1858; d. Jan. 20, 1896. Issue:

a) PRINCE ALEXANDER ALBERT MOUNTBATTEN of Battenberg, Marquess of Carisbrooke, Earl of Berkhampsted, Viscount Launceston, G.C.B., G.C.V.O., b. Nov. 23, 1886; m., 1917, Irene Frances Adza Denison, G.B.E., dau. of the 2nd Earl of Londesborough, and have issue;

b) PRINCESS VICTORIA EUGENIA JULIA ENA of Battenberg, b. Oct. 24, 1887; m. at Madrid, May 31, 1906, Alphonso XIII, King of Spain, of Castile, of Leon, of Aragon, of the Two Sicilies, Jerusalem, Navarre, &c., b. at Madrid, May 17, 1886; d. at Rome, Feb. 28, 1941. (Issue listed under Spain.)

ITALY

CHARLEMAGNE

See Page 34

FRANCIS I (STEPHEN), Emperor of Germany in 1745; Duke of Lorraine, Grand Duke of Tuscany, King of Hungary and Bohemia, Archduke of Austria; b. Dec. 8, 1708; d. Aug. 18, 1765; m., Feb. 12, 1736, Maria Theresa, b. May 13, 1717; d. Nov. 29, 1780; Queen of Hungary and Bohemia; eldest dau. of Charles VI, Emperor of Germany,

LEOPOLD II, Emperor of Germany, Grand Duke of Tuscany, &c., b. May 5, 1747; d. Mar. 1, 1792; m., Aug. 5, 1765, Maria Louisa, b. Nov. 24, 1745; d. May 15, 1792; dau. of Charles III, King of Spain, by Princess Marie Amelia, eldest dau. of Augustus III, King of Poland, Elector of Saxony,

FERDINAND III, Grand Duke of Tuscany, Elector of Salzburg and of Wurzburg, &c., b. May 6, 1769; d. June 18, 1824; m., first, Sept. 19, 1790, Princess Louise Amelia, b. July 27, 1773; d. Sept. 19, 1802; dau. of Ferdinand I, King of the Two Sicilies,

MARIA THERESA FRANCES, Princess of Tuscany, Archduchess of Austria, b. Mar. 21, 1801; d. Jan. 12, 1855; m., Sept. 30, 1817, Charles Albert, Duke of Savoy Carigan, King of Sardinia, b. Oct. 29, 1798; d. July 28, 1849,

VICTOR EMMANUEL II, King of Italy, b. Mar. 14, 1820; d. Jan. 9, 1878; m., first, Apr. 12, 1842, Marie Adelaide, Archduchess of Austria, b. June 3, 1822; d. Jan. 20, 1855.

HUMBERT (UMBERTO) I, King of Italy, b. Mar. 14, 1844; d. July 29, 1900; m., Apr. 22, 1868, Marguerite (Margherita), b. Nov. 20, 1851; d. Jan. 4, 1926; dau. of Prince Ferdinand of Savoy, 1st Duke of Genoa,

VICTOR EMMANUEL III, King of Italy, Sardinia, and Cyprus, King of Jerusalem, Duke of Savoy, Prince of Carignan, Piedmont, &c., Duke of Genoa, &c., b. at Naples, Nov. 11, 1869; m., Oct. 24, 1896, Helena (Elena), Princess Petrovitch Niegoch, b. Dec. 27, 1872, dau. of the late Nicholas I, King of Montenegro. Issue:

1.) PRINCESS YOLANDA MARGUERITE of Savoy, b. June 1, 1901; m., Apr. 9, 1923, George Carlo, Count Calvi di Bergolo, b. Mar. 15, 1887, and have issue:

    a) MARIA LUDOVICA, b. 1924;

    b) VICTORIA FRANCES, b. 1927;

    c) GUJA ANNA, b. 1930;

    d) PIER FRANCIS, b. 1933.

2.) PRINCESS MAFALDA MARIE ELIZABETH of Savoy, b. Nov. 19, 1902; m., Sept. 23, 1925, Philippe, Prince of Hesse, b. Nov. 6, 1896, son of Prince Frederick Charles Louis Constantine, Landgrave of Hesse, &c., and his wife Marguerite, Princess of Prussia, and have issue:

    a) PRINCE MAURICE FREDERICK of Hesse, b. Aug. 6, 1926;

    b) PRINCE HENRY WILLIAM of Hesse, b. Oct. 30, 1927;

    c) PRINCE OTHO ADOLPH of Hesse, b. June 3, 1937.

3.) PRINCE HUMBERT (UMBERTO) NICHOLAS of Savoy, Crown Prince of Italy, Prince of Piedmont, &c., b. Sept. 15, 1904; m., Jan. 8, 1930, Marie Jose, Princess of Belgium, b. Aug. 4, 1906, and have issue:

    a) PRINCESS MARIA PIA ELIZABETH of Savoy, b. Sept. 24, 1934;

    b) PRINCE VICTOR EMMANUEL of Savoy, Prince of Naples, b. Feb. 12, 1937.

4.) PRINCESS IOANNA (GIOVANNA) of Savoy, b. Nov. 13, 1907; m., Oct. 25, 1930, Boris III, King of the Bulgarians, Duke of Saxony, &c., b. Jan. 30, 1894, and have issue:

    a) PRINCESS MARIE LOUISE of Bulgaria, b. Jan. 13, 1933;

    b) PRINCE SIMEON of Bulgaria, Prince de Tirnovo, Crown Prince, b. June 16, 1937.

5.) PRINCESS MARIE FRANCISCA of Savoy, b. Dec. 26, 1914.

LUXEMBURG

GEORGE II (GEORGE AUGUSTUS), King of Great Britain, France, and Ireland; m. Wilhelmina Carolina, dau. of John Frederdick, Marggrave of Brandenburg-Anspach, by his second wife, Eleanor, dau. of John George, Duke of Saxe-Eisenach,

PRINCESS ANNE of Great Britain, m. William IV (Charles Henry Frisco), Prince of Orange, Staathalter von Holland, &c.,

PRINCESS CAROLINA, b. Feb. 28, 1743; d. May 6, 1787.; m., Mar. 5, 1760, Charles, Prince of Nassau-Weilburg, b. Jan. 16, 1735; d. Nov. 28, 1788; son of Charles Augustus, Prince of Nassau-Weilburg,

FREDERICK WILLIAM, Prince of Nassau-Weilburg, b. Oct. 25, 1768; d. Jan. 9 or Feb. 5, 1816; m., about 1788, Louisa Isabella Alexandrina Augusta of Kirchberg, dau. of Burggrave William George of Kirchberg, Count of Sayn-Hachemburg,

WILLIAM GEORGE AUGUSTUS HENRY, Duke of Nassau, b. June 14, 1792; d. Aug. 20, 1839; m., first, June 24, 1813, Louisa, Princess of Saxe-Hildburghausen (afterwards Saxe-Altenburg), b. Jan. 28, 1794; d. April 6, 1825,

ADOLPHUS WILLIAM CHARLES AUGUST FREDERICK, Grand Duke of Luxemburg, Duke of Nassau, Pfalzgraf bei Rhein, &c., b. July 24, 1817; d. Nov. 17, 1905; m., 2ndly, at Dessau, April 23, 1851, Adelheid Marie, Princess of Anhalt, b. at Dessau, Dec. 25, 1833; d. Nov. 24, 1916; dau. of Frederick, Prince of Anhalt, &c., and his wife Marie, Princess of Hesse-Cassel,

WILLIAM ALEXANDER, Grand Duke of Luxemburg, Duke of Nassau, &c., b. April 22, 1852; d. Feb. 25, 1912; m., June 21, 1893, Maria Anna, Princess of Braganza, Infanta of Portugal, b. at Bronnbach, July 13, 1861; living in March 1941; dau. of Michael I, King of Portugal from June 30, 1828, until May 26, 1834. Issue:

   1.) MARIE ADELAIDE THERESE HILDA ANTONIE WILHELMINA, Grand Duchess of Luxemburg, Duchess of Nassau,

&c., b. June 14, 1894; renounced the throne, Jan. 15, 1919, in favor of her sister, Grand Duchess Charlotte; d. Jan. 24, 1924;

2.) CHARLOTTE (ALDEGONDA ELISE MARIE WILHELMINA), Sovereign Grand Duchess of Luxemburg, Duchess of Nassau, Princess de Bourbon de Parma, Countess Palatine of the Rhine, Countess of Sayn, Konigstein, Katzenelnboden and Dietz, Burggravine of Hammerstein, Lady of Mahlberg, Wiesbaden, Idstein, Merenberg, Limburg and Eppstein, &c., Royal Highness, b. in Berg Castle, Luxemburg, Jan. 23, 1896; m. at Luxemburg, Nov. 6, 1919, Felix Maria Vincent, Prince de Bourbon de Parma, Prince of Luxemburg, b. at Schwarzau am Steinfelde, Sept. 28, 1893, son of Robert, Duke of Parma. Issue:

> a) JOHN (JEAN BENOIT WILLIAM ROBERT ANTON LOUIS MARIA ADOLPHE MARC D'AVIANO), Hereditary Grand Duke of Luxemburg, Hereditary Duke of Nassau, Prince de Bourbon de Parma, &c., b. in Berg Castle, Jan. 5, 1921;

> b) PRINCESS ELIZABETH HILDA ZITA MARIE ANNE ANTONIA FREDERIQUE WILHELMINA LOUISE of Luxemburg and of Nassau, Princess de Bourbon de Parma, b. Dec. 22, 1922;

> c) PRINCESS MARIE ADELAIDE LOUISE THERESE WILHELMINA of Luxemburg and of Nassau, Princess de Bourbon de Parma, b. May 21, 1924;

> d) PRINCESS MARIE GABRIELLA ALDEGONDA WILHELMINA LOUISE of Luxemburg and of Nassau, Princess de Bourbon de Parma, b. Aug. 2, 1925;

> e) PRINCE CHARLES FREDERICK LOUIS WILLIAM MARIA of Luxemburg and of Nassau, Prince de Bourbon de Parma, b. Aug. 7, 1927;

> f) PRINCESS ALIX MARIE ANNE ANTONIA CHARLOTTE GABRIELLA of Luxemburg and of Nassau, Princess de Bourbon de Parma, b. Aug. 24, 1929.

3.) HILDA SOPHIA MARIE ADELAIDE WILHELMINA, Princess of Luxemburg and of Nassau, b. Feb. 15, 1897; m.,

Oct. 29, 1930, Adolph John Maria Francis Joseph Hubert, Hereditary Prince of Schwarzenberg, b. Aug. 18, 1890, son of John Nepomuk Adolph Maria Hubert Maximin, 9th Prince of Schwarzenberg, Duke zu Krumau, Princely Count in Kleggau, Count of Sulz, &c., and his wife Therese, Countess of Trauttmansdorff-Weinsberg;

4.) ANTOINETTE ROBERTA SOPHIA WILHELMINA, Princess of Luxemburg and of Nassau, b. Oct. 7, 1899; m., April 7, 1921, (his second wife), Rupert (Rupprecht) Maria Luitpold Ferdinand, Crown Prince of Bavaria, Duke of Bavaria, Franconia and of Swabia, Count Palatine of the Rhine, &c., b. at Munchen, May 18, 1869, son and heir of Louis III, King of Bavaria, and his wife, Archduchess Maria Theresa of Austria-Este, Princess of Hungary and Bohemia, dau. of H.I. & R.H. Archduke Ferdinand of Austria-Este. Issue:

  a) PRINCE HENRY (HEINRICH) FRANCIS WILLIAM of Bavaria, b. March 28, 1922;

  b) PRINCESS IRMGARD MARIE JOSEPHA of Bavaria, May 29, 1923;

  c) PRINCESS EDITH MARIE GABRIELLA ANNA of Bavaria, b. Sept. 16, 1924;

  d) PRINCESS HILDA HILDEGARDE MARIE GABRIELLA of Bavaria, b. March 24, 1926;

  e) PRINCESS GABRIELLA ADELGONDA MARIE THERESA ANTONIA of Bavaria, b. May 10, 1927;

  f) PRINCESS SOPHIA MARIA THERESA of Bavaria, b. June 20, 1935.

5.) ELIZABETH MARIA WILHELMINA, Princess of Luxemburg and of Nassau, b. March 7, 1901; m., Nov. 14, 1922, Louis Philip Maria Frederick Joseph Maximilian Anthony Ignac Lamoral, Prince of Thurn and Taxis, b. Feb. 2, 1901; d. April 22, 1933; son of Albert, 8th Prince of Thurn and Taxis, Prince zu Buchau, &c., and his wife, Archduchess Marguerite (Margarete) of Austria, Princess of Hungary and Bohemia, dau. of Joseph Charles Louis, Archduke of Austria, Prince of

Hungary, &c., and his wife Clotilda, Princess of Saxe-Coburg and Gotha. Issue:

a) ANSELME ALBERT LOUIS MARIA LAMORAL, Prince of Thurn-et-Taxis, b. April 14, 1924;

b) INIGA ANNA MARGIT WILHELMINA LOUISE, Princess of Thurn-et-Taxis, b. Aug. 25, 1925.

6.) SOPHIA CAROLINE MARIE WILHELMINA, Princess of Luxemburg and of Nassau, b. Feb. 14, 1902; m., April 12, 1921, Ernest Henry Ferdinand Francis Joseph Otho Maria Melchiades, Prince of Saxony, Duke of Saxony, b. at Dresden, Dec. 9, 1896, son of the late Frederick August III, King of Saxony. Issue:

a) ALBRECHT FREDERICK AUGUST JOHN GREGORY DEDO, Prince of Saxony, Duke of Saxony, b. May 9, 1922;

b) GEORGE TIMO MICHAEL NICHOLAS MARIA, Prince of Saxony, Duke of Saxony, b. Dec. 2, 1923;

c) RUPERT (RUPPRECHT) HUBERT GERO MARIA, Prince of Saxony, Duke of Saxony, b. Sept. 12, 1925.

NETHERLANDS

HENRY III, King of England, b. Oct. 1, 1206/7; d. Nov. 16, 1272; m., Jan. 14, 1236, Eleanor, dau. and heiress of Raymond Berenger, Count of Provence,

EDWARD I, King of England, b. June 17, 1239; d. July 7, 1307; m., first, 1254, Eleanor, b. about 1244; d. Nov. 29, 1290; dau. of Ferdinand III, the Saint, King of Castile and Leon,

EDWARD II, King of England, d. Sept. 21, 1327; m., Jan. 25, 1307/8, Princess Isabel (Isabella), d. Aug. 22, 1358, dau. of Philippe IV, surnamed *le Bel*, King of France and Navarre,

EDWARD III, King of England, b. Nov. 13, 1312; d. June 21, 1377; m. Jan. 24, 1327/8, Philippa of Hainault, b. about 1312; d. Aug. 14/5, 1369; dau. of William III, Count of Hainault and Holland, and his wife Joanna (Jane) of Valois, dau. of Charles, Count of Valois, and granddau. of Philippe III, King of France,

PRINCE EDMUND, "of Langley," Duke of York, Earl of Cambridge, K.G., b. June 5, 1344; d. Aug. 1, 1402; m., first, Isabel (Isabella), b. about 1355; d. 1392/3; dau. and co-heiress of Peter (Pedro) the Cruel, King of Castile and Leon,

PRINCE RICHARD, "of Conisburgh," or "of York," Earl of Cambridge, Almoner of England, &c., b. about 1375/6; beheaded Aug. 5/6, 1415; m., first, about 1406, Anne de Mortimer, b. Dec. 27, 1390; d. about 1411; dau. of Roger de Mortimer, 4th Earl of March, Earl of Ulster,

PRINCE RICHARD, Earl of Cambridge, Duke of York, sometime Regent of France, K.G., b. Sept. 20, 1410/11/12; slain at Wakefield, Dec. 30/1, 1460; m., about 1437, Cecily, b. May 3, 1415; d. May 31, 1495; dau. of Ralph de Neville, 1st Earl of Westmorland, K.G.,

EDWARD IV, King of England, b. April 28, 1442; d. April 9, 1483; m., May 4, 1464, (her second husband), Elizabeth Wydeville (Woodville), b. about 1437; d. June 7, 1492;

81

widow of John, Lord Ferrers of Groby, and dau. of Sir Richard Wydeville (Woodville), Earl of Rivers, K.G.,

PRINCESS ELIZABETH, b. Feb. 11, 1465/6; d. in the Tower of London, Feb. 11, 1502/3; m., Jan. 18, 1485/6, Henry VII, King of England, b. July 26, 1456; d. April 21, 1509,

PRINCESS MARGARET TUDOR, d. Oct. 18, 1541; m., first, James IV, King of Scots, b. March 17, 1472/3; killed at the battle of Flodden, Sept. 9, 1513,

JAMES V, King of Scots, b. April 10, 1512; d. Dec. 14, 1542; m., 2ndly, 1538, Marie de Lorraine, Duchess of Longueville, d. June 10, 1560, eldest dau. of Charles (or Claude) of Lorraine, Duke of Guise, and widow of Louis d'Orleans, Duke de Longueville,

MARY, Queen of Scots, b. Dec. 7/8, 1542; beheaded Feb. 8, 1586/7; widow of Francis II, King of France; m., 2ndly, July 29, 1565, her cousin, Henry Stewart, Lord Darnley, murdered at Edinburgh, Feb. 10, 1566/7,

JAMES I, King of England, (and VI of Scotland), m. Princess Anne, dau. of Frederick II, King of Denmark and Norway, and his wife Sophia, dau. of Ulric, Duke of Mecklenburg,

PRINCESS ELIZABETH, m. Frederick V, Duke of Bavaria, Elector Palatine of the Rhine, and King of Bohemia,

PRINCESS SOPHIA, m. Ernest Augustus, Duke of Brunswick-Luneburg, Elector of Hanover,

GEORGE I, (GEORGE LOUIS), Elector of Hanover, King of Great Britain, France, and Ireland, m. Sophia Dorothy, b. Sept. 5/15, 1666; d. Nov. 2/13, 1726; only surviving dau. and heiress of George William, Duke of Brunswick-Luneburg and of Zelle, and his wife Eleonore d'Emiers, dau. of Alexander d'Olbreuse,

PRINCESS SOPHIA DOROTHY (DOROTHEA), b. March 16/27, 1686/7; d. June 28, 1757; m. at Berlin, Nov. 28, 1706, Frederick William I, King of Prussia, b. Aug. 15, 1688; d. May 31, 1740,

AUGUSTUS WILLIAM, Prince of Prussia, b. Aug. 9, 1722; d. June 12/4, 1758; m., Jan. 6, 1742, Louisa Amelia, Princess of Brunswick-Wolfenbuttel, b. Jan. 29, 1722; d. Jan. 13, 1780; dau. of Ferdinand Albert, Duke of Brunswick, and his wife

Antoinette Amelia, youngest dau. of Louis Rudolph, Duke of Brunswick,

FREDERICK WILLIAM II, King of Prussia, Elector of Branden-burg, b. at Berlin, Sept. 25, 1744; d. Nov. 16, 1797; m., 2ndly, July 14, 1769, Frederica Louisa, Princess of Hesse-Darm-stadt, b. Oct. 16, 1751; d. Feb. 25, 1805; dau. of Louis IX, Landgrave of Hesse-Darmstadt, and his wife Henrietta Carolina, dau. of Christian III, Duke of Deux-Ponts,

PRINCESS FREDERICA LOUISA WILHELMINA, b. Nov. 18, 1774; d. Oct. 12, 1837; m., Oct. 1, 1791, William Frederick, Grand Duke of Luxemburg, afterwards as William I was proclaimed King of the Netherlands, b. Aug. 24, 1772; d. Dec. 12, 1843; son of William V, Prince of Orange, and his wife Frederica Sophia Wilhelmina, only dau. of Augustus William, Prince of Prussia, and had,

1.) WILLIAM II (FREDERICK GEORGE LOUIS), King of the Netherlands (Holland), b. at The Hague, Dec. 6, 1792; d. at Tilburg, March 17, 1849; m., Feb. 21, 1816, Anne Paulovna of Russia, b., at St. Petersburg, Jan. 18, 1795; d. March 1, 1865; youngest dau. of Paul I, Emperor of Russia, and his wife Princess Sophia Dorothea (Maria Feodorovna), eldest dau. of Fred-erick Eugene, Duke of Wurtemberg, by his wife, Princess Frederica, eldest dau. of Frederick William, Markgraf of Brandenburg-Schwedt. Issue:

   a) WILLIAM III (ALEXANDER PAUL FREDERICK LOUIS), King of the Netherlands, b. Feb. 19, 1817; d. Nov. 23, 1890; m., 2ndly, at Arolsen, Jan. 7, 1879, Princess Emma, b. Aug. 2, 1858; d. March 20, 1934; dau. of George Victor, Prince of Waldeck-Pyrmont, and his wife, Princess Helen, dau. of William, Duke of Nassau. Issue:

      i WILHELMINA (HELENA PAULINA MARY), Queen of the Netherlands, Princess of Orange-Nassau, Duchess of Mecklenburg, &c., Majesty, b. at The Hague, Aug. 31, 1880; m. at The Hague, Feb. 7, 1901, Henry, Duke of Mecklenburg, Prince of the Netherlands, &c., b. at Schwerin, April 19, 1876; naturalized in the Netherlands, Jan.

23, 1901; d. at The Hague, July 3, 1934; youngest son of Frederick Francis II, Grand Duke of Mecklenburg-Schwerin. Issue:

1. JULIANA LOUISE EMMA MARIE WILHELMINA, Crown Princess of the Netherlands, Princess of Orange-Nassau, Duchess of Mecklenburg, Princess of Lippe-Biesterfeld, Ph.D., b. at The Hague, April 30, 1909; m. at The Hague, Jan. 7, 1937, Bernhard Leopold Frederick Eberhard Jules Curt Charles Godfrey Peter, Prince of Lippe-Biesterfeld, Prince of the Netherlands, b. at Jena, Germany, June 29, 1911; naturalized as a citizen of the Netherlands, Nov. 27, 1936; son of Prince Bernhard Casimir of Lippe-Biesterfeld. Issue:

   a) PRINCESS BEATRIX;

   b) PRINCESS IRENE.

2.) PRINCE FREDERICK of the Netherlands, Prince of Orange-Nassau, &c., b. Feb. 28, 1797; d. Sept. 8, 1881; m., May 21, 1825, Louise Augusta Wilhelmina Amelia, Princess of Prussia, b. Feb. 1, 1808; d. Dec. 6, 1870; dau. of Frederick William III, King of Prussia, and his wife Louise Augusta Wilhelmina Amelia, dau. of Charles Louis Frederick, Duke of Mecklenburg-Strelitz. Issue:

   a) PRINCESS WILHELMINA FRIEDERIKA ANNA ELIZABETH MARIE of the Netherlands, b. at Wassenaar, July 5, 1841; d. June 22, 1910; m. at Wassenaar, July 18, 1871, William Adolphus Maximilian Charles, Prince zu Wied, Prince of the Holy Roman Empire, Count of Isemburg, Lord of (Herr auf) Runkel and Neuerburg; Hereditary Member and President of the Prussian House of Lords; b. at Neuwied, Aug. 22, 1845; d. Oct. 22, 1907; son of Hermann, Prince zu Wied, Prince of the Holy Roman Empire, Count of Isemburg, &c., and his wife Marie Wilhelmina, Princess of Nassau, dau. of

William, Duke of Luxemburg and Nassau, and his first wife, Louise, Princess of Saxe-Hildburghausen. Issue:

i WILLIAM FREDERICK HENRY, Prince zu Wied, Highness, b. at Neuwied, March 26, 1876; Sovereign Prince of Albania, Feb. 6, 1914, and ascended the throne of Albania on March 7, 1914, as William I; reserved all rights to the Throne of Albania for himself and his descendants; m. at Waldenburg, Nov. 30, 1906, Sophia, Princess of Schonburg-Waldenburg, b. at Potsdam, May 21, 1885; d. Feb. 3, 1936; dau. of Victor, Hereditary Prince of Schonburg-Waldenburg, and his wife Lucie, Princess of Sayn-Wittgenstein-Berleburg. Issue:

1.) PRINCESS MARIE ELEONORE ELIZABETH CECILE MATHILDA LUCIE ZU WIED, b. at Potsdam, Feb. 19, 1909; Dr. rer. pol.; m. at Munchen, Nov. 16, 1937, Alfred, Prince of Schonburg-Waldenburg, b. at Droyssig, Oct. 30, 1905, son of Henry, Prince of Schonburg-Waldenburg, Lord of the *seigneuries* of Droyssig and Quessnitz, Lord of Szelejewo, and his first wife, Princess Olga, dau. of Prince Alfred of Lowenstein-Wertheim-Freudenberg;

2.) PRINCE CHARLES VICTOR WILLIAM FREDERICK ERNEST GONTHIER ZU WIED, Prince of Albania, b. at Potsdam, May 19, 1913; Doctor of Laws.

NORWAY

JOHN, King of England, m., 2ndly, Isabella, dau. and heiress of Aymer de Taillefer, Count d'Angouleme, and his wife Alice, dau. of Peter (Pierre) de Courtenay, Prince of France, and granddau. of Louis VI, *le Gros*, King of France,

PRINCESS ISABELLA, b. 1214; d. Dec. 1/10, 1241; m., 1234/5, Frederick II, Emperor of Germany, b. Dec. 26, 1194; d. Dec. 13, 1250; son of Emperor Henry VI, and his wife Constance, dau. of Roger, King of Sicily,

PRINCESS MARGARET, b. Dec. 1, 1241; d. Aug. 8, 1270; m., (his first wife), Albert Degener, Landgrave of Thuringia, Markgraf of Meissen, b. about 1240; d. about 1314; son and heir of Henry, Landgrave of Thuringia and Markgraf of Meissen (Misnia), and his wife Constance, dau. of Leopold VII, Duke of Austria,

FREDERICK, Landgrave of Thuringia, Markgraf of Meissen (Misnia), b. about 1257; d. 1325/6; m., 2ndly, 1301, Elizabeth, Countess of Arensberg, d. about 1345,

FREDERICK, surnamed the Grave, Landgrave of Thuringia, Markgraf of Misnia, d. Feb. 2, 1349; m., 1328/9, Mathilda, d. July 2, 1349, dau. of Louis, Emperor of Germany, and his wife Beatrice, dau. of Henry III, Duke of Glogau,

FREDERICK, surnamed the Valiant, Landgrave of Thuringia, Markgraf of Misnia, b. Oct. 6/16, 1331; d. May 26, 1380/1; m., 1346, Catherine, dau. of Henry, Count of Henneberg, who brought Coburg into her husband's family,

FREDERICK, surnamed the Bellicose, Markgraf of Misnia, Elector of Saxony, d. Jan. 4, 1428; m. Catherine, d. Dec. 28, 1422, dau. of Henry I, Duke of Brunswick (Braunschweig), and his wife Sophia, dau. of Wratislaus VI, Duke of Pomerania,

FREDERICK, surnamed Placidus, Elector of Saxony, b. Aug. 24, 1411; d. Feb. 7, 1464; m., June 23, 1432, Margaret of Austria, d. Feb. 12, 1486, dau. of Ernest, Duke of Carinthia, and his wife Zimburg (or Cimburga), dau. of Ziemovito, Duke of Mazovia,

ERNEST, Elector of Saxony, Landgrave of Thuringia, b. March 25, 1441; d. Aug. 26, 1486; m., 1462, Elizabeth, d. Feb. 23, 1484, dau. of Albert III, Duke of Bavaria, and his wife Anne, dau. of Erich, Duke of Brunswick-Grubenhagen,

JOHN, surnamed the Constant, Elector of Saxony, b. June 30, 1467; d. Aug. 16, 1532; m., first, Oct. 23, 1499, Sophia, d. July 12, 1503, dau. of Magnus, Duke of Mecklemburg, and his wife Sophia, dau. of Erich, Duke of Pomerania,

JOHN FREDERICK I, surnamed the Magnanimous, Elector of Saxony, b. June 30, 1503; d. March 3, 1554; was deprived of his Electorate in 1547, having been defeated and taken prisoner by Charles V; m., June 2, 1527, Sibylla, b. about 1510; d. Feb. 21, 1554; dau. of John, Duke of Cleves, and his wife Maria, only dau. and heiress of William, Duke of Juliers,

JOHN WILLIAM, Duke of Saxe-Weimar, b. March 11, 1530; d. March 2, 1573; m., Dec. 10, 1560, Dorothy Susanna, b. 1544; d. March 29, 1592; dau. of Frederick III, Elector Palatine,

FREDERICK WILLIAM I, Duke of Saxe-Altenburg, b. April 25, 1562; d. July 7, 1602; m., 2ndly, Aug. 29, 1591, Anne Marie, d. Feb. 1, 1643, dau. of Philip Louis, Palatine of Neuburg, and his wife Anne, dau. of William, Duke of Juliers,

JOHN PHILIP, Duke of Saxe-Altenburg, b. 1597; d. April 1, 1639; m., Oct. 25, 1618, Elizabeth, b. June 23, 1593; d. March 25, 1650, widow of Augustus, son of Christian I, Elector of Saxony, and dau. of Henry Julius, Duke of Brunswick, and his wife Elizabeth, dau. of Frederick II, King of Denmark,

ELIZABETH SOPHIA, b. Oct. 10, 1619; d. Dec. 20, 1680; m., Oct. 24, 1636, Ernest I, the Pious, Duke of Saxe-Gotha, b. Dec. 25, 1601; d. March 1675; son of John, Duke of Saxe-Weimar, and his wife Dorothy Mary, Princess of Anhalt,

FREDERICK I, Duke of Saxe-Gotha, b. July 15, 1646; d. Aug. 2, 1691; m., Nov. 14, 1669, Magdalena Sibylla, b. Sept. 2, 1648; d. Jan. 7, 1681; dau. of Augustus, Duke of Saxe-Halle, and his wife Anne Mary, dau. of Adolphus Frederick I, Duke of Mecklenburg-Strelitz,

FREDERICK II, Duke of Saxe-Gotha, b. July 28, 1676; d. March 23, 1732; m., June 7, 1696, Magdalena Augusta, b. Oct. 12, 1679; d. Oct. 11, 1740; dau. of Charles William, Prince of

Anhalt-Zerbst, and his wife Sophia, dau. of Augustus, Duke of Saxe-Halle,

FREDERICK III, Duke of Saxe-Gotha, b. April 14, 1699; d. March 10, 1772; m., Aug. 8, 1729, Louisa Dorothy, b. Aug. 10, 1710; d. Oct. 22, 1767; dau. of Ernest Louis I, Duke of Saxe-Meiningen, and his wife Dorothy Mary, dau. of Frederick I, Duke of Saxe-Gotha,

ERNEST (LOUIS) II, Duke of Saxe-Gotha, b. Jan. 30, 1745; d. April 20, 1804; m., March 21, 1769, Mary Charlotte Amelia Ernestine, b. Sept. 11, 1751; d. April 25, 1827; 7th dau. of Anthony Ulric, Duke of Saxe-Meiningen, and his wife Charlotte Emilia, dau. of Charles, Landgrave of Hesse-Philippsthal,

EMILIUS LEOPOLD AUGUSTUS, Duke of Saxe-Gotha, b. Nov. 23, 1772; d. May 17, 1822; m. Oct. 21, 1797, Louisa Charlotte, b. Nov. 19, 1779; d. Jan. 4, 1801; eldest dau. of Frederick Francis I, Grand Duke of Mecklenburg-Schwerin, and his wife Louisa, dau. of Prince John Augustus of Saxe-Gotha,

DOROTHY LOUISA PAULINE CHARLOTTE FREDERICA AUGUSTA, only child and heiress, b. Dec. 31, 1800; d. Aug. 30, 1831; m., July 13, 1817, Ernest I (Anthony Charles Louis), Duke of Saxe-Coburg and Gotha, b. Jan. 2, 1784; d. Jan. 29, 1844; son of Francis, Duke of Saxe-Coburg-Saalfeld, and his wife Augusta Carolina Sophia, dau. of Henry XXIV, Count of Reuss Ebersdorf,

FRANCIS ALBERT AUGUSTUS CHARLES EMANUEL, Prince of Saxe-Coburg-Gotha, Duke of Saxony, 2nd and youngest son, b. Aug. 26, 1819; d. Dec. 14, 1861; m., Feb. 10, 1840, Victoria (Alexandrina), Queen of Great Britain and of Ireland, Empress of India, &c., b. May 24, 1819; d. Jan. 22, 1901,

EDWARD VII, King of Great Britain and of Ireland, Emperor of India, &c., m. Princess Alexandra (Caroline Mary Charlotte Louisa Julia), dau. of Christian IX, King of Denmark,

PRINCESS MAUD (CHARLOTTE MARIE VICTORIA) of Great Britain and of Ireland, b. Nov. 26, 1869; m., Buckingham Palace, London, July 22, 1896, Prince Christian Frederick Charles George Waldemar Axel of Denmark, elected King of Norway on Nov. 18, 1905, crowned June 22, 1906, ascended the throne as Haakon VII, King of Norway, b. Aug. 3, 1872, 2nd son of

Fredreick VIII, King of Denmark, by his wife, Princess Louise, only dau. of Charles IV and XV, King of Norway and Sweden,

PRINCE OLAV ALEXANDER EDWARD CHRISTIAN FREDERICK, Crown Prince of Norway, b. at Appleton House, Sandringham, July 2, 1903; m. at Oslo, March 21, 1929, Martha, Princess of Sweden, b. at Stockholm, March 28, 1901, dau. of Prince Oscar Charles William of Sweden, Duke of Westgotland, and his wife Princess Ingeborg, dau. of Frederick VIII, King of Denmark. Issue:

1.) PRINCESS RAGNHILD ALEXANDRA, b. at Oslo, June 9, 1910;

2.) PRINCESS ASTRID MAUD INGEBORG, b. at Oslo, Feb. 12, 1932;

3.) PRINCE HARALD, b. at Skaugum Asker, Feb. 21, 1937.

Saxony

HENRY II, King of England, m. Eleanor, Duchess of Aquitaine, d. Mar. 31, 1204. dau. of William V, Duke of Aquitaine, the divorced wife of Louis VII, King of France,

MATHILDA (OR MAUD), eldest dau., b. 1156; d. June 28, 1189; m., Feb. 1, 1167/8, Henry, surnamed the Lion, Duke of Saxony and Bavaria, b. 1129; d. Apr. 1, 1195,

HENRY, surnamed the Long, Duke of Saxony, Count Palatine of the Rhine, eldest son and h., b. 1170; d. May 5, 1227; m., 1193, Agnes, dau. and h. of Conrad of Swabia, Count Palatine of the Rhine, and his wife Ermengarde, dau. of Berthold, Count of Henneberg,

AGNES, eldest dau. and co-heiress, b. 1201; d. 1262; m., 1225, Otto The Illustrious, Duke of Bavaria, d. Nov. 29, 1253, son of Louis I, Duke of Bavaria, and his wife Ludomilla, dau. of Ladislaus II, King of Bohemia, and widow of Albert, Count of Bogen,

LOUIS II, Duke of Bavaria, Count and Elector Palatine of the Rhine, eldest s. and h., b. 1229; d. Jan. 1, 1294; m., thirdly, 1273, Mathilda, dau. of Rudolph of Habsburg, Emperor of Germany, and his wife Gertrude (or Anne) of Hohenberg,

RUDOLPH I, Count and Elector Palatine of the Rhine, eldest s. and h., b. 1274; d. Aug. 11, 1319; m., 1294, Mathilda, d. 1315, dau. of Adolph of Nassau, Emperor of Germany, and his wife Imogene, dau. of Gerlac, Lord of Limburg,

ADOLPH, surnamed the Simple, Elector Palatine of the Rhine, eldest s. and h., b. Sept. 27, 1306; d. Feb. 17, 1327; m., Irmengarde, dau. of Louis, Count of Oetingen,

RUPERT II, surnamed "the Little" and "the Tenacious," Elector Palatine of the Rhine, only s. and h., d. Feb. 14, 1398; m. Beatrix, d. 1366, dau. of Pierre II d'Aragon, King of Sicily, and his wife Elizabeth of Carinthia, and widow of John Henry, Count of Goritz,

Rupert III, Elector Palatine of the Rhine, and afterwards Emperor of Germany, Aug. 24, 1400; only s. and h., b. 1352; d. May 18, 1410; m., 1374, Elizabeth, d. June 26, 1409, dau. of Frederick V, Burggrave of Nuremburg, and his wife Elizabeth, dau. of Frederick, Markgraf of Misnia and Landgrave of Thuringia,

Louis III, Elector Palatine of the Rhine, eldest surviving s. and h., d. Dec. 29, 1436; m., secondly, Nov. 3, 1417, Mathilda, d. May 14, 1436, dau. of Amadeus of Savoy, Prince of Acaia, and his wife Catherine, dau. of Amadeus, Count of Geneva,

Louis IV, the Good, Elector Palatine of the Rhine, b. 1424; d. Aug. 13, 1449; m., Oct. 22, 1445, Margaret, Queen of Sicily, d. Sept. 30, 1479; 4th dau. of Amadeus VIII, Duke of Savoy, and his wife Mary, 4th dau. of Philip, Duke of Burgundy, and widow of Louis III, d'Anjou, King of Sicily,

Philip, Elector Palatine of the Rhine, b. July 14, 1448; d. Feb. 18/28, 1508; m., Mar. 11, 1474, Margaret, d. Feb. 25, 1501, dau. of Louis (Dives), Duke of Lower Bavaria at Landshut, and his wife Amelia, dau. of Frederick II, Elector of Saxony,

Elizabeth, eldest dau., b. 1483; d. June 24, 1522; she m., first, William III, Landgrave of Hesse, who d. Feb. 17, 1500; she m., secondly, 1503, Philip, 4th son of Christopher, Markgrave of Baden, and his wife Otilie of Catzenellenbogen,

Marie Jacqueline, only dau. and h., b. June 25, 1507; d. Nov. 15, 1580; m., 1522/23, William, Duke of Bavaria, b. Nov. 13, 1493; d. Mar. 6, 1550; s. and h. of Albert IV, Duke of Bavaria, and his wife Cunegonda, dau. of Emperor Frederick III,

Albert III, Duke of Bavaria, surnamed the Magnanimous, b. Mar. 1, 1528; d. Oct. 24, 1579; m., July 4, 1546, Anne of Austria, b. June 7, 1528; d. Oct. 18, 1587; dau. of Ferdinand I, Emperor of Germany, and his wife Anne, dau. of Ladislaus, King of Hungary and Bohemia,

William II, Duke of Bavaria, b. Sept. 29, 1548; d. Feb. 7, 1626; m., Feb. 22, 1568, Renata (Rénée); d. May 23, 1602, dau. of Francis, Duke of Lorraine, and his wife Christina, youngest dau. of Christian II, King of Denmark,

MAXIMILIAN I, First Elector of Bavaria, b. Apr. 17, 1573; d. Sept. 17/27, 1651; m., secondly, July 15, 1635, Marie Anne of Austria, b. Jan. 13, 1610; d. Sept. 18/20, 1665; dau. of Ferdinand II, Emperor of Germany, and his wife Marie Anne, dau. of William II, Duke of Bavaria,

FERDINAND, Elector of Bavaria, b. Oct. 31, 1636; d. May 26, 1679; m., June 22, 1652, Henrietta Adelaide of Savoy, b. Nov. 6, 1636; d. Mar. 18, 1676, 3rd dau. of Victor Amadeus I, Duke of Savoy, and his wife Princess Christina, 2nd dau. of Henry IV, King of France,

MAXIMILIAN EMANUEL, Elector of Bavaria, b. July 11, 1662; d. Feb. 26, 1726; m., secondly, Jan. 2, 1695, Theresa Cunegonda Sobieska, b. Mar. 4, 1676; d. Mar. 11, 1730; dau. of John Sobieski, King of Poland, and his Marie Casimire Louise, dau. of Henry de la Grange, Marquis d'Arquien,

CHARLES ALBERT, Elector of Bavaria, afterwards Emperor of Germany, b. Aug. 6, 1697; d. Jan. 20, 1745; m., Oct. 5, 1722, Marie Amelia of Austria, b. Oct. 22, 1701; d. Dec. 11, 1756; dau. of Joseph I, Emperor of Germany, and his wife Wilhelmina Amelia, youngest dau. of John Frederick, Duke of Hanover,

MARIE ANTOINETTE of Bavaria, eldest dau., b. July 18, 1724; d. Apr. 23, 1780; m., June 13, 1747, Prince Frederick Christian Leopold, Elector of Saxony, b. Sept. 5, 1722; d. Sept. 17, 1763; eldest surviving son of Augustus III, King of Poland, and his wife Mary Josephine, eldest dau. of Joseph I, Emperor of Germany,

MAXIMILIAN MARIA JOSEPH, 5th son, b. Apr. 13, 1759; d. Jan. 3, 1838; m., May 9, 1792, Caroline Marie Theresa Josephine, b. Nov. 22, 1770; d. Mar. 1, 1804; eldest dau. of Ferdinand, Duke of Parma, and his wife Archduchess Marie Amelia, 6th dau. of Francis I, Emperor of Germany, and of the Empress Maria Theresa,

JOHN, King of Saxony, 3rd and youngest son, b. Dec. 12, 1801; d. Oct. 29, 1873; succeeded his brother, Frederick Augustus II, in 1854 as King of Saxony; m., Nov. 21, 1822, Amelia Augusta, b. Nov. 13, 1801; d. Nov. 8, 1877; 5th dau. of Maximilian I, King of Bavaria, and his wife Princess Caroline, 2nd dau. of Charles Louis, Hereditary Prince of Baden,

GEORGE, King of Saxony 3rd but 2nd surviving son, b. Aug. 8, 1832; d. Oct. 15, 1904; succeeded his brother, Albert, as King of Saxony in 1902; m., May 11, 1859, Marie Anne, b. July 21, 1843; d. Feb. 5, 1884; 2nd dau. of Maria II, Queen of Portugal, and her husband King Ferdinand, Prince of Saxe-Coburg,

FREDERICK AUGUSTUS III, King of Saxony, eldest s. and h., b. May 25, 1865; d. Feb. 18, 1932; m., at Vienna, Nov. 21, 1891, Archduchess Louisa Antoinette Marie, b. at Salzburg, Sept. 2, 1870, 2nd dau. of Ferdinand IV, Grand Duke of Tuscany, (divorced Feb. 11, 1903, and the Queen assumed the name and title of Countess de Montignoso; she is actually known as Countess d'Ysette). Issue:

1.) PRINCE FREDERICK AUGUSTUS GEORGE FERDINAND ALBERT CHARLES ANTHONY MARIA PAUL MARCELLA, b. at Dresden, Jan. 15, 1893; entered the religious life and is now known as Father George, S.J.;

2.) PRINCE FREDERICK CHRISTIAN ALBERT LEOPOLD ANNO SYLVESTER MACAIRE, Crown Prince of Saxony, Duke of Saxony, Markgrave of Misnia, b. at Dresden, Dec. 31, 1893; m., June 16, 1923, Elizabeth Helena, Princess of Thurn and Taxis, b. Dec. 15, 1903; and have:

   a) PRINCE MARIA EMANUEL, b. Jan. 31, 1926;

   b) PRINCESS MARIE JOSEPHINE, b. Sept. 20, 1928;

   c) PRINCESS MARIE ANNE JOSEPHINE, b. Dec. 13, 1929;

   d) PRINCE ALBERT JOSEPH MARIE FRANCIS XAVIER, b. Nov. 30, 1934;

   e) PRINCESS MATHILDE MARIE JOSEPHINE ANNE XAVIERE, b. Jan. 17, 1936.

3.) PRINCE ERNEST HENRY FERDINAND FRANCIS JOSEPH OTTO MARIA MELCHIADES, b. at Dresden, Dec. 9, 1896; m., Apr. 12, 1921, Sophia, Princess of Luxemburg and Nassau, b. Feb. 14, 1902, and have:

   a) PRINCE ALBERT (ALBRECHT) FREDERICK AUGUSTUS JOHN GREGORY DEDO, b. at Munchen, May 9, 1922;

b) Prince George Timo Nicholas Maria, b. at Munchen, Dec. 2, 1923;

c) Prince Rupert (Rupprecht) Hubert Gero Maria, b. at Munchen, Sept. 12, 1925.

4.) Princess Marguerite Carola Wilhelmina Victoria Adelheid Albertina Petrusa Bertram Paula, b. at Dresden, Jan. 24, 1900; m., June 2, 1920, Prince Frederick Victor Pius Alexander Leopold Charles Theodore Ferdinand de Hohenzollern, Burggrave de Nuremburg, Count of Sigmaringen and Veringen, Count de Berg, b. Aug. 30, 1891, son of Prince William de Hohenzollern and his first wife, Marie Theresa, Princess de Bourbon and Sicily, and have:

a) Princess Benoite Marie Antoinette Mathilda, b. Feb. 19, 1921;

b) Princess Marie Aldegonde Alice Louise Josephine, b. Feb. 19, 1921;

c) Princess Marie Theresa Louise Cecil Zita Elizabeth Hilda Agnes, b. Oct. 11, 1922;

d) Prince Frederick William Ferdinand Joseph Maria Manuel George Meinrad Fidelis Benedict Michael Hubert, b. Feb. 3, 1924;

e) Prince Francis Joseph Hubert Maria Mainrad Michael, b. Mar. 15, 1926;

f) Prince John George Carol Leopold Eitel Frederick Meinrad Maria Hubert Michael, b. July 31, 1932.

5.) Princess Marie Alice Luitpolde Anne Henrietta Germaine Agnes Damienne Michelle, b. at Dresden, Sept. 27, 1901; m., May 25, 1921, Prince Francis Joseph Louis Maria Charles Anthony Tassillon de Hohenzollern, b. Aug. 30, 1891, and have:

a) Prince Charles Anthony Frederick William Louis Maria George Manuel Rupert Henry Benedick Tassillon, b. at Munchen, Jan. 28, 1922;

b) Prince Meinrad Leopold Maria Frederick Christian Ferdinand Albert, b. at Sigmaringen, Jan. 17, 1925;

c) Princess Marie Marguerite Anne Victoria Louise Josephine Mathilda Theresa, b. at Sigmaringen, Jan. 2, 1928;

d) Prince Emanuel Joseph Maria William Ferdinand Burchard, b. at Munchen, Feb. 23, 1929.

6.) Princess Anne Monique Pie, b. at Lindau, May 4, 1903; m., Oct. 4, 1924, Dr. Joseph Francis, Archduke of Austria, b. at Brunn, Mar. 28, 1895, and have:

a) Archduchess Marguerite, b. at Budapest, Aug. 17, 1925;

b) Archduchess Ilona, b. at Budapest, Apr. 20, 1927;

c) Archduchess Anne Theresa Gabriella, b. at Budapest, Apr. 19, 1928;

d) Archduke Joseph Arpad Benedick Ferdinand Francis Maria Gabriel, b. at Budapest, Feb. 8, 1933;

e) Archduke Istvan Domokos Anthony Hubert, b. July 1, 1934.

SAXE—COBURG AND GOTHA

VICTORIA (ALEXANDRINA), Queen of Great Britain and of Ireland, Empress of India, &c., m. Prince Francis Albert Augustus Charles Emanuel of Saxe-Coburg-Gotha, Prince Consort,

ALFRED ERNEST ALBERT, Prince of the United Kingdom of Great Britain and of Ireland, Duke of Saxony, Duke of Edinburgh, Earl of Kent, Earl of Ulster, reigning Duke of Saxe-Coburg and Gotha (succeeded his paternal uncle, Ernest II, 1893), K.G., K.T., G.C.M.G., G.C.V.O., &c., b. Aug. 6, 1844; d. July 30, 1900; m., Jan. 11/23, 1874, Grand Duchess Marie Alexandrovna, b. Oct. 5, 1853; d. Oct. 14, 1920; dau. of Alexander II, Emperor of Russia, by Marie, dau. of Ludwig II, Grand Duke of Hesse. Issue, among others:

1.) PRINCESS ALEXANDRA LOUISE OLGA VICTORIA, b. at Coburg, Sept. 1, 1878; m., April 20, 1896, Ernest, 7th Prince of Hohenlohe-Langenburg, Count of Hohenlohe, Count of Gleichen, &c., b. at Langenburg, Sept. 13, 1863. Issue:

    a) PRINCE GODEFROY HERMANN of Hohenlohe-Langenburg, b. March 24, 1897; m. April 20, 1931, Marguerite, Princess of Greece and Denmark, b. at Athens, April 18, 1905, and have issue:

        i PRINCE KRAFT ALEXANDER, b. June 25, 1935;

        ii PRINCESS BEATRIX, b. July 10, 1936.

    b) PRINCESS MARIE MELITA, b. Jan. 18, 1899; m. at Coburg, Feb. 15, 1916, Frederick, Duke of Schleswig-Holstein-Glucksburg, b. Aug. 23, 1891, and have issue:

        i PRINCE HANS, b. May 12, 1917;

        ii PRINCE FREDERICK, b. April 30, 1922;

        iii PRINCESS MARIE, b. July 9, 1927.

    c) PRINCESS ALEXANDRA BEATRICE LEOPOLDINE, b. April 2, 1901;

d) PRINCESS IRMA HELEN, b. July 4, 1902.

2.) PRINCESS BEATRICE LEOPOLDINE VICTORIA, b. at East-well Park, April 20, 1884; m., July 15, 1909, Alphonso, Prince of Orleans, Duke of Galliera, Infant of Spain, b. at Madrid, Nov. 12, 1886, son of Prince Anthony of Orleans, 1st Duke of Galliera, Infant of Spain, and his wife, Infanta Eulalia of Spain, dau. of Isabella II, Queen of Spain. Issue:

   a) PRINCE ALVARO ANTHONY of Orleans, b. at Co-burg, April 20, 1910; m. at Rome, July 10, 1937, Carta Parodi Delfino;

   b) PRINCE ATAULFO ISABELLO, b. Madrid. Oct. 20, 1913.

Saxe—Coburg and Gotha

Victoria (Alexandrina), Queen of Great Britain, Ireland, &c., Empress of India; m. Prince Francis Albert Augustus Charles Emanuel of Saxe-Coburg-Gotha, Duke of Saxony, Prince Consort of Great Britain,

Prince Leopold, 1st Duke of Albany, Earl of Clarence, Baron Arklow, &c., K.G., K.T., G.C.S.I., G.C.M.G., P.C.; b. at Claremont, Esher, April 7, 1853; d. at Cannes, March 28, 1884; m. at Windsor, April 27, 1882, Princess Helen, b. at Arolsen, Feb. 17, 1861; d. at Hinterriss, Tryol, Sept. 1, 1922, dau. of George Victor, Prince of Waldeck and Pyrmont. Issue:

1.) Princess Alice Marie Victoria Augusta Pauline of Great Britain and Ireland, b. at Windsor Castle, Feb. 25, 1883; m. at Windsor, Feb. 10, 1904, Prince Alexander Augustus Frederick William Alfred George Cambridge of Teck, 1st Earl of Athlone, K.G., G.C.B., G.C.M.G., G.C.V.O., D.S.O., P.C., Viscount Trematon, &c., Governor of Windsor Castle since 1931; Chancellor of London University, 1932; Grand Master of Order of St. Michael and St. George since 1936; Governor General of the Union of South Africa, 1923-31; now Governor General of the Dominion of Canada; b. at Kensington Palace, April 14, 1874, 3rd son of Francis, Prince and Duke of Teck, and his wife, Princess Mary Adelaide Wilhelmina Elizabeth, dau. of Adolphus Frederick, Prince of Great Britain, Duke of Cambridge, Duke of Brunswick and Luneburg, &c., 7th and youngest son of George III, King of Great Britain, France, and Ireland. Issue:

   a) Princess May Helen Emma, b. at Claremont, Jan. 23, 1906;

   b) Prince Rupert Alexander George Augustus, b. at Claremont, Aug. 24, 1907.

2.) Prince Charles Edward of Great Britain and Ireland, Duke of Saxe-Coburg-Gotha, Duke of Albany, Duke of Juliers, Cleves and Berg, Engern, and Westphalia,

Landgrave in Thuringia, Marquess of Meissen, Prince-
ly Count of Henneberg, Earl of Clarence, Baron Ark-
low, &c., b. at Claremont, July 19, 1884; K.G., G.C.V.O.,
&c.; succeeded his uncle, Duke Alfred I, as reigning
Duke of Coburg and Gotha; m., Oct. 11, 1905, Princess
Victoria Adelaide, b. Dec. 31, 1885, dau. of Frederick
Ferdinand, Duke of Schleswig-Holstein-Sonderburg-
Glucksburg. Issue:

a) PRINCE JOHN LEOPOLD WILLIAM ALBERT FERDI-
NAND VICTOR of Saxe-Coburg and Gotha, b. at
Callenberg Castle, Aug. 2, 1906; m. at Dresden,
March 14, 1932, Feodora Marie Alma Mar-
guerite, Baroness de Horst, divorced wife of
Baron Pergler de Perglas. Issue:

i PRINCESS CAROLINE MATHILDE ADELHEID
SIBYLLA MARIANNE ERIKA of Saxe-Coburg
and Gotha, b. April 5, 1933;

ii PRINCE ERNEST LEOPOLD EDWARD WILLIAM
JOSIAS of Saxe-Coburg and Gotha, b. Jan.
14, 1935.

b) PRINCESS SIBYLLA CALMA MARIE ALICE BATHIL-
DIS FEODORA of Saxe-Coburg and Gotha, b. Jan.
18, 1908; m. at Coburg, Oct. 20, 1932, Gustave
Adolph, Prince of Sweden, Duke of Vasterbot-
ten, b. at Stockholm, April 22, 1906, son of
Prince Oscar Frederick William Olaf Gustave
Adolph of Sweden, Duke of Scanie, and his
first wife Marguerite, Princess Royal of Great
Britain and Ireland, and have issue;

c) PRINCE DIETMAR HUBERT FREDERICK WILLIAM
PHILIPPE of Saxe-Coburg and Gotha, b. at Cha-
teau of Reinhardsbrunn, Aug. 24, 1909;

d) PRINCESS CAROLINE MATHILDE HELEN LUDWIGA
AUGUSTA BEATRICE of Saxe- Coburg and Gotha,
b. in Callenberg Castle, near Coburg, June 22,
1912; m. at Coburg, Dec. 14, 1931, Frederick
Wolfgang, Count of Castell-Rudenhausen, b. at
Berlin, June 27, 1906, and have issue;

e) PRINCE FREDERICK JOSIAS CHARLES EDWARD
ERNEST CYRILLE HARALD of Saxe-Coburg and
Gotha, b. in Callenberg Castle, Nov. 29, 1918.

SPAIN

JAMES I, King of England, (and VI of Scotland), b. June 19, 1566; d. March 27, 1625; succeeded his cousin, Queen Elizabeth, March 24, 1602/3, as King of England; m. Anne, dau. of Frederick II, King of Denmark and Norway,

CHARLES I, King of England, &c., b. Nov. 19, 1600; executed Jan. 30, 1648/49; m., May 1/11 or June 22, 1625, Princess Henrietta Maria de Bourbon, b. Nov. 25/6, 1609; d. Aug. 10 or Sept. 10, 1669; dau. of Henry IV, King of France, and his wife, Marie de Medicis, dau. of Francis I de Medicis, Grand Duke of Tuscany, by his wife, Archduchess Joanna, youngest dau. of Ferdinand I, Emperor of Germany,

PRINCESS HENRIETTA MARIA ANNE, b. June 10/6, 1664; d. June 30, 1670; m. at Paris, March 31, 1661, (his first wife), Prince Philippe, Duke of Orleans, b. Sept. 21, 1640; d. June 9, 1701; youngest son of Louis XIII, King of France, and only brother of King Louis XIV of France,

PRINCESS ANNE MARIE, MADEMOISELLE DE VALOIS, b. Aug. 27, 1669; d. Aug. 26, 1728; m. by proxy, April 10, 1684, Victor Amadeus, Duke of Savoy; declared King of Sardinia, Aug. 18, 1718; b. May 14, 1666; d. Oct. 31, 1732,

PRINCESS MARIE ADELAIDE of Savoy, b. at Turin, Dec. 16, 1685; d. Feb. 12, 1711/2; m. at Versailles, Dec. 7, 1697, Prince Louis of France, Duke of Burgundy, Dauphin of France, b. Aug. 6, 1682; d. Feb. 18, 1712; eldest son and heir of Louis, Dauphin of Viennois, and grandson of Louis XIV, King of France,

LOUIS, Duke of Anjou, ascended the Throne of France as King Louis XV, Sept. 1, 1715; b. Feb. 15, 1710; d. May 16, 1774; m., 1725, Maria Charlotte Sophie Felicite Leczinska, b. June 23, 1703, only dau. of Nicholas Stanislas Leczinski, King of Poland 1704, and his wife, Catherine, Countess de Bnin-Opolinski,

MARIE LOUISE ELIZABETH (MADAME ROYALE), b. Aug. 14, 1727; d. Dec. 6, 1759; m., Oct. 25, 1739, her cousin, Philippe, Duke of Parma, Plaisance et Guastalla, b. March 15, 1720; d. July 18, 1765; son of Philip V, King of Spain, Duke of Anjou, and his second wife, Elizabeth, Princess Farnese,

LOUISE MARIE THERESE, b. Dec. 9, 1751; m., Sept. 4, 1765, Charles des Asturies, afterwards King of Spain as Charles IV, b. Nov. 12, 1748; d. Jan. 19, 1819,

FERDINAND, Prince des Asturies, King Ferdinand VII of Spain after March 19, 1808; b. Oct. 14, 1784; d. Sept. 29, 1833; m., Dec. 11, 1829, (Maria) Christina Ferdinanda, dau. of Francis I, King of the Two Sicilies,

ISABELLA II (MARIE ISABELLA LOUISE), Queen of Spain, b. Oct. 10, 1830; d. April 9, 1904; m., Oct. 10, 1846, Francis d'Assise, titular King of Spain, b. May 13, 1822; d. April 16, 1902. Issue:

1.) ALPHONSO XII, proclaimed King of Spain on Dec. 29, 1874; b. Nov. 28, 1857; d. Nov. 25, 1885; m., 2ndly, Nov. 29, 1879, Maria Christina, Archduchess of Austria, b. July 21, 1858; d. Feb. 6, 1929; dau. of Charles Ferdinand, Archduke of Austria. Issue:

a) ALPHONSO XIII, King of Spain, King of Castile, Leon, Aragon, the Two Sicilies, Jerusalem, Navarre, Granada, Toledo, Valencia, Galicia, &c., b. May 17, 1886; d. Feb. 28, 1941, at Rome, Italy; m., May 31, 1906, Victoria Eugenia Julia Ena, Princess of Battenberg, b. Oct. 24, 1887, dau. of Henry Maurice, Prince of Battenberg, and his wife, Beatrice Marie Victoria Feodora, Princess of Great Britain and of Ireland. Issue:

i INFANT JAIME LUITPOLD, DUKE of Ségovie, b. June 23, 1908; renounced his rights to succession to the throne, June 11, 1933; m., March 4, 1935, Emanuela de Dampierre of the Dukes of San Lorenzo, b. at Rome, Nov. 8, 1913. Issue:

1. ALPHONSO JAIME de Bourbon-Ségovie, Infant of Spain, b. at Rome, April 20, 1936;

2. GONZALO VICTOR de Bourbon-Ségovie, Infant of Spain, b. at Rome, June 5, 1937.

ii INFANTA BEATRIZ ISABEL, b. June 22, 1909; m. at Rome, Jan. 14, 1935, Alexander Torlonia, Principe di Civitella Cesi;

iii INFANTA MARIA CHRISTINA, b. Dec. 12, 1911;

iv INFANT JEAN (JUAN), Prince des Asturies, heir to the Throne of Spain, b. June 20, 1913; m. at Rome, Oct. 12, 1935, Marie Mercedes, Princess de Bourbon-Sicily, b. at Madrid, Dec. 23, 1910. Issue:

    1. INFANTA MARIA DEL PILAR, b. at Cannes, July 30, 1936;

    2. INFANTA MARIE CHRISTINA, b. at Rome, March 11, 1939.

b) INFANTA MARIA DE LAS MERCEDES, Princess des Asturies, b. at Madrid, Sept. 11, 1880; d. Oct. 17, 1904; m. Feb. 14, 1901, (his first wife), Charles, Prince de Bourbon-Sicily, Infant of Spain, b. Nov. 10, 1870, son of Alphonso, Count Caserta, Head of the Royal House of the Two Sicilies. Issue:

i INFANT ALPHONSO of Spain, Prince de Bourbon-Sicily, b. at Madrid, Nov. 30, 1901; m. at Vienna, April 16, 1936, Alice, Princess de Bourbon de Parma, b. at Vienna, Nov. 13, 1917, dau. of Elie Robert, Prince de Bourbon de Parma, and his wife, Marie Anne, Archduchess of Austria, &c. Issue:

    1. THERESA MARIE, Princess de Bourbon-Sicily, b. Feb. 1937.

ii INFANTA ISABELLA ALPHONSINE of Spain, Princess de Bourbon-Sicily, b. Oct. 16, 1904; m., March 9, 1929, John de Kanty, Count Zamoyski.

c) INFANTA MARIA THERESE of Spain, b. Nov. 12, 1882; d. Sept. 23, 1912; m., Jan. 12, 1906, Ferdinand Maria Louis Francis d'Assise, Prince of Bavaria, Infant of Spain, b. at Madrid, May 10, 1884. Issue:

    i PRINCE LOUIS ALPHONSO of Bavaria, Infant of Spain, b. Dec. 12, 1906;

    ii PRINCE JOSEPH EUGENE of Bavaria, Infant of Spain, b. March 26, 1909; m., July 25, 1933, Maria Solange de Mesia y Lesseps des Condes de Mora, b. at London, Sept. 30, 1911;

    iii PRINCESS MARIA DE LAS MERCEDES of Bavaria, Infanta of Spain, b. Oct. 3, 1911.

2).) INFANTA MARIE DE LA PAZ JEANNE AMELIA, Princess de Bourbon, b. June 23, 1862; m., April 2, 1883, Louis Ferdinand, Prince of Bavaria, b. at Madrid, Oct. 22, 1859, son of Prince Adalbert William George Louis of Bavaria, and his wife, Amelia, Infanta of Spain. Issue:

    a) FERDINAND MARIA LOUIS FRANCIS D'ASSISE, Prince of Bavaria, Infant of Spain, b. May 10, 1884; m., first, at Madrid, Jan. 12, 1906, Infanta Maria Therese of Spain (above mentioned), b. Nov. 12, 1882; d. Sept. 23, 1912, (see above for issue of this marriage) ; m., 2ndly, Oct. 1, 1914, Maria Louise de Silva y Fernandez de Henestrosa, 2nd Duchess of Talavera de la Reine, Infanta of Spain, b. at Madrid, Dec. 3, 1880.

3.) INFANTA MARIE EULALIE FRANCES D'ASSISE, Princess de Bourbon b. Feb. 12, 1864; m., March 6, 1886, Anthony Louis Philippe, Prince of Orleans, Infant of Spain, Duke di Galliera, b. at Seville, Feb. 23, 1866; d. at Paris, Dec. 24, 1930; son of Anthony, Duke de Montpensier, Infant of Spain, and his wife, Louise, Infanta of Spain. Issue:

    a) ALPHONSO MARIA FRANCIS ANTHONY DIEGO, Prince of Orleans, Infant of Spain, Duke di Galliera, b. Nov. 12, 1886; m., July 15, 1909, Beatrice, Princess de Saxe-Coburg and Gotha,

b. at Eastwell Park, April 20, 1884, dau. of Alfred, Duke of Saxe-Coburg and Gotha, Duke of Edinburg, and his wife, Marie Alexandrovna, Grand Duchess of Russia. Issue:

    i PRINCE ALVARO ANTHONY CHARLES PHILIPPE, Duke di Galliera, b. at Coburg, April 20, 1910; m., July 10, 1937, Carta Parodi Delfino;

    ii PRINCE ALONSO MARIA, b. May 28, 1912; d. in battle in Spain, Nov. 18, 1936;

    iii PRINCE ATAULFO ISABELLO CHARLES, b. Oct. 20, 1913.

b) LOUIS FERDINAND MARIA ZACHARIAS, Prince of Orleans, Infant of Spain, b. Nov. 5, 1888; m. at London, Sept. 19, 1930, Marie, widow of Prince Amadeus de Broglie, née Say.

ALLYN—NEWBERRY—MOSELEY—MATHER— TURNER—HOOKER

ISABEL DE VERMANDOIS, m. first, 1096, Robert de Beaumont I, Seigneur of Beaumont, Pont-Audemer, Vatteville, and Brionne, Count of Meulan in the French Vexin, 1st Earl of Leicester, d. June 5, 1118,

WALERAN, Count of Meulan, Earl of Worcester, b. ca. 1104; d. Apr. 9/10, 1166; m. ca. 1141, Agnes, d. Dec. 15, 1187, dau. of Amauri de Montfort, Comte d'Evreux, and his wife Agnes, a niece of Stephen de Garlande,

ROBERT, Count of Meulan, d. ca. 1207; m., ca. 1165, Maud, dau. and co-heiress of Reynold de Dunstanville, Earl of Cornwall, (natural son of Henry I, King of England),

MABEL, m. William de Reviers, called de Vernon, (also de Redvers), Earl of Devon, Lord of the Isle of Wight, d. Sept. 8/10, 1217, 3rd but only surviving son of Baldwin de Reviers (de Redvers), 1st Earl of Devon, Lord of the Isle of Wight,

MARY, eventually sole heiress, m. Pierre de Preaux (Peter Prouz), of Eastervale, Devonshire,

WILLIAM PROUZ, father of,

WALTER PROUZ, m. a dau. of Baron Dinham,

WILLIAM PROUZ, m. a dau. and heiress of Giles de Gidley,

SIR WILLIAM PROUZ, Knt., of Gidley, m. Alice (?), dau. and h. of Sir Fulk Ferrers (or Ferners), of Throwleigh,

SIR WILLIAM PROUZ, Knt., of Orton, Devonshire, m. Alice, dau. and h. of Sir Hugh Widworthy (or co-heiress of William de Reyny),

ALICE PROUZ, m. first, ca. 1316, Sir Roger Mules (or de Moels, of Lustleigh, co. Devon, d. ca. 1323); she m. secondly, Sir John Damerell (or Dammerel),

JOHANNA (OR JOAN), heiress, m. John Wotton, of Widworthy, Devonshire,

JOHN WOTTON, of Widworthy, m. Engaret, dau. and h. of Walter Dymoke (or Dymock),

ALICE WOTTON, m. Sir John Chichester, Knt.,

RICHARD CHICHESTER, m. Margaret, dau. of Sir Nicholas Keynes,

NICHOLAS CHICHESTER, m. Christian, dau. of Sir William (or Nicholas) Pawlet (or Poulett),

JOHN CHICHESTER, of Rawleigh Manor, Devon, m. secondly, Joan dau. of Robert Brett (or Bright),

AMIAS CHICHESTER, of Arlington Manor, Devon, m. Jane, dau. of Sir Roger Giffard, of Brightley,

FRANCES CHICHESTER, m. John Wyatt, of Braunton, Devon, Member of the Inner Temple, London,

MARGARET WYATT, m. in the Parish Church of Braunton, Devon, England, Feb. 2, 1625/6, Matthew Allyn, b. at Braunton, Apr. 15, 1605; came to America, *ca.* 1632; Representative to the General Court in 1626; one of the founders of Windsor; Representative, 1648-57; Magistrate, 1657-67; Commissioner for the United Colonies of New England, 1660-64; d. at Windsor, Conn., Feb. 1, 1670/1,

MARY ALLYN, b. at Braunton, co. Devon, *ca.* 1628; d. Dec. 14, 1703; m. at Windsor, Conn., June 11, 1646, Captain Benjamin Newberry, of Dorchester, Mass., and Windsor, Conn., Deputy to the General Court of Connecticut, etc., d. at Windsor, Sept. 11, 1689,

MARY NEWBERRY, b. Mar. 10, 1647/8, m. Dec. 14, 1664, Lieutenant John Moseley (Maudsley), d. Aug. 18, 1690,

JOSEPH MOSELEY, b. Dec. 21, 1670; m., Sept. 13, 1696, Abigail Root, b. June 26, 1680, dau. of Thomas Root,

DAVID MOSELEY, b. at Westfield, Mass., Feb. 9, 1705; d. at Westfield, Jan. 3, 1768; m., 1729, Margaret Dewey, b. at Westfield, Feb. 12, 1706; d. there Jan. 14, 1762,

GRACE MOSELEY, b. at Westfield, May 16, 1739; m. at Westfield, July 30, 1761, Dr. Samuel Mather, b. at Northampton, Mass., June 10, 1737; d. Apr. 27, 1808,

JOHN MATHER, b. at Westfield, Feb. 27, 1775/6; d. there Oct. 25, 1847; m. there Feb. 22, 1798, Sophia Taylor, b. at Westfield, Nov. 19, 1774; d. there Jan. 24, 1847; dau. of Major Edward Taylor, by Sarah Ingersoll,

ROLAND MATHER, b. at Westfield, May 31, 1809; d. at Hartford, Conn., May 10, 1897; m. at Royalton, Vt., May 30, 1837; Mary Francis, b. at Royalton, June 15, 1818: d. Oct. 17, 1873,

JULIA FRANCIS MATHER, b. at Hartford, Aug. 10, 1839; d. at Philadelphia, July 20, 1925; m. at Hartford, Oct. 6, 1858, Dr. Charles Peaslee Turner, b. at Hartford, Feb. 5, 1826; d. at Philadelphia, Apr. 12, 1910,

MARY MATHER TURNER, b. at Philadelphia, Feb. 26, 1864; d. at Hartford, May 13, 1939; m. at Philadelphia, Nov. 12, 1889, Edward Williams Hooker, b. at Hartford, Oct. 19, 1865; d. at Eastern Point, Conn., Sept. 3, 1915,

ROLAND MATHER HOOKER, b. at Hartford, Sept. 10, 1900; Ph.B., M.A., Dignitary (Commander) and one of the Priors of Order of the Crown of Charlemagne; Member of Order of the Founders and Patriots of America, Society of Colonial Wars, Pennsylvania State Society of the Cincinnati, S.R., S.A.R., Society of Mayflower Descendants, British Association of Descendants of Knights of the Garter, M. O. F. W., Royal Society of Literature of the United Kingdom, Baronial Order of Runnemede, Saint Nicholas Society of New York, Hereditary Order of Descendants of Colonial Governors Prior to 1750; Huguenot Society of America, Grand Prix Humanitaire (Commander), Order of Washington, Society of American Wars, Descendants of Delegates to the Continental Congress, Order of the Crown in America, Colonial Order of the Acorn, Military Order of the Crusades, Institute of American Genealogy; President of Conn. Society of the War of 1812, etc., m., first, Oct. 22, 1921, Winifred Cartwright Holahan, of Durham, N. C., (marriage dissolved by divorce, Oct. 19, 1935) ; m., secondly, at Poughkeepsie, N. Y., June 27, 1936, Loua Bedell Hooker.
Issue by first wife:

1.) EDWARD GORDON HOOKER, b. at Oxford, England, Apr. 7, 1923;

2.) MARGARET CARMICHAEL HOOKER, b. at New York, N. Y., Jan. 14, 1925; d. at New York, July 8, 1940.

BATTE—JETER—BIRDWELL—EASON—DOLL—DICKSON

CHARLEMAGNE

See Page 133

ROGER DE QUINCY, 2nd Earl of Winchester, Constable of Scotland, &c., m., first, Helen (or Elena), dau. and co-h. of Alan, Lord of Galloway, Constable of Scotland,

ELIZABETH (often referred to as Isabel and Marjory) de Quincy, 2nd dau. and co-h., m. Alexander Comyn, Earl of Buchan, Constable of Scotland, Justiciar in Scotland, d. 1290; son and heir of William Comyn, Earl of Buchan, Justiciar, by Margaret, Countess of Buchan,

ELIZABETH COMYN (sometimes referred to as Agnes), d. before Feb. 17, 1328/9; m. Gilbert de Umfreville, Earl of Angus, Lord Umfreville, Governor of Angus and of Dundee and Forfar Castles, &c., son and heir of Gilbert de Umfreville, Lord of Prudhoe and Redesdale in Northumberland, Earl of Angus in right of his wife, by Maud, *suo jure* Countess of Angus, widow of John Comyn, Earl of Angus, and dau. and heiress of Malcolm, Earl of Angus, and his wife Mary, dau. and h. of Sir Humphrey Berkeley,

ROBERT DE UMFREVILLE, Lord Umfreville, Earl of Angus, d. 1325; m., 2ndly, Alianor, d. Mar. 31, 1368,

THOMAS DE UMFREVILLE, of Hessle, co. York, and Holmside, co. Durham, inherited the Castle of Harbottle and the Manor of Otterburn, d. May 21, 1387; m. Joan, dau. of Adam de Roddam,

SIR THOMAS DE UMFREVILLE, of Harbottle Castle, &c., Sheriff of Northumberland 1388-89, and M. P. for that county in the Parliaments which met Feb. 3, 1387/8 and Jan. 17, 1389/90; d. 1390/1; m. Agnes, d. Oct. 25, 1420, probably dau. of Sir Thomas de Grey, of Heton,

MARGARET DE UMFREVILLE, d. June 23, 1444, widow of William Lodington, of Gunby, co. Lincoln, Justice of the Common Pleas; m., 2ndly, 1423, Sir John Constable, Knt., of Halsham in Holderness,

108

SIR JOHN CONSTABLE, Knt., of Halsham in Holderness; will dated Dec. 20, 1472, proved Mar. 18, 1472/3; m. Lora, widow of John Musgrave, and dau. of Sir William FitzHugh, and his wife Margery, dau. of William, Baron Willoughby de Eresby, co. Lincoln, by his 1st wife, Lucy, dau. of Sir Roger La Straunge, Lord La Straunge, of Knockin, Salop,

JOAN (OR JANE) CONSTABLE, m. Sir William Mallory, Knt., of Stewdley, Yorkshire,

SIR JOHN MALLORY, Knt., of Stewdley, Yorkshire, m., first, Margaret, dau. of Edward Thwaytes, of Laund,

SIR WILLIAM MALLORY, Knt., of Stewdley, m. Jane (or Joanna), dau. of Sir John Conyers, alias Norton, Knt., of Norton, High Sheriff of the co. York in 1507, 1508, and in 1514,

SIR WILLIAM MALLORY, Knt., of Stewdley, m., (her 1st husband), Ursula, dau. of George Gale, Esq., Lord Mayor of York in 1534 and 1546, Master of the Mint there,

REVEREND THOMAS MALLORY, Dean of Chester, d. at the Deanery-house, Chester, Apr. 3, 1644; m. Elizabeth, dau. of the Rt. Rev. Richard Vaughan, Bishop of Chester,

MARTHA (sometimes referred to as KATHARINE) MALLORY, m. Capt. (or Col.) John Batte (Batt), of Okewell Hall, near Birstall in the Wapentake of Agbrigg and Morley, Yorkshire, Justice of the Peace in the West Riding, son of Robert Batte (Batt), Fellow and Vice-Master of the University College, Oxford, &c., and his wife Mary, dau. of John Parry, of the Golden Valley in Herefordshire,

CAPTAIN HENRY BATTE, of Okewell Hall, came to Virginia about 1646; Member of the Va. House of Burgesses, 1685-86 and 1692-93; Justice of Charles City County, Va., 1693; m. Mary, dau. of Henry Lound, of Henrico County, Va.,

MARY BATTE, m. John Poythress, Burgess for Charles City County, Va., 1723; resided in Charles City County until his death in 1723/4,

THOMAS POYTHRESS, m. Elizabeth Pleasants Cocke, dau. of James Cocke, of "Curles," Va., Clerk of Court and Burgess about 1699, (and his wife Elizabeth, dau. of John Pleasants, of Henrico County, Va.), and granddau. of Captain Thomas Cocke, J. P., Sheriff of Henrico County, Member of the Va.

House of Burgesses, (and his wife Margaret, widow of Jones, dau. of Major General Abraham Wood, one of the four Major Generals commanding the Military Establishment, Member of the Governor's Council) and great-grand-dau. of Lieutenant-Colonel Richard Cocke, of "Bremo," Henrico County, Va.,

SUSANNAH POYTHRESS, m. William Hall, of Buckingham County, Va., b. about 1700,

DR. ROBERT HALL, b. in Buckingham County, Va., resided in the colony of Chonan County, Edenton, N. C., 1742-80./86; Surgeon in Third N. C. Infantry Regiment, commissioned Apr. 17, 1774; d. at Edenton, N. C., about 1780/86; m., about 1742, Anne Leary, presumably dau. of Cornelius Leary, Jr., and his wife Elizabeth, dau. of Thomas Haughton,

SICILY (OR CECILY) ANN HALL, m., about 1772, John Agee, b. in Buckingham County, Va., about 1749; d. there about 1810; son of James Agee, a soldier in the Revolutionary War, and his wife Mary (or Elizabeth) Ford, presumably dau. of James Ford and his wife Ann Bondurant,

ELIZABETH AGEE, b. in Va., March 5, 1790; d. at Houston, Texas, Nov. 28, 1874; m., Jan. 8/18, 1807, Nehemiah McAshan II, b. Dec. 15, 1784; d. June 23, 1846, son of Nehemiah McAshan I,

ANN WATKINS McASHAN, b. in Buckingham County, Va., Sept. 9, 1814; d. at Petit Prairie Bayou, St. Landry Parish, La., July 28, 1878; widow of William Guerrant; m., 2ndly, in Amelia County, Va., Feb. 20, 1839, (his 2nd wife), John Tinsley Jeter, b. in Amelia County, Va., Nov. 13, 1798; d. at Memphis, Tenn., May 13, 1862; son of Capt. John Jeter, of Amelia County, Va., Captain of Artillery of Va. Militia in the War of 1812,

JOHN WARRICK JETER, b. at New Orleans, La., Oct. 23, 1850; d. at Bossier Parish, La., Dec. 18, 1903; served as President of Levy Board, member of School Board and represented his co. in the Legislature; m., Feb. 23, 1876, Marie Louise Dirmeyer, b. at New Orleans, La., Sept. 9, 1856; d. at Shreveport, La., Jan. 18, 1917; dau. of Dr. George Dirmeyer and his wife Rosa Bright, widow of George Lynch, and dau. of George T. Bright and his wife Lodoiska de Maupassant, dau. of Pierre Francois Valentine de Maupassant. Issue, among others:

110

1.) MARIE LOUISE JETER, b. Dec. 29, 1876; Dame Companion of the Order of the Crown of Charlemagne; m., Feb. 17, 1897, John Nixon Birdwell, d. Dec. 31, 1931. Issue:

    a) WARRIE RUSSELL BIRDWELL, b. Apr. 11, 1901; m., 1921, Gladys Baumgardner. Issue:

        i WARRIE RUSSELL BIRDWELL, JR., b. 1922;

        ii JOHN ROLAND BIRDWELL, b. 1924;

        iii CAROLINE LOUISE BIRDWELL, b. 1927;

        iv GLADYS G. BIRDWELL, b. 1929.

    b) THOMAS MALVIN BIRDWELL, b. Dec. 7, 1902; m., June 30, 1924, Erie Kelley. Issue:

        i JACQUELYN BIRDWELL, b. 1925;

        ii THOMAS MALVIN BIRDWELL, JR., b. 1929.

    c) MARY LOUISE BIRDWELL, b. Nov. 12, 1904; now Sister Mary Fidelis, Daughter of the Cross, St. Vincent's College and Academy, Shreveport;

    d) MADELINE ELIZABETH BIRDWELL, b. March 7, 1906; m., Sept. 19, 1931, Walter Miller White. Issue:

        i ELIZABETH ANN WHITE, b. Jan. 10, 1933;

        ii WALTER MILLER WHITE, JR., b. July 13, 1935;

        iii MARIE LOUISE WHITE, b. Apr. 21, 1939.

    e) JOHN NIXON BIRDWELL, b. July 4/14, 1907; m., Sept. 27, 1928, Erie R. Black;

    f) MAURICE JETER BIRDWELL, b. Dec. 2, 1908; m., Nov. 9, 1935, Gladys Winn. Issue:

        i MAURICE NIXON BIRDWELL, b. Sept. 16, 1937;

        ii BARBARA ANNE BIRDWELL, b. Nov. 8, 1939.

2.) JOHN WARRICK JETER II, b. Sept. 11, 1878; m., Feb. 8, 1905, Jessie Elizabeth Herndon, b. Sept. 11, 1885; d. at Shreveport, La., May 5, 1940. Issue:

a) BEVERLY ARDIS JETER, b. Aug. 18, 1907; m. Joseph E. Marshall, b. July 2, 1901. Issue:

   i Jo ANN MARSHALL, b. Nov. 26, 1926;

   ii JOHN CULLEN MARSHALL, b. Oct. 4, 1930.

3.) JOHN TINSLEY JETER, b. July 1, 1880; m., 1901, Lillie Belle Gribble, b. Sept. 30, 1884. Issue:

a) JAMES TINSLEY JETER, b. Mar. 30, 1903; m., first, 1924, Marie Louise Howell, b. Feb. 11, 1902, (marriage dissolved by divorce); m., 2ndly, Mary West. Issue by 1st wife:

   i JAMES TINSLEY JETER, JR., b. Jan. 17, 1928;

Issue by 2nd wife:

   ii JUDITH JETER.

b) JOHN ROBERT JETER, b. Jan. 28, 1906; m. Bebbie West.

4.) ANNIE CARMOUCHE JETER, b. at Brownlee, La., Mar. 16, 1885; Dame Companion of the Order of the Crown of Charlemagne; Member of D.A.C., D.A.R., U.D.C., &c.; m. at Shreveport, La., Dec. 27, 1905, Andrew Wilson Eason, b. at Olive Branch, Miss., Jan. 6, 1879. Issue:

a) WILSON JETER EASON, b. at Memphis, Tenn., Mar. 27, 1907; attended Memphis University and Carnegie Institute of Technology at Pittsburgh, Pa.; Member of Scarab Architecture Honorary Society; m. at Memphis, Tenn., Dec. 6, 1938, Lois Elizabeth Nickey, b. at Memphis, Nov. 17, 1917, graduated from Randolph-Macon Women's College, Lynchburg, Va., member of Alpha Omicron Pi, dau. of Samuel Mossman Nickey and his wife Lois Metsker.

5.) DAISY ELIZABETH JETER, b. Mar. 3, 1887; Dame Dignitary, one of the Priors and Delegate of the Order of the Crown of Charlemagne; Member of National Society of the Colonial Dames of America in the State of La. (Corresponding Secretary, Shreveport Committee), D.A.C. (Corresponding Secretary, La. State Society), U.D.C., &c.; m., Jan. 2, 1908, Francis

Theodore Doll, b. at Shreveport, July 7, 1883, son of the late Howard Frederick Doll and his wife, the late Ludeweka Josephine Bercher. Issue:

a) HOWARD FRANCIS DOLL, b. at Riverton, Wyo., Nov. 27, 1908; B.S.E.E., Notre Dame University, 1929; Companion (Knight) of the Order of the Crown of Charlemagne; m., Nov. 30, 1933, Mary Alyce Cecilia Jeanmougin, dau. of Henry Francis Jeanmougin and his wife Johanna McCarthy. Issue:

i HOWARD FRANCIS DOLL, JR., b. at Chicago, Feb. 18, 1936;

ii HENRY THEODORE DOLL, b. at Chicago, Oct. 10, 1940.

b) FREDRICKA ADELAIDE MARIE JETER DOLL, b. at Shreveport, La., Mar. 4, 1914; Dame Dignitary First Class (Grand Officer) and Delegate of the Order of the Crown of Charlemagne; Member of National Society of the Colonial Dames of America in the State of La., D.A.C., D.A.R., U.D.C., Daughters of Colonial Wars, Huguenot Society of New England (life member), Advisory Council of General Court of Patriotic Societies of America, &c.; National Organizing Secretary, National Society Children of the American Colonists, 1939-42; Awarded British Coronation Medal, 1937; Awarded Diploma and Insignia of the Papal Order of St. John the Lateran, &c.; m., Aug. 5, 1933, (his 2nd wife), Marcellus Donald Alexander R. von Redlich, LL.B., D.C.L., J.D., LL.D., Ph.D., D.Lit., &c., b. Aug. 15, 1893, only son and heir of the late Baron Harold Ignatius Sigismund R. von Redlich, and his wife the late Sarah Katharine Maria, née Baroness (Freiin) von Heim. Issue:

i FREDRICKA LORETTA MARIE ELIZABETH VON REDLICH, b. May 30, 1935.

c) DAISY LOUISE DOLL, b. at Shreveport, La., Aug. 25, 1916; B.A., La. State University; Dame Companion of the Order of the Crown of

Charlemagne; Member of National Society of the Colonial Dames of America in the State of La.; m. at Shreveport, Feb. 1, 1939, William Henry Martin, Jr., B.A., b. at Houston, Texas, Feb. 3, 1907, son of William Henry Martin, M.D., of Houston, and his first wife Gertrude Brinkley, d. Sept. 3, 1913. Issue:

i LOUISE DOLL MARTIN, b. at Mt. Vernon, Ill., Nov. 24, 1939.

6.) ROBERT MCLEAN JETER, b. Feb. 5, 1891; m., Oct. 4, 1917, Marion Hearne, b. Dec. 11, 1892, dau. of George M. Hearne and his wife Luella Applegate, dau. of William Clarke Applegate. Issue:

a) ROBERT MCLEAN JETER, Jr., b. Aug. 18, 1918;

b) HORACE HEARNE JETER, b. Feb. 14, 1922;

c) JOHN MARION JETER, b. July 26, 1935.

7.) ADELAIDE SCANLAND JETER, b. Jan. 6, 1894; Dame Dignitary First Class of the Order of the Crown of Charlemagne; Member of National Society of the Colonial Dames of America in the State of La. (member of Board of Managers, La. State Society), D.A.C. (Registrar, La. State Society), D.A.R., U.D.C., Order of the Crown in America, National Society Daughters of the Barons of Runnemede, &c.; m., Oct. 11, 1916, Donald Coty Dickson, LL.B., b. Feb. 28, 1890, son of George Bennett Dickson and his wife Lucile Coty (dau. of Thomas Davenport Coty, and granddau. of James Lucas Coty), and grandson of Major Bennett Smith Dickson. Issue:

a) DONALD COTY DICKSON, JR., LL.B., Second Lieutenant U.S.A., b. at Shreveport, Nov. 17, 1917;

b) WARRICK JETER DICKSON, b. at Shreveport, Dec. 13, 1920;

c) ADELAIDE LUCILE DICKSON, b. at Shreveport, Jan. 16, 1923;

d) BENNET KETH DICKSON, b. at Shreveport, Jan. 1, 1927.

BATTE—JETER—GILMER

CHARLEMAGNE

See Page 110

ANN WATKINS MCASHAN, widow of William Guerrant; m., 2ndly, (his 2nd wife), John Tinsley Jeter,

ANNIE TINSLEY JETER, b. in Va., July 27, 1843; d. at Shreveport, La., June 16 or July 28, 1921; m. at New Orleans, La., Apr. 28, 1864, Capt. Emile A. Carmouche, of Point Coupee Parish, La., b. Jan. 5, 1836; d. July 3, 1884,

BESSIE CARMOUCHE, b. May 20, 1870; d. at Shreveport, Apr. 6, 1935; m., Jan. 15, 1890, George Edwin Gilmer, b. Oct. 21, 1863, son of Peachy Ridgeway Gilmer and his wife Elizabeth Dooley, of LaFayette County, Arkansas, and a grandson of Dr. John Thornton Gilmer, of Amherst County, Va., and his wife Martha Gaines Harvey. Issue:

1.) ANNIE ELIZABETH GILMER, b. Feb. 12, 1891; m., Dec. 30, 1914, Oswald E. La Cour, of Point Coupee Parish, La., b. July 20, 1884, son of Edgar La Cour and his wife Adele Hatkinson. Issue:

    a) OSWALD EDGAR LA COUR, JR., b. Mar. 16, 1917;

    b) ANNIE JETER LA COUR, b. Jan. 12, 1919;

    c) GEORGE GILMER LA COUR, b. June 8, 1920;

    d) WILLIAM CARMOUCHE LA COUR, b. May 6, 1922;

    e) MARIE ADELE LA COUR, b. May 10, 1924;

    f) ROBERT HATKINSON LA COUR, b. June 11, 1925;

    g) FRANCES ELIZABETH LA COUR, b. Oct. 28, 1927.

2.) GEORGE TINSLEY GILMER, b. Mar. 27, 1894; B.A., Tulane University, 1915, LL.D., 1917; m., Oct. 2, 1920, Mrs. Edna Clary Ebey, b. at Hickory, Okla., Jan. 30, 1900.

3.) PEACHY RIDGEWAY GILMER, b. Dec. 8, 1897; B.S., Tulane University, 1917, and M.D., 1921; m., June 6,

115

1929, Julia Morrow Church, b. Oct. 4, 1899, dau. of Judge John Church, of "The Groves," in Strabane, co. Londonderry, Ireland, and afterwards of McKinney, Texas, and his wife Julia Summerville Coffee. Issue:

    a) PEACHY RIDGEWAY GILMER, JR., b. July 26, 1932.

4.) WILLIAM CARMOUCHE GILMER, b. May 14, 1906; Bachelor of Architecture, Tulane University, 1931.

BATTE—LIGON—JONES—WHEELER

CHARLEMAGNE

See Page 109

CAPTAIN HENRY BATTE, of Okewell Hall, came to Va. about 1646; m. Mary, dau. of Henry Lound, of Henrico County, Va.,

ELIZABETH BATTE, m. William Ligon II,

WILLIAM LIGON III, m. Ann,

THOMAS LIGON, m. Tabitha,

ANNE (NANCY) LIGON, b. about 1765; d. about 1842; m., about 1781, Harrison Jones,

RICHARD JONES, b. in Cumberland County, Va., June 29, 1793; d. at Wheeler, Ala., Feb. 3, 1883; m., about 1818, Lucy Wilkinson Early, d. at Wheeler, Ala., Oct. 31, 1869, dau. of Governor Early,

DANIELLA JONES, b. in Ala., Aug. 20, 1841; d. at Washington, D.C., May 19, 1896; m., Feb. 8, 1866, General Joseph Wheeler (C.S.A.), b. at Augusta, Ga., Set. 10, 1836; d. at Brooklyn, N. Y., Jan. 25, 1906,

ANNIE EARLY WHEELER, b. in Ala., July 31, 1868; Dame Companion of the Order of the Crown of Charlemagne; Member of D.A.C. (Vice-Regent, Ala. State Society), National Society Daughters of the Barons of Runnemede, &c.

BRAGANZA

CHARLEMAGNE

See Page 35

FRANCES II (JOSEPH CHARLES JOHN), Emperor of Germany, 1st
Emperor of Austria in 1804, &c., b. Feb. 12, 1768; d. March
2, 1835; m., 2ndly, Sept. 19, 1790, Maria Theresa, b. June 6,
1772; d. April 13, 1807; eldest dau. of Ferdinand I, King of
the Two Sicilies,

ARCHDUCHESS MARIE LEOPOLDINE, b. Jan. 22, 1797; d. Dec. 11,
1826; m., Nov. 6, 1817, Pedro IV, King of Portugal, Prince
of Brazil, b. Oct. 12, 1798; d. Sept. 24, 1834; proclaimed
Emperor of Brazil and ascended the throne as Pedro I, Oct.
12, 1822; abdicated as King of Portugal in favor of his dau.,
Maria da Gloria II, May 2, 1826,

PEDRO II, Emperor of Brazil until Nov. 15, 1889; Infant of
Portugal, Prince of Braganza; b. Dec. 2, 1825; d. Dec. 5,
1891; m. at Rio de Janeiro, Sept. 4, 1843, Theresa, Princess
de Bourbon-Sicily, b. March 14, 1822; d. Dec. 28, 1889,

ISABELLA CHRISTINA LEOPOLDINE AUGUSTINA, Princess of Bra-
ganza, Princess of Brazil, &c., b. at Rio de Janeiro, July 29,
1846; d. Nov. 14, 1921; m. at Rio de Janeiro, Oct. 15, 1864,
Louis Philippe Maria Ferdinand Gaston, Prince of Orleans,
Count d'Eu, b. April 28, 1842; d. Aug. 28, 1922; son of Louis,
Duke de Nemours, and his wife, Victoria, Princess of Saxe-
Coburg and Gotha. Issue:

1.) PRINCE PIERRE D'ALCANTARA LOUIS PHILIPPE of Orleans,
Prince of Braganza, b. Oct. 15, 1875; renounced his
rights to the succession to the throne of Brazil in
favor of his brother, Prince Louis, Oct. 30, 1908; m.,
Nov. 14, 1908, Marie Elizabeth Adelaide, Countess
Dobrzensky de Dobrzenicz, b. Dec. 7, 1875. Issue:

a) PRINCESS ISABELLA MARIE AMELIA of Orleans,
Princess de Braganza, b. Aug. 13, 1911; m. at
Palermo, April 8, 1931, Henry Robert Ferdi-
nand Maria Louise Philippe, Count of Paris,
Prince of France, &c., b. July 5, 1908, son of

John Peter (Jean Pierre) Clement Maria, Prince of Orleans, Duke of Guise, Chief of the Royal House of France, and his wife, Isabella, Princess of France, &c. Issue:

    i Princess Isabella Marie Laura Victoria of Orleans and of France, b. April 8, 1932;

    ii Prince Henry Philippe Peter Maria of Orleans and of France, b. June 14, 1933;

    iii Princess Helen Astrid Leopoldine Marie of Orleans and of France, b. Sept. 17, 1934;

    iv Prince Francis Gaston Michael Maria of Orleans and of France, b. Aug. 15, 1935.

b) Prince Peter (Pierre d'Alcantara) Gaston John Maria of Orleans, Prince de Braganza, b. Feb. 19, 1913;

c) Princess Marie Frances Amelia of Orleans and of Braganza, b. Sept. 8, 1914;

d) Prince John Maria Philippe Gabriel of Orleans and of Braganza, b. Oct. 15, 1916;

e) Princess Theresa Marie Theodora of Orleans and of Braganza, b. June 18, 1919.

2.) Prince Louis Maria Philippe of Orleans, Prince of Braganza, &c., b. Jan. 26, 1878; d. at Cannes, France, March 26, 1920; m. at Cannes, Nov. 4, 1908, Marie Pia, Princess of Bourbon-Sicily, b. at Cannes, Aug. 12, 1878, dau. of Alphonso, Count of Caserta, Head of the Royal House of the Two Sicilies, and his wife, Princess Antoinette, dau. of Prince Francis de Paul of the Two Sicilies, Count of Trapani. Issue:

a) Prince Peter (Pierre) Henry Alphonso Philippe Maria of Orleans and of Braganza, b. Sept. 13, 1909; m., Aug. 19, 1937, Princess Marie Elizabeth Frances of Bavaria, b. Sept. 9, 1914, dau. of Prince Francis Marie Luitpold of Bavaria, and his wife Isabella, Princess de Croy and a granddau. of Louis III, King of Bavaria;

b) Princess Pia Marie Reniere Isabella of Orleans and of Braganza, b. Mar. 4, 1913.

BRUEN—BALDWIN—CRANE—BOYD

CHARLEMAGNE, King of the Franks and Emperor of the West, b. April 2, 747; d. Jan. 28, 814; m., 771, the Swabian Princess Hildegard, d. April 30, 783,

PEPIN, King of Italy, b. April 773; d. July 8, 810; father of,

BERNARD, King of Italy Sept. 813, abdicated Dec. 817; b. about 797; d. April 17, 818; (according to Thegan and others he was *ex concubina natus*, but this statement cannot definitely be substantiated and seems improbable); m. Cunigunde, d. about 835,

PEPIN, b. 817/8; d. after 840; father of,

HERBERT I, Count of Vermandois, b. about 840; murdered about 902; m. Berthe de Morvois,

HERBERT II, Count of Vermandois and of Troyes, d. about 943; m. Liégeard, dau. of Robert I, King of France,

ALBERT I, the Pious, Count of Vermandois, b. about 920; d. 987/8; m. Princess Gerberga[1], dau. of Louis IV, *d'Outre-mer*, King of France, and his wife Gerberga, widow of Gisilbert, Duke of Lorraine, and dau. of Henry I, the Fowler, Emperor of Germany,

HERBERT III, Count of Vermandois, b. about 955; d. about 1000; m., (her second husband), Irmgard (Ermengarde), dau. of Reinald, Count of Bar,

OTHO, Count of Vermandois, b. about 1000; d. May 25, 1045; m. Pavie,

HERBERT IV, Count of Vermandois and of Valois, b. about 1032; d. about 1080; m. Adela de Vexin, dau. of Raoul III, the Great, Count of Valois, Vexin, &c.,

ADELAIDE (ADELHEID), Countess of Vermandois and of Valois, m. Hugh the Great, Duke of France and Burgundy, Marquis

---

[1] It is contended by the latest authorities that this Gerberga was the the daughter of Gerberga by her first husband, Gisilbert, Duke of Lorraine, and not by her 2nd husband, King Louis IV. However, the line is good either way.

of Orleans, Count of Amiens, Chaumont, Paris, Valois, Vermandois, &c., son of Henry I, King of France, by Anne, dau. of Yaroslav I, Grand Prince of Kiev,

ISABEL DE VERMANDOIS, Countess of Leicester, d. Feb. 13, 1131; m., 2ndly, William de Warenne, 2nd Earl of Surrey, d. 1135/8,

GUNDRED DE WARENNE, m., first, Roger de Newburgh, Earl of Warwick, Crusader, d. June 12, 1153, son of Henry de Newburgh, Earl of Warwick,

WALERAN DE NEWBURGH, 4th Earl of Warwick, d. about 1204/5; m., 2ndly, Alice, dau. of John de Harcourt, and widow of John de Limesi,

ALICE DE NEWBURGH, m. William, Baron Mauduit, of Hanslape, co. Buckingham, d. April 1257,

ISABEL DE MAUDUIT, sister and heiress of William de Mauduit, Earl of Warwick, m. William, 5th Baron Beauchamp, of Elmley Castle,

WILLIAM DE BEAUCHAMP, 6th Baron Beauchamp, of Elmley Castle, Earl of Warwick, d. at Elmley Castle, co. Worcester, June 5/9, 1298; m. Maud, d. April 16/8, 1301, widow of Sir Gerard de Furnivalle, Lord of Hallamshire, and dau. of Sir John FitzGeoffrey, of Shere and Shalford, Surrey, Fambridge, Essex, &c., Justiciar of Ireland 1245-56, (d. Nov. 23, 1258), and his wife Isabel, widow of Gilbert de Lacy, of Ewyas Lacy, co. Hereford, and dau. of Hugh le Bigod, Earl of Norfolk,

GUY DE BEAUCHAMP, 2nd Earl of Warwick, d. at Warwick, Aug. 10/2, 1315; m., Feb. 12/3, 1309/10, Alice, d. Jan. 1, 1324/5, dau. and eventually heiress of Ralph de Toni, of Castle Maud, Flamstead, Herts, and widow of Thomas Leyburne,

MAUD DE BEAUCHAMP, d. 1369; m., first, Geoffrey de Say, 2nd Baron Say, Knight - Banneret, Admiral of the King's Fleet, d. June 26, 1359,

IDONEA DE SAY, d. about 1384; m., (his first wife), Sir John de Clinton, 3rd Baron Clinton, of Amington and Maxstoke, co. Warwick, d. Sept. 6, 1398; Constable of Warwick Castle, 1390-97; son and heir of John, 2nd Baron Clinton, and his wife Margery, dau. of Sir William Corbet, of Chaddesley Corbet, co. Worcester,

MARGARET DE CLINTON, m. Sir Baldwin de Montfort (Mont-ford), of Coleshill Manor, co. Warwick,

SIR WILLIAM DE MONTFORT, of Coleshill Manor, m. presumably Margaret Peche,

ROBERT MONTFORT, Esq., of Bescote, co. Stafford, and Monks-path, co. Warwick, father of,

KATHARINE MONTFORT, dau. and heiress, m. Sir George Booth (Bothe), of Dunham Massie, co. Chester, d. 1483, son of Sir William Booth (Bothe), of Dunham Massie, Sheriff of Cheshire, and his wife Maud, dau. of John de Dutton, Esq., of Dutton,

SIR WILLIAM BOOTH, Knt., of Dunham Massie, d. Nov. 9, 1519; m., 2ndly, Ellen, dau. of Sir John Montgomery, of Throwley, co. Stafford,

JANE (OR JOAN) Booth, widow of Hugh Dutton, of Dutton; m., 2ndly, Sir Thomas Holford, of Holford, nigh Nether Tabley, co. Chester,

DOROTHY HOLFORD, m,. (his second wife), John Bruen (Bruyn), Esq., of Bruen Stapleford, co. Chester, d. May 14, 1580/7, son of John Bruyn, Esq., of Bruen Stapleford, and grand-son of James Bruyn, Esq., of Bruen Stapleford,

JOHN BRUEN III, of Bruen Stapleford, b. about 1560; d. Jan. 18, 1625/6; m., 2ndly, Anne, dau. of John Fox,

OBADIAH BRUEN, bapt. at Tarvin, England, Dec. 25, 1606; d. at Newark, N. J., about 1682/90; m., 2ndly, Sarah, d. about March 25, 1684,

HANNAH BRUEN, b. at Gloucester, Mass., Jan. 9, 1643; d. at Newark, about 1695; m. at New London, Oct. 3, 1663, John Baldwin, b. at Milford, Conn., about 1640; d. at Newark, about 1703,

JONATHAN BALDWIN, b. at Newark, about 1691; d. at Newark, Aug. 9, 1726; m. Phebe Roberts,

JOANNA BALDWIN, m. Isaac Nutman, b. 1714; died at Newark, 1749,

PHEBE NUTMAN, b. at Elizabethtown, N. J., about 1742; d. at Orange, Dec. 28, 1826; m. Matthias Pierson, M.D., b. at Orange, June 20, 1734; d. at Orange, N. J., May 9, 1809.

FANNY PIERSON, b. at Orange, N. J., March 20, 1773; d. at Bloomfield, N. J., Aug. 19, 1828; m. Israel Crane, b. Mar. 14, 1774; d. at Bloomfield, Mar. 25, 1858,

MATTHIAS CRANE, b. at Bloomfield, about 1802; d. at Montclair, N. J., June 28, 1882; m. Susan Baldwin, b. at Orange, N. J., about 1812; d. at Montclair, Feb. 5, 1880,

KATE CRANE, b. at West Bloomfield, N. J., Nov. 19, 1839; d. at Montclair, N. J., June 17, 1935; m. at West Bloomfield, Nov. 9, 1859, Robert Munro Boyd, b. at Winsted, Conn., Aug. 12, 1834; d. at Montclair, Dec. 19, 1917,

ROBERT MUNRO BOYD, JR., b. at West Bloomfield, N. J., May 5, 1863; Dignitary (Commander) and Judge Advocate General of the Order of the Crown of Charlemagne; Governor General, General Society of Colonial Wars; Former Governor General of the General Society of Mayflower Descendants; Former Governor of Huguenot Society in State of New Jersey; Member of Order of Colonial Governors, &c.; m. at New London, Conn., Oct. 26, 1898, Edith Bancroft, b. at San Francisco, California, June 21, 1875; Associate Dame Companion of the Order of the Crown of Charlemagne; dau. of Eugene G. Bancroft and Eleanor Croes, his wife.

BRUEN—DAVIS—COE—PARKER—WESTON

CHARLEMAGNE, King of the Franks and Emperor of the West,

LOUIS I, the Pious, *le Debonnaire,* King of the Franks and Emperor of the West; m., 1st, about 794/8, Irmengarde, d. about Oct. 3, 818, dau. of Ingeramun, Count of Hasbaye,

LOUIS LE GERMANIQUE, King of Bavaria, 817; b. about 806; d. Aug. 28, 876; m. Emma, d. Jan. 31, 876, (she was a sister of his stepmother, Judith, who married, as second wife, Emperor Louis I), dau. of Guelph I, Count of Altdorf and Duke of Bavaria,

CARLOMAN, King of Bavaria, 876; b. about 829; d. Sept. 29, 880, father of,

ARNULPH, Emperor of Germany, d. Nov. 29, 899; m. Oda (or Utade), dau. of Theudon, Count in Bavaria,

HEDWIGE of Germany, m. Otho I, the Illustrious, Duke of Saxony, d. Nov. 12/3, 912, son of Ludolph I, the Great, Duke of Saxony,

HENRY I, the Fowler, (*l'Oiseleur*), Emperor of Germany, Duke of Saxony, Brunswick and Zelle, b. about 876; d. July 2, 936; m., 2ndly, about 911, Mathilda, dau. of Dietrich, Count of Ringelheim, and sister of Siegfried, 1st Count (Markgraf) of Brandenburg,

PRINCESS HATWIDE (Hatwin or Hawise), m., (his third wife), Hugh the Great, surnamed *the White,* Duke of France, Count of Paris, &c., d. about June 17 - July 1, 956, son of Robert, Duke of France, Marquis of Orleans, who was crowned King of France June 29, 922, and was killed in battle, about June 15, 923,

HUGH CAPET, King of France, b. about 939/46, d. Oct. 24, 996; m. Adelaide,

ROBERT II, the Pious, King of France, b. about 970/1; d. July 20, 1031; m., 2ndly, Constance, dau. of William Taillefer, Count of Toulouse, by Blanche d'Anjou, his wife,

HENRY I, King of France, d. Aug. 4/24, 1060; m., about 1044, Anne of Kiev, d. about 1075, dau. of Yaroslav I, Grand Prince of Kiev, and his wife Ingegarde, dau. of Olave III, King of Sweden,

HUGH THE GREAT, Duke of France and Burgundy, Marquis of Orleans, Count of Amiens, Chaumont, Valois, Vermandois, &c., Crusader; m. Adelaide (Adelheid), Countess of Vermandois and of Valois, dau. of Herbert IV, Count of Vermandois,

ISABEL DE VERMANDOIS, m., first, 1096, Robert de Beaumont, Seigneur of Beaumont, Pont-Audemer, Brionne, and Vatteville in Normandy, Count of Meulan in the French Vexin, Earl of Leicester, b. about 1046; d. June 5, 1118; son and heir of Roger de Beaumont, called *de Bello Monte*, Seigneur of Beaumont and Pont-Audemer, and his wife Adeline (dau. of Waleran and sister of Hugh, Counts of Meulan), and grandson of Humphrey de Vieilles (de Vetulis), Seigneur of Vieilles and Pont-Audemer in Normandy,

ROBERT DE BEAUMONT II, called *le Bossu* or *le Goczen*, Earl of Leicester, b. about 1104; d. April 5, 1168; Steward of England and of Normandy, Justiciar, Viceroy, &c.; m. about 1120 Amice, dau. of Ralph, Seigneur of Gael and Montfort in Brittany,

HAWISE DE BEAUMONT, d. April 24, 1197; m. about 1150 William FitzRobert, Earl of Gloucester, Lord of the Manor of Glamorgan and Cardiff Castle, d. Nov. 23, 1183, 1st son and heir of Robert *"de Caen,"* Earl of Gloucester, and his wife Mabel (also called Matilda), dau. and heiress of Robert FitzHamon, Lord of Tewkesbury, Lord of Creully in Calvados, Hereditary Governor of Caen, and his wife Sibyl, dau. of Roger de Montgomery, Earl of Shrewsbury,

AMICE, Countess of Gloucester, d. Jan. 1, 1224/5; m. Richard de Clare, Earl of Hertford, generally known as Earl of Clare, d. 1217, son and heir of Roger de Clare, Earl of Hertford, (and his wife Maud, dau. and heiress of James de St. Hilary), and grandson of Richard FitzGilbert, Lord of Clare, &c., and his wife Adeliz (or Alice), dau. of Ranulph Le Meschin, Earl of Chester, Vicomte de Bayeux in Normandy,

GILBERT DE CLARE, Earl of Gloucester and Hertford, b. about 1180; d. Oct. 25, 1230; m., Oct. 9, 1217, Isabel, d. Jan. 17,

1239/40, dau. of William Mareschal, Earl of Pembroke, and his wife Isabel, dau. and heiress of Richard de Clare, known as "Strongbow," Earl of Pembroke,

RICHARD DE CLARE, Earl of Gloucester and Hertford, b. Aug. 4, 1222; d. July 15, 1262; m., 2ndly, 1237/8, Maud, dau. of John de Lacy, Earl of Lincoln, and his wife Margaret, dau. of Robert de Quincy, and granddau. of Saire de Quincy, Earl of Winchester,

GILBERT DE CLARE, Earl of Gloucester and Hertford, "the Red Earl," b. Sept. 2, 1243; d. Dec. 7, 1295; m., 2ndly, April 30 or May 2, 1290, Princess Joan Plantaganet, styled "of Acre," b. at Acre, Palestine, about 1272; d. 1307; dau. of Edward I, King of England, by Eleanor of Castile,

MARGARET DE CLARE, d. April 9, 1342, widow of Piers de Gavaston, Earl of Cornwall; m., 2ndly, April 28, 1317, Hugh de Audley, Lord Audley; cr. Earl of Gloucester, March 16, 1336/7; d. *s.p.m.* Nov. 10, 1347; son of Hugh de Audley, Lord Audley, and his wife Isolt, dau. of Edmund de Mortimer, of Wigmore,

MARGARET DE AUDLEY, *de jure,* apparently *suo jure,* Baroness Audley, m. about 1335/6 Ralph, Lord Stafford; cr. Earl of the County of Stafford, March 5, 1350/1; d. Aug. 31, 1372,

MARGARET DE STAFFORL, m. Sir John de Stafford, Knt.,

RALPH DE STAFFORD, m. Maud de Hastang, b. at Chebsey, co. Stafford, and bapt. there Feb. 2, 1358/9, dau. and co-heiress of Sir John Hastang,

JOAN DE STAFFORD, m. Sir Nicholas Beke, Knt.,

ELIZABETH BEKE, m. Sir Robert de Swynnerton, Knt., of Swynnerton, co. Stafford, d. about 1395,

MAUD (OR MATHILDA) DE SWYNNERTON, only dau. and heiress; m., first, about 1450, Sir John Savage, of Clifton, d. Aug. 1, 1450,

MARGARET SAVAGE, m. Sir John de Dutton, of Dutton, co. Chester,

MAUD DE DUTTON, m. Sir William Booth (Bothe), Knt., of Dunham-Massie, co. Chester, Sheriff of Cheshire, d. about 1476,

SIR GEORGE BOOTH, Lord of Dunham Massie, co. Chester, d. 1483; m. Katharine, dau. and heiress of Robert Montfort, Esq., Lord of Bescote, co. Stafford, and Monks-path in Warwickshire, and granddau. of Sir William Montfort, Knt., of Coleshill in Warwickshire,

SIR WILLIAM BOOTH, Knt., of Dunham Massie, d. Nov. 9, 1519; m., 2ndly, Ellen, dau. of Sir John Montgomery, of Throwley, co. Stafford,

JANE (OR JOAN) BOOTH, widow of Hugh Dutton, of Dutton; m., 2ndly, Thomas Holford, Esq., of Holford, nigh Nether Tabley, co. Chester,

DOROTHY HOLFORD, m., (his second wife), John Bruen (Bruyn), of Bruen Stapleford, d. May 14, 1580/7, son of John Bruyn, Esq., of Bruen Stapleford, and grandson of James Bruyn, Esq., of Bruen Stapleford,

JOHN BRUEN III, of Bruen Stapleford, b. about 1560; d. Jan. 18, 1625/6; m., 2ndly, Anne, dau. of John Fox,

OBADIAH BRUEN, bapt. at Tarvin, England, Dec. 25, 1606; d. at Newark, N. J., about 1682/90; m. Sarah, d. about Mar. 25, 1684,

JOHN BRUEN IV, b. June 2, 1646; d. at Newark, N. J., about 1696; m. Esther, dau. of Richard Lawrence,

JOSEPH BRUEN, b. at Newark, N. J., about 1667; d. there Feb. 1, 1753, father of,

RUTH BRUEN, b. at Newark, about 1717/8; d. there June 5, 1793; m. Caleb Davis, b. at Newark, about 1717; d. there Oct. 18, 1783,

JOSEPH DAVIS, b. at Newark, about 1753; d. at Bloomfield, N. J., June 5, 1827; m., first, at Bloomfield, Abby Farrand, b. at Newark, about 1756; d. at Bloomfield, May 2, 1790,

SALLY DAVIS, b. at Bloomfield, May 13, 1774; d. at Newark, Feb. 13, 1853; m. at Bloomfield, about 1795, Sayres Coe, b. at Newark, April 26, 1772; d. there Feb. 1, 1851,

AARON COE, b. at Newark, Sept. 27, 1810; d. there March 3, 1890; m. at Newark, Oct. 29, 1834, Julia Baldwin, b. at Newark, Sept. 21, 1814; d. there Sept. 25, 1904,

CORNELIA BALDWIN COE, b. at Newark, Jan. 10, 1852; d. there June 19, 1934; m. at Newark, April 3, 1873, Franklin Monroe Parker, b. at Newark, June 13, 1846; d. there Jan. 26, 1927,

EDITH ROSS PARKER, b. at Newark, N. J., Jan. 1, 1874; Dame Companion of the Order of the Crown of Charlemagne; Member of National Society of the Colonial Dames of America in the State of New Jersey, D.A.R., Daughters of Founders and Patriots of America, Society of Daughters of Holland Dames, Huguenot Society, &c.; m. at Newark, May 10, 1906, Edward Faraday Weston, b. at Newark, Oct. 23, 1878, son of Edward Weston and his wife Wilhelmina, née Seidel. Issue.

    1.) CORNELIA WESTON, b. at Elizabeth, N. J., May 25, 1907; m. at Lake Placid, N. Y., June 23, 1938, Philip Harry Cummings, b. at Hardwick, Vt., Nov. 19, 1906, son of Harry Foster Cummings and his wife Addie Sarah, née Smith. Issue:

        a) CORNELIA FRANCES CUMMINGS, b. at Glen Ridge, N. J., Oct. 11, 1939.

    2.) FRANCES ROSS WESTON, b. at Elizabeth, N. J., Nov. 15, 1908.

Bruen—Hayes—Jacobs—Newkirk—Boden

Charlemagne
See Page 125

Robert de Beaumont II, called *le Bossu* or *le Goczen*, Earl of Leicester, b. about 1104; d. April 5, 1168; m. Amice, dau. of Ralph, Seigneur of Gael and Montfort in Brittany, and granddau. of Ralph, Earl of Norfolk, by Emma, dau. of William FitzOsbern,

Robert de Beaumont III, Earl of Leicester, Steward of England and Normandy, styled *ès Blanchemains*, Crusader, d. on his return journey from Jerusalem in 1190 at Durazzo; m. Pernel (or Petronilla), d. April 1, 1212, heiress of the Norman honor of Grandmesnil, great-granddau. of Hugh de Grandmesnil, the Domesday tenant,

Margaret de Beaumont, d. Jan. 12, 1235/6; m. Saier de Quincy, 1st Earl of Winchester, Justiciar, Magna Charta Surety, Crusader, d. Nov. 3, 1219, in the Holy Land,

Robert de Quincy, Crusader, d. 1217; m. Hawise, Countess of Lincoln, d. 1242/3, sister of Ranulph "de Blundeville," Earl of Chester and Earl of Lincoln, also Vicomte d'Avranches, &c., and dau. of Hugh, "of Kevelioc," Earl of Chester, Vicomte d'Avranches in Normandy, by Bertrade, his wife, dau. of Simon, Count d'Evreux,

Margaret de Quincy, d. 1266; m., first, 1221, (his second wife), John de Lacy, Constable of Chester, Earl of Lincoln in right of his wife, d. July 22, 1240, son and heir of Roger de Lacy, by Maud de Clare, his wife,

Maud de Lacy, d. 1288/9; m., 1237/8, (his second wife), Richard de Clare, Earl of Gloucester and Hertford, b. Aug. 4, 1222; d. July 15, 1262,

Gilbert de Clare, Earl of Gloucester and Hertford, "the Red Earl," b. Sept. 2, 1243; d. Dec. 7, 1295; m., 2ndly, April 30 or May 2, 1290, Princess Joan Plantagenet, styled "of Acre," daughter of Edward I, King of England,

MARGARET DE CLARE, d. April 9, 1342, widow of Piers de Gavaston, Earl of Cornwall; m., 2ndly, April 28, 1317, Hugh de Audley, Lord Audley; cr. Earl of Gloucester, March 16, 1336/7; d. *s.p.m.* Nov. 10, 1347,

MARGARET DE AUDLEY, *de jure,* apparently *suo jure,* Baroness Audley, m. about 1335/6, Ralph, Lord Stafford; cr. Earl of the County of Stafford, March 5, 1350/1; d. Aug. 31, 1372,

MARGARET DE STAFFORD, m. Sir John Stafford, Knt.,

RALPH DE STAFFORD, m. Maud de Hastang, b. at Chebsey co. Stafford, and bapt. there Feb. 2, 1358/9, dau. and co-heiress of Sir John Hastang,

JOAN DE STAFFORD, m. Sir Nicholas Beke, Knt.,

ELIZABETH BEKE, m. Sir Robert de Swynnerton, Knt., of Swynnerton, co. Stafford, d. about 1395,

MAUD (or Mathilda) de Swynnerton, m., first, Sir John Savage, of Clifton,

MARGARET SAVAGE, m. Sir John de Dutton, of Dutton,

MAUD DE DUTTON, m. Sir William Booth (Bothe), Knt,. of Dunham-Massie,

SIR GEORGE BOOTH, Lord of Dunham-Massie, m. Katharine Montfort,

SIR WILLIAM BOOTH, Knt., m., 2ndly, Ellen Montgomery,

JANE (or Joan) BOOTH, widow of Hugh Dutton, of Dutton; m., 2ndly, Thomas Holford, Esq.,

DOROTHY HOLFORD, m. (his second wife), John Bruen (Bruyn), of Bruen Stapleford, d. May 14, 1580/7, son of John Bruyn, Esq., of Bruen Stapleford, and grandson of James Bruyn, Esq., of Bruen Stapleford,

JOHN BRUEN III, of Bruen Stapleford, b. about 1560; d. Jan. 18, 1625/6; m., 2ndly, Anne, dau. of John Fox,

ODADIAH BRUEN, bapt. at Tarvin, England, Dec. 25, 1606; d. at Newark, N. J., about 1682/90; m., 2ndly, Sarah (said to be Lawrence), d. about March 25, 1684,

JOHN BRUEN IV, b. June 2, 1646; d. about 1696; m. Esther, dau. of Richard Lawrence.

JOHN BRUEN V, b. about 1690; d. Sept. 1, 1767; m. Mary Tompkins,

SARAH BRUEN, b. about 1737; d. June 3, 1803; m. Major Samuel Hayes, b. about 1738; d. June 2, 1801,

SAMUEL HAYES, M.D., b. about 1776; d. 1839; m. Elizabeth Ogden Keen,

SARAH HAYES, b. about 1815; d. 1881; m., 1876, the Rev. Melancthon Williams Jacobs (or Jacobus), D.D., LL.D., b. Sept. 15, 1816; d. Oct. 28, 1876,

ELIZA HAYES JACOBS, b. Oct. 12, 1840; d. July 19, 1911; m., 1865, the Rev. Matthew Newkirk, D.D., S.T.D., b. Sept. 23, 1838; d. Dec. 24, 1910,

MARGARET HEBERTON NEWKIRK, b. Oct. 11, 1867; d. Oct. 17, 1923; m., 1888, Harry Clark Boden, b. Nov. 1, 1857; d. Jan. 16, 1892,

HARRY CLARK BODEN, b. Jan. 24, 1892; graduate with degree of Expert in Architecture, 1917, University of Pennsylvania; Lieutenant of Cavalry, U.S.A., 1917-19; member of Society of Colonial Wars, S.A.R., M.O.F.W., Huguenot Society, Society of the War of 1812, &c.; m., June 22, 1937, (her second husband), Marguerite du Pont Ortiz, whose lineage appears elsewhere in this book.

BULKELEY—BATES—CLEVELAND—BRADFORD— DU PONT—ORTIZ

CHARLEMAGNE, King of the Franks and Emperor of the West, b. April 2, 747; d. Jan. 28, 814; m. 771, the Swabian Princess Hildegard,

LOUIS I, the Pious, surnamed *le Debonnaire*, King of the Franks and Emperor of the West, b. 778; d. June 20, 840; m., 2ndly, 819, Judith, d. April 19, 843, dau. of Guelph I, Count of Altdorf (Altorff) and Duke of Bavaria,

CHARLES II, *le Chauve*, King of the Franks 843; Emperor 875; b. June 23, 823; d. Oct. 6, 877; m. first, Ermintrude (Irmtrude), d. Oct. 6, 869, dau. of Odo (Vodon), Count of Orleans,

LOUIS II, *le Begue*, King of the Franks 877; Emperor 878; d. April 10, 879; m., 2ndly, 868/70, Adelheid (or Adelaide), presumably sister of Abbot Wulfard of Flavigny,

CHARLES III, *le Simple*, King of the Franks 898-923; b. Nov. 17, 879; d. Oct. 7, 929; m., 2ndly, 918/9, Eadgifu (or Edgiva), dau. of Edward the Elder, King of England, and granddau. of Alfred the Great, King of England,

LOUIS IV, *d'Outre Mer*, King of the Franks 936; b. about 921; d. Sept. 10, 954; m., 939, Princess Gerberga, d. May 5, 984, widow of Gisilbert, Duke of Lorraine, and dau. of Henry I, the Fowler, Emperor of Germany, and his wife Mathilda, dau. of Dietrich, Count of Ringelheim,

PRINCESS GERBERGA, m. Albert I, the Pious, Count of Vermandois, b. about 920; d. Sept. 9, 987/8; son of Herbert II, Count of Vermandois and of Troyes,

HERBERT III, Count of Vermandois, b. about 955; d. about 1000; m., (her second husband), Irmgard (Ermengarde), dau. of Reinald, Count of Bar,

OTHO, Count of Vermandois, b. about 1000; d. May 25, 1045; m. Pavie,

HERBERT IV, Count of Vermandois and of Valois, b. about 1032; d. about 1080; m. Adela de Vexin, dau. of Raoul III, the Great, Count of Valois, Vexin, &c.,

ADELAIDE (or Adelheid), Countess of Vermandois and of Valois, m. Hugh the Great, Duke of France and Burgundy, Marquis of Orleans, Count of Amiens, Chaumont, Paris, Valois, Vermandois, &c., son of Henry I, King of France, by Anne, dau. of Yaroslav I of Kiev,

ISABEL DE VERMANDOIS, m., first, 1096, Robert de Beaumont, Seigneur of Beaumont, Pont-Audemer, Brionne and Vatteville in Normandy, Count of Meulan in the French Vexin, Earl of Leicester, b. about 1046; d. June 5, 1118; son and heir of Roger de Beaumont, called *de Bello Monte*, Seigneur of Beaumont and Pont Audemer, and his wife Adeline, dau. of Waleran and sister of Hugh, Counts of Meulan.

ROBERT DE BEAUMONT II, surnamed *le Bossu* or *le Goczen*, 2nd Earl of Leicester, Steward of England and of Normandy, Justiciar, b. about 1104; d. April 5, 1168; m., about 1120, Amice, dau. of Ralph, Seigneur of Gael and Montfort in, Brittany, and granddau. of Ralph, Earl of Norfolk, by Emma, dau. of William FitzOsbern,

ROBERT DE BEAUMONT III, styled *ès Blanchemains*, 3rd Earl of Leicester, Steward of England and Normandy, Crusader, only son and heir; d. on his return journey from Jerusalem, 1190, at Durazzo; m. Pernel (or Petronilla), d. April 1, 1212, heiress of the Norman honor of Grandmesnil, great-granddau. of Hugh de Grandmesnil, the Domesday tenant,

MARGARET DE BEAUMONT, d. Jan. 12, 1235/6; m. Saier de Quincy, 1st Earl of Winchester, Justiciar, Magna Charta Surety, Crusader, d. Nov. 3, 1219, in the Holy Land,

ROGER DE QUINCY, 2nd Earl of Winchester, Constable of Scotland, d. 1264; m., first, Helen, dau. and co-heiress of Alan, Lord of Galloway, Constable of Scotland,

ELENA (Ela) de Quincy, d. about 1296, m. Alan La Zouche, Baron Zouche of Ashby de la Zouche, co. Leicester, Constable of the Tower of London, d. about 1269,

SIR ROGER LA ZOUCHE, Baron Zouche of Ashby, d. about 1285; m. Ela Longespée, granddau. of William Longespée, Earl of Salisbury, believed to be a natural son of Henry II, King of England,

ALAN LA ZOUCHE, Baron Zouche of Ashby de la Zouche, co. Leicester, and of North Molton, co. Devon, Governor of Rockingham Castle and Steward of Rockingham Forest, d. 1313/4; m. Eleanor, presumably dau. of Nicholas Segrave,

ELENA (or Eleanor) La Zouche, m., first, Nicholas St. Maur, Lord Saint Maur, who d. 1316/7; m., 2ndly, about 1317, Sir Alan de Charlton, Knt., of Apley (or Appley), Shropshire, d. Dec. 3, 1360, probably brother of John, 1st Baron Charlton of Powys,

ALAN DE CHARLTON, d. May 3, 1349; m. Margery FitzAer, b. April 4, 1314; d. about 1349,

THOMAS DE CHARLTON, d. Oct. 6, 1387, father of,

ANNA DE CHARLTON, b. about 1380; d. about 1399; m. William de Knightley,

THOMAS DE KNIGHTLEY, heir of the Charltons of Apley Castle, adopted the surname of Charlton, b. March 30, 1394; d. Jan. 4, 1460; m. Elizabeth, dau. and heiress of Sir Adam Francis (or Fraunceys), Knt., of London,

ROBERT DE CHARLTON, b. about 1430; d. about 1471; m. Mary, dau. of Robert Corbet, of Morton (Moreton), Shropshire,

RICHARD DE CHARLTON, d. about 1522; m. Anne, dau. of William Mainwaring of Ightfield, Shropshire,

ANNE DE CHARLTON, m., about 1500, Randall Grosvenor, of Bellaport, Shropshire,

ELIZABETH GROSVENOR, m. Thomas Bulkeley, of Woore, Shropshire, d. about 1591,

REV. EDWARD BULKELEY, D.D., d. about Jan. 5, 1620/1; m. Olive Irby, buried at Odell, March 10, 1614/5, dau. of John Irby and his wife Rose Overton,

FRANCES BULKELEY, m., about 1595, Richard Welby (or Welbie),

OLIVE WELBY (or Welbie), b. about 1604; d. about 1691; m., about 1629, Henry Farwell, d. about 1670, came from England to Concord, Mass., about 1635,

MARY FARWELL, b. at Concord, Mass., about 1642; d. at Chelmsford, Mass., about 1713/4; m. at Chelmsford, about 1665, John Bates, b. at Boston, about 1641/2; d. at Chelmsford, about 1722,

MARY BATES, b. at Chelmsford, about 1667; d. at Canterbury, Conn., about 1743; m., about 1689, Josiah Cleveland, d. at Canterbury, about 1709,

JOSIAH CLEVELAND II, b. at Chelmsford, about 1690; d. at Canterbury, about 1762; m. at Canterbury, about 1710, Abigail Payne, b. at Eastham, Conn., about 1686; d. at Canterbury, about 1762,

MARY CLEVELAND, b. at Canterbury, about 1720; d. there about 1765; m. there, 1743, William Bradford, b. about 1718, d. at Canterbury, 1780,

REV. EBENEZER BRADFORD, b. at Canterbury 1746; d. at Rowley, Mass., 1801; m. at Hanover, N. J., 1776, Elizabeth Greene, b. at Hanover, 1758; d. at Rowley, 1825,

MOSES BRADFORD, b. at Rowley, 1788; d. in New Castle County, Del., 1874; m. in New Castle County, Del., 1817, Phoebe George, b. in Cecil County, Md., 1794; d. in New Castle County, Del., 1840,

JUDGE EDWARD GREENE BRADFORD, b. in New Castle County, Del., 1819; d. there 1884; m. there, 1852, Elizabeth Roberts Canby, b. in New Castle County, Del., 1843; d. there in 1914,

ELIZABETH CANBY BRADFORD, b. in New Castle County, Del., 1852; d. there in 1925; m. there in 1875, Dr. Alexis Irenée du Pont,, b. in New Castle County, Del., 1843; d. there in 1904,

ALICE EUGENIE DU PONT, b. at Louisville, Ky., 1876; d. in New Castle County, Del., Nov. 5, 1940; m. at Wilmington, Del., Jan. 20, 1906, Julien Ortiz, b. at Paris, France, Nov. 18, 1868,

MARGUERITE DU PONT ORTIZ, b. in New Castle County, Del., July 20, 1907; Dame Companion and one of the Priors of the Order of the Crown of Charlemagne; Regent General of Order of Three Crusades; Member of National Society of the Colonial Dames of America, D.A.R., Society of Mayflower Descendants, Huguenot Society, United Daughters of 1812, Hereditary Order of Descendants of Colonial Governors, National Society Women Descendants of the Ancient and Honorable Artillery Company, National Society of New England Women, &c.; Associate Member of National Society Daughters of the Founders and Patriots of America; Corresponding Secretary of National Society Daughters of Colonial Wars in the State of Del., &c., m., first, June 5,

1926, Forrester Holmes Scott, of Philadelphia; m., 2ndly, June 22, 1937, Harry Clark Boden, of Philadelphia, a descendant of the Emperor Charlemagne, whose pedigree appears elsewhere in this book.

Issue by first husband:

1.) EVE SCOTT, b. June 17, 1931;

2.) ZOE ZENGER SCOTT, b. May 29, 1934.

BULKELEY—EGLIN—STOLTZE

CHARLEMAGNE

See Page 133

MARGARET DE BEAUMONT, m. Saier de Quincy, 1st Earl of Winchester,

ROBERT DE QUINCY, m. Hawise, *suo jure* Countess of Lincoln,

MARGARET DE QUINCY, d. 1266; m. first, about 1221, (his 2nd wife) John de Lacy, Earl of Lincoln, Constable of Chester, b. about 1192; d. July 22, 1240; s. & h. of Roger de Lacy, by Maud de Clare, his wife,

MAUD DE LACY, d. about 1288; m., 1237/8, (his 2nd wife), Richard de Clare, Earl of Gloucester and Hertford, b. Aug. 4, 1222; d. July 15, 1262,

GILBERT DE CLARE, Earl of Gloucester and Hertford, surnamed "the Red Earl," b. Sept. 2, 1243; d. Dec. 7, 1295; m., 2ndly, 1290, Joan of Acre, d. Apr. 23, 1307, dau. of Edward I, King of England, by Eleanor of Castile,

ALIANORE (Eleanor) de Clare, b. 1292; d. June 30, 1337; m., 1306, Sir Hugh Le Despenser, Baron Le Despenser, hanged Nov. 24, 1326, son of Sir Hugh Le Despenser, of Loughborough, Arnesby, Parlington, Ryhall, etc., Baron Le Despenser, cr. Earl of Winchester on May 10, 1322,

ISABEL LE DESPENSER, m., Feb. 9, 1320/21, (his first wife), Richard FitzAlan, Earl of Arundel, called "Copped Hat," b. c 1313; d. Jan. 24, 1375/6,

ISABEL FITZALAN, m. John Le Strange, Baron Strange of Blackmere,

ANKARET LE STRANGE, Baroness Strange of Blackmere, m. Richard Talbot, Baron Talbot, son of Gilbert Talbot, 3rd Baron Talbot, and grandson of Sir Richard Talbot, 2nd Baron Talbot, of Goderich Castle, co. Hereford, a Banneret, Steward of the King's Household, and his wife Elizabeth Comyn, dau. of John Comyn, Lord of Badenoch, (by his wife Joan, dau. of William de Valence, Earl of Pembroke), and a granddau. of Sir John Comyn, Lord of Baden-och, by his wife Alianore, sister of John de Baliol, King of Scots,

SIR JOHN TALBOT, 7th Baron Talbot, Baron Furnivalle(in right of his wife) ; cr. Earl of Shrewsbury, May 20, 1442; slain in battle at Castillon on the Dordogne, July 17, 1453; m., first, 1406/7, Maud de Neville, dau. and h. of Thomas de Neville, Baron Furnivalle,

SIR JOHN TALBOT, 2nd Earl of Shrewsbury, Baron Furnivalle, killed at the battle of Northampton, July 10, 1460; m., 2ndly, Elizabeth, d. Sept. 8, 1473, dau. of James Butler, Earl of Ormond, by his wife Elizabeth, dau. of William de Beauchamp, Baron Abergavenny,

SIR GILBERT TALBOT, of Grafton, co. Worcester; Knight Banneret, Governor of Calais, K.G.; d. Sept. 19, 1516/8; m., 2ndly, Audrey (or Etheldreda), dau. of Sir John Cotton, of Landwade, co. Cambridge,

SIR JOHN TALBOT, of Albrighton, Shropshire, afterwards of Grafton, co. Worcester, Sheriff of Shropshire, d. Sept. 10, 1549; m., first, Margaret, dau. of Adam Troutbeck, of Mobberley, co. Cheshire, by his wife Margaret, dau. of Sir John Butler, of Bewsey in Warrington, co. Lancaster,

ANNE TALBOT, m. Thomas Needham, of Shavington in Adderley, Shropshire, son of Sir Robert Needham, of Cranage, afterward of Shavington, and his wife Agnes, dau. of John Manwaring, of Over-Pover, co. Cheshire,

ROBERT NEEDHAM, of Shavington, m. Frances Aston, dau. of Sir Edward Aston, of Tixall, co. Stafford, and his first wife, Joan, dau. of Sir Thomas Bowles, of Penho, co. Carnarvon, (Sir Edward Aston was son of Sir John Aston, K.B., of Tixall, and his wife Joan Lyttelton, of Frankley, co. Worcester),

DOROTHY NEEDHAM, m. Sir Richard Chetwood, of Warkworth, co. Northampton, son of Richard Chetwood and his wife Agnes de Wahull, dau. of Anthony de Wahull, of Warkworth, co. Northampton,

GRACE CHETWOOD, d. at New London, Conn., Apr. 21, 1669; m., 1635, (his second wife), Rev. Peter Bulkeley, b. Jan. 31, 1582/3; d. at Concord, Mass., Mar. 9, 1658/9; son of the Rev. Edward Bulkeley, D.D.,

PETER BULKELEY, b. at Concord, Mass., Aug. 12, 1643; d. at Fairfield, Conn., 1691; m. Margaret,

CAPTAIN GERSHOM BULKLEY, b. c 1676; d. at Fairfield, Conn., Apr. 9, 1753; m., 2ndly, Rachel Talcott,

PETER BULKLEY, bapt. at Fairfield, Conn., Feb. 5, 1715/6; d. at Fairfield, May 12, 1804; m., Apr. 9, 1740, Ann Hill, d. at Fairfield, Apr. 11, 1795,

GERSHOM BULKLEY, b. at Fairfield, May 9, 1748; d. at Rye, N. Y., Feb. 22, 1820; m., first at Fairfield, (Greens Farms), June 3, 1773, Elizabeth Chapman, b. at Fairfield, Aug. 12, 1751; d. there, May 26, 1795,

WILLIAM BULKLEY, b. at Fairfield, May 16, 1787; d. at Rye, N. Y., Aug. 29, 1860; m. at Rye, 1809, Mary Bartram Osborn, b. at Fairfield, Mar. 27, 1790; d. at Rye, Jan. 10, 1850,

PHILEMON CARPENTER BULKLEY, b. Dec. 15, 1828; d. Apr. 1904; m., June 13, 1855, Mary Jane Moody,

LOUIS CARLETON BULKLEY, b. at Westchester County, N. Y., Sept. 19, 1863; d. at Shreveport, La., Dec. 24, 1930; m. at Cincinnati, Ohio, Mar. 19, 1894, Caroline Rogers Kemper, b. at Louisville, Ky., Dec. 8, 1865, Member (Vice- President) of National Society of the Colonial Dames of America in the State of Louisiana, Honorary State Regent of Louisiana Society of Daughters of the American Colonists, Member of D.A.R., First Families of Virginia, etc., and had,

   1.) LOUISE BULKLEY, b. at St. Louis, Mo., Feb. 28, 1895; m. at Shreveport, La., June 18, 1919, Ralph Burton Eglin, b. July 10, 1890, and have issue:

      a) DOROTHY LOUISE EGLIN, b. June 27, 1920;

      b) RICHARD CARLETON EGLIN, b. Oct. 20, 1921.

   2.) GRACE CHETWODE BULKLEY, b. at St. Louis, Mo., Dec. 4, 1897; m., Mar. 28, 1921, John Robert Stoltze, b. Nov. 22, 1896, son of Frederick Hawes Stoltze, of Madison, Wis., and his first wife, Elizabeth May Robert, and have issue:

      a) ELIZABETH ROBERT STOLTZE, b. at Shreveport, La., Jan. 7, 1922;

b) Robert Bulkley Stoltze, b. at Shreveport, Oct. 10, 1923;

c) Carolyn Kemper Stoltze, b. at Shreveport, Feb. 3, 1927;

d) Sarah Ward Stoltze, b. at St. Paul, Minn., Feb. 19, 1930;

e) Louise Stoltze, b. at St. Paul, Dec. 19, 1931.

Bulloch—Roosevelt—Longworth—Roosevelt

Edward III, King of England, m. Philippa of Hainault,

John, "of Gaunt," Duke of Lancaster, K.G., assumed title of King of Castile and Leon; cr. Duke of Aquitaine or Guienne, Mar. 2, 1390; d. Feb. 3/4, 1398/9; m., 3rdly, Jan. 1396, Katharine, widow of Sir Hugh Swynford, and dau. of Sir Paon Roet, Guienne King of Arms,

John Beaufort, Marquess of Dorset, Marquess of Somerset, Earl of Somerset, Knight-Banneret, K. G., P. C., Crusader (against Tunis), d. Apr. 21, 1410; m., (her first husband), Margaret de Holand, d. about Dec. 30, 1429, dau. and eventually co-heiress of Thomas de Holand, Earl of Kent, Lord Woodstock, Holand, and Wake, K.G., and his wife Alice, dau. of Richard FitzAlan, Earl of Arundel, by his wife Eleanor, dau. of Henry, Earl of Lancaster,

Joan Beaufort, d. July 15, 1445; m., first, James I, King of Scots, b. Dec. 1394; assassinated 1436/7; son of Robert III, King of Scots, and his wife Annabella, dau. of Sir John Drummond, of Stobhall,

Joan Stewart, (also called Joanna), 3rd dau., m., 1458/9, James Douglas, Lord Dalkeith; cr. Earl of Morton, Mar. 14, 1457/8; d. 1493,

Janet Douglas, m., 1480/1, (his first wife), Sir Patrick Hepburn, of Dunsyre; cr. Earl of Bothwell, Oct. 17, 1488; Keeper of the Castle of Edinburgh; High Admiral in Scotland, &c.; d. Oct. 18, 1508; son of Adam Hepburn, Master of Hailes, and his wife Helen, dau. of Alexander, Lord Home,

Janet Hepburn, d. after May 10, 1558; m., before Dec. 1506, George, Lord Seton, killed at the battle of Flodden, Sept. 9, 1513,

George Seton, Lord Seton; m., first, Elizabeth Hay, dau. of John Hay; cr. Lord Hay of Yester, co. Haddington, Jan. 29, 1487/8,

BEATRIX SETON, m. Sir George Ogilivie (or Ogilvy), of Dunlugus and of Boyne, co. Banff,

JANET OGILVIE, m. William Forbes, Laird of Tolquohon,

THOMAS FORBES, 1st Laird of Watertown in Aberdeenshire, father of,

GRIZEL FORBES, m. John Douglas, of Tilquhille (or Tiliwhilly),

JOHN DOUGLAS, of Tilquhille, m. Agnes, dau. of the Rev. James Horn, of Westhall, Minister of Elgin, and his wife Isabel Ramsey, of Balmain,

EUPHEMIA DOUGLAS, d. Dec. 21, 1766; m., about 1733, Charles Irvine, of Cults, near Aberdeen, Scotland, d. Mar. 28, 1779,

JOHN IRVINE, M.D., b. Sept. 15, 1742; came to Georgia about 1765 and was a member of the last Royal Assembly in 1780; d. at Savannah, Ga., Oct. 15, 1808; m., first at Sunbury, Ga., Sept. 5, 1765, Ann Elizabeth Baillee, dau. of Col. Kenneth Baillee.

ANN IRVINE, b. Jan. 14, 1770; m., first, April 13, 1786, Capt. James Bulloch of Savannah, Ga., b. about 1765; d. Feb. 9, 1806; son of Archibald Bulloch, President and Commander-in-Chief of Georgia 1767-77,

MAJOR JAMES STEPHENS BULLOCH, of Roswell, Ga., m., 2ndly, Martha Stewart, dau. of General Daniel Stewart,

MARTHA BULLOCH, b. July 8, 1834; d. Feb. 12, 1884; m. at Roswell, Ga., Dec. 22, 1853, Theodore Roosevelt, b. at New York, N. Y., Sept. 22, 1831; d. Feb. 9, 1878; Collector of the Port of New York, &c.,

1.) COLONEL THEODORE ROOSEVELT, President of the United States, b. at New York, N. Y., Oct. 27, 1858; d. at Oyster Bay, L. I., N. Y., Jan. 6, 1919; Governor of State of New York, 1898-1900; Vice-President of the United States, 1900, and became President of the United States upon the assassination of President McKinley; elected President of the United States, 1904; awarded Nobel Peace Prize, 1906; m., first, Oct. 27, 1880, Alice Hathaway Lee, b. July 29, 1861; d. at New York, Feb. 14, 1884; dau. of George Cabot Lee, of Boston, Mass., and his wife Caroline Haskell; he m., 2ndly, at London, England, Dec. 2,

1886, Edith Kermit Carow, b. Aug. 6, 1861, dau. of Charles Carow, of New York, and his wife Gertrude Elizabeth Tyler.

Issue by first wife:

a) ALICE LEE ROOSEVELT, b. Feb. 12, 1884; m. in the White House, Washington, D. C., Feb. 17, 1906, Nicholas Longworth, of Cincinnati, Ohio, Member and Speaker of the U. S. House of Representatives, d. April 9, 1931. Issue:

    i PAULINE LONGWORTH, b. Feb. 14, 1925.

Issue by second wife:

b) LIEUTENANT-COLONEL THEODORE ROOSEVELT, JR., B.A., M.A., D.S.C., D.S.M., &c., b. in Oyster Bay, L.I., N.Y., Sept. 13, 1887; Assistant Secretary of the Navy, 1921-24; Governor of Puerto Rico, 1929-32; Governor General of the Philippine Islands, 1932-33; m., June 20, 1910, Eleanor Butler Alexander, only dau. of Henry Addison Alexander, of New York, and his wife Grace Green. Issue:

    i GRACE GREEN ROOSEVELT;

    ii THEODORE ROOSEVELT;

    iii CORNELIUS VAN SCHAACK ROOSEVELT;

    iv QUENTIN ROOSEVELT.

c) CAPTAIN KERMIT ROOSEVELT, B.A., &c., b. in Oyster Bay, L. I., N. Y., Oct. 10, 1889; m., June 11, 1914, Belle Wyatt Willard, of Richmond, Va.

d) ETHEL CAROW ROOSEVELT, b. Aug. 10, 1891; m., April 4, 1913, Richard Derby, B.A., M.D., b. at New York, N. Y., April 7, 1881, son of Richard Henry Derby and his wife Sarah Coleman Alden. Issue:

    i EDITH ROOSEVELT DERBY;

    ii SARAH ALDEN DERBY;

    iii JUDITH QUENTIN DERBY.

e) Captain Archibald Bulloch Roosevelt, B.A., b. at Washington, D. C., Apr. 9, 1894; m. Grace S. Lockwood. Issue:

    i Archibald Bulloch Roosevelt, Jr.;

    ii Theodora Roosevelt;

    iii Nancy Dabney Roosevelt;

    iv Edith Roosevelt.

2.) Elliott Roosevelt, b. at New York, N. Y., Feb. 28, 1860; d. at New York, Sept. 1893; m., Oct. 1883, Anna Hall. Issue:

a) Anna Eleanor Roosevelt, D.H.L., b. at New York, N. Y., Oct. 11, 1884; m., Mar. 17, 1905, Franklin Delano Roosevelt, of Hyde Park, N. Y., b. Jan. 30, 1882, B.A., LL.D., Litt.D., 32nd President of the United States of America, elected Nov. 8, 1932, re-elected Nov. 3, 1936, and re-elected for third term on Nov. 5, 1940; son of James Roosevelt (d. Dec. 8, 1900) and his wife Sara Delano (b. Sept. 21, 1854; d. Sept. 7, 1941), dau. of Warren Delano and his wife Katherine Robbins Lyman. Issue:

    i Anna Eleanor Roosevelt, b. May 3, 1906; m., 1st, June 5, 1926, Curtis B. Dall, of New York, (marriage dissolved by divorce, 1934); m., 2ndly, Jan. 18, 1935, John Boettiger, b. at Chicago, Mar. 25, 1900, son of Adam Charles Boettiger and Dorothy Ott, his wife. Issue by first husband:

        1. Anna Eleanor Dall,

        2. Curtis Roosevelt Dall.

    ii Captain James Roosevelt, b. Dec. 23, 1907; m., 1st, June 6, 1930, Betsey, dau. of Dr. Harvey Cushing, of Boston, (marriage dissolved by divorce, Mar. 1941); m., 2ndly, Apr. 14, 1941, Romelle Theresa Schneider. Issue by first wife:

144

1. SARA DELANO ROOSEVELT,

2. KATE ROOSEVELT.

iii CAPTAIN ELLIOTT ROOSEVELT, b. Sept. 23, 1910; m., 1st, Jan. 16, 1931, Elizabeth Browning Donner, of Bryn, Mawr, Pa., (marriage dissolved by divorce, July 17, 1933); m., 2ndly, July 22, 1933, Ruth Josephine Googins, of Fort Worth, Texas.

Issue by first wife:

1. WILLIAM DONNER ROOSEVELT,

Issue by second wife:

2. RUTH CHANDLER ROOSEVELT,

3. ELLIOTT M. ROOSEVELT.

iv FRANKLIN DELANO ROOSEVELT, JR., b. Aug. 17, 1914; Ensign, U. S. Navy; m., June 30, 1937, Ethel du Pont, dau. Eugene du Pont, of Wilmington, Del.;

v JOHN A. ROOSEVELT, b. Mar. 16, 1916; Ensign, U. S. Navy; m., June 18, 1938, Anne L. Clark, of Nahant, Mass.

CALVERT—HYDE—MITCHELL—COOKE—FREEMAN
JONES—COOKE

PHILIPPE III, *le Hardi* and *Coeur de Lion,* King of France,

PRINCESS MARGARET, m., (his 2nd wife), Edward I, King of England,

THOMAS, "of Brotherton," Earl of Norfolk, &c., b. June 1, 1300; d. 1338; m., first, about 1320, Alice, dau. of Sir Roger de Hales, Coroner of Norfolk, 1303-13,

MARGARET, *suo jure* Countess of Norfolk; cr. in Parliament, in her absence, Duchess of Norfolk, Sept. 29, 1397; d. Mar. 24, 1398/9; m., first, 1337/8, John Segrave, Lord Segrave, d. 1353,

ELIZABETH, *suo jure* Baroness Segrave, m. John de Mowbray, Lord Mowbray, d. 1368,

THOMAS DE MOWBRAY, Lord Mowbray and Segrave; cr. Earl of Nottingham, Feb. 12, 1382/3; K. G.; cr. Duke of Norfolk, Sept. 29, 1397; Earl Marshal of England; b. Mar. 22, 1365/6; d. Sept. 22, 1399; m., 2ndly, 1384, Elizabeth, d. July 8, 1425, widow of Sir William de Montagu, and dau. of Richard FitzAlan, Earl of Arundel, by his 1st wife, Elizabeth, dau. of William Bohun, Earl of Northampton,

MARGARET DE MOWBRAY, m. Sir Robert Howard, of Stoke Neyland, Suffolk,

JOHN HOWARD, Lord Howard; M.P. for Norfolk, 1455; K.G., 1472; cr. Duke of Norfolk and Earl Marshal of England, June 28, 1483; Admiral of England, Ireland and Aquitaine; Steward of the Duchy of Lancaster; P.C.; slain at the battle of Bosworth, Aug. 22, 1485; m., first, Catherine, d. Nov. 3 1465, dau. of Sir William de Moleyns,

THOMAS HOWARD, Sheriff of Norfolk and Suffolk 1476; M.P. for Norfolk, 1478; K.B., 1477/8; P.C. and K.G., 1483; cr. Earl of Surrey, June 28, 1483; cr. Earl Marshal of England for life, July 10, 1510; cr. Duke of Norfolk, Feb. 1, 1513/4; b. 1443; d. May 21, 1524; m., first, Apr. 30, 1472, Elizabeth,

d. Apr. 4, 1497, widow of Sir Humphrey Bourchier, and dau. and h. of Sir Frederick Tylney, of Ashwellthorpe, co. Norfolk, and his wife Elizabeth, dau. of Lawrence Cheney, of Ditton, co. Cambridge, by Elizabeth, dau. of Sir John Cokayne,

EDMUND HOWARD, Marshal of the Horse in the battle of Flodden, 1513; m., first, Joyce, dau. and co-h. of Sir Richard Culpepper,

MARGARET HOWARD (sister of Katherine, wife of Henry VIII, King of England), m. Sir Thomas Arundell, Knt., of Wardour Castle, co. Wilts, beheaded Feb. 26, 1552;

SIR MATTHEW ARUNDELL, of Wardour Castle, m. Margaret Willoughby, dau. of Sir Henry Willoughby, Knt., of Wollaton, co. Nottingham,

SIR THOMAS ARUNDELL, surnamed the Valiant, he served as a volunteer in the Imperial Army in Hungary, cr. Count of the Holy Roman Empire by Emperor Rudolph .II, Dec. 14, 1595, in recognition of his having captured the Turkish standard at the battle of Gran; cr. Baron Arundell of Wardour, May 4, 1605, by King James I; d. Nov. 7, 1639; m., 2ndly, July 1, 1608, Anne, d. June 28, 1637, dau. of Miles Philipson, of Crook, co. Westmorland,

ANNE ARUNDELL, d. July 23, 1649; m. Cecil Calvert, 2nd Baron Baltimore of Baltimore, bapt. Mar. 2, 1605/6; d. Dec. 1675; s. and h. of George Calvert, of Danbywiske, co. York, 1st Baron Baltimore of Baltimore, by his first wife Anne, dau. of George Mynne, of Hertingfordbury, Herts., and his wife Elizabeth, dau. of Sir Thomas Wroth,

CHARLES CALVERT, 3rd Baron Baltimore, b. Aug. 27, 1637; d. Feb. 21, 1714/5; Governor of Maryland, 1661-75, 1676, and again 1679-84; Brigadier General, 1696; Major General, 1704; m., secondly, c 1667, Jane, d. Jan. 1700/01, widow of Henry Irwell, M.D., and dau. of Nicholas Lows, of Denby, co. Derby,

BENEDICT LEONARD CALVERT, 4th Baron Baltimore, b. Mar. 21, 1679; d. at Epsom, Surrey, Apr. 16, 1715; M.P. for Harwich, 1714-15; m., Jan. 2, 1698/9, Charlotte, b. Mar. 13, 1678; d. Jan. 22, 1720/21; 1st dau. of Edward Henry Lee, 1st Earl of Lichfield, and his wife Charlotte FitzRoy, natural dau. of Charles II, King of England,

JANE CALVERT, m. Colonel John Hyde, of Kingston Lisle,

MARY CALVERT HYDE, m. c 1766, George Mitchell, of Ireland,

GEORGE CALVERT MITCHELL, b. in Ireland, 1772; came to the United States c 1800, and settled at Royalton, N. Y. c 1810, father of,

GEORGE MITCHELL, b. at Royalton, N. Y., c 1810; d. at Royalton, c 1838; m. Rhoda Marvin, b. at Rutland, Vt., c 1816; d. at Colon, Mich., c 1865,

GEORGE MARVIN MITCHELL, b. at Royalton, c 1836; d. at Middleville, Mich., 1883; m. at Middleville, Mary Alice (von) Walrath, b. at Ogdensburg, N. Y., c 1834; d. at Sturgis, Mich., 1901,

CORA MAY MITCHELL, b. at Middleville, Mich., Oct. 4, 1864; m., first, 1882, George Freeman, and had issue as appears below; m., secondly, in Barry County, Mich., Dec. 29, 1886, Joseph Robert George Cooke, b. in Barry County, Mich., July 7, 1828; d. at Sturgis, Mich., Apr. 4, 1910, and had issue as appears below; m., thirdly, June 25, 1925, Bishop Hevey Schriber.

Issue by 1st husband:

1.) FLOYD MILFORD FREEMAN, M.D., b. at Middleville, Mich., Nov. 24, 1883; m. at Sturgis, Nov. 30, 1911, Elizabeth Miller, b. Oct. 26, 1886, and have issue:

a) ELEANOR MILLER FREEMAN, b. at Goshen, Ind., May 25, 1913; m. at Goshen, 1936, Charles Champion, b. June 11, 1902, and have issue:

i CHARLES KOHLER CHAMPION, b. at Goshen, Feb. 25, 1938;

ii ELIZABETH VIRGINIA CHAMPION, b. at Goshen, Mar. 11, 1940.

b) CARMENA MITCHELL FREEMAN, b. at Goshen, Aug. 27, 1914;

c) VIRGINIA KATHRYN FREEMAN, b. at Goshen, July 30, 1917.

Issue by 2nd husband:

2.) MILDRED MITCHELL COOKE, b. at Middleville, Mich., July 25, 1893; m. at Kalamazoo, Mich., Feb. 23, 1918,

148

Wallace Jones, b. at Goshen, Ind., July 31, 1892, son of Emory Jones, and have issue:

- a) MARILYN ELOISE JONES, b. at Sturgis, Mich., Dec. 13, 1921;

- b) LENORE ADELE JONES, b. at Sturgis, Jan. 20, 1923;

- c) EMORY JONES, b. at Sturgis, Dec. 12, 1926.

3.) ROBERT GEORGE COOKE, b. at Sturgis, Mich., Oct. 31, 1906; Companion First Class (Officer) of Order of the Crown of Charlemagne; m. at North St. Paul, Minn., Aug. 1, 1935, Helen Marie Mullery, b. at Duluth, Minn., Feb. 18, 1911, dau. of Valentine Mullery, and have issue:

- a) MARY ALICE WALDORF COOKE, b. at St. Paul, Sept. 7, 1936.

CARLETON—BOWDITCH—MORIARTY

EDWARD III, King of England, m., 1327/8, Philippa of Hainault, dau. of William, Count of Hainault and Holland,

JOHN, "of Gaunt," Duke of Lancaster, K.G., assumed style of King of Castile and Leon; cr. Duke of Aquitaine or Guienne, Mar. 2, 1390; d. Feb. 3/4, 1398/9; m., thirdly, Jan. 1396, Katharine, widow of Sir Hugh Swynford and dau. of Sir Paon Roet, Guienne King of Arms,

JOAN BEAUFORT, m., first, Sir Robert de Ferrieres, of Willisham, Wem and Oversley, b. 1374; d. Nov. 29, 1396,

MARY FERRERS, d. Jan. 25, 1457/8, m. Sir Ralph Neville, of Oversley, 2nd son of Ralph Neville, Earl of Westmorland, by his first wife, Margaret, dau. of Hugh Stafford, 2nd Earl Stafford,

JOHN NEVILLE, of Althorpe, co. Lincoln, Oversley, co. War., and Wormesley, co. Yorks, M.P., d. Mar. 17, 1481/2; m., first, Elizabeth, dau. and h. of Robert Newmarch, of Wormesley, co. Yorks,

JANE NEVILLE, h. of Oversley and Wormesley, m. about 1448/50, Sir William Gascoigne, of Gawthorpe, co. Yorks, d. about 1463/4,

MARGARET GASCOIGNE, m. Sir Christopher Ward, of Givendale, d. Dec. 31, 1521,

ANNE WARD, d. Feb. 4, 1522/3, m. Ralph Neville, Esq., of Thornton Brigg, co. Yorks, d. Oct. 27, 1522,

KATHERINE NEVILLE, co-heiress, b. about 1500; m., first, Sir Walter Strickland, of Sizergh, co. Westmorland, d. Jan. 9, 1527/8,

WALTER STRICKLAND, Esq., of Sizergh, b. Apr. 5, 1516; d. Apr. 6, 1569, father of,

ELLEN STRICKLAND, alive 1522; m., secondly, about 1577, John Carleton, gent., Stewart of Beaford Manor, co. Yorks, 1586-1619, buried Jan. 27, 1622/3,

WALTER CARLETON, gent., of Hornsea, co. Yorks, bapt. Dec. 29, 1582; d. Oct. 4, 1623; m., 1607, Jane, b. about 1594/5, dau. of Peter Gibbon, of Gt. Hatfield and Hornsea,

"MR." EDWARD CARLETON, of Barmston, co. Yorks, bapt. Oct. 20, 1610; d. in England 1650/61; went to Rowley, Mass., 1638/9, returned to England 1649; m. at York, England, Nov. 3, 1636, Ellen Newton, bapt. at Hedon, co. Yorks, Feb. 24, 1613/4, alive in 1661, dau. of Lancelot Newton, gent., of Heden, Mayor of that town,

LIEUTENANT JOHN CARLETON, b. 1637; d. at Haverhill, Mass., Jan. 22, 1668/9; m., (probably at Rowley, Mass.), 1658/9, Hannah, b. at Rowley, Mass., Apr. 15, 1641; d. after Nov. 27, 1706; dau. of Joseph Jewett, of Rowley,

JOHN CARLETON, yeoman, b. about 1660/61; d. at Andover, Mass., Oct. 5, 1745; m. at Andover, Mass., Aug. 27, 1688, Hannah, b. at Andover, d. there Feb. 1733/4, dau. of Captain Christopher Osgood,

CAPTAIN SAMUEL CARLETON, b. at Andover, Mass., June 3, 1696; d. at Salem, Mass., Jan. 30 - Apr. 7, 1767; m. at Andover, June 20, 1726, Deborah Stevens, of Andover,

MARY CARLETON, b. (probably at Salem) 1737; d. at Salem, Mass., Dec. 22, 1805; m. at Salem, Feb. 11, 1759, John Bowditch, gent., of Salem, Mass., b. at Salem, Apr. 3, 1732; d. at sea 1793,

DEBORAH BOWDITCH, b. at Salem, Oct. 10, 1767; d. there July 24, 1823; m. at Salem, Oct. 3, 1782, Captain Thomas Moriarty, b. in Ireland 1760; d. at sea (South Atlantic) 1787,

JOHN MORIARTY, gent., b. at Salem, Oct. 12, 1783; d. there Mar. 16, 1835; m. there Dec. 26, 1806, Abigail Moseley, b. at Salem June 2, 1786; d. at Boston, Aug. 15, 1858,

JOHN MOSELEY MORIARTY, A.M., M.D., b. at Salem, Oct. 14, 1807; d. at Boston, Oct. 20, 1865; m. at Salem, Oct. 2, 1834, Nancy Page Andrews, b. at Salem Sept. 28, 1807; d. at Boston, Sept. 2, 1866,

GEORGE ANDREWS MORIARTY, b. at Brooklyn, N. Y., Sept. 29, 1846; d. April 19, 1914; m. at Roxbury, Mass., May 4, 1882, Mary Sheffield, b. Sept. 16, 1850; d. at Newport, R. I., July 1938,

GEORGE ANDREWS MORIARTY, b. at Newport, R. I., Feb. 14, 1883; A.B. *cum laude,* Harvard, 1905 (as of 1906), A.M., 1907, LL.B., 1916; Christ Church Oxford, 1905-06; American Consular Agent, Vice and Deputy Consul at Fiume, 1907-09; Third and Second Secretary, American Embassy, Mexico City, 1909-10; Secretary, American Legation, Guatemala, 1910-11; Captain of Military Intelligence, U. S. A., 1918-19; Dignitary (Commander) and Genealogist General, Order of the Crown of Charlemagne; Fellow of Society of Antiquaries of London, Society of Genealogists of London, Manorial Society of London, and Colonial Society of Mass.; Member of the Society of Colonial Wars, Rhode Island and Virginia Historical Societies, etc.; Vice-President of New England Historic Genealogical Society and Chairman of the Committee on English and Foreign Research of same; m., first, at Budapest, Hungary, 1908, Olga Gillming, dau. of Josef Gillming; m., 2ndly, Sept. 19, 1931, Louise, dau. of John Dittemore, of Indianapolis, Ind., and Boston, Mass., by Edith Louise Bingham, his wife.

CLARKE—GREENMAN—DU BOIS—JONES

EDWARD I, King of England, m. Eleanor, dau. of Ferdinand III, King of Castile and Leon,

PRINCESS JOAN, "of Acre," d. Apr. 23, 1307; m., first, May 1290, Gilbert de Clare, Earl of Gloucester and Hertford, (his second wife), b. Sept. 2, 1243; d. Dec. 7, 1295; son and heir of Richard de Clare, Earl of Gloucester and Hertford, by his second wife, Maud, dau. of John de Lacy, Earl of Lincoln,

ELIZABETH DE CLARE, d. Nov. 4, 1360; m., secondly, Feb. 3, 1315/6, ('his second wife), Theobald, 2nd Baron Verdon, d. July 27, 1316,

ISABEL VERDON, b. posthumously Mar. 21, 1316/7, only dau. by second wife, d. July 25, 1349; m., before Feb. 20, 1390/1, Henry de Ferrers, Baron Ferrers of Groby, d. Sept. 15, 1343,

WILLIAM, Baron Ferrers of Groby, b. and bapt. Feb. 28, 1332/3; d. Jan. 8, 1370/1; m., first, before Apr. 25, 1344, Margaret, dau. of Robert d'Ufford, Earl of Suffolk,

HENRY, Baron Ferrers of Groby, b. Feb. 16, 1355/6; d. Feb. 3, 1387/8; m., before Apr. 27, 1371, Joan, d. May 30, 1394, dau. (probably) of Sir Thomas de Hoo, of Luton Hoo and Stopsley, Beds, by Isabel, dau. and h. of Sir John de Seint Leger, of Offley, Herts,

WILLIAM, Baron Ferrers of Groby, bapt. Apr. 25, 1372; d. May 18, 1445; m., first, after Oct. 10, 1388, Philippa, dau. of Sir Roger de Clifford, sometimes called Lord Clifford, by Maud, dau. of Thomas de Beauchamp, Earl of Warwick,

THOMAS FERRERS, inherited the manors and advowsons of Walton and Tettenhall, and the manors of Champeyns in Woodham Ferris, Flecknoe, Hethe, and Claverley, d. Jan. 6, 1458/9; m. Elizabeth, dau. of Sir Baldwin Freville, of Tamworth Castle, co. Warwick,

SIR HENRY FERRERS, Knt., of the manor of Hambleton, Rutland, d. Dec. 28, 1500; m. Margaret, dau. and co-heiress of

William Heckstall, of East Peckham, and widow of William Whetenhall,

ELIZABETH FERRERS, m., about 1508, James Clerke, gent., of Ford Hall, d. about Sept. 20, 1553, son of John Clerke, of Ford, near Wrotham, Kent,

GEORGE CLERKE, gent., of Ford Hall, d. Mar. 8, 1558; m., about 1533, Elizabeth, dau. of Thomas Wilsforde, of Hartridge, Parish of Cranbrook, Kent,

JAMES CLERKE, gent., of East Farleigh, d. about 1614; m., about 1566, Mary, dau. of Sir Edward Saxby (Saxilby),

WILLIAM CLERKE, gent., of East Farleigh, Kent, and St. Botolph Aldgate, London; m. at St. Andrew's, Holborn, Feb. 10, 1598/9, Mary, dau. of Sir Jerome Weston,

JEREMY CLERKE (or Clarke), bapt. at East Farleigh, Kent, Dec. 1, 1605; d. at Newport, R. I., Nov. 1651; President Regent of Rhode Island; one of the founders of Newport, R. I.; Treasurer of Newport, 1644-47; Lieutenant and afterwards Captain of Militia, m., about 1637, Frances, bapt. in Parish of Kempston, co. Bedford, England, Feb. 15, 1609/10; d. Sept. 1677; widow of William Dungan, and dau. of Lewis Latham,

JEREMIAH CLARKE b, about 1643; d. Jan. 16, 1729; Deputy Governor of Rhode Island, 1696-1705; m. Anne Audley, d. Dec. 15, 1732,

ANNE CLARKE, m., about 1703, William Greenman,

JEREMIAH GREENMAN, m. Sarah Blackman,

AMEY GREENMAN, b. Oct. 24, 1727; d. June 2, 1807; m., 1758, Captain Peter Du Bois, b. Apr. 10, 1734; d. Aug. 21, 1795,

JEREMIAH DU BOIS, b. Nov. 22, 1760; d. Dec. 29, 1844; m. Sarah, b. Feb. 18, 1761; d. Sept. 5, 1813; dau. of William Shute,

JEREMIAH GREENMAN DU BOIS, b. Feb. 8, 1785; m., May 13, 1804, Hannah Timberman,

JEREMIAH DU BOIS, b. Feb. 8, 1807; d. June 20, 1874; m., Mar. 14, 1829, Hannah Turner Nordike, b. July 16, 1810; d. Apr. 13, 1872,

WILLIAM FRANKLIN DU BOIS, b. Apr. 23, 1840; d. May 27, 1885; m. at Bridgeton, N. J., Sept. 20, 1860, Harriet Amanda, b.

Apr. 10, 1842; d. Jan. 2, 1873; dau. of Enoch Sayre and his wife Mary McGee Roorke,

MARY LINCOLN DU BOIS, b. at Bridgeton, N. J., Apr. 7, 1865; d. there Feb. 28, 1938; m. there Dec. 8, 1891, William Madara Wilmer Jones, b. in Salem County, N. J., May 19, 1868; d. at Bridgeton, N. J., July 19, 1921,

CHARLES MARTIN JONES, b. at Bridgeton, N. J., Sept. 2, 1894; Member of Evening Star Lodge No. 97 Free and Accepted Masons of Bridgeton, Delta Chapter No. 6 Royal Arch Masons of Wilmington, St. John's Commandery No. 1 Knights Templar of Wilmington (past commander), Ancient Accepted Scottish Rite 32nd Degree Masons of Wilmington, Del. Swedish Colonial Society of Wilmington (registrar), Swedish Colonial Society of Penn., Society of Colonial Wars in State of N. J., Huguenot Society of Washington, D. C.

CLARKE—GREENMAN—DU BOIS—HENDRIXSON— NEWSOME

EDWARD I, King of England

See Page 154

AMEY GREENMAN, m. Captain Peter Du Bois, b. Apr. 10, 1734; d. Aug. 21, 1795,

JOEL DU BOIS, b. Oct. 22, 1759; d. June 29, 1808; m., (her first husband), Elizabeth Sparks, b. July 6, 1764; d. about 1834,

RACHEL DU BOIS, b. about 1787; d. May 28, 1867; m. William Holston,

MARIA DU BOIS HOLSTON, b. June 20, 1812; d. about 1889; m., Nov. 28, 1833, Isaac Hendrixson, Jr., b. Apr. 17, 1808; d. Sept. 11, 1880; son of Isaac Hendrixson and Prudence, his wife,

WILLIAM HOLSTON HENDRIXSON, b. Nov. 8, 1836; d. Mar. 4, 1910; m., Aug. 29, 1861, Miranda Richman Ford, b. May 20, 1840; d. Oct. 14, 1924; dau. of James Grubb Ford and Martha Kandle Oxenbaker, his wife,

FLORINE BAILEY HENDRIXSON, b. Nov. 2, 1877; m., June 19, 1901, Frank Newsome, b. Apr. 2, 1872; d. Oct. 22, 1935; son of Sam Newsome (born in Yorkshire, England, Aug. 18, 1842; d. Aug. 6, 1908), and his wife, Lydia Jane Glenn (b. May 9, 1847; d. Dec. 29, 1916), dau. of Jesse Glenn,

SAMUEL HENDRIXSON NEWSOME, b. at Chester, Penn., June 2, 1902.

Deighton—Bird—Macomber—Little—Sears

Margaret de Beaumont, m. Saier de Quincy, 1st Earl of Winchester,

Robert de Quincy, d. 1217, m. Hawise, Countess of Lincoln, d. 1242/3, sister of Ranulph "de Blundeville," Earl of Chester and Earl of Lincoln, Vicomte d'Avranches, and dau. of Hugh, styled "of Kevelioc," Earl of Chester, Vicomte d'Avranches in Normandy,

Margaret de Quincy, d. 1266; m., first, 1221, (his second wife), John de Lacy, Constable of Chester, Earl of Lincoln in right of his wife, d. July 22, 1240,

Maud de Lacy, d. 1288/9, m., 1237/8, (his second wife), Richard de Clare, Earl of Gloucester and Hertford, b. Aug. 4, 1222; d. July 15, 1262,

Gilbert de Clare, Earl of Gloucester and Hertford, "the Red Earl," b. Sept. 2, 1243; d. Dec. 7, 1295; m., secondly, Apr. 30 or May 2, 1290, Princess Joan Plantagenet, styled "of Acre," dau. of Edward I, King of England, by his wife, Eleanor, daughter of Ferdinand III., the Saint, King of Castile and Leon,

Margaret de Clare, d. Apr. 9, 1342, widow of Piers de Gavaston, Earl of Cornwall; m., secondly, Apr. 28, 1317, Hugh de Audley, Lord Audley; cr. Earl of Gloucester, Mar. 16, 1336/7; d. *s. p. m.* Nov. 10, 1347,

Margaret, *de jure*, apparently *suo jure* Baroness Audley, m., c 1335/6, Ralph, Lord Stafford; cr. Earl of Stafford, Mar. 5, 1350/1; d. Aug. 31, 1372,

Margaret de Stafford, m. Sir John de Stafford, Knt., of Bramshall, co. Stafford,

Ralph de Stafford, of Grafton, co. Worcester, m., Maud, b. at Chebsey co. Stafford, and bapt. there Feb. 2, 1358/9; dau. and co-heiress of Sir John Hastang,

SIR HUMPHREY DE STAFFORD, of Grafton, m. Elizabeth, dau. of Sir John Bindette, of Huncote and Leire, co. Leicester,

SIR HUMPHREY DE STAFFORD, of Grafton, m. Eleanor, dau. of Sir Thomas Aylesbury, of Blatherwick, Northampton,

ELIZABETH DE STAFFORD, m. at Beauchamp's Court, Jan. 27, 1446/7, Richard de Beauchamp, Baron Beauchamp of Powick, d. Jan. 19, 1502/3, son and heir of John, 1st Baron Beauchamp of Powick, co. Worcester, K.G., Constable of Gloucester Castle, Justice of South Wales, Lord Treasurer from 1450 to 1452, by his wife, Margaret, sister of Richard Ferrars,

ANNE DE BEAUCHAMP, d. 1535, m. Sir Richard Lygon, of Arle Court, Gloucester,

SIR RICHARD LYGON, m. Margaret, dau. of William Greville, of Arle Court, Gloucester,

HENRY LYGON, d. c 1577, m. Elizabeth, dau. of Sir John Berkeley, of Upton St. Leonard, Gloucester,

ELIZABETH (or Isabel) LYGON, m. Edward Basset, of Uley, Gloucester, d. c 1602,

JANE BASSET, d. c 1631, m. Dr. John Deighton, of St. Nicholas, Gloucester, d. c 1640,

FRANCES DEIGHTON, bapt. at St. Nicholas, Gloucester, England, Mar. 1, 1611; d. at Taunton, Mass., c Feb. 1705/06; m. at Witcombe Magna, Gloucester, England, Feb. 11, 1632, Richard Williams, bapt. at Wotten-Under-Edge, England, Jan. 28, 1607; d. at Taunton, Mass., c Aug. 1693,

ELIZABETH WILLIAMS, b. at Taunton, Mass., c 1647; d. at Dorchester, Mass., Oct. 20, 1724; m., c 1670, John Bird, b. at Dorchester, Mass., Mar. 11, 1641; d. there Aug. 2, 1732,

DIGHTON BIRD, b. at Dorchester, Mass., Nov. 10, 1687; m., c 1711, Isaac Merrick, b. at Taunton, Mass., c 1678; d. there c 1748,

ISAAC MERRICK, b. at Taunton, c 1712; d. there c Oct. 1765; m., c 1736, Hannah Hathaway, b. at Freetown, Mass., Mar. 30, 1718; d. at Taunton, after Dec. 5, 1762,

DIGHTON MERRICK, bapt. at Freetown, Mass., Sept. 9, 1750; m. at Freetown, Feb. 1, 1770, David Millard (or Miller), b. at Freetown, Mar. 30, 1739,

HANNAH MILLER, b. at Freetown, c 1776; d. at Westport, Mass., Sept. 1851; m. at Westport, Jan. 31, 1805, Ephraim Macomber, b. at Dartmouth, Mass., Oct. 20, 1776; d. at Westport, Mar. 1841,

RUTH HANNAH MACOMBER SLADE, b. at Dartmouth, Oct. 19, 1806; d. at Westport, June 14, 1882; m., secondly, at Dartmouth, Jan. 31, 1835, Esek Little, b. at Dartmouth, Jan. 9, 1812; d. at Westport, Aug. 4, 1883,

SARAH AUGUSTA LITTLE, b. at Dartmouth, Aug. 12, 1844; d. at Fall River, Mass., Jan. 19, 1924; m. at Westport, Nov. 30, 1871, Isaiah Francis Sears, b. at East Dennis, Mass., Jan. 20, 1844; d. at Fall River, Sept. 12, 1925,

ELMER SNOW SEARS, b. at Fall River, Mar. 13, 1874; d. at Swansea, Mass., Sept. 23, 1937; m., secondly, at Swansea, Sept. 12, 1905, Mima Carr Gray, b. at Somerset, Mass., Mar. 4, 1883,

FRANCIS RICHMOND SEARS, b. at Fall River, November 5, 1906; LL.B.; Companion (Knight) of the Order of the Crown of Charlemagne; Member of Order of the Founders and Patriots of America, Society of Mayflower Descendants, &c.

De La Warr—West—Sackville-West—Bedford

Henry III, King of England, m. Eleanora, dau. and h. of Raymond Berenger, Count of Provence,

Prince Edmund, Earl of Lancaster, Leicester and Derby, surnamed "Crouchback," m., secondly, Blanche, widow of Henry I, King of Navarre, and only dau. of Robert, Count d'Artois (son of Louis VIII, King of France), and his wife Maud, dau. of Henry II, Duke of Brabant,

Prince Henry, Earl of Lancaster and Leicester, etc.; m. Maud, only dau. and h. of Sir Patrick Chaworth, Knt., Lord of Kidwelly, and his wife Isabel, daughter of William de Beauchamp, Earl of Warwick,

Princess Joan, d. 1349; m., (his first wife), John de Mowbray, b. Nov. 29, 1310; d. Oct. 4, 1361,

Alianore de Mowbray, d. 1387, m., first, 1358, (his third wife), Roger La Warre, Lord De La Warre, b. Nov. 30, 1326; d. Aug. 27, 1370; s. and h. of Sir John La Warre, and his wife Margaret, dau. of Sir Robert de Holand, Lord Holand, of West Derby, co. Lancaster,

Joan, d. Apr. 24, 1404; m. Sir Thomas West, Baron West, of Oakhanger, Newton, Valence, and Winkton, Hants, Wolveton, Compton Valence, and Hinton Martell, Dorset, Blatchington, Sussex, etc.,

Reynold West, Lord De La Warr and Baron West, b. Sept. 7, 1395; d. 1433; m., first, 1428/9, Margaret, d. 1433, dau. and h. of Robert Thorley, of Tybeste, Cornwall, by his first wife, Anne (or Amy) Lisle,

Richard West De La Warr, Lord De La Warr and Baron West, b. Oct. 28, 1430; d. Mar. 10, 1475/6; m., 1451, Katherine, d. May 12, 1493, dau. of Sir Robert Hungerford, sometimes called Lord Hungerford, of Haytesbury, Wilts, by Margaret, dau. and h. of Sir William Botreaux, of Boscastle, Cornwall,

SIR THOMAS WEST, LORD DE LA WARR, BARON WEST, K.G., K.B., d. Oct. 11, 1525; m., secondly, Eleanor, dau. of Sir Roger Copley, of Roughway, Sussex, and his wife Anne, dau. and co-h. of Thomas Hoo, Baron Hoo and Hastings,

SIR GEORGE WEST, of Warbleton, Sussex, m. Elizabeth, 1st dau. and co-h. of Sir Robert Morton, of Lechdale, co. Gloucester,

WILLIAM WEST, b. 1520; d. Dec. 30, 1595; cr. Baron De La Warr, Feb. 5, 1569/70; m., first, Elizabeth, dau. of Thomas Strange, of Chesterton, co. Gloucester,

THOMAS WEST, 2ND BARON DE LA WARR, d. Mar. 24, 1601/2; m., Nov. 19, 1571, Anne, dau. of Sir Francis Knollys, K.G., and his wife Mary, dau. of William Cary,

THOMAS WEST, 3RD BARON DE LA WARR, b. July 9, 1577; d. June 7, 1618; Governor and Captain-General of Virginia, Feb. 28, 1610; m., Nov. 25, 1602, Cecily, 6th and youngest dau. of Sir Thomas Shirley, of Wiston, Sussex, and his wife Anne, daughter of Sir Thomas Kempe,

CAPTAIN HENRY WEST, 4th Baron De La Warr, b. Oct. 3, 1603; d. June 1, 1628; m., 1624/5. Isabella, b. at Brussels, 1607, 1st dau. and co-h. of Sir Thomas Edmunds, Treasurer of the Household,

CHARLES WEST, 5th Baron De La Warr, d. Dec. 22, 1687; m., Sept. 25, 1642, Anne, dau. of John Wild, of Droitwich, co. Worcester,

JOHN WEST, 6th Baron De La Warr, 1st Gentleman of the Bed-chamber to Prince George of Denmark, Treasurer of the Excise, d. May 26, 1723; m., 1691, Margaret, d. Jan. 31, 1737/8, dau. and h. of John Freeman, Merchant, of London, and widow of Thomas Salwey.

JOHN WEST, only s. and h., 7th Lord De La Warr, b. Apr. 4, 1693; d. Mar. 16, 1766; Clerk extraordinary of the Privy Council, M.P. for Grampound, K.B., P.C., Treasurer of the Household; Governor of New York in 1737; Governor of Gravesend and Tilbury Fort, 1747-52; cr. Viscount Cantelupe and Earl De La Warr, Mar. 18, 1761; m., first, May 25, 1721, Charlotte, d. Feb. 7, 1734/5; dau. of Donogh MacCarthy, 4th Earl of Clancarty, and his wife Elizabeth, dau. of Robert Spencer, 2nd Earl of Sunderland,

LIEUTENANT GENERAL JOHN WEST, 2nd Earl De La Warr, Viscount Cantelupe, Baron De La Warr, b. 1729; d. Nov. 22, 1777; m., Aug. 8, 1756, Mary d. Oct. 27, 1784, dau. of Lieutenant-General John Wynyard,

JOHN RICHARD WEST, 4th Earl De La Warr, b. July 28, 1758; d. July 28, 1795; m., Apr. 22, 1783, Catherine, d. May 27, 1826, dau. and h. of Henry Lyell, of Bourne, co. Cambridge, and his wife Catherine, only child of George Allestrie, of Alvaston, Devon,

GEORGE JOHN WEST, afterwards Sackville-West, 5th Earl De La Warr, b. Oct. 26, 1791; d. Feb. 23, 1869; Lord of the Bedchamber to King George III and King George IV, Lord Chamberlain of the Household, P.C., etc.; m., June 21, 1813, Elizabeth, b. Aug. 11, 1795; d. Jan. 9, 1870; cr. Baroness Buckhurst of Buckhurst, Apr. 27, 1864; dau. of John Frederick Sackville, 3rd Duke of Dorset, and his wife Arabella Diana, dau. of Sir Charles Cope, Bart., and had:

    1.) REGINALD WINDSOR SACKVILLE-WEST, 3rd son, 7th Earl De La Warr, Baron Buckhurst, b. Feb. 21, 1817; d. Jan. 15, 1896; m., 1867, Constance Mary Elizabeth, b. Feb. 7, 1846, 1st dau. of Alexander Dundas Ross (Cochrane-Wishart-Baillie), 1st Baron Lamington, and his wife Annabella Mary Elizabeth, dau. of Andrew Robert Drummond, of Cadlands, Hants, and had,

        a) GILBERT GEORGE REGINALD SACKVILLE, 8th Earl De La Warr, Viscount Cantelupe, Baron De La Warr, Baron Buckhurst, 2nd and only surviving s. and h., b. Mar. 22, 1869; d. 1915; m., first, Aug. 4, 1891, Muriel Agnes, b. Apr. 21, 1872; d. 1930; dau. of Thomas Brassey, 1st Baron Brassey of Bulkeley, and his first wife Anne, dau. of John Allnutt; (marriage dissolved by divorce, 1902), and had issue, among others:

            i HERBRAND EDWARD DUNDONALD BRASSEY SACKVILLE, 9th Earl De La Warr, Baron De La Warr, Baron West, Viscount Cantelupe, Baron Buckhurst, P.C., J.P. East Sussex, b. June 20, 1900; Lord Privy Seal since 1937; Lord-in-Waiting to H.M., 1924 and 1929-31; Mayor of Bexhill, 1932-33; Deputy Minister of Fisheries, 1930-35;

Parliamentary Under Secretary of State
for the Colonies, 1936-37, etc., m., 1920,
Diana, dau. of the late Gerard Leigh, and
have issue, among others,

a LORD WILLIAM HERBRAND SACKVILLE
BUCKHURST, b. Oct. 16, 1921.

2.) ELIZABETH, extra lady of the Bedchamber to Queen Victoria, d. Apr. 22, 1897; m., Jan. 18, 1844, Francis
Charles Hastings, 9th Duke of Bedford, K.G., M.P.
for Bedfordshire, etc., b. Oct. 16, 1819; d. Jan. 14,
1891, and had,

a) HERBRAND ARTHUR RUSSELL, 2nd son, 11th Duke
of Bedford, K.G., K.B.E., Marquess of Tavis-
stock, Earl of Bedford, Baron Russell of Chen-
ies, Baron Russell of Thornhaugh, Baron Howland of Streatham, Lord Lieutenant of the
County of Middlesex, 1898-1926; First Mayor
of Holborn, 1900; A.D.C., to King Edward VII
and King George V, 1908-20; b. Feb. 19, 1858;
m., 1888, Mary du Caurroy, b. Sept. 13, 1865; d.
Mar. 22, 1937; dau. of the late Ven. W. H. Tribe,
Archdeacon of Lahore, and had issue:

i HASTINGS WILLIAM SACKVILLE RUSSELL,
Marquess of Tavistock, b. in Cairnsmore,
Scotland, Dec. 21, 1888; author; m., Nov.
21, 1914, Louisa Crommelin Roberta Jowitt
Whitwell, and have issue:

a LORD JOHN ROBERT RUSSELL HOWLAND,
b. May 24, 1917;

b LADY DAPHNE CROMMELIN, b. Sept. 2,
1920;

c LORD HUGH HASTINGS, b. Mar. 29, 1923.

DENNE—HANCOCK—GARWOOD—ADAMS

CHARLEMAGNE, King of the Franks and Emperor of the West, b. Apr. 2, 747; d. Jan. 28, 814; m., 771, Princess Hildegard of Swabia.

LOUIS I, the Pious, *le Debonnaire*, King of the Franks and Emperor of the West, d. June 20, 840; m., 2ndly, 819, Judith, d. Apr. 19, 843, dau. of Guelph I, Count of Altdorf (Altorff) and Duke of Bavaria,

CHARLES II, the Bald, King of the Franks 843, Emperor 875; b. June 23, 823; d. Oct. 6, 877; m., first 842, Ermintrude (Irmtrud), d. Oct. 6, 869, dau. of Odo (or Vodon), Count of Orleans,

LOUIS II, King of the Franks 877, Emperor 878; d. Apr. 10, 879; m., 2ndly, 868/70, Adelheid (or Adelaide), d. 901, presumably a sister of Abbot Wulfard of Flavigny,

CHARLES III, the Simple, King of the Franks, b. Nov. 17, 879; d. Oct. 7, 929; m., 2ndly, 919, Edgina (or Eadgifu), dau. of Edward the Elder, King of England, and granddau. of Alfred the Great, King of England,

LOUIS IV, *d'Outre Mer*, King of France, d. Sept. 10, 954; m., 939, Princess Gerberga, d. May 5, 984, widow of Gisilbert, Duke of Lorraine, and dau. of Henry I., the Fowler, Emperor of Germany, and his wife Mathilda von Ringelheim,

CHARLES, Duke of Nether Lorraine, m. Bonna, Countess of Ardennes, dau. of Godefroy, the Old, Count of Verdun and Ardennes,

GERBERGA of Lorraine, m., Lambert I, Barbatus, Count of Mons and Louvain, son of Regnier III, Count of Hainault,

MAHAUT (or Maud) de Louvain, m. Eustace I, Count of Boulogne, d. *c* 1049,

LAMBERT, Count of Lens in Artois, Count of Louvain, slain in battle at Lille in 1054; m., (her second husband), Adelaide (or Adeliz), widow of Enguerrand II, Count of Ponthieu and Sire d'Aumale, and dau. of Robert, Duke of Normandy, and she was sister to William, the Conquerer, King of England,

JUDITH of Lens, m. 1070, Waltheof, Earl of Huntingdon, Northampton and Northumberland, beheaded on St. Giles' Hill, Winchester, May 31, 1076, son of Syward, Earl of Northumberland, and his wife Aelfled, dau. of Aldred of Bernicia,

MAUD, Countess of Huntingdon and Northampton, d. 1130/31, m., first, c 1090, Simon de St. Liz I, Earl of Huntingdon and Northampton in right of his wife, d. on his second journey to Jerusalem, at the Priory of La Charité c 1111, (she m., 2ndly, 1113, David I, the Saint, King of Scotland),

MAUD DE ST. LIZ, d. 1140, m. Robert FitzRichard, d. 1134, younger son of Richard FitzRichard, styled *de Bienfaite*, of Clare and de Tonbridge, and grandson of Gilbert, Count of Brionne in Normandy,

WALTER FITZROBERT, Lord of Dunmow Castle, m., first Mathilda (or Maud), Lady of Diss, Norfolk, dau. of Richard de Lucy, Justiciar of England,

ALICE, m. Sir Gilbert Peche,

HAMO PECHE, m. Eva,

GILBERT PECHE, of Westcliff, co. Kent, m. Joan, dau. of Sir Simon de Gray,

MARGERY PECHE, m., 1271/2, Sir Nicholas de Criol (or Kiriel), of Eynsford, Stockbury, Westenhanger, etc., co. Kent, and of Croxton Kerrial, co. Leicester, d. Oct. 12, 1303, son and heir of Nicholas de Criol, of Croxton, and of Cherry Hinton, co. Cambridge, by his first wife, Joan, dau. and heiress of William d'Auberville, of Eynsford, co. Kent,

SIR NICHOLAS DE CRIOL, m. Rohesia,

SIR JOHN DE CRIOL, m. Lettice,

IDA CRIOL, m. Sir John Brockhull, Knt.,

WILLIAM BROCKHULL, father of,

NICHOLAS BROCKHULL, m. Katharine, dau. of Adam Wood,

WILLIAM BROCKHULL, m. Elizabeth, dau. of Thomas Hever,

EDWARD BROCKHULL, m. Mildred Ellis, of Kennington, co Kent,

MARION BROCKHULL, m. Thomas Harfleet,

HENRY HARFLEET, m. Mary Slaughter, dau. of George Slaughter,

MARTHA HARFLEET, m. John Halsnode, by license dated Nov. 6, 1608,

JOHN HALSNODE, m. Margaret Ladd, by license dated Feb. 4, 1633,

MARGARET HALSNODE, m., first, John Denne, of St. Alphange, Canterbury, bapt. at Ripple, co. Kent, June 24, 1636; d. c June 24, 1685; son of James Denne (or Den), of Ripple, co. Kent, and his wife Ann Elgare, and grandson of John Denne (or Den), of Great Mongeham, co. Kent, and afterwards of Estry, and his wife Joan Foche, of Worth, co. Kent, (they were m. on Aug. 8, 1601), and great-grandson of Peter Denne (or Den), of Deal, co. Kent,

ELIZABETH DENNE, bapt. at St. Alphange, Mar. 19, 1662/3; m. first, at Salem, Nov. 28, 1680, (his second wife), Richard Hancock, of Bromley-by-Bow, co Middelsex, and later of Salem, N. J., d. Cohansey, Cumberland County, N. J., 1689,

MARGARET HANCOCK, b. in Salem County, N. J., c 1684; m. in Salem County, N. J., Feb. 23, 1705, Thomas Garwood, d. in Burlington County, N. J., c 1752,

THOMAS GARWOOD, b. in Burlington County, N. J., Mar. 2, 1707; d. at Great Egg Harbor, N. J., June 27, 1796; m. in Burlington County, N. J., 1733, (Friend's Record), Mary Ballinger, d. at Great Egg Harbor April 6, 1764,

MARGARET GARWOOD, b. in Burlington County, N. J., Aug. 30, 1704; d. at Great Egg Harbor, Apr. 29, 1825; m. at Great Egg Harbor, 1763, John Adams, b. at Great Egg Harbor, c 1738, d. there in 1798,

DANIEL ADAMS, b. at Great Egg Harbor, Apr. 1, 1773, d. there Feb. 17, 1863; m. there Dec. 1, 1818, Elizabeth Good Bartlett, b. at Great Egg Harbor, Nov. 4, 1799, d. there Nov. 17, 1862,

JAMES READING ADAMS, b. at Great Egg Harbor, N. J., May 6, 1835; d. at Pleasantville, N. J.; m. at Great Egg Harbor, Jan.

31, 1857, Marietta English, b. at English Creek, N. J., July 5, 1840; d. at Camden, N. J., Feb. 9, 1912,

PROFESSOR ARTHUR ADAMS, b. at Pleasantville, N. J., May 12, 1881; A.B. (Rutgers), A.M. (Yale), Ph.D. (Yale), B.D., S.T.M., F.R.S.L., F.S.A., F.S.G.; Grand Dignitary (Knight Grand Cross), Registrar General and Prior General of the Order of the Crown of Charlemagne; Registrar General, General Society of Colonial Wars; Formerly Governor General and now Registrar General, Order of the Founders and Patriots of America; Member of Committee on Heraldry, New England Historic Genealogical Society; Member of S.R., Saint Nicholas Society, American Historical Society, Modern Language Association of America, Conn. Historical Society, etc.; m. at Ocean City, N. J., June 22, 1910, Emma Guerin Steelman, b. at Mays Landing, N. J., Jan. 30, 1880, and have issue:

1.) ESTHER STEELMAN ADAMS, b. at Hartford, Conn., Dec. 30, 1912; Dame Companion of the Order of the Crown of Charlemagne;

2.) RICHARD HANCOCK ADAMS, b. at Hartford, Conn., Nov. 16, 1916.

EDEN

EDWARD III, King of England; m., 1328, Philippa of Hainault,

LIONEL "of Antwerp," Duke of Clarence, K.G., b. Nov. 29, 1338; d. Oct. 17, 1368; m., first (in his fourth year), Sept. 9, 1342, Elizabeth de Burgh, b. July 6, 1332, d. at Dublin, 1363; dau. and h. of William de Burgh, 3rd Earl of Ulster, and his wife Maud, dau. of Henry, Earl of Lancaster,

PHILIPPA, sole heiress, b. 1355; d. 1382; m., 1368, Edmund de Mortimer, 3rd Earl of March, Lord Mortimer, b. at Llangoed in Llyswen, co. Brecon, Feb. 1, 1351/2; d. Dec. 27, 1381; he became, in right of his wife, Lord of Ulster and of Connaught, Lord of Clare in Suffolk, Earl of Ulster, etc.,

ELIZABETH DE MORTIMER, b. at Usk, Feb. 12, 1370/1; d. Apr. 20, 1417; m., first, 1379, Sir Henry de Percy, surnamed *Hotspur*, b. May 20, 1364; d. July 21, 1403; K.G., K.B.,

HENRY DE PERCY, Earl of Northumberland, b. Feb. 3, 1392/3; d. May 22, 1455; m., 1414, Eleanor, widow of Richard Le Despenser, Lord Le Despenser, and dau. of Ralph de Neville, Earl of Westmorland, and his second wife, Joan de Beaufort,

HENRY DE PERCY, Earl of Northumberland, b. July 25, 1421; d. Mar. 29, 1461; m., 1435, Eleanor de Poynings,, d. 1483/4, dau. of Richard de Poynings,

HENRY DE PERCY, Earl of Northumberland, K.G., P.C., only son and heir, b. c 1449; murdered Apr. 28, 1489; m., c 1476, Maud Herbert, d. 1485, dau. of William Herbert, Earl of Pembroke, and his wife Anne, dau, of Sir Walter Devereux,

HENRY ALGERNON DE PERCY, Earl of Northumberland, Lord Poynings, etc., K.B., K.G., b. Jan. 14, 1477/8; d. May 19, 1527; m., c 1502, Catherine Spencer, dau. and co-heiress of Sir Robert Spencer, of Spencercombe, co. Devon, and his wife Eleanor, dau. of Edmund Beaufort, Duke of Somerset,

MARGARET DE PERCY, m., c 1516, Henry de Clifford, Lord Clifford; cr. Earl of Cumberland, June 18, 1525; K.G., 1537; b. in 1493; d. Apr. 22, 1542,

CATHERINE DE CLIFFORD, d. 1598; m., first, John, Lord Scrope of Bolton, d. 1549,

MARGARET LE SCROPE, m. Sir John Constable, of Kirby Knowle, d. 1579,

SIR HENRY CONSTABLE, of Burton Constable, co. York, d. 1607; m., c 1575, Margaret Dormer, dau. of Sir William Dormer, of Wing, Bucks,

KATHERINE CONSTABLE (sister of Henry, 1st Viscount of Dunbar), m., c 1594, Thomas, 1st Viscount Fairfax of Emley, co. Tipperary. b. 1574; d. Dec. 23, 1636,

MARY FAIRFAX, m., c 1615, Sir Thomas Layton, of Laton and Sexhow, co. York, d. 1651,

CATHERINE LATON, b. 1618; d. c 1686, m. John Eden, of West Auckland and Windleston, co. Durham,

SIR ROBERT EDEN, 1st Bart., of West Auckland, M.P. for Durham, d. 1720; m. Margaret, d. July 2, 1730, dau. of John Lambton, of the city of Durham,

SIR JOHN EDEN, 2nd Bart., M.P. for co. Durham, d. May 2, 1728; m., Jan. 31, 1715, Catherine, dau. of Mark Shafto, of Whitworth,

SIR ROBERT EDEN, 3rd Bart., d. June 25, 1755; m., May 8, 1739, Mary Davison, d. Jan. 31, 1794, dau. of William Davison, of Beamish,

SIR ROBERT EDEN, 2nd son, Governor of Maryland, cr. a Bart., Oct. 19, 1776, d. Sept. 2, 1784; m., Apr. 26, 1763, Caroline Calvert, d. c 1803, sister and co-heiress of Frederick Calvert, 7th Baron Baltimore, and dau. of Charles, 6th Baron Baltimore,

SIR FREDERICK MORTON EDEN, 2nd Bart., of Maryland, b. c 1767; d. Nov. 14, 1809; m. Jan. 10, 1792, Anne, d. July 14, 1808, dau. and h. of James Paul Smith, of New Bond Street,

SIR WILLIAM EDEN, 4th Bart., and 6th Bart. of West Auckland, b. Jan. 31, 1803; d. Oct. 20, 1873; m., Apr. 23, 1844, Elfrida Susanna Harriet, d. July 8, 1882, youngest dau. of Colonel William Iremonger, of Wherwell Priory, co. Hants,

Sir William Eden, 5th Bart., and 7th Bart. of West Auckland, J.P., D.L., b. Apr. 4, 1849; m. July 20, 1886; Sybil Frances, dau. of Sir William Grey, K.C.S.I.,

Rt. Hon. Robert Anthony Eden, P.C., M.C., J.P., D.C.L., M.P., b. June 12, 1897; Secretary of State for Foreign Affairs, 1935-38; Secretary of State for Dominion Affairs, 1939; Secretary of State for War, 1940, etc.; m. 1923, Beatrice Helen, dau. of Sir Gervase Beckett, 1st Bart., and his wife Lady Marjorie, and have issue.

Esterhazy de Galantha

Edward IV, King of England, m. Elizabeth Wydeville (Woodville),

Princess Elizabeth, m. Henry VII, King of England,

Princess Mary Tudor, widow of Louis XII, King of France; m., secondly, Charles Brandon, Duke of Suffolk, K.G.,

Eleanor Brandon, youngest dau. and co-h., d. Sept. 27, 1547; m. (his first wife), 1537, Henry Clifford, 2nd Earl of Cumberland, K.B., d. Jan. 2, 1569/70, son of Henry Clifford, Lord Clifford, 1st Earl of Cumberland, and his second wife Margaret, dau. of Henry de Percy, 5th Earl of Northumberland, by his wife Catherine, dau. and co-h. of Sir Robert Spencer, of Spencer Combe, Devon,

Margaret de Clifford, only surviving child and h., d. Sept. 29, 1596; m., Feb. 7, 1555, Henry Stanley, 4th Earl of Derby, K.G., b. 1531; d. Sept. 25, 1593,

Ferdinando Stanley, Lord Stanley, Lord Strange of Knokin, Lord Mohun of Dunster, 5th Earl of Derby, Sovereign Lord of the Isle of Man, b. c 1559; d. Apr. 16, 1594; m., c 1580, Alice Spencer, d. Jan. 23, 1636/7, dau. of Sir John Spencer, of Althorpe, Northants, and his wife Katherine, dau. of Sir Thomas Kitson, of Hengrave, Suffolk,

Frances Stanley, b. 1583; d. Mar. 11, 1635/6; m., c 1601, John Egerton, 1st Earl of Bridgwater, K.B., Baron of the Exchequer of Chester, Lord President of Wales, d. Dec. 4, 1649,

John Egerton, 2nd Earl of Bridgwater, Lord Lieutenant of Bucks, High Steward of the University of Oxford, P.C., b. 1623; d. Oct. 26, 1686; m., July 22, 1641, Elizabeth Cavendish, d. June 14, 1663, dau. of William Cavendish, 1st Duke of Newcastle, and his first wife Elizabeth, dau. and h. of William Bassett, of Blore, co. Stafford,

John Egerton, 3rd Earl of Bridgwater, K.B., b. Nov. 9, 1646; d. Mar. 19, 1700/1; m., secondly, Apr. 2, 1673, Jane Powlett,

d. May 23, 1716, dau. of Charles Powlett, 1st Duke of Bolton, and his second wife Mary,

SCROOP EGERTON, 4th Earl of Bridgwater, 1st Marquess of Brackley, and 1st Duke of Bridgwater, b. Aug. 11, 1681; d. Jan. 11, 1744/5; m., first, Feb. 9, 1703, Elizabeth, 3rd dau. and co-h. of John Churchill, Duke of Marlborough, and his wife Sarah, dau. and co-h. of Richard Jennings,

ANNE EGERTON, d. June 22, 1762, widow of Wriothesley Russell, Duke of Bedford; m., secondly, June 23, 1733, William, 6th Viscount Grandison of Ireland, 3rd Earl of Jersey, d. Aug. 28, 1769,

GEORGE BUSSY, 4th Earl of Jersey, Lord of the Admiralty, Lord Chamberlain of the Household, b. June 9, 1735; d. Aug. 22, 1805; m., Mar. 26, 1770, Frances Twysden, d. July 25, 1821, only dau. and h. of the Right Rev. Philip Twysden, D.D., Bishop of Raphoe,

GEORGE, 5th Earl of Jersey, twice Lord Chamberlain to King William IV, b. Aug. 19, 1773; d. Oct. 3, 1859; m., May 23, 1804, Sarah Sophia Fane, d. Jan. 26, 1867, eldest dau. of John, 10th Earl of Westmorland, and his wife Sarah Anne, dau. and h. of Robert Child, of Osterley Park, Middlesex,

SARAH FREDERICA CAROLINE VILLIERS, b. Aug. 12, 1822; d. Nov. 17, 1853; m., Feb. 8, 1842, Nicholas, Prince Esterházy de Galántha, b. June 25, 1817; d. Jan. 28, 1894; eldest son of Prince Paul Anthony Esterházy,

PAUL ANTON NICHOLAS, 10th Prince Esterházy de Galántha, Princely Count of Edelstetten, Count von Forchtenstein, b. at Vienna, Mar. 21, 1843; Knight of the Austrian Order of the Golden Fleece; d. Aug. 22, 1898; m., first, at Vienna, Oct. 21, 1868, Marie, Countess von Trauttmansdorff, b. Apr. 21, 1847; d. Apr. 1, 1876,

NICHOLAS, 11th Prince Esterházy de Galántha, Princely Count of Edelstetten, Count von Forchtenstein, b. July 5, 1869; d. Apr. 6, 1920; m., Nov. 16, 1898, Marguerite, Countess Cziráky de Czirák et Dénesfalva, b. Aug. 11, 1874; d. Aug. 18, 1910, and had, among others:

1.) PAUL MARIE ALOYSE ANTHONY NICHOLAS VICTOR, 12th Prince Esterházy de Galántha, Princely Count of Edelstetten, Count von Forchtenstein, etc., Dr. Jur. et Pol., b. Mar. 23, 1901;

2.) PRINCE ANTHONY MARIE PAUL NICHOLAS ESTERHÁZY DE GALÁNTHA, b. July 22, 1903; m. at Budapest, Oct. 22, 1935, Gabriella, Countess de Nagy-Appony, b. Apr. 25, 1910;

3.) PRINCE LADISLAS ANTHONY NICHOLAS MARIE PAUL QUIRINUS ESTERHÁZY DE GALÁNTHA, b. June 4, 1905; Dr. Pol.; m. at Budapest, Nov. 17, 1929. Marie (Mariette), Countess Erdödy de Monyorókerék et Monoszló b. Feb. 26, 1905, and have issue.

    a) PRINCESS ELIZABETH MARGUERITE BERNADETTE ALEXANDRA MARIE AGATHA, b. at Budapest, Feb. 5, 1931;

    b) PRINCE NICHOLAS LADISLAS PAUL ANTHONY ALEXANDER MARIE MICHAEL, b. at Budapest, Sept. 29, 1932;

    c) PRINCESS MARGUERITE MARIE BERNADETTE ELIZABETH HELEN, b. at Budapest, Apr. 11, 1936.

Gurdon—Saltonstall

Edward I, King of England, m., secondly, Princess Margaret, dau. of Philip III, King of France,

Thomas, styled "of Brotherton," Earl of Norfolk, Marshal of England, Keeper of England, b. at Brotherton, Yorks, June 1, 1300; d. c 1338; m. Alice, d. c 1330, dau. of Sir Roger de Hales, Coroner of Norfolk,

Margaret, *suo jure* Countess of Norfolk; cr. Duchess of Norfolk, Sept. 29, 1397; d. March 24, 1398/9; m. first, 1337/8, John Segrave, Lord Segrave, d. March 20, 1353,

Elizabeth de Segrave, b. Oct. 25, 1338; m., c 1349, John de Mowbray, Baron de Mowbray, of Axholme, b. June 25, 1340; slain by the Saracens in 1368; son and heir of John de Mowbray, of the Isle of Axholme, d. Oct. 4, 1361, and his first wife Joan, dau. of Henry, Earl of Lancaster and Leicester, son of Edmund, styled "Crouchback," Earl of Lancaster, Earl of Leicester, Count of Champagne and Brie in France, (by his second wife Blanche, widow of Henry, King of Navarre, and dau. of Robert, Count of Artois, who was son of Louis VIII, King of France), and grandson of Henry III, King of England,

Thomas de Mowbray, Duke of Norfolk, Earl of Norfolk, Earl of Nottingham, Earl Marshal of England, K.G., b. Mar. 22, 1365/6; d. at Venice, Sept. 22, 1399; m., secondly, 1384, Elizabeth FitzAlan, d. July 8, 1425, widow of Sir William Montagu, and dau. of Sir Richard FitzAlan, Earl of Arundel, K.G., Admiral of England, beheaded Sept. 21, 1397, and his first wife Elizabeth, dau. of William de Bohun, Earl of Northampton,

Margaret de Mowbray, m. Sir Robert Howard, Knt., of Stoke Neyland, co. Suffolk, d. c 1436; son of Sir John Howard, Knt., Sheriff of the counties of Essex and Hertford,

John Howard, Lord Howard, K.G.; cr. Duke of Norfolk and Earl Marshal of England, June 28, 1483; Admiral of England, Ireland, and Aquitaine; Steward of the Duchy of

Lancaster, P.C.; d. Aug. 22, 1485; m., secondly, Margaret, widow of John Norreys, of Bray, Berks, relict of Nicholas Wyfold, Lord Mayor of London, and dau. of Sir John Chedworth,

KATHARINE HOWARD, d. Mar. 12, 1535/6; m. Sir John Bourchier, 2nd Baron Berners, K.B., Chancellor of the Exchequer 1516-27, d. at Calais, March 16/19, 1532/3; son and heir of Sir Humphrey Bourchier, slain at the battle of Barnet on Apr. 14, 1471, and his wife Elizabeth, dau. and sole h. of Frederick Tylney, of Boston, co. Lincoln, (this Elizabeth was afterwards the first wife of Thomas Howard, Duke of Norfolk), and grandson of Sir John Bourchier, 1st Baron Berners, K.G., and great-grandson of Sir William Bourchier, Count of Eu in Normandy, by his wife Anne, dau. of Thomas, "of Woodstock," Duke of Gloucester,

JANE BOURCHIER, of Ashwellthorpe, co. Norfolk, *de jure* Baroness Berners, d. Feb. 17, 1561/2; m. Edmund Knyvett, Esquire, Sergeant Porter to King Edward III, d. April 1539,

JOHN KNYVETT, of Plumstead, co. Norfolk, and of Thetford, m. Agnes, dau. of Sir John Harcourt, of Stanton Harcourt, co. Oxon,

SIR THOMAS KNYVETT, *de jure* Baron Berners; Sheriff of Norfolk, 1579-80; b. *c* 1539; d. Feb. 9, 1617/8; m. Muriel, d. Apr. 25, 1616, dau. of Sir Thomas Parry, Treasurer of the Household to Queen Elizabeth,

MURIEL (OR ABIGAIL) KNYVETT, m., (his second wife), Martin Sedley, of Morley, son of Martin Sedley, Gent. of Morley,

MURIEL SEDLEY, m., (his second wife), Brampton Gurdon, Esquire, of Assington Hall, co. Suffolk, and of Letton, co. Norfolk, High Sheriff for Suffolk in 1625, son of John Gurdon, of Assington Hall, High Sheriff for Suffolk, and his wife Amy, dau. and h. of William Brampton, of Letton, co. Norfolk,

MURIEL GURDON, m., June 1633, Richard Saltonstall, Esquire, of Yorkshire, afterwards of Ipswich, Mass., Deputy to the General Court in 1635-37, b. at Woodsome, Yorkshire, England, *c* 1610; d. at Hulme, Lancaster, Apr. 29, 1694; son of Sir Richard Saltonstall, Knt., of Huntwicke, Lord of the Manor of Ledsham, near Leeds, England, he commenced the settlement of Watertown in 1630, one of the original patentees of Connecticut, and his first wife Grace Kaye, dau. of Robert Kaye, of Woodsome, Yorkshire.

NATHANIEL SALTONSTALL, b. at Ipswich, Mass., c 1639; d. May 21, 1707; Colonel of the Essex Regiment, 1679-86; Town Clerk of Haverhill; Member of the Council; Judge Oyer and Terminer Court, 1692; m., Dec. 28, 1663, Elizabeth Ward, b. April 9, 1647; d. Apr. 29, 1741; dau. of the Rev. John Ward, of Haverhill, and his wife Alice Edmunds,

COLONEL RICHARD SALTONSTALL, b. Apr. 25, 1672; d. Apr. 22, 1714; m., March 25, 1702, Mehitabel, dau. of Captain Simon Wainwright, of Haverhill, and granddau. of Francis Wainwright, of Ipswich,

JUDGE RICHARD SALTONSTALL, b. at Haverhill, Mass., June 24, 1703; d. Oct. 20, 1756; Colonel, 1726; Judge of the Superior Court, 1736 until his death; m., thirdly, Mary Cooke, dau. of Elisha Cooke, Jr., and his wife Jane, granddau. of Richard Middlecott, Esq., of Boston,

NATHANIEL SALTONSTALL, Physician, b. Feb. 10, 1746; d. May 15, 1815; m., Oct. 21, 1780, Anna White, b. Apr. 12, 1752; d. Oct. 21, 1841; dau. of Samuel White, of Haverhill,

LEVERETT SALTONSTALL, LL.D., b. June 13, 1783; d. May 8, 1845; Speaker of the House of Representatives; President of the Senate; 1st Mayor of Salem, etc.; m., March 7, 1811, Mary Elizabeth, b. Feb. 29, 1788; d. Jan. 11, 1858; dau. of Thomas Sanders, Esq., of Salem,

LEVERETT SALTONSTALL, A.M. ,LL.B., b. at Salem, Mar. 16, 1825; m., Oct. 19, 1854, Rose S. Lee, b. Jan. 24, 1835, dau. of John Clarke Lee, of Salem,

RICHARD MIDDLECOTT SALTONSTALL, b. Oct. 28, 1859; m., Oct. 17, 1891, Eleanor Brooks, b. Sept. 18, 1867, dau. of Peter Chardon Brooks, of West Medford. Issue:

> 1.) LEVERETT SALTONSTALL, b. at Chestnut Hill, Mass., Sept. 1, 1892; A.B., Harvard, 1914, and LL.B., 1917; Member of Board of Alderman, Newton, 1920-22; Assistant District Attorney, Middlesex County, Mass., 1921-22; Speaker of Mass. House of Representatives, 1929-36; Governor of Mass., 1939 - Jan. 1941; m., June 27, 1916, Alice Wesselhoeft, of Jaffrey, N. H., and have issue:

a) LEVERETT SALTONSTALL;

b) EMILY B. SALTONSTALL;

c) PETER B. SALTONSTALL;

d) WILLIAM L. SALTONSTALL;

e) SUSAN SALTONSTALL.

2.) ELEANOR SALTONSTALL, b. Oct. 10/19, 1894;

3.) MURIEL GURDON SALTONSTALL, b. Mar. 26, 1896;

4.) RICHARD SALTONSTALL, b. July 23, 1897.

MURIEL GURDON, m., June 1633, Richard Saltonstall, Esq,. of Yorkshire, afterwards of Ipswich, Mass., son of Sir Richard Saltonstall, Knt., of Huntwicke, Lord of the Manor of Ledsham,

NATHANIEL SALTONSTALL, b. at Ipswich, Mass., c 1639; d. May 21, 1707; m. Dec. 28, 1663, Elizabeth Ward, dau. of the Rev. John Ward, of Haverhill,

GURDON SALTONSTALL, b. at Haverhill, Mass., Mar. 27, 1666; d. Sept. 20, 1724; Governor of Connecticut, 1708 until his death; m., secondly, Elizabeth Rosewell, d. Sept. 12, 1710, dau. and sole 'h. of William Rosewell, of Branford, and his wife Catherine, dau. of Hon. Richard Russell, of Charlestown,

GURDON SALTONSTALL, b. Dec. 22, 1708; Brigadier General in the Revolutionary War, afterwards Collector of the Port of New London; m., Mar. 15, 1732/3, Rebecca Winthrop, dau. of John Still Winthrop, and granddau. of Hon. Waitstill Winthrop, and had,

1.) DUDLEY SALTONSTALL, b. Sept. 8, 1738; d. in the West Indies in 1796; Commodore in the Revolutionary War; m., 1765, Frances, dau. of Dr. Joshua Babcock, of Westerly, R. I., and had,

a) JOSHUA SALTONSTALL, m. Abbie Lewis, dau. of Thomas Lewis, of Farmington, Conn., and had,

i DUDLEY GILBERT SALTONSTALL, b. Sept. 10, 1808; m., 1845, Sophia A. M. de Zocieur, and had,

1. DUDLEY EDWARD SALTONSTALL, of Rye,
N. Y., m. Annie, dau. of Samuel H.
Satterlee, and had:

 a) SATTERLEE SALTONSTALL, b. July
  19, 1870;

 b) DUDLEY SALTONSTALL, b. June
  22, 1874.

2.) ROSEWELL SALTONSTALL, b. Aug. 29, 1741; d. at New
York, Jan. 12, 1804; m., Mar. 4, 1763, Elizabeth Stewart, dau. of Matthew Stewart, of New London, and
had,

 a) WILLIAM SALTONSTALL, d. at Pensacola, Aug.
  26, 1842; m. Maria Hudson, and had,

  i MARY SUSAN SALTONSTALL, m. Thomas
  Marston Beare, of Meridian, Conn., d. Oct.
  1, 1869, and had,

   1. ISABEL BEARE, m. George Benjamin
   Mickle, of Bayside, L. I., and had,

    a ANDREW H. MICKLE, of Flushing,
    b. Oct. 5, 1856, adopted surname
    of Saltonstall; m. Susan S. Hun-
    ter, of Berkeley Springs, W. Va.,
    and had,

     i SOPHIA FOREST SALTONSTALL,
     b. Aug. 14, 1893.

GURDON—SALTONSTALL—BROOKS—ADAMS— MORGAN—HOMANS—ABBOTT—PERKINS

EDWARD III, King of England, m. Philippa, dau. of William, Count of Hainault and Holand,

THOMAS, surnamed "of Woodstock," 6th son, Duke of Gloucester, Earl of Essex and Buckingham, Constable of England, K.G., b. Jan. 7, 1354/5; d. *c* 1397; m., *c* 1376, Alianore (Eleanor), d. Oct. 3, 1399, elder dau. and co-heiress of Humphrey de Bohun, Earl of Hereford and Essex, Earl of Northampton, Constable of England, and his wife Joan, dau. of Richard FitzAlan, Earl of Arundel,

ANNE, Countess of Buckingham, Hereford and Northampton, widow of Edmund de Stafford, Earl of Stafford, m., thirdly Sir William Bourchier, Count of Eu in Normandy, d. at Troyes, May 28, 1420, Constable of the Tower of London, son and heir of Sir William Bourghchier and his wife Alianore, dau. and co-heiress, eventually sole heiress of Sir John de Lovayne, of Little Easton and Broxted, co. Essex, and Bildeston, co. Suffolk,

SIR JOHN BOURCHIER, Baron Berners, K.G., Constable of Windsor Castle, d. May 16/21, 1474; m. Margery, d. Dec. 18, 1475, widow of John Ferreby and dau. and h. of Sir Richard Berners, of West Horsley, co. Surrey, and his wife Philippa, dau. of Sir Edward Dalyngridge,

SIR HUMPHREY BOURCHIER, slain at the battle of Barnet, Apr. 14, 1471, m. Elizabeth (she was afterwards the first wife of Thomas Howard, Duke of Norfolk), dau. and sole h. of Frederick Tylney, of Boston, co. Lincoln,

SIR JOHN BOURCHIER, 2nd Baron Berners, K.B., a distinguished soldier and author, Chancellor of the Exchequer 1516-27, d. at Calais, Mar. 16/19, 1532/3; m. Katharine Howard, d. Mar. 12, 1535/6, dau. of John Howard, Duke of Norfolk, and his second wife Margaret, dau. of Sir John Chedworth,

JANE BOURCHIER, *de jure* Baroness Berners, 2nd but only surviving dau. and h., of Ashwellthorpe, co. Norfolk, d. Feb. 17,

1561/2; m. Edmund Knyvett, Sergeant Porter to King Henry VIII, d. Apr. 1539,

JOHN KNYVETT, *d.v.m.*, m. Agnes, dau. of Sir John Harcourt, of Stanton Harcourt, co. Oxon,

SIR THOMAS KNYVETT, *de jure* Baron Berners, Sheriff of Norfolk 1579-80, b. *c* 1539; d. Feb. 9, 1617/8; m. Muriel, d. Apr. 25, 1616, sister and co-heiress of Sir Thomas Parry, of Welford, Berks, and dau. of Sir Thomas Parry, Treasurer of the Household to Queen Elizabeth,

MURIEL KNYVETT, m. Martin Sedley, of Morley, co. Norfolk,

MURIEL SEDLEY, m., (his second wife), Brampton Gurdon, Esq., of Assington Manor, co. Suffolk, and of Letton, co. Norfolk, son of John Gurdon, of Assington, and his wife Amy Brampton (dau. of William Brampton, of Letton, co. Norfolk), and grandson of Robert Gurdon, of Assington, and his wife Rose (Sexton) Appleton, dau. of Robert Sexton and widow of William Appleton,

MURIEL GURDON, m. Richard Saltonstall, Esq., of Yorkshire, afterwards of Ipswich, Mass.,

NATHANIEL SALTONSTALL, b. at Ipswich, Mass., *c* 1639; d. May 21, 1707; m., Dec. 28, 1663, Elizabeth Ward, dau. of the Rev. John Ward, of Haverhill,

ELIZABETH SALTONSTALL, b. Sept. 17, 1668; d. at Boston, July 8, 1726; m., secondly, 1690, Rev. Roland Cotton, of Sandwich, b. Dec. 27, 1667, son of Rev. John J. Cotton, of Plymouth, and his wife Joanna Rossiter,

JOANNA COTTON, m. the Rev. John Brown, of Haverhill, d. Dec. 2, 1742,

ABIGAIL BROWN, d. Nov. 29, 1800; m., *c* 1764, the Rev. Edward Brooks, d. May 6, 1781,

PETER CHARDON BROOKS, of Boston, b. Jan. 6, 1767; d. Jan. 1, 1849; m., *c* 1792, Ann Gorham, d. Feb. 21, 1830, dau. of Nathaniel Gorham,

ABIGAIL BROWN BROOKS, b. Apr. 25, 1808; m., *c* 1829, Charles Francis Adams, LL.D., author, diplomat and statesman, b. at Boston, Aug. 18, 1807; d. at Boston, Nov. 21, 1886; son of John Quincy Adams, President of the United States, and

180

grandson of John Adams, President of the United States. Issue:

1.) JOHN QUINCY ADAMS, b. at Boston, Sept. 22, 1833; d. at Quincy, Mass., Aug. 14, 1894; m., Apr. 29, 1861, Fanny Cadwallader Crowninshield, b. at Boston, Oct. 15, 1839; d. at Boston, May 16, 1911, and had issue, among others:

   a) CHARLES FRANCIS ADAMS, b. at Quincy, Mass., Aug. 2, 1866; Secretary of the Navy, 1929-33; m. at Washington, D. C., Apr. 3, 1899, Frances Lovering, of Taunton, Mass., and have issue:

      i CATHERINE ADAMS, b. Jan. 13, 1902; m. at Concord, Mass., June 26, 1923, Henry Sturgis Morgan, b. at London, England, Oct. 24, 1900, son of John Pierpont Morgan and his wife Jane Norton Grew, and have issue:

         a HENRY STURGIS MORGAN;

         b CHARLES FRANCIS MORGAN;

         c MILES MORGAN;

         d JOHN ADAMS MORGAN.

      ii CHARLES FRANCIS ADAMS, b. May 5, 1910.

   b) ARTHUR ADAMS, b. at Quincy, Mass., May 20, 1877; m., Oct. 5, 1921, Mrs. Margery (Lee) Sargent, b. in Brookline, Mass., May 2, 1893, dau. of George and Eva (Ballerina) Lee, and widow of Francis Williams Sargent;

   c) ABIGAIL ADAMS, b. at Quincy, Mass., Sept. 6, 1879; m., June 10, 1907, Robert Homans, b. at Boston, Oct. 3, 1873, son of John and Helen Amory (Perkins) Homans, and have issue:

      i GEORGE GASPAR HOMANS, b. Aug. 11, 1910;

      ii FANNY CROWNINSHIELD HOMANS, b. Aug. 21, 1911;

      iii HELEN AMORY HOMANS, b. Oct. 29, 1913;

      iv ROBERT HOMANS, b. Oct. 25, 1918.

2.) COLONEL CHARLES FRANCIS ADAMS, author and lawyer, b. at Boston, May 27, 1835; d. at Washington, D. C.,

March 20, 1915; m. at Newport, R. I., Nov. 7, 1865, Mary H. Ogden, b. Feb. 23, 1843, dau. of Edward Ogden, of Newport and New York, and his wife Caroline Callender. Issue:

a) MARY ADAMS, b. July 27, 1867; m., Sept. 30, 1890, Grafton St. Loe Abbott, b. at Lowell, Nov. 14, 1856; d. at Concord, Feb. 27, 1915, and have issue:

    i HENRY LIVERMORE ABBOTT, b. at Lewiston, Maine, Apr. 12, 1892;

    ii MARY OGDEN ABBOTT, b. at Concord, Mass., Oct. 12, 1894;

    iii JOHN ADAMS ABBOTT, b. at Concord, July 11, 1902.

b) LOUISA CAROLINE ADAMS, b. Dec. 28, 1871; m., June 6, 1900, Thomas Nelson Perkins, b. at Milton, Mass., May 6, 1870; d. Oct. 7, 1937; son of Edward Cranch Perkins, and his wife Jane Sedgwick Watson, and have issue:

    i ELLIOTT PERKINS, b. at Westwood, Mass., Mar. 16, 1901;

    ii JAMES HANDASYD PERKINS, b. at Westwood, Nov. 17, 1903;

    iii THOMAS NELSON PERKINS, b. Apr. 30, 1907.

c) ELIZABETH OGDEN ADAMS, b. at Quincy, Mass., Dec. 3, 1873;

d) JOHN ADAMS, b. July 17, 1875; m., Oct. 3, 1905, Marian Morse, and have issue:

    i MARY ADAMS, b. Aug. 15, 1906;

    ii JOHN QUINCY ADAMS, b. July 15, 1907;

    iii THOMAS BOYLSTON ADAMS, b. July 25, 1910;

    iv FREDERICK OGDEN ADAMS, b. Sept. 13, 1912;

    v ABIGAIL ADAMS, b. June 3, 1915.

3.) HENRY ADAMS, author, American historian, Professor of History in Harvard College, b. at Boston, Feb. 16, 1838; d. at Washington, D. C., Mar. 27, 1918; m., June 27, 1872, Marian Hooper, b. at Boston, Sept. 13, 1843; d. Dec. 6, 1885; dau. of Dr. Robert W. Hooper.

HALIFAX

CHARLEMAGNE, King of the Franks and Emperor of the West, father of,

LOUIS I, the Pious, King of the Franks and Emperor of the West; m., first, ca. 794, Ermengarde (Irmgard), d. Oct. 3, 818, dau. of Ingeramun (Ingram), Count of Hasbaye,

LOTHARIUS I, King of Italy and Emperor of the West, b. ca. 795; d. Sept. 29, 855; m., first, Oct. 15, 821, Ermengarde (Irmgard), d. Mar. 20, 851, dau. of Hugo II, Count of Tours, (or of Alsace),

LOTHARIUS II, King of Lorraine (Lotharingien - Lothierregne - Lotharingia), b. ca. 835; d. Aug. 8, 869; m., secondly, ca. 862, Waldrade (formerly his concubine), who d. as a nun in Remiremont ca. 868,

PRINCESS BERTHA, b. ca. 863; d. Mar. 8, 925; m., first, ca. 879, Theobald (Thibault), Count of Arles,

BOSO, Count of Arles, 926-31; Markgraf of Tuscany, 931-36; b. ca. 885; d. ca. 938; m. Willa,

WILLA, m. ca 936, Berenger II, King of Italy, Markgraf of Ivrea, d. Aug. 6, 966, son of Adalbert, Markgraf of Ivrea, and his wife Princess Gisela, dau. of Berenger I, King of Italy and Emperor of the West,

PRINCESS SUSANNA, (often referred to as Rosela), m., first, Arnolph II, Le Jeune, Count of Flanders, son of Baldwin III, Count of Flanders, and his wife Mathilda, dau. of Hermann Billung, Duke of Saxony,

BALDWIN IV, Le Barbu, Count of Flanders, b. ca. 980; d. May 30, 1035; m., first, ca. 1012, Ogive (Otgive), d. Feb. 21, 1030, dau. of Frederick, Count of Luxemburg,

BALDWIN V, the Pious, Count of Flanders, b. ca. 1012; d. Sept. 1, 1067; m., ca. 1028, Adele (Adelheid), d. Jan. 8, 1079, dau. of Robert II, King of France, and widow of Richard III, Duke of Normandy,

MATHILDA (OR MAUD) of Flanders, b. *ca.* 1032; d. Nov. 2/3, 1083; m., *ca.* 1050/53, William I, Duke of Normandy, The Conqueror, King of England, b. *ca.* 1027; d. Sept. 9, 1087,

HENRY I, *Beauclerc,* King of England, b. 1068; d. Dec. 1/2, 1135; m., first, Nov. 11, 1100, Princess Mathilda, b. 1079; d. May 1, 1118; dau. of Malcolm III, *Canmore,* King of Scotland, by his second wife, Saint Margaret, dau. of Prince Edward the Exile and his wife Agatha,

PRINCESS MATHILDA (OR MAUD), b. 1104; d. Sept. 10, 1169; widow of Henry V, Emperor of Germany; m., secondly, May 22, 1127/8, Geoffrey Plantagenet, Count of Anjou, b. Aug. 24, 1113/4; d. Sept. 7, 1151,

HENRY II, King of England, b. Mar. 5, 1132/3; d. July 3, 1189; m. May 1, 1152, Eleanor, Duchess of Aquitaine and Queen of France, d. Mar. 31, 1204, the divorced wife of Louis VII, King of France, and dau. of William, Duke of Aquitaine and Count of Poitou,

JOHN, King of England, b. Dec. 24, 1166; d. Oct. 19, 1216; m., secondly, Aug. 24, 1200, Isabella, d. May 31, 1246, only dau. and h. of Aymer de Valence, Count of Angouleme, and his wife Alice, dau. of Peter de Courtenay, and granddau. of Louis VI, King of France,

HENRY III, King of England, b. Oct. 1, 1207; d. Nov. 16, 1272; m., Jan. 14, 1236, Eleanor, b. *c* 1217; d. June 24, 1291; dau. and co-h. of Raymond Berenger, Count of Provence,

PRINCE EDMUND, styled "Crouchback," Earl of Lancaster and of Leicester, Count of Champagne and Brie in France, b. Jan. 16, 1244/5; d. at Bayonne, June 5, 1296; m., secondly, 1276, Blanche, d. at Paris, May 2, 1302, widow of Henry, King of Navarre, (who d. July 22, 1274), and dau. of Robert, Count of Artois, (son of Louis VIII, King of France), and his wife Mathilda (or Maud), dau. of Henry II, Duke of Brabant, by his first wife, Mary of Hohenstauffen, dau. of Philip II, Emperor of Germany,

HENRY, 3rd Earl of Lancaster and of Leicester, Steward of England, b. *c* 1281; d. Sept. 22, 1345; m., first, Maud, d. *c* 1322, dau. and h. of Sir Patrick de Chaworth, of Kidwelly, and his wife Isabel, dau. of William de Beauchamp, Earl of Warwick,

JOAN PLANTAGENET, d. c July 7, 1349; m., (his first wife), John de Mowbray, 3rd Baron Mowbray, b. at Hovingham, Yorks, Nov. 29, 1310; d. Oct. 4, 1361; s. and h. of John, 2nd Baron Mowbray, and his wife Aline, dau. and co-h. of William de Braose, lord of Gower in Wales and of Bramber in Sussex,

SIR JOHN DE MOWBRAY, 4th Baron Mowbray, b. June 25, 1340; slain by the Saracens in 1368; m., c 1349, Elizabeth, dau. and co-h. of John de Segrave, Baron Segrave, and his wife Margaret, eldest dau. and eventually h. of Thomas "of Brotherton," Earl of Norfolk and Marshal of England, (son of Edward I, King of England, by his 2nd wife, Princess Margaret, dau. of Philippe III, King of France),

THOMAS DE MOWBRAY, 6th Baron Mowbray, Baron Segrave; cr. Earl of Nottingham, Feb. 12, 1382/3; cr. Earl Marshal of England, June 30, 1385, and Duke of Norfolk, Sept. 29, 1397; K.G., d. at Venice, Sept. 22/30, 1399/1400; m., secondly 1384, Elizabeth, widow of Sir William de Montagu, and dau. of Richard FitzAlan. Earl of Arundel,

MARGARET DE MOWBRAY, m. Sir Robert Howard, Knt., of Stoke Neyland, Suffolk, d. c 1436,

JOHN HOWARD, Lord Howard, K.G., M.P. for Norfolk in 1455; cr. Duke of Norfolk and Earl Marshal of England, June 28, 1483; slain at Bosworth, Aug. 22, 1485; m., first, Catherine, d. Nov. 3, 1465, dau. of Sir William Moleyns (who died June 8, 1425),

THOMAS HOWARD, K.B., K.G., P.C., b. c 1443; d. May 1/21, 1524; M.P. for Norfolk, 1478; cr. Earl of Surrey, June 28, 1483; Earl Marshal of England, July 10, 1510; cr. Duke of Norfolk, Feb. 1, 1513/4; commanded the English forces at Flodden; m., secondly, Agnes, sister and h. of Sir Philip Tylney, Knt., of Boston, and dau. of Hugh Tylney, of Skirbeck and Boston, co. Lincoln,

WILLIAM HOWARD, K.G., cr. Baron Howard of Effingham, Mar. 11, 1553/4; b. c 1510; d. Jan. 11/12, 1572/3; m., secondly, Margaret, d. May 18, 1581, dau. of Sir Thomas Gamage, Knt., of Coity, co. Glamorgan, and his wife Margaret, dau. of Sir John St. John, of Bletsoe,

SIR WILLIAM HOWARD, of Lingfield, buried at Reigate, Sept. 2, 1600; m. Frances, buried at Reigate, 1615/6, dau. of William Gouldwell, of Gouldwell Hall, co. Kent,

Sir Francis Howard, of Eastwick in Great Bookham, Surrey, knighted at Chatham, July 4, 1604; d. July 7, 1651; m. Jane, dau. of Sir William Monson, of Kinnersley,

Sir Charles Howard, of Eastwick in Great Bookham, d. Mar. 20, 1672; m., Aug. 5, 1641, Frances, d. May 6, 1681, dau. of Sir George Courthope, of Whiligh in Ticehurst, Sussex,

Francis Howard, 5th Baron Howard of Effingham, Governor of Virginia 1683-93; bap. Sept. 17, 1643; d. Mar. 30, 1695; m., first, July 8, 1673, Philadelphia, bap. Oct. 6, 1654; d. Aug. 13, 1685; dau. of Sir Thomas Pelham, Bart., of Laughton, Sussex, and his third wife, Margaret, dau. of Sir Henry Vane,

Francis Howard, 7th Baron Howard of Effingham; cr. Earl of Effingham, Dec. 8, 1731; bap. Oct. 20, 1683; d. Feb. 12, 1742/3; m., first Feb. 23, 1712/3, Diana, dau. of Lieutenant General Fergus O'Farrel of Ireland,

Thomas Howard, 2nd Earl of Effingham, Baron Howard of Effingham, d. Nov. 19, 1763; m., Feb. 14, 1744/5, (her first husband), Elizabeth, d. Oct. 13, 1791, dau. of Peter Beckford, of Jamaica, Speaker of the House of Assembly, and his wife Bathshua, dau. and co-h. of Colonel Julines Hering,

Elizabeth Howard (sister and co-h. of the 4th Earl of Effingham), d. Oct. 31, 1815; m., Jan. 24, 1774, Henry Reginald Courtenay, D.D., Bishop of Bristol and Exeter, b. Nov. 27, 1741; d. June 9, 1803,

William Courtenay, 10th (or 20th) Earl of Devon, M.P. for Exeter 1812-26, b. June 19, 1777; d. Mar. 19/29, 1859; m., first, Nov. 29, 1804, Harriet Leslie, b. June 1, 1777; d. Dec. 16, 1839; dau. of Sir Lucas Pepys, Bart., physician to King George III, and his wife, Jane Elizabeth, *suo jure* Countess of Rothes, dau. of John, 9th Earl of Rothes, Lord Leslie, Major General at the battle of Dettingen, Commander-in-Chief of the Forces in Ireland at this death, K.T., and his wife Hannah, dau. and co-h. of Matthew Howard, of Hackney, co. Middlesex,

William Reginald Courtenay, 11th (or 21st) Earl of Devon, D.C.L., M.P. for South Devon 1841-49; Chancellor of the Duchy of Lancaster, July 1866 - May 1867; P.C., etc.; b. Apr. 14, 1807; d. Nov. 18, 1888; m., Dec. 27, 1830, Elizabeth, b. July 10, 1801; d. Jan. 27, 1867; youngest dau. of Hugh,

1st Earl of Fortescue, K.G., and his wife, Hester, dau. of the Rt. Hon. George Grenville, Chancellor of the Exchequer and Prime Minister (1763-65), and his wife Elizabeth, dau. of the Rt. Hon. Sir William Wyndham, 3rd Bart., of Orchard Wyndham, Somerset, by his first wife, Katherine, dau. of Charles Seymour, 6th Duke of Somerset,

AGNES ELIZABETH COURTENAY, only dau., b. May 1, 1838; d. July 4, 1919; m., Apr. 22, 1869, Charles Lindley Wood, 2nd Viscount Halifax of Monk Bretton, b. at the Admiralty, June 7, 1839; d. 1934; Groom of the Bedchamber to the Prince of Wales, 1862-77; s. and h. of Charles Wood, 3rd Bart., of Barnsley, co. York; cr. Viscount Halifax of Monk Bretton, Feb. 21, 1866; B.A., M.A.; M.P. for Great Grimsby 1826-31, for Wareham 1831-32, for Halifax 1832-65, and for Ripon 1865-66; Chancellor of the Exchequer 1846-52; P.C., President of the Board of Control for India 1852-55; First Lord of the Admiralty 1855-58; Secretary of State for India 1859-66; Lord Privy Seal 1870-74; G.C.B.; and his wife Mary, dau. of Charles Grey, 2nd Earl of Grey, K.G., by Mary Elizabeth, dau. of William Brabazon Ponsonby, 1st Baron Ponsonby of Imokilly,

EDWARD FREDERICK LINDLEY WOOD, 3rd Viscount Halifax of Monk Bretton, M.A., K.G., P.C., G.C.S.I., G.C.I.E., 1st Baron Irwin of Kirby Underdale, b. Apr. 16, 1881; Colonel late Yorkshire Dragoons; Viceroy of India, 1926-31; President of Board of Education, 1922-24 and 1932-35; Minister of Agriculture, 1924-25; M.P. (U.) for Ripon Division, West Ridenig, Yorks, 1910-25; Chancellor of the University of Oxford since 1933; Secretary of State for War, 1935; Lord Privy Seal, 1935-37; Leader of the House of Lords, 1935-38; Lord President of the Council, 1937-38; Secretary of State for Foreign Affairs, 1938-40; Ambassador Extraordinary and Plenipotentiary to the United States, 1941 ——; m., Sept. 21, 1909, Dorothy Evelyn Augusta Onslow, C.I., b. Mar. 7, 1885, youngest dau. of William Hillier Onslow, 4th Earl of Onslow, and his wife, Florence Coulston, 1st dau. and co-h. of Alan Legge Gardner, 3rd Baron Gardner, of Uttoxeter, and have issue three sons, the heir being:

    1.) HON. CHARLES INGRAM COURTENAY WOOD, b. Oct. 3, 1912; M.P. (U.) for York since 1937; Second Lieutenant, Royal Horse Guards, 1934-37, etc.; m., 1936, Ruth Primrose, and have issue two daughters.

LOVELACE—GORSUCH—PHELPS—RUSSEL

CHARLEMAGNE

See Page 133

MARGARET DE BEAUMONT, d. Jan. 12, 1235/6; m. Saier de Quincy, 1st Earl of Winchester, Justiciar, Magna Charta Surety, Crusader, d. Nov. 3, 1219, in the Holy Land,

ROGER DE QUINCY, 2nd Earl of Winchester, Constable of Scotland, 2nd son, d. about April 25, 1264; m., first, before 1234, Helen, dau. and co-h. of Alan, Lord of Galloway, Constable of Scotland,

MARGARET DE QUINCY, d. about 1280/1; m., about 1238, (his second wife), William de Ferrers, Earl of Derby, Constable of Bolsovar Castle, d. Mar. 24/8, 1254,

JOAN DE FERRERS, d. Mar. 19, 1309/10; m., 1267, Thomas de Berkeley, feudal Lord of Berkeley, Vice-Constable of England in 1297; b. 1245; d. July 23, 1321; son of Maurice de Berkeley, Lord of Berkeley, and his wife Isabel, dau. of Richard FitzRoy, by Rohcse, dau. and heiress of Robert of Dover,

MAURICE DE BERKELEY, Lord of Berkeley, Chief Justiciar of South Wales in 1316; Seneschal of Aquitaine in 1320; b. about 1281; d. May 31, 1326; m., first, 1289, Eve, d. Dec. 5, 1314, sister of William La Zouche, Lord Zouche of Haryngworth, and dau. of Eudes La Zouche, by his wife Milicent de Cantelou (Cantelupe),

ISABEL DE BERKELEY, only dau., d. July 25, 1362; m., first, 1328, Robert de Clifford, Lord Clifford, b. Nov. 5, 1305; d. May 20, 1344; son of Robert de Clifford, Lord Clifford, Captain General of the Marches of Scotland in 1299, and his wife Maud, dau. of Thomas de Clare (2nd son of Richard de Clare, Earl of Gloucester and Hertford), and his wife Julian, dau. of Sir Maurice FitzMaurice, Lord Justice of Ireland,

ROGER, Lord Clifford, Sheriff of Cumberland and Governor of Carlisle Castle in 1377; b. July 10, 1333; d. July 13, 1389;

m. Maud de Beauchamp, d. 1402/3, dau. of Thomas de Beau-champ, Earl of Warwick, K.G., and his wife Catherine, dau. of Roger de Mortimer, 1st Earl of March,

THOMAS, Lord Clifford, Sheriff of Westmorland, Governor of Carlisle Castle for life, d. Aug. 18, 1391; m. Elizabeth, d. 1424, dau. of Thomas de Ros, Lord Ros, by Beatrice, dau. of Ralph de Stafford, 1st Earl of the County of Stafford,

JOHN, Lord Clifford, K.G., d. Mar. 13, 1421/2; m., (her first husband), Elizabeth, d. Oct. 26, 1437, dau. of Sir Henry de Percy, "Hotspur," and his wife Elizabeth, dau. of Edmund de Mortimer, Earl of March,

THOMAS, Lord Clifford, b. Mar. 25, 1414; slain at the battle of St. Albans, May 22, 1455; m., 1424, Joan, dau. of Thomas, Lord Dacre, of Gilsland (Gillesland), and his wife Philippa, dau. of Ralph de Neville, Earl of Westmorland,

JOAN DE CLIFFORD, m. Richard de Musgrave, d. Aug. 10, 1491; son and heir of Thomas de Musgrave (and his wife Joan, dau. and co-heiress of William Stapilton, of Edenhall), and grandson of Sir Richard de Musgrave, J.P., Under Sheriff of Westmorland, and his wife Elizabeth, dau. of Sir Thomas Beetham, of Beetham,

SIR EDWARD DE MUSGRAVE, who fought at, and was knighted after the battle of Flodden, Sept. 9, 1513; d. May 23, 1542; m., 2ndly, about 1496, Joan, dau. and eventually co-heiress of Sir Christopher Ward, of Givendale in Ripon,

SIR WILLIAM DE MUSGRAVE, Keeper of the Castle of Bewcastle, Cumberland; knighted at Jedburgh, Sept. 25, 1523; d. Oct. 18, 1544; m. Elizabeth, widow of Thomas Tamworth, and dau. of Sir Thomas Curwen, of Workington,

SIR RICHARD DE MUSGRAVE, Knt., b. about 1524; d. at Edenhall, Sept. 10/1, 1555; m. Anne, dau. of Thomas Wharton, Lord Wharton,

ELEANOR DE MUSGRAVE, b. about 1546; d. July 23, 1623; m., first, William Thornborough (Thornburgh), Esq., of Selside (she m., 2ndly, as his second wife, Robert Bowes, of Aske, Yorks),

WILLIAM THORNBOROUGH, Esq., of Gampsfield, co. Lancaster, father of,

ROWLAND THORNBOROUGH, Esq., of Hampsfield, m. Jane, dau. of Thomas Dalton, Esq., of Turnham,

ANNE THORNBOROUGH, m., (his second wife), Thomas Roos,

ANNE ROOS, m. John Dixon, of London,

MARGARET DIXON, m. George Sandys, of London and Estwaite Furnese, co. Lancaster, son of William Sandys, of Cumberland, and his wife Margaret, dau. and heiress of John Gerard, of Turvey, co. Bedford,

EDWIN SANDYS, of Garthwaite Hall, in the parish of Hawkshead, Lancashire, D.D., Vicar of Haversham, Archbishop of York, &c., d. 1588; m., 2ndly, Cicely Wilford, of Cranbrook, co. Kent, sister of Sir Thomas Wilford,

ANNE SANDYS, b. about June 21, 1570; m. Sir William Barne, Knt., of Woolwich, co. Kent, son of Sir George Barne, Knt., Lord Mayor of London in 1586,

ANNE BARNE, m. Sir William Lovelace, Knt., of Lovelace, co. Kent,

ANNE LOVELACE, b. about 1611; d. in Va., about 1657; m., about 1628, the Rev. John Gorsuch, D.D., of Walkerne, co. Hertfordshire, killed in 1647 by the rebels under Fairclough of Weston,

RICHARD GORSUCH, father of,

ANNE GORSUCH, b. about 1666; d. about 1711; m., 1680/1, William Phelps, b. about 1656; d. about 1748,

JOHN PHELPS, b. about 1683, d. about 1747; m. Margaret,

THOMAS PHELPS I, d. about 1754; m., about 1720, Elizabeth Patterson,

THOMAS PHELPS II, m. Sarah Moore (or More),

GEORGE PHELPS, b. about 1757; d. 1803; m., about 1787, Tabitha Simmons,

SAMUEL PHELPS, b. about 1788; d. 1852; m., about 1822, Tabitha Taylor, b. about 1800, d. 1869,

THOMAS PHELPS III, b. 1838, d. 1908; m., 1865, Sarah Winifred Cobb,

MINERVA PARKE PHELPS, b. near Richmond, Madison County, Ky., Jan. 15, 1870, Dame Companion First Class and Member of the Ladies Advisory Council of the Order of the Crown of Charlemagne; Honorary President of National

Society of the Colonial Dames of America in the State of Florida (served as President, Registrar, Genealogist) ; Member of D.A.R. (Chaplain and Parliamentarian), Huguenot Society of Manikintowne, Jacksonville Junior League; Fellow of the American Institute of Genealogy, &c.; m., first, May 8, 1901, General John Hooe Russel, b. 1842; d. Jan. 1903; son of Dr. Albert Russel, of Huntsville, Ala.; m., 2ndly, June 15, 1907, Frank E. Jennings, LL.B., Member and Speaker of the House of Representatives of Florida in 1921.

Issue by first husband:

ALBERT LACY RUSSEL, b. Feb. 2, 1902; A.B., LL.B.; m. at Cincinnati, Ohio, Nov. 29, 1933, Caroline How Collier, issue:

1.) MARY ALLEN RUSSEL, b. Feb. 14, 1935;

2.) ANNE IVANUS HOW RUSSEL, b. Aug. 25, 1937;

3.) ELIZABETH COLLIER RUSSEL, b. May 14, 1940.

LUDLOW—BREWSTER—CALDWELL

EDWARD I, King of England

See Page 197

EDITH DE WINDSOR, m. George Ludlow, Esq., of Hill Deverell, co. Wilts,

THOMAS LUDLOW, of Dinton (or Denton), and Baycliffe, d. about 1607; m., about 1581, Jane Pyle, dau. of Thomas Pyle, and sister of Sir Gabriel Pyle,

ROGER LUDLOW, (brother of Gabriel Ludlow), bapt. about Mar. 7, 1590; d. about 1664/5; Deputy Governor of the Massachusetts Bay Colony, first Deputy Governor of Conn., &c.; m. Mary Cogan, dau. of Philobert Cogan,

SARAH LUDLOW, d. at Brookhaven, L. I., N. Y., about 1695; m., about 1656, (his 2nd wife), Nathaniel Brewster, d. about 1618; d. at Brookhaven, about Dec. 18, 1690,

TIMOTHY BREWSTER, b. about 1658; d. at Brookhaven, 1741/5; m., about 1685, Mary Hawkins, dau. of Zachariah Hawkins,

NATHANIEL BREWSTER, b. at Brookhaven, about 1689; d. there Nov. 6, 1732; m., about 1712, Phebe Smith, dau. of Samuel Smith, by Hannah Longbotham, his wife,

SAMUEL BREWSTER, b. at Brookhaven, July 8, 1718/20; d. in Orange County, N.Y., Feb. 10, 1802; Member of the Provincial Congress, 1775-76; Chairman of Committee on Safety of the Precinct of New Windsor, N. Y., 1775-79; m. Mary,

SAMUEL BREWSTER, b. at Brookhaven, about 1740; d. at Haverstraw, N. Y., Nov. 29, 1824; State Senator from Middle District of N. Y., 1805-08; m., 2ndly, about 1775, Freelove Williams, b. at Huntingdon, L. I., N. Y., about 1754; d. at Haverstraw, Dec. 4, 1815; dau. of Jonas Williams,

HARRIET BREWSTER, b. at Haverstraw, Jan. 2, 1789; d. at Salisbury, N. Y., June 26, 1846; m. Aug. 30, 1815, Andrew James Caldwell, b. at Ballimony, co. Antrim, Ireland, about Oct. 10, 1782; d. at Salisbury Mills, N. Y., Jan. 9, 1862,

SAMUEL BREWSTER CALDWELL, b. at Salisbury Mills, Aug. 22, 1822; d. at London, England, Jan. 7, 1901; m. at New Windsor, N. Y., Oct. 11, 1849, Susan Elizabeth Roe, b. at Moodna, Orange County, N. Y., Oct. 18, 1826; d. at Brockville, Canada, Sept. 12, 1907; dau. of Peter Roe,

ANDREW JAMES CALDWELL, b. at Brooklyn, N. Y., May 1, 1858; d. at New York, N. Y., May 10, 1909; m. at Minneapolis, Oct. 1, 1890, (her 1st husband), Rosana McCarthy, b. at Ironton (Hanging Rock), Ohio, Dec. 24, 1869; d. at Washington, D. C., Oct. 10, 1928. Issue:

1.) MARGARET SHAPTER CALDWELL, b. at Irvington, N. Y., Aug. 15, 1891; President of Society of Daughters of Colonial Wars in the State of Ga.; Member of D.A.R., D.A.C. (first Regent of James Edward Oglethorpe Chapter in Atlanta, 1935-37), U.S.D. of 1812 (State Corresponding Secretary), National Society Sons and Daughters of the Pilgrims (Deputy Governor General), New England Historic Genealogical Society; Registrar of Ga. State Society of Children of the American Colonists, &c.; m. at Newburg, N. Y., June 5, 1911, Samuel Montague Page Rees, b. at Richmond, Va., Aug. 3, 1882, son of James Conway Rees, by Ann Page, his wife;

2.) ROSALINE DEERING CALDWELL, b. at New Windsor, Orange County, N. Y., Aug. 3, 1895; m. at Washington, D. C., June 3, 1916, John Brewer. Issue:

    a) RICHARD CALDWELL BREWER, b. at Washington, D. C., July 31, 1923.

3.) ELIZABETH ROE CALDWELL, b. at New Windsor, N. Y., July 18, 1899; m. at New York, July 8, 1921, Robert Penneman Lewis, Lieutenant-Commander U.S.N. Issue:

    a) EDWARD CALDWELL LEWIS, b. at Seattle, Wash., Aug. 4, 1923;

    b) ROBERTA PENNEMAN LEWIS, b. at Guam, Dec. 9, 1925.

LUDLOW—CARTER—HARRISON—McKEE—WALKER

EDWARD I, King of England

See Page 197

COLONEL ROBERT CARTER, of "Corotoman," called "King Carter," Speaker of the Va. House of Burgesses, Rector of William and Mary College, &c.; m., 2ndly, Elizabeth (or Betty) Landon, dau. of Thomas Landon, and widow of a Willis,

ANNE CARTER, m. Benjamin Harrison, of "Berkeley," Charles City County, Va., Sheriff and Burgess, d. about 1744,

BENJAMIN HARRISON, of "Berkeley," d. Apr. 24, 1791; Signer of the Declaration of Independence; Governor of Va., 1782-84; Member of the Continental Congress, &c.; m. Elizabeth Bassett,

GENERAL WILLIAM HENRY HARRISON, President of the United States of America, b. at "Berkeley," Feb. 9, 1773; d. at Washington, D. C., Apr. 4, 1841; m., Nov. 22, 1795, Anna Tuthill Symmes, b. near Morristown, N. J., July 25, 1775; d. Feb. 25, 1864; dau. of Col. John Cleves Symmes and his wife, Anna Tuthill,

JOHN SCOTT HARRISON, b. at Vincennes, Oct. 4, 1804; d. 1878; resided at North Bend, Ohio, and was twice elected to Congress; m., 2ndly, Aug. 12, 1831, Elizabeth P. Irwin,

GENERAL BENJAMIN HARRISON, President of the United States of America, b. at North Bend, Ohio, Aug. 20, 1833; d. at Indianapolis, Ind., Mar. 13, 1901; m., first, Caroline, b. at Oxford, Ohio, 1832; d. in the White House, Washington, Oct. 25, 1892; dau. of Professor John Witherspoon Scott, D.D.; he m., 2ndly, Apr. 6, 1896, Mary Scott Lord, b. at Honesdale, Pa., Apr. 30, 1858/9, widow of Walter Erskine Dimmick, and dau. of Russell Farnham Lord and his wife. Elizabeth Scott.

Issue by first wife:

1.) RUSSELL BENJAMIN HARRISON, b. about 1854; d. Dec. 13, 1936; m., Jan. 8, 1884, Mary Angeline, dau. of

Alvin Saunders. Issue:

    a) MARTHENA HARRISON.

2.) MARY SCOTT HARRISON, m., Nov. 25, 1884, James Robert McKee, of Indianapolis. Issue:

    a) BENJAMIN HARRISON McKEE;

    b) MARY LODGE McKEE.

Issue by second wife:

3.) ELIZABETH HARRISON, m. James Blaine Walker, Jr.

Ludlow—Carter—Moon—Butts

Edward I, King of England, b. June 17/8, 1239; d. July 7, 1307; m., first, 1254, Eleanor of Castile, d. Nov. 29, 1290, dau. of Ferdinand III, the Saint, King of Castile and Leon, by his 2nd wife, Joanna, dau. of Simon Dammartin, Count of Ponthieu and Aumale,

Princess Elizabeth, b. 1282; d. May 5, 1316; widow of John I, Count of Holland and Zealand; m., 2ndly, Nov. 14, 1302, Humphrey de Bohun, Earl of Hereford and Essex, Lord of Brecknock, and Constable of England, killed at Boroughbridge, Mar. 16, 1321/2; son and h. of Humphrey de Bohun, Earl of Hereford and Essex, Constable of England, and his wife, Maud, dau. of Enguerrand de Fiennes, Seigneur de Fiennes in Guisnes,

Margaret de Bohun, b. Apr. 3, 1311; d. Dec. 16/27, 1391; m., Aug. 11, 1325, Sir Hugh Courtenay, Earl of Devon, Lord Courtenay, Chief Warden of Devon in 1373, b. July 12, 1303; d. May 2, 1377; son and h. of Sir Hugh Courtenay, of Okehampton, Devon, Earl of Devon, Lord Courtenay, a Knight Banneret, and his wife, Agnes, dau. of John de St. John, of Basing, Hants, by Alice, dau. of Reynold FitzPiers,

Elizabeth Courtenay, d. Aug. 7, 1395, widow of Sir John de Vere; m., 2ndly, about 1359, Sir Andrew Luttrell (or Luterel), of Chilton, co. Devon,

Hugh Luttrell, of Chilton, co. Devon, b. about 1364; d. Mar. 24, 1428; m. Catherine, d. Aug. 28, 1435, widow of John Streche, and dau. of Sir John Beaumont, Knt., of Devonshire,

Elizabeth Luttrell, widow of William Harleston; m., 2ndly, John Stratton, Esq., of London, d. about June 14, 1448,

Elizabeth Stratton, m. John Andrews, Esq., of Baylham, co. Suffolk,

Elizabeth Andrews, m., first, Thomas Windsor (Wyndsore), Esq., of Stanwell, s. and h. of Miles de Wyndsore, and his

196

wife Joan, presumably dau. of Walter Green, Esq., of Bridgenorth,

SIR ANDREWS DE WINDSOR, 1st Baron Windsor, K.B., of Stanwell, a Knight Banneret, &c., m. Elizabeth Blount, dau. of William Blount, Knight of the Shire for Derby in 1417, and his wife, Margaret, (her first husband), dau. of Thomas de Echyngham, of Echyngham (now Etchingham), by his wife, Margaret, believed to be a dau. of Reginald West, Lord De La Warr,

EDITH DE WINDSOR, m. George Ludlow, Esq., of Hill Deverell, co. Wilts, High Sheriff of Wiltshire in 1567, d. about 1580, will proved Feb. 4, 1580,

THOMAS LUDLOW, of Denton (or Dinton), and Baycliffe, d. at Dinton, about 1607, will proved Jan. 1608; m. Jane Pyle, (will proved July 8, 1650), dau of Thomas Pyle, and sister of Sir Gabriel Pyle,

GABRIEL LUDLOW, Esq., Bencher in c. 1637; believed to have been appointed "Particular Receiver of the Duchy of Lancaster Possessions in Norfolk," resigned about 1639; d. about 1639; m. Phyllis,

SARAH LUDLOW, d. in co. Lancaster, Va., about 1668; m., (his 3rd or 4th wife), Colonel John Carter, of "Corotoman," Lancaster County, Va., member of the Va. House of Burgesses and of the Governor's Councli,

COLONEL ROBERT CARTER, of "Corotoman," called "King Carter," b. about 1663; d. 1732; Member and Speaker of the Va. House of Burgesses, Councillor and Acting Governor, &c.; m., about 1688, Judith Armistead, dau. of Colonel John Armistead, of "Hesse," Gloucester County, Va.,

ELIZABETH CARTER, b. about 1688; d. at Williamsburg, Va., about 1721; m., 2ndly, Dr. George Nicholas, of the Royal Navy, d. at Williamsburg, Va., about 1734,

JUDGE ROBERT CARTER NICHOLAS, of Hanover County, Va., b. at Williamsburg, about 1726; d. there about 1788; Treasurer of Va., and Presiding Judge of the Court of Appeals of Va., &c.; m. Ann Cary, dau. of Colonel William Cary, of "Celey's," Elizabeth City County, Va.,

CAPTAIN LEWIS VALENTINE NICHOLAS, of "Alta Vista," Albemarle County, Va., b. at Williamsburg, Va., about 1766; d.

at "Alta Vista," 1840; m. Frances Harris, dau. of Major William Harris,

SARAH NELSON NICHOLAS, b. at "Alta Vista," June 8, 1804; d. at "Locust Shades," Albemarle County, Va., Oct. 13, 1863; m., May 16, 1820, John Harris Coleman, b. at "Oak Grove," Albemarle County, Va., Dec. 7, 1798; d. at "Locust Shades," Dec. 25, 1870,

ANN CARY COLEMAN, b. at "Locust Shades," May 18, 1840; d. at "Shirland," Albemarle County, Va., Dec. 27, 1921; m., Sept. 20, 1866, James Nelson Moon, b. at "Mt. Ayr," Albemarle County, Va., Dec. 15, 1836; d. at "Shirland," Sept. 20, 1898,

FRANCES MOON, b. at "Shirland," near Scottsville, Albemarle County, Va., Aug. 20, 1877; Dame Companion of the Order of the Crown of Charlemagne; B.A., M.A., Ph.D.; Member of D.A.R., D.A.C., U.D.C., First Families of Virginia, &c.; m., July 14, 1898, Dr. Charles Shannon Butts, of Greenville, W. Va., d. 1915. Issue:

    1.) CHARLES SHANNON BUTTS II, D.D.S., b. Oct. 17, 1901; m., 1928, Vera Hickman, of Oakland, Fla., and have issue:

        a) CHARLES SHANNON BUTTS III, b. Mar. 23, 1938.

MANCHESTER

EDWARD III, King of England, m. Philippa of Hainault,

LIONEL, "of Antwerp," Duke of Clarence, K. G., Earl of Ulster, Chief Governor of Ireland, b. Nov. 29, 1338; d. Oct. 17, 1368; m., first, Sept. 9, 1342, Elizabeth, b. July 6, 1332; d. 1363; only dau. and h. of William de Burgh, 3rd Earl of Ulster, and his wife Maud, dau. of Henry, Earl of Lancaster,

PHILIPPA, only dau. and h., b. Aug. 16, 1355; m., 1368, Edmund de Mortimer, Earl of March, Lord Mortimer, b. Feb. 1, 1351/2; d. Dec. 27, 1381,

ELIZABETH DE MORTIMER, b. at Usk, Feb. 12, 1370/1; d. Apr. 20, 1417; m., first, 1379, Sir Henry Percy, Lord Percy, K.G., K.B., surnamed "Hotspur," b. May 20, 1364; d. July 21, 1403,

HENRY DE PERCY, cr. in Parliament, Mar. 16, 1415/6, Earl of Northumberland, Constable of England, etc., b. Feb. 3, 1392/3; slain at the first battle of St. Albans, May 22, 1455; m., 1414, Eleanor, widow of Richard Le Despenser, (son of Thomas, Earl of Gloucester), and dau. of Ralph de Neville, Earl of Westmorland, and his second wife, Joan Beaufort, sister of the half-blood of King Henry IV,

KATHERINE DE PERCY, b. May 28, 1423; m., 1458/9, Edmund de Grey, Lord Grey of Ruthin, Earl of Kent, b. Oct. 26, 1416; d. May 22, 1490; s. and h. of Sir John de Grey, K.G., and his wife Constance, dau. of John Holand, Duke of Exeter,

ANNE, m., (his first wife), John Grey, Lord Grey of Wilton, d. Apr. 3, 1499, s. and h. of Reynold Grey, Lord Grey of Wilton, and his wife Thomasine (or Tacine), natural dau. of John Beaufort, Duke of Somerset,

EDMUND GREY, Lord Grey of Wilton, d. May 5, 1511; m., 1505, Florence, 1st dau. and co-h. of Sir Ralph Hastings, of Harrowdon, Northants, and of Kirby, co. Leicester, (younger brother of William, Lord Hastings),

ELIZABETH, d. Dec. 29, 1559; m. John Brydges, Baron Chandos of Sudeley, b. Mar. 9, 1491/2; d. Apr. 12, 1557.

EDMUND BRYDGES, 2nd Baron Chandos of Sudeley, K.G., d. Mar. 11, 1572/3; m., c 1548, Dorothy, d. Oct. 31, 1605, 5th dau. of Edmund Bray, Lord Bray, and his wife Jane, dau. and h. of Sir Richard Halighwell, or Halywell, of Holwell,

GILES BRYDGES, 3rd Baron Chandos of Sudeley, d. Feb. 21, 1593/4; m. Frances, d. Sept. 12, 1623, 5th dau. of Edward Clinton, 1st Earl of Lincoln, and his second wife, Ursula, dau. of William Stourton, Baron Stourton,

CATHERINE BRYDGES, d. Jan. 29, 1656/7; m., Feb. 26, 1608/9, Francis Russell, Earl of Bedford, Baron Russell of Thornhaugh, b. 1593; d. May 9, 1641; only s. and h. of William, Lord Russell of Thornhaugh, and his wife Elizabeth, dau. and h. of Henry Long,

CATHERINE, d. c 1676; m., c 1630, Robert Greville, Baron Brooke of Beauchamps Court, b. 1607; d. Mar. 2, 1642/3,

ROBERT GREVILLE, Baron Brooke of Beauchamps Court, d. Feb. 17, 1676/7; m. Ann, d. 1690/1, dau. and eventually sole h. of John Dodington, of Breamore, Hants,

DODINGTON, youngest dau. and co-h., b. Feb. 20, 1671/2; d. Feb. 6, 1720/1; m., 1690/1, Charles Montagu, Earl of Manchester, Viscount Mandeville; cr. Duke of Manchester, Apr. 28, 1719; b. c 1662; d. Jan. 20, 1721/2; 1st surviving s. of Robert Montagu, Earl of Manchester, and his wife Anne, dau. of Sir Christopher Yelverton, 1st Bart., of Easton Mauduit, Northants,

ROBERT MONTAGU, 3rd Duke of Manchester, Earl of Manchester, b. c 1710; d. May 10, 1762; m., Apr. 3, 1735, Harriet, d. Feb. 25, 1755, dau. and co-h. of Edmund Dunch, of Little Wittenham, Berks, and his wife Elizabeth, dau. of Colonel Charles Godfrey and Arabella, his wife, sister of John Churchill, 1st Duke of Marlborough,

GEORGE MONTAGU, 4th Duke of Manchester, Earl of Manchester, b. Apr. 6, 1737; d. Sept. 2, 1788; m., Oct. 23, 1762, Elizabeth, d. June 26, 1832, 1st dau. of Sir James Dashwood, 2nd Bart., of Kirtlington Park, Oxon, and his wife Elizabeth, dau. of Edward Spencer, of Rendlesham, co. Suffolk,

WILLIAM MONTAGU, 5th Duke of Manchester, Earl of Manchester, b. Oct. 21, 1771; d. at Rome, Mar. 18, 1843; Governor of Jamaica, 1808-27; m. Oct. 7, 1793, Susan, b. Feb. 2, 1774; d. Aug. 26, 1828; 3rd dau. of Alexander, 4th Duke of Gordon, and his wife Jane, dau. of Sir William Maxwell, 3rd Bart.,

GEORGE MONTAGU, 6th Duke of Manchester, Earl of Manchester, b. July 9, 1799; d. Oct. 2, 1893; m., first, Oct. 8, 1822, Millicent, b. Jan. 25, 1798; d. Nov. 21, 1848; only dau. of Brigadier-General Robert Bernard Sparrow, of Brampton Park, Hunts, and his wife Olivia, 1st dau. of Arthur Acheson, 1st Earl of Gosford,

WILLIAM DROGO MONTAGU, 7th Duke of Manchester, Earl of Manchester, b. Oct. 15, 1823; d. at Naples, Mar. 22, 1890; m., July 22, 1852, Louisa Frederica Augusta, Countess von Alten, b. Jan. 15, 1832; d. July 15, 1911; dau. of Charles Francis Victor, Count von Alten, of Hanover, and his wife Hermina de Schminke,

GEORGE VICTOR DROGO MONTAGU, 8th Duke of Manchester, Earl of Manchester, b. June 17, 1853; d. Aug. 18, 1892; m., May 22, 1876, at Grace Church, New York, N. Y., Consuelo, d. Nov. 20, 1909, dau. of Antonio Yznaga Del Valle, of Ravenswood, La., of New York, and of Cuba,

WILLIAM ANGUS DROGO MONTAGU, 9th Duke of Manchester, Earl of Manchester, Viscount Mandeville, Baron Montagu of Kimbolton, etc., P.C., J.P. and D.L. co. Armagh; served in the World War, 1914-18; m., first, at London, Nov. 14, 1900, Helena Zimmerman, of Cincinnati, Ohio, only dau. of Eugene Zimmerman, of Cincinnati, (marriage dissolved by divorce, 1931, and the Duchess m., 1937, Arthur George Keith-Falconer, 11th Earl of Kintore); m., secondly, Dec. 17, 1931, Kathleen Dawes. Issue by first marriage, among others:

1.) ALEXANDER GEORGE FRANCIS DROGO MONTAGU, Viscount Mandeville, Lieutenant-Commander R.N., b. Oct. 2, 1902; m., May 5, 1927, Nell, dau. of Sydney Vere Stead, of Melbourne, Australia, and have issue:

a) SIDNEY ARTHUR ROBIN GEORGE DROGO MONTAGU, Lord Montagu of Kimbolton, b. Feb. 5, 1929.

2.) LORD EDWARD EUGENE FERNANDO MONTAGU, b. July 26, 1906; m., first, Aug. 10, 1929, Norah Margaret Macfarlane Potter (marriage dissolved by divorce, **Aug. 25, 1937**) ; m., secondly, Aug. 28, 1937, Dorothy Peters.

Issue by first marriage:

    a) RODERICK EDWARD ALEXANDER MONTAGU, b. June 1, 1930.

3.) LADY ELLEN MILICENT LOUISE MONTAGU, b. Jan. 5, 1908; m., 1936, Herman Martin Hofer.

MARLBOROUGH

EDWARD IV, King of England, m. Elizabeth Wydeville (Woodville),

See Page 224

CATHERINE COCHRANE, d. at Bath, Mar. 15, 1786; m., Jan. 5/7, 1728/9, (his 2nd wife), Alexander Stewart, 6th Earl of Galloway, &c.,

JOHN STEWART, 7th Earl of Galloway, Lord Garlies, K.T.; cr. Baron Stewart of Garlies, June 6, 1796; b. Mar. 15, 1735/6; d. Nov. 13, 1806; m., 2ndly, June 13, 1764, Anne, d. Jan. 8, 1830, 2nd dau. of Sir James Dashwood, 2nd Bart., of Kirtlington, by Elizabeth, dau. and co-h. of Edward Spencer, of Rendlesham, Suffolk, and had Susan, b. Apr. 10, 1767; d. Apr. 2, 1841, who m., Sept. 15, 1791, George Spencer, afterwards Spencer-Churchill, 5th Duke of Marlborough, and,

GEORGE STEWART, 8th Earl of Galloway, Lord Garlies, Baron Stewart of Garlies, K.T., b. Mar. 24, 1768; d. Mar. 27, 1834; m., Apr. 18, 1797, Jane Paget, b. Sept. 1, 1774; d. June 30, 1842; sister of Henry William Paget, 1st Marquess of Anglesey, and dau. of Henry Paget, 1st Earl of Uxbridge,

JANE STEWART, b. Mar. 29, 1798; d. Oct. 12, 1844; m., Jan. 13, 1819, her cousin, (his 1st wife), George Spencer-Churchill, 6th Duke of Marlborouh, &c., b. Dec. 27, 1793; d. July 1, 1857,

JOHN WINSTON SPENCER-CHURCHILL, 7th Duke of Marlborough, K.G., &c., P.C., Lord Lieutenant of Oxon, Viceroy of Ireland, &c., b. June 2, 1822; d. July 5, 1883; m., July 12, 1843, Frances Anne Emily, b. Apr. 15, 1822; d. Apr. 16, 1899; dau. of Charles William Vane, 3rd Marquess of Londonderry, by his 2nd wife, Frances Anne Emily, dau. and h. of Sir Henry Vane-Tempest, Bart.,

GEORGE CHARLES SPENCER-CHURCHILL, 8th Duke of Marlborough, &c., b. May 13, 1844; d. Nov. 9, 1892; m., first, Nov. 8, 1869, Albertha Frances Anne, b. July 29, 1847, 6th dau. of James Hamilton, 1st Duke of Abercorn, by Louisa Jane, dau. of John Russell, 6th Duke of Bedford.

CHARLES RICHARD JOHN SPENCER-CHURCHILL, 9th Duke of Marlborough, &c., K.G., P.C., Paymaster General of the Forces, 1899-1902; Under Secretary of State for the Colonies, 1903-05; Lt.-Col. attached to General Staff, 1914-18; b. Nov. 13, 1871; d. 1934; m., first, at New York, N. Y., Nov. 6, 1896, Consuelo, dau. of William Kissam Vanderbilt, of New York, (marriage dissolved by divorce, 1921); m., 2ndly, June 25, 1921, Gladys, dau. of Edward Parke Deacon, of Boston.

Issue by first wife:

JOHN ALBERT EDWARD WILLIAM SPENCER-CHURCHILL, 10th Duke of Marlborough, Earl of Marlborough, Marquess of Blanford, Earl of Sunderland, Baron Spencer, Baron Churchill, Prince of Mindelheim in Swabia, &c.; Capt. 1st Life Guards, served in first World War, 1914-18; b. Sept. 18, 1897; b., Feb. 17, 1920. Alexandra Mary Hilda, dau. of Henry Arthur Cadogan, Viscount Chelsea, by his wife, Mildred Cecilia Harriet, dau. of Henry Gerard Sturt, 1st Baron Alington of Crichel, and have issue three daughters and,

JOHN GEORGE VANDERBILT HENRY SPENCER-CHURCHILL, Marquess of Blandford, b. Apr. 13, 1926.

Norfolk

Edward I, King of England, m., 2ndly, Princess Margaret, dau. of Philippe III, King of France,

See Page 146

Thomas Howard, Sheriff of Norfolk and Suffolk 1476; M.P. for Norfolk, 1478; K.B., P.C. and K.G.; cr. Earl of Surrey, June 28, 1483; cr. Earl Marshal of England for life, 1510; cr. Duke of Norfolk, 1513/4; b. 1443; d. May 21, 1524; m., first, Apr. 30, 1472, Elizabeth, widow of Sir Humphrey Bourchier, and dau. and h. of Sir Frederick Tylney, of Ashwellthorpe, co. Norfolk,

Thomas Howard, Lord Howard, Earl of Surrey, Duke of Norfolk, Earl Marshal of England, b. 1473; d. Aug. 25, 1554; Lord High Admiral, &c.; attainted in 1546/7, and fully restored in 1553; m., 2ndly, 1512/3, Elizabeth, d. Nov. 30, 1558, dau. of Edward Stafford, Duke of Buckingham, by Eleanor, dau. of Henry Percy, Earl of Northumberland,

Sir Henry Howard, Earl of Surrey, K.B., K.G., b. 1517; executed Jan. 19, 1546/7; he acted as Earl Marshal at the trial of Queen Anne Boleyn, May 15, 1536; m., 1531/2, Frances de Vere, d. June 30, 1577, dau. of John de Vere, Earl of Oxford, by Elizabeth, dau. and h. of Sir John Trussell,

Thomas Howard, Earl of Surrey, 4th Duke of Norfolk, and Earl Marshal of England, K.B., K.G., b. Mar. 10, 1537/8; restored in blood and honors, Sept. 2, 1553; beheaded June 2, 1572; m., first, 1555, Mary, b. 1540; d. Aug. 25, 1557; dau. of Henry FitzAlan, Earl of Arundel, by his first wife, Catherine, dau. of Thomas Grey, Marquess of Dorset.

Philip Howard, Earl of Arundel, b. June 28, 1557; inherited in right of his mother the feudal Earldom of Arundel, &c., and was placed in Parliament as Premier Earl; m. Anne, sister and co-h. of George, 5th Lord Dacre of Gillesland,

Thomas Howard, Earl of Arundel, Earl of Surrey, and Lord Mautravers; cr. Earl of Norfolk, June 6, 1644; b. July 7,

1585; d. 1646; m. Alathea, dau. and eventually sole h. of Gilbert, 7th Earl of Shrewsbury,

HENRY FREDERICK HOWARD, Earl of Arundel, Surrey and Norfolk, &c., b. Aug. 15, 1608; d. Apr. 17, 1652; m., 1625/6, Elizabeth Stewart, b. July 17, 1610; d. Jan. 23, 1673/4; dau. of Esme, 3rd Duke of Lennox, by Catherine, dau. and h. of Gervase, Lord Clifton of Leighton-Bromswold,

BERNARD, Lord Howard, b. Oct. 16, 1641; d. Oct. 21, 1717; m., June 14, 1672, Katherine, d. Apr. 8, 1727, dau. and co-h. of George Tattershall, of Finchampstead, Berks, and widow of Sir Richard Lichford,

BERNARD HOWARD, of Glossop, b. Mar. 14, 1674; d. Apr. 22, 1735; m., June 24, 1710, Anne Roper, d. 1744, dau. of Christopher, Lord Teynham,

HENRY HOWARD, of Glossop, co. Derby, b. Apr. 9, 1713; d. Nov. 11, 1787; m., Oct. 30, 1764, Juliana, d. June 12, 1808, dau. of Sir William Molyneux, Bart., of Weollow, Notts,

BERNARD EDWARD HOWARD, Earl of Arundel, Surrey and Norfolk, &c., Duke of Norfolk and Earl Marshal of England, b. Nov. 21, 1765; d. Mar. 16, 1842; m., Apr. 24, 1789, Elizabeth Balasyse, b. Jan. 17, 1770, 3rd dau. and co-h. of Henry, Earl of Fauconberg of Newborough, by his first wife, Charlotte, dau. of Sir Matthew Lamb, 1st Bart.,

HENRY CHARLES HOWARD, Duke of Norfolk, Earl of Arundel, Surrey and Norfolk, and Earl Marshal of England, K.G., P.C., b. Aug. 12, 1791; d. Feb. 16, 1856; m., Dec. 27, 1814, Charlotte Sophia, b. June 8, 1788; d. July 7, 1870; dau. of George Granville (Leveson-Gower), 1st Duke of Sutherland, by Elizabeth, *suo jure* Countess of Sutherland,

HENRY GRANVILLE FITZALAN HOWARD, Duke of Norfolk, Earl of Arundel, Surrey and Norfolk, Earl Marshal, &c., b. Nov. 7, 1815; d. Nov. 25, 1860; m., June 19, 1839, Augusta Mary Minna Catherine, b. Aug. 1, 1821; d. Mar. 22, 1886; youngest dau. of Edmund Lyons, 1st Baron Lyons of Christchurch, by Augusta Louisa, 2nd dau. of Capt. Josiah Rogers,

HENRY FITZALAN HOWARD, Duke of Norfolk, Earl of Arundel, Surrey and Norfolk, Premier Duke and Premier Earl, Earl Marshal, &c., K.G., G.C.V.O., P.C., b. Dec. 27, 1847; d. Feb. 11, 1917; m., 2ndly, Feb. 15, 1904, Gwendolen Mary, *suo jure* Baroness Herries, b. Jan. 11, 1877, elder dau. of Marmaduke Francis, Baron Herries, by Angela Mary Charlotte, 2nd dau. of Edward George, Lord Howard of Glossop,

BERNARD MARMADUKE FITZALAN HOWARD, Duke of Norfolk, Earl of Arundel, Surrey and Norfolk, Lord Mautravers, Lord FitzAlan, Clun and Oswaldestre, Premier Duke and Premier Earl, Earl Marshal and Hereditary Marshal of England, and Chief Butler of England, K.G., P.C., b. at Arundel Castle, May 31, and bapt. June 1, 1908; succeeded his father, 1917; m., 1937, Hon. Lavinia Mary Strutt, eldest dau. of Algernon Henry Strutt, 3rd Baron Belper, and granddau. of the 2nd Baron Belper and his wife Lady Margaret Coke, dau. of Thomas William Coke, 2nd Earl of Leicester of Holkham, &c., and have issue.

Nourse—Cooke—Winn—Hall—Probert

Edward III, King of England, m. Philippa of Hainault,

Prince Lionel, "of Antwerp," Duke of Clarence, Earl of Ulster, K.G., Chief Governor of Ireland, &c., b. at Antwerp, Nov. 29, 1338; d. at Alba, Piedmont, Italy, Oct. 17, 1368; m., first, Elizabeth, b. July 6, 1332; d. 1363; only dau. and heiress of William de Burgh, 3rd Earl of Ulster, Lord of Connaught, &c., by his wife Maud, dau. of Henry, Earl of Lancaster, (son of Edmund, styled "Crouchback," Earl of Lancaster, Earl of Leicester, and grandson of Henry III, King of England, by Eleanor, dau. and co-h. of Raymond Berenger, Count of Provence),

Philippa, only dau. and heiress, b. Aug. 16, 1355; m., 1368, Edmund de Mortimer, Lord Mortimer, 3rd Earl of March, Lord of Ulster and of Connaught, Lord of Clare in Suffolk, b. Feb. 1, 1351/2; d. Dec. 27, 1381,

Roger de Mortimer, 4th Earl of March, Earl of Ulster, Lord Mortimer, b. Apr. 11, 1374; d. July 20, 1398; m., about 1388, (her first husband), Eleanor, d. Oct. 6/18, 1405, dau. of Thomas de Holand, Earl of Kent,

Anne de Mortimer, m., (his first wife), Prince Richard, styled "of Conisburgh," or "of York," Earl of Cambridge, Almoner of England, &c., beheaded Aug. 5/6, 1415, son of Edmund styled "of Langley," Earl of Cambridge, Duke of York, K.G., (by his first wife Isabel, dau. and co-heiress of Pedro the Cruel, King of Castile and Leon), and grandson of Edward III, King of England, by Philippa of Hainault, dau. of William, Count of Hainault and Holland, by his wife Joanna, dau. of Charles, Count of Valois, and granddau. of Philippe III, King of France,

Prince Richard, Earl of Cambridge, Duke of York, sometime Regent of France, K.G., &c.; d. Dec. 30, 1460, slain at the battle of Wakefield; m. Cecily, dau. of Ralph de Neville. 1st Earl of Westmorland, K.G.,

Princess Anne (sister of Edward IV, King of England), b. Aug. 10, 1439; d. Jan. 12/4, 1475/6; m., first, 1447, Henry Holand (or Holland), Duke of Exeter, Earl of Huntingdon, whom she divorced on Nov. 12, 1472; m., 2ndly, Thomas Seint Leger (or Selenger), Knt.,

Anne Seint Leger, d. May 21, 1526; m., about 1490, Sir George Manners, of Belvoir and Helmsley, otherwise Hamlake, Lord Ros (or Roos), &c., d. Oct. 27, 1513,

Thomas Manners, Lord Ros (or Roos), K.G.; cr. Earl of Rutland, June 18, 1525; d. Sept. 20, 1543; m., 2ndly, Eleanor, dau. of Sir William Paston, of Paston, co. Norfolk,

Frances Manners, m., (his first wife), Henry de Neville, 6th Lord Abergavenny (Bergavenny), K.B., d. Feb. 10, 1586/7; son of George de Neville, 5th Lord Albergavenny, K.G., by his third wife Mary, dau. of Edward de Stafford, Duke of Buckingham, by Eleanor, dau. of Henry Percy, Earl of Northumberland,

Mary de Neville, *suo jure* Baroness Le Despenser, b. Mar. 25, 1554; d. June 28, 1626; m., Dec. 12, 1574, (his second wife), Sir Thomas Fane, of Badsell, co. Kent, d. Mar. 13, 1588/9,

Francis Fane, cr. Earl of Westmorland and Baron Burghersh, Dec. 29, 1624; Lord Le Despenser, K.B.; d. Mar. 23, 1628/9; m., 1599, Mary, dau. and eventually sole heiress of Sir Anthony Mildmay, of Apethorpe, co. Northampton,

Elizabeth Fane, m., 2ndly, William Cope, Esq., of Icome,

Rachel Elizabeth Cope, m. Thomas Geers, Serjent-at-Law,

Elizabeth Geers, m. Sir William Gregory, Knt.,

Elizabeth Gregory, m. John Nourse, Esq.,

James Nourse, Esq., m. Sarah La Fouace,

Catherine Burton Nourse, b. at London, England, May 9, 1759; d. at Lexington, Ky., June 1833; m., April 30, 1778, (his second wife), John Cooke, d. in Woodford County, Ky., about 1817, son of Mordecai Cooke and his wife Elizabeth, dau. of Francis Whiting,

Maria Bull Cooke, b. in Berkeley County, Va., Mar. 4, 1784; d. in Hickman County, Ky., Oct. 2, 1853; m. in Woodford County, Ky., Sept. 15, 1811, Thomas Winn, b. in Hanover

County, Va., about 1786; d. in Hickman County, Ky., July 7, 1862,

MARTHA ANN WINN, b. in Woodford County, Ky., May 12, 1820; d. in Hickman County, Ky., Oct. 26, 1907; m., 2ndly, In Ky., Feb. 26, 1856, William Keel Hall, b. at Trenton, Tenn., Jan. 25, 1827; d. in Columbus, Ky., April 28, 1877,

JOHN FRANKLIN HALL, b. in Dyer County, Tenn., May 6, 1860; d. at Louisville, Ky., April 4, 1930; m. at Fulton, Ky., Oct. 4, 1884, (her second husband), Virginia Eleanor (Greif) Robinson, b. at Paducah, Ky., Aug. 4, 1858; d. at Detroit, Mich., Feb. 19, 1934,

MARTHA BESS HALL, only child, b. at Union City, Tenn., Mar. 16, 1886; Dame Companion and Delegate in Michigan of the Order of the Crown of Charlemagne; Member of Society of Daughters of Colonial Wars, D.A.R., U.D.C., Huguenot Society of Michigan, U.S.D. 1812, &c.; m. at Louisville, Ky., April 3, 1910, Sidney Chinnock Probert, b. at Cleveland, Ohio, Sept. 4, 1888. Issue:

1.) SIDNEY HALL PROBERT, b. at Springfield, Ohio, May 15, 1914;

2.) ANNA VIRGINIA PROBERT, b. at Detroit, Mich., July 25, 1918;

3.) MARTHA ELIZABETH PROBERT, b. at Detroit, Mich., Oct. 17, 1920; m. at Napoleon, Ohio, Oct. 12, 1940, Douglas Charles McNally, b. Apr. 30, 1921, son of Charles E. and Gertrude (Campbell) McNally. Issue:

a) SUSAN ELIZABETH McNALLY, b. May 22, 1941.

READE—WARNER—LEWIS—COBB—JACKSON—
GRANT—SLATON

CHARLEMAGNE

See Page 133

ROGER DE QUINCY, 2nd Earl of Winchester, Constable of Scotland; m., first, Helen, dau. and co-heiress of Alan, Lord of Galloway, Constable of Scotland,

ELIZABETH (often referred to as Isabel) DE QUINCY, m. Alexander Comyn, Earl of Buchan, Constable of Scotland, Justiciar in Scotland, d. 1290; son and heir of William Comyn, Earl of Buchan, Justiciar, by Margaret, Countess of Buchan.

ELIZABETH COMYN, d. before Feb. 17, 1328/9; m. Gilbert de Umfreville, Earl of Angus, Lord Umfreville, Governor of Angus and of Dundee and Forfar Castles, b. about 1244; d. before Oct. 13, 1307; son and heir of Gilbert de Umfreville, Lord of Prudhoe and Redesdale in Northumberland, and his wife, (her 2nd husband), Maud, *suo jure* Countess of Angus, dau. and heiress of Malcolm, Earl of Angus, and his wife, Mary, dau. and heiress of Sir Humphrey Berkeley,

ROBERT DE UMFREVILLE, Earl of Angus, Lord Umfreville, d. 1325; m., first, 1303, Lucy, dau. and in her issue heiress of Sir Philip de Kyme, 1st Lord Kyme, by his wife Joan, dau. of Sir Hugh Le Bigod, Chief Justiciar of England,

ELIZABETH DE UMFREVILLE, m. Gilbert de Boroughdon or Borrowdon, Sheriff of Northumberland 1323-24 and 1339-41,

ALIENOR (OR ELEANOR), *de jure* Baroness Kyme, dau. and heiress, m. Henry Tailboys, d. Feb. 23, 1368/9, son of William Tailboys,

SIR WALTER TAILBOYS, Lord Kyme, Sheriff of co. Lincoln in 1389, d. Sept. 20/1, 1417; m. Margaret,

WALTER TAILBOYS, *de jure* Lord Kyme, Sheriff of co. Lincoln in 1423, Justice of the Peace of co. Lincoln 1442-43, d. Apr. 13, 1444; m. Alice, d. 1448, widow of Sir Henry Cheyney, Knt., and dau. of Sir Humphrey Stafford, Knt,

211

SIR WILLIAM TAILBOYS, of Kyme, co. Lincoln, *de jure* Lord Kyme, b. about 1415; beheaded about May 26, 1464; m. Elizabeth, d. Feb. 14, 1490/1, dau. of William, Lord Bonville,

SIR ROBERT TAILBOYS, Knt., of Kyme and of Redesdale, *de jure* Lord Kyme, M. P. for co. Lincoln in 1472 and 1477/8, Sheriff of co. Lincoln in 1480, d. Jan. 30, 1494/5; m. Elizabeth, dau. of Sir John Heron,

SIR GEORGE TAILBOYS, *de jure* Lord Kyme, d. Sept. 21, 1538; m., 2ndly, before Apr. 1493, Elizabeth, dau. of Sir William Gascoigne,

ANNE TAILBOYS, m., first, Sir Edward Dymoke, of Schrivelsby, co. Lincoln, Sheriff of co. Lincoln about 1536, Champion to Queen Elizabeth, d. about 1566; son and heir of Sir Robert Dymoke, Knight Banneret, the King's Champion,

FRANCES DYMOKE, m. Sir Thomas Windebank, Knt., of Haynes Hall, Hurst Parish, Berkshire,

MILDRED WINDEBANK, m., about 1600, (his 2nd or 3rd wife), Robert Reade, of Linkenholt Manor,

COLONEL GEORGE READE, m. Elizabeth, dau. and co-heiress of Captain Nicholas Martiau,

MILDRED READE, m. Colonel Augustine Warner, Jr., of Warner Hall, Gloucester County, Va.,

ELIZABETH WARNER, b. Nov. 24, 1672; d. Feb. 5, 1710/20; m. Major John Lewis, b. Nov. 30, 1669; d. Nov. 14, 1725; Member and Speaker of the Va. House of Burgesses, Member of the Governor's Council in 1715,

COLONEL CHARLES LEWIS, of "The Byrd," Gloucester County, Va., d. about 1779; m. Mary, dau. of John Howell.

MAJOR HOWELL LEWIS, of "The Byrd," and afterwards of Granville County, N.C., b. Sept. 13, 1731; d. about 1814; State Senator in N.C.; m., his cousin, Mary Isabel, b. at Fredericksburg, Va., June 10, 1733; d. in Granville County, N. C., about 1813, dau. of Colonel Henry Willis, of Fredericksburg, Va.,

MILDRED LEWIS, m. in Granville County, N. C., Sept. 6, 1769, Major John Cobb, of "The Sand Hills," Augusta, Ga., son of Colonel John Cobb and his wife Susannah, dau. of Admiral John Addison of the British Navy,

MILDRED LEWIS COBB, d. Mar. 3, 1853; m., about 1808, Colonel William Henry Jackson, of Savannah, Ga., b. June 3, 1786; d. Aug. 8, 1875; State Senator, First Alumnus of the University of Ga., and Trustee for 40 years; son of Major General James Jackson, of Savannah, Ga., Governor of Ga., &c., and his wife Mary Charlotte Young,

MARTHA COBB JACKSON, b. Jan. 29, 1816; d. Sept. 26, 1893; m., Dec. 23, 1834, Colonel John Thomas Grant, b. Dec. 13, 1813; d. Jan. 18, 1887; son of Daniel Grant, of Athens, Ga.,

CAPTAIN WILLIAM DANIEL GRANT, of Atlanta, Ga., b. Aug. 6/16, 1837; d. Nov. 7, 1901; m., June 13, 1866, Sarah Francis Ried, b. Feb. 22, 1839; d. Sept. 2, 1920; dau. of William Ried. Issue:

1.) JOHN WILLIAM GRANT, b. July 26. 1867; deceased; m., April 11, 1893, Annie M. Inman, and had issue.

2.) SARAH FRANCES GRANT, b. at West Point, Troupe County, Ga., Jan. 1, 1870; Member of National Society of the Colonial Dames of America in the State of Ga. (Chairman of Atlanta Town Committee in 1939-40), D.A.C., U.D.C., D.A.R. (Charter Member) &c.; m., first, Colonel Thomas Cobb Jackson; m., 2ndly, July 12, 1898, John Marshall Slaton, b. in Meriwether County, Ga., Dec. 25, 1866; M.A., Knight of the Legion of Honor of France; Member of the Ga. House of Representatives, 1896-1909 (Speaker 4 years); Member of Ga. State Senate, 1909-13 (President 4 years); Acting Governor of Ga., 1911-12, and Governor 1913-15; son of William Franklin Slaton and his wife Nancy Jane Martin.

READE—WARNER—LEWIS—DALE—ROBERTSON—ANDERSON

ROGER DE QUINCY, 2nd Earl of Winchester

See Page 212

COLONEL CHARLES LEWIS, of "The Byrd," co. Gloucester, Va., m. Mary Howell,

ANNE LEWIS, b. Mar. 2, 1733; m. Edmund Taylor, b. July 5, 1723; d. about 1808; son of John Taylor,

FRANCES TAYLOR, b. about 1763; d. Jan. 26, 1815; m. the Rev. Nathaniel Moore, of Granville County, N. C., afterwards of Columbia, Tenn.,

ANNE LEWIS MOORE, b. Nov. 3, 1796; d. Feb. 13, 1828; m., May 22, 1815, Edward Washington Dale, of Columbia, Tenn., b. Nov. 11, 1790; d. July 7, 1840,

ANNE LEWIS DALE, b. May 14, 1821; d. Feb. 17, 1888; m., Oct. 9, 1845, James Robertson, of Ayrshire, Scotland, b. Dec. 8, 1816; d. at Memphis, Tenn., May 26, 1898. Issue:

1.) JEAN ROBERTSON, b. Sept. 1, 1846; d. about 1923; m., Feb. 11, 1869, Col. Keller Anderson, of Memphis, b. Sept. 21, 1842; d. about 1918. Issue:

    a) CLAUDE DESHA ANDERSON, m. Mary Simmons, and had,

        i CLAUDE DESHA ANDERSON, Jr., b. Aug. 11, 1897.

    b) JEAN KELLER ANDERSON, b. at Memphis, Feb. 14, 1883; Member D.A.R., U.S.D. of 1812, &c.

2.) JAMES THOMAS ROBERTSON, m. Anne Bibb Wright. Issue:

MARY DALE ROBERTSON, m. Paul Burrus Benham.

Reade—Washington—Lewis—Stevens

Charlemagne
See Page 219

Maud de Lacy, d. 1288/9; m., 1237/8, (his second wife), Richard de Clare, Earl of Gloucester and Hertford, b. Aug. 4, 1222; d. July 15, 1262; son and heir of Gilbert de Clare, Earl of Gloucester and Hertford,

Sir Thomas de Clare, 2nd son, Crusader, d. in Ireland 1287/8; m. Julian, dau. of Sir Maurice FitzMaurice, Lord Justice of Ireland,

Maud de Clare, 2nd and youngest dau., d. 1326/7; m., first, 1295, Robert de Clifford, Lord Clifford, Governor of Nottingham Castle, Captain General of the Marches of Scotland, &c., b. about 1274; d. June 24, 1314; son and heir of Roger de Clifford, by Isabel, dau. and co-heiress of Robert de Vipont, Hereditary Sheriff of Westmorland,

Robert de Clifford, Lord Clifford, Sheriff of Westmorland, b. Nov. 5, 1305; d. May 20, 1344; m., June 1328, (her first husband), Isabel, d. July 25, 1362, dau. of Maurice de Berkeley, Lord Berkeley, and his first wife, Eve, dau. of Eudes La Zouche,

Roger de Clifford, Lord Clifford, Sheriff of Westmorland, Governor of Carlisle Castle, Knight Banneret, Warden of the East and West Marches; b. July 10, 1333; d. July 13, 1389; m. Maud, d. 1402/3, dau. of Thomas de Beauchamp, Earl of Warwick, by Catherine, dau. of Roger de Mortimer, 1st Earl of March,

Katherine de Clifford, d. Apr. 23, 1413; m. Ralph de Greystoke, Lord Greystoke and Lord FitzWilliam, Warden of the West Marches; Justice, Steward, and Keeper of the lordship of Annandale, &c.; b. 1353; d. Apr. 6, 1418; son and heir of William de Greystoke, Lord Greystoke and Lord FitzWilliam, and his 2nd wife, Joan, dau. of Sir Henry FitzHenry, of Ravensworth, by his wife, Joan, youngest dau. of

215

Sir Richard de Fourneux, of Carlton in Lindrick, Kingston, and Bothamsall, Notts, and Beighton, co. Derby,

MAUD DE GREYSTOKE, m. Eudo de Welles, eldest son of Sir John de Welles, of Gainsby, Lord Welles, presumably by his second wife, said to be Eleanor (Alienore) de Mowbray, eldest dau. of John de Mowbray, 4th Lord Mowbray of Axholme, by Elizabeth, *suo jure* Baroness Segrave, dau. and eventually heiress of John de Segrave, Lord Segrave, by his wife Margaret, eldest dau. of Thomas, "of Brotherton," Earl of Norfolk and Marshal of England (son of Edward I, King of England, by his 2nd wife, Margaret, dau. of Philippe III, King of France),

SIR LEO (or Lionel) DE WELLES, Lord Welles, Chief Governor of Ireland 1438-42; K.G.; slain at the battle of Towton, Mar. 29, 1461; m., first, about 1426, Joan (Joanne), dau. of Robert Waterton, of Waterton and Methley, co. York, and heiress of her brother, Sir Robert Waterton, Knt.,

MARGARET DE WELLES, d. before 1504, m. Sir Thomas Dymoke, Knt., of Schrivelsby, co. Lincoln, son of Sir Philip Dymoke,

SIR ROBERT DYMOKE, of Scrivelsby, Knight Banneret, m., 2ndly, Jane, dau. and heiress of John Sparrow,

SIR EDWARD DYMOKE, of Scrivelsby, Champion to Queen Elizabeth; m., (her first husband), Anne, dau. of Sir George Tailboys, *de jure* Lord Kyme, Sheriff of co. Lincoln, &c., and his 2nd wife, Elizabeth, dau. of Sir William Gascoigne,

FRANCES DYMOKE, m. Sir Thomas Windebank, Knt., of Haynes Hill, Hurst Parish, Berkshire,

MILDRED WINDEBANK, m., about 1600, (his 2nd or 3rd wife), Robert Reade, of Linkenholt Manor.

COLONEL GEORGE READE, b. about 1608; came to Virginia about 1637; d. about 1671; Acting Governor of the Colony, 1638, 1639; Burgess from James City County, 1649, and from York, 1655/6; Member of the Governor's Council, 1657-71; m. Elizabeth, dau. and co-heiress of Captain Nicholas Martiau, of York County, Va., Burgess and Justice, and his wife, Jane Berkeley,

MILDRED READE, m. Colonel Augustine Warner, Jr., of Warner Hall, Gloucester County, Va., Member and Speaker of the Va. House of Burgesses, &c., b. July 3, 1642/3; d. June

10/19, 1681; son of Captain Augustine Warner, Burgess, Member of the Council, &c.,

MILDRED WARNER, m., first, Captain Lawrence Washington, b. about 1659; d. 1697/8; son of Colonel John Washington, by his wife, Anne Pope, dau. of Lieutenant-Colonel Nathaniel Pope, of Charles County, Maryland,

CAPTAIN AUGUSTINE WASHINGTON, of Stafford County, Va., b. about 1694; d. Apr. 12, 1743; m., 2ndly, Mar. 6, 1730/1, Mary Ball, b. 1707/8; d. Aug. 25, 1789; dau. of Colonel Joseph Ball, of "Epping Forest," Lancaster County, Va.,

ELIZABETH "BETTY" WASHINGTON, (sister of General George Washington, 1st President of the United States), b. at "Wakefield," Westmoreland County, Va., June 20, 1733; d. at "Western View," Culpeper County, Va., Mar. 31, 1797; m. at Fredericksburg, Va., May 7, 1750, (his second wife), Colonel Fielding Lewis, of "Kenmore," near Fredericksburg, Spottsylvania County, Va., b. July 7, 1725; d. 1781/2; son of Colonel John Lewis, of "Warner Hall," Gloucester County, Va., by his wife, Frances Fielding, only dau. of Henry Fielding, of King and Queen County,

MAJOR LAWRENCE LEWIS, b. at "Kenmore," near Fredericksburg, Va., Apr. 4, 1767; d. at "Arlington," on the Potomac, Va., Nov. 20, 1839; m. at Mount Vernon, Va., Feb. 22, 1799, Eleanor Parke Custis, b. at "Abingdon," on the Potomac, Fairfax County, Va., Mar. 21, 1779; d. at "Audley," near Berryvile, Va., July 1852,

LORENZO LEWIS, b. at "Woodlawn," Fairfax County, Va., Nov. 13, 1803; d. at "Audley," near Berryville, Va., Aug. 27, 1847; m. at Philadelphia, Penn., June 6, 1827, Esther Maria Coxe, b. at Philadelphia, Aug. 10, 1804; d. at "Audley," June 23, 1885,

GEORGE WASHINGTON LEWIS, b. at Philadelphia, Feb. 12, 1829; d. at "Monterey," near Berryville, Va., Feb. 5, 1885; m. at Baltimore, Md., Mar. 25, 1852, Emily C. Johnson, b. at Baltimore, July 31, 1832; d. at Berryville, Va., Apr. 1, 1909,

EMILY C. LEWIS, b. at "Monterey," near Berryville, Va., Dec. 29, 1857; d. at Bedminster, N. J., Oct. 25, 1931; m. at Berryville Va., Oct. 28, 1879, Colonel Edwin A. Stevens, b. at Philadelphia, Mar. 14, 1858; d. at Washington, D. C., Mar.

8, 1918; son of Edwin A. Stevens and his wife Martha Bayard Dod, dau. of Professor the Reverend Albert Baldwin Dod, and granddau. of Daniel Dod, and great-granddau. of Capt. Lebbeus Dod (and his wife Mary Baldwin, dau. of Caleb Baldwin, and granddau. of Samuel Baldwin, and great-granddau. of John Baldwin and his wife Hannah Bruen, dau. of Obadiah Bruen, a descendant of the Emperor Charlemagne),

Colonel Basil Martiau Stevens, b. at Castle Point, Hoboken, N. J., Dec. 28, 1888; Companion First Class (Officer) and one of the Priors of the Order of the Crown of Charlemagne; Officer in U. S. A. during World War; Capt. Officers' Reserve Corps; Lieutenant-Colonel, Infantry, National Guard of N. J.; United States Commissoner for the District of N. J., 1932-35; Special Master in Chancery of N. J. and a Commissioner of the Supreme Court of N. J.; Member of the Order of the Founders and Patriots of America, Society of Colonial Wars in N. J. (Chancellor), S.A.R. (President of Montclair, N. J. Chapter), Order of Colonial Lords of Manors in America, M.O.W.W., American Legion, Officer's Reserve Association of the United States, Saint Nicholas Society of the City of New York, Huguenot Society of America, &c.; m. at New Castle, Penn., Oct. 28, 1913, Helen Clendenin Ward, b. at New Castle, Penn., Mar. 5, 1891, dau. of Edward Hadnett Ward (a descendant of Andrew Ward, who settled at Watertown, Mass. about 1632), and Mary E. Clendenin, his wife. Issue:

1.) Emily Custis Lewis Stevens, b. on Castle Point Terrace, Hoboken, N. J., May 22, 1915; Member of the Order of Colonial Lords of Manors in America;

2.) Edwin Augustus Stevens IV, b. at Bernardsville, N. J., Mar. 8, 1917; B.A., University of Colorado, 1941; Member of the Order of Colonial Lords of Manors in America.

St. Leger—Horsmanden—Byrd

CHARLEMAGNE

See Page 133

MARGARET DE BEAUMONT, m. Saier de Quincy, 1st Earl of Winchester,

ROBERT DE QUINCY, d. 1217; m. Hawise, Countess of Lincoln, d. 1242/3, sister of Ranulph "de Blundeville," Earl of Chester, 1st Earl of Lincoln, and dau. of Hugh, "of Kevelioc," Earl of Chester, Vicomte d'Avranches, and his wife Bertrade, dau. of Simon, Count d'Evreux,

MARGARET DE QUINCY, d. 1266; m. first, 1221, (his 2nd wife) John de Lacy, Earl of Lincoln, Constable of Chester, b. about 1192; d. July 22, 1240,

MAUD DE LACY, m., (his 2nd wife), Richard de Clare, Earl of Gloucester and Hertford, b. Aug. 4, 1222; d. at John de Criol's Manor of Ashenfield in Waltham, near Canterbury, July 15, 1262,

GILBERT DE CLARE, Earl of Clare, Hertford and Gloucester, b. Sept. 2, 1243; d. Dec. 7, 1295; m. 2ndly, 1290, Joan of Acre, d. April 23, 1307, dau. of Edward I, King of England,

ELEANOR (or Alianor) de Clare, m. first, 1306, Sir Hugh Le Despenser, Lord Despenser, hanged Nov. 24, 1326, son of Sir Hugh Le Despenser, of Loughborough, Arnesby, Parlington, Ryhall, Wycombe, Lord Le Despenser, and his wife Isabel, widow of Sir Patrick de Chaurces or Chaworces, and dau. of William de Beauchamp, Earl of Warwick, by Maud, dau. of Sir John FitzGeoffrey, of Shere and Fambridge,

SIR EDWARD LE DESPENSER, 2nd son of Buckland, Bucks, Eyworth; it is believed that he was killed in battle at Morlaix, Sept. 30, 1342; m. at Groby, April 20, 1335, Anne, d. Aug. 8, 1367, dau. of Sir William de Ferrers, Lord Ferrers of Groby,

SIR EDWARD LE DESPENSER, Lord le Despenser, K.G., b. Mar. 24, 1336; d. Nov. 11, 1375; m., 1354, Elizabeth, dau. and heiress of Sir Bartholomew de Burghersh, Lord Burghersh, of

219

Ewias Lacy, co. Hereford, and his first wife Cicely, dau. of
Sir Richard de Weyland, of Blaxhall and Cockfield, Suffolk,

THOMAS LE DESPENSER, Lord Le Despenser, K.G., b. Sept. 22,
1373; beheaded Jan. 13, 1399/1400; cr. Earl of Gloucester,
Sept. 29, 1397; m. Constance, d. Nov. 28, 1416, dau. of Edmund of Langley, Earl of Cambridge, afterwards Duke of
York,

ISABEL LE DESPENSER, b. July 26, 1400; d. Dec. 27, 1439; m.
first, July 27, 1411, Richard de Beauchamp, Lord of Abergavenny, Earl of Worcester, K.B., d. Mar. 18, 1421/2, son of
William de Beauchamp, Lord of Abergavenny, K.G., Justiciar of South Wales and Governor of Pembroke, and his
wife Joan, dau. of Richard FitzAlan, Earl of Arundel, by
Elizabeth, his wife, dau. of William de Bohun, Earl of Northampton,

ELIZABETH DE BEAUCHAMP, Baroness Abergavenny, only dau.
and heiress, b. Sept. 16, 1415; d. June 18, 1448; m. Sir Edward de Neville, Lord of Abergavenny, K.G., d. Oct. 18, 1476,
son of Ralph, 1st Earl of Westmorland, by his second wife
Joan Beaufort, Dowager Lady Ferrers de Wemme, the legit-
imated dau. of John of Gaunt, Duke of Lancaster,

GEORGE DE NEVILLE, Lord of Abergavenny, d. Sept. 20, 1492;
m., first, Margaret, dau. and heiress of Sir Hugh Fenne, of
Sculton Burdeleys, Norfolk, Treasurer of the Household to
King Henry IV,

GEORGE DE NEVILLE, Lord of Abergavenny, K.B., K.G., P.C., d.
1535; m., 3rdly, Mary, dau. of Edward de Stafford, 3rd Duke
of Buckingham, K.G., and his wife Eleanor de Percy, dau.
of Henry, 4th Earl of Northumberland, by Lady Maud Herbert, his wife,

URSULA DE NEVILLE, m., (his first wife), Sir Warham St. Leger,
Knt., of Ulcombe; Sheriff of Kent, 1560; President of Munster
in Ireland,

SIR ANTHONY ST. LEGER, of Ulcombe, d. 1603; m., c 1578, Mary,
dau. of Sir Thomas Scott,

SIR WARHAM ST. LEGER, of Ulcombe, d. c 1631; m. Mary, d.
1662, dau. of Sir Rowland Heyward, Knt., Lord Mayor of
London, and his wife Joan, dau. and heiress of William Tyllf-
worth,

URSULA ST. LEGER, d. c 1672; m., c 1627, Rev. Daniel Horsmanden, D.D., Rector of Ulcombe, Whipsnade, 1622; Vicar of
Goudhurst, Kent, 1625, and of Ulcombe, Kent, until 1645;
came to Virginia during the civil war and settled in Charles
City County, served as Burgess from Charles City County
and was a member of the Governor's Council in 1657; d. c
1655,

COLONEL WARHAM HORSMANDEN, of Purleigh, Essex, came to
Virginia c 1649, afterwards returned to England and d.
there; member of Governor's Council, 1658, father of,

MARIA HORSMANDEN, d. Nov. 9, 1699; m., 2ndly, c 1673, Colonel
(or Captain) William Byrd I, of London, England, and of
Virginia, b. c 1652; d. in Virginia, Dec. 4, 1704,

COLONEL WILLIAM BYRD II, of "Westover," Charles City
County, Va., b. March 10, 1674; d. at Westover, Va., Aug. 26,
1744; Member of the House of Burgesses; Receiver General of
Virginia, 1705-16; Member of the Governor's Council, 1707-44;
m., 2ndly, at Kensington, near London, May 9, 1724,
Maria Taylor, b. at Kensington, Nov. 10, 1698; d. in Virginia,
Aug. 28, 1771; dau. of Thomas Taylor, of Kensington, Eng-
land,

COLONEL WILLIAM BYRD III, of "Westover," b. in Va., Sept. 6,
1728; d. in Va., Jan. 1, 1777; m., first, in Va., Apr. 14, 1748,
Elizabeth Hill Carter, b. at Shirley, Va., 1731; d. in Va.,
July 25, 1760; dau. of Colonel John Carter, of Shirley, and
his wife Elizabeth, dau. of Edward Hill, King's Counsel,

CAPTAIN THOMAS TAYLOR BYRD, b. in Va., Jan. 17, 1752; d. in
Clarke County, Va., Aug. 19, 1821; m., March 13, 1786, Mary
Anne Armistead, b. Gloucester County, Va., 1766; d. in
Clarke County, Va., Sept. 29, 1824; dau. of William Arm-
istead, of "Hesse," Gloucester County, Va., and his wife
Maria, dau. of Colonel Charles Carter, of "Cleve," by his
second wife Anne Byrd,

RICHARD EVELYN BYRD, b. in Clarke County. Va., Dec. 29, 1801;
d. in Frederick County, Va., Jan. 1, 1872; m. in Va., Apr. 6,
1826, Ann Harrison, b. at Brandon, Va., 1802; d. in Clarke
County, Va., 1842,

COLONEL WILLIAM BYRD, of Winchester, d. at Winchester, Va.,
1899; m. at Austin, Texas, 1859, Jennie M. Rivers, b. 1839;
d. at Baltimore, Md., March 24, 1930,

RICHARD EVELYN BRYD, b. at Austin, Texas, Aug. 13, 1860; d. at Richmond, Va., Oct. 25, 1925; m. in Appomattox County, Va., Sept. 15, 1886, Eleanor (or Elinor) Bolling Flood, of Appomattox County, and had issue:

1.) HARRY FLOOD BYRD, b. at Martinsburg, W. Va., June 10, 1887, Governor of the Commonwealth of Virginia, 1926-30; Senator of the United States from Virginia, 1933-; m., Oct. 7, 1913, Anne Douglas Beverley, of Winchester, Va. Issue:

    a) HARRY FLOOD BYRD,

    b) WESTWOOD BYRD,

    c) BEVERLEY BYRD,

    d) RICHARD EVELYN BYRD.

2.) ADMIRAL RICHARD EVELYN BYRD, Explorer, b. at Winchester, Va., Oct. 25, 1888; m., Jan. 20, 1915, Marie D. Ames, of Boston, Mass. Issue:

    a) E. BOLLING BYRD,

    b) KATHARINE A. BYRD,

    c) HELEN A. BYRD,

    d) RICHARD EVELYN BYRD, JR.

SOMERSET

See Pages 120-21 and 132-33

ISABEL DE VERMANDOIS, m., 1st, 1096, Robert de Beaumont, Count of Meulan, 1st Earl of Leicester,

ISABEL (or Elizabeth) de Beaumont, m., 1st, Gilbert de Clare, cr., 1138, Earl of Pembroke, d. Sept. 14, 1148/9,

RICHARD DE CLARE, surnamed "Strongbow," 2nd Earl of Pembroke, d. ca. Apr. 5, 1176; m. Eva, dau. of Dermot MacMurrough, King of Leinster,

ISABEL DE CLARE, m., Aug. 1189, Sir William Marshall (Mareschal), Earl of Pembroke, Marshal of England, Regent of the Realm, &c., d. May 14, 1219,

SYBIL MARESCHAL, d. 1280/1; m., 1219, (his 1st wife), William de Ferrieres or de Ferrers, 5th Earl of Derby, of Chartley Castle, Constable of Bolsover Castle, d. Mar. 24/8, 1254,

MAUD DE FERRERS, d. Mar. 12, 1298/9; m., 2ndly, William de Vivonne (or Vivonia) in Poitou, of Chewton, d. May 22, 1259,

CICELY (or Cecily) de Vivonne (or Vivonia), b. ca. 1257; d. Jan. 10, 1320/1; m. John de Beauchamp, of Hatch (or Hache), co. Somerset, d. Oct. 24, 1283,

JOHN DE BEAUCHAMP, b. July 27, 1274; d. Jan. 1, 1336/7; m. Joan, d. Feb. 9, 1327, said to have been dau. of Chenduit,

JOHN DE BEAUCHAMP, 2nd Lord Beauchamp, of Hatch (or Hache), d. May 14/9, 1343; m. Margaret, d. Nov. 19, 1361, probably dau. of John St. John, 1st Lord St. John, of Basing, and his wife Isabel, dau. of Sir Hugh Courtenay,

CICELY (or Cecily) de Beauchamp, d. June 7, 1394; m., 1st, Sir Roger (de St. Mauro) Seymour,

SIR WILLIAM SEYMOUR, d. Aug. 25, 1391; m. Margaret, dau. and h. of Simon de Brockbury (or Brockburn), and his wife Joan, sister and h. of Sir Peter de la Mare,

ROGER SEYMOUR, m. Maud, dau. and co-h. of Sir William Esturmi, of Chadham, Wilts, Lord of Wolf Hall,

JOHN SEYMOUR, m. Isabel, dau. and h. of Mark William (or William MacWilliam),

JOHN SEYMOUR, m. Elizabeth, dau. and h. of Sir Robert Coker, Knt., of Lawrence Lydiard, Somerset,

JOHN SEYMOUR, m., 1st, Elizabeth, dau. of Sir George Darrell, of Littlecote, Wilts,

SIR JOHN SEYMOUR, Knt., of Wolf Hall, Wilts; Knight-Banneret, 1513; d. Dec. 21/4, 1536; m. Margaret (or Margery), 2nd dau. of Sir Henry Wentworth, K. B., of Nettlested, co. Suffolk,

SIR EDWARD SEYMOUR, 1st Duke of Somerset, K. B., K. G.; cr. Viscount Beauchamp, June 5, 1536; cr. Earl of Hertford,

Oct. 18, 1537; cr. Baron Seymour, Feb. 15, 1546/7, and the next day advanced to the Dukedom; Lord Great Chamberlain; Lord Treasurer of England; Earl Marshal; Protector of the Realm; P.C.; beheaded Jan. 22, 1551/2; m., 1st, ca. 1527, Catherine, dau. and co-h. of Sir William Fillol, of Fillol's Hall in Langton Wash, co. Essex, whom he divorced in 1535,

SIR EDWARD SEYMOUR, Knt., of Berry Pomeroy, co. Devon, d. May 6, 1593; m. Margaret, dau. and co-h. of John Walsh, of Cathanger, co. Somerset, Justice of the Common Plea,

SIR EDWARD SEYMOUR. 1st Bart., of Berry Pomeroy, cr. a Baronet, June 29, 1611; d. Apr. 11, 1613; m., ca. 1576, Elizabeth. dau. of Sir Arthur Champernowne, Knt., of Dartington, co. Devon,

SIR EDWARD SEYMOUR, 2nd Bart., of Berry Pomeroy, d. Oct. 5, 1659; m., ca. 1600, Dorothy, dau. of Sir Henry Killegrew, Knt.,

SIR EDWARD SEYMOUR, 3rd Bart., of Berry Pomeroy, bapt. Sept. 10, 1610; d. Dec. 7, 1688; m. Anne, dau. of Sir John or William Portman,

SIR EDWARD (or Edmund) Seymour, 4th Bart., of Berry Pomeroy, P.C.; b. ca. 1633; d. Feb. 17, 1707/8; Treasurer of the Navy; m., 1st, Margaret, dau. and co-h. of Sir William Wale. Knt., Alderman of London,

SIR EDWARD SEYMOUR, 5th Bart., of Berry Pomeroy, M.P., b. ca. 1663; d. Dec. 29, 1741; m. Laetitia, only dau. of Sir Francis Popham, K.B., of Littlecote, co. Wilts,

SIR EDWARD SEYMOUR, 6th Bart., of Berry Pomeroy, 8th Duke of Somerset, Baron Seymour; claimed the Dukedom upon the demise of his kinsman, and was summoned to Parliament Nov. 23, 1750; bapt. Jan. 17, 1694/5; d. Dec. 15, 1757; m., Mar. 8, 1716, Mary, buried Feb. 6/23, 1768, only dau. and h. of Daniel Webb, of Monckton-Farley, co. Wilts, by Elizabeth, dau. of John and sister and co-h. of Edward Somner, of Seend, co. Wilts,

VERY REV. FRANCIS SEYMOUR, Dean of Wells, b. ca. 1726; d. Feb. 16, 1799; m., ca. 1749, Catherine, d. Dec. 24, 1801, dau. of the Rev. Thomas Payne,

COLONEL FRANCIS COMPTON SEYMOUR, d. ca. 1822; m., ca. 1787. Leonora, d. June 27, 1795, widow of John Hudson,

CAPTAIN FRANCIS EDWARD SEYMOUR, R.N., b. Sept. 21, 1788; d. July 26, 1866; m., Feb. 4, 1815, Elizabeth, d. July 11, 1851, 2nd dau. of Charles Cooke,

REV. FRANCIS PAYNE SEYMOUR, Rector of Havant, b. Dec. 23, 1815; d. July 4, 1870; m., 1st, Sept. 13, 1848, Jane Margaret. d. Oct. 25, 1860, youngest dau. of the Rev. Alexander Robert Charles Dallas,

EDWARD SEYMOUR, 16th Duke of Somerset, Baron Seymour, b. May 19, 1860; d. May 5, 1931; m. July 28, 1881, Rowena, dau. of the late George Wall, of Ceylon,

EVELYN FRANCIS EDWARD SEYMOUR, 17th Duke of Somerset, Baron Seymour, b. May 1, 1882; J.P., Wilts; Deputy- Lieutenant, co. Devon; Lieutenant Colonel retired; D.S.O., O.B.E., Grand Dignitary (Knight Grand Cross) and Honorary Prior General of the Order of the Crown of Charlemagne; m., Jan. 3, 1906, Edith Mary Parker, dau. of William Parker, J.P., of Whittington Hall, Derbyshire, and have issue:

1.) PERCY HAMILTON SEYMOUR, Lord Seymour, b. Sept. 27, 1910; B.A.;

2.) LADY SUSAN MARY SEYMOUR, b. Apr. 26, 1913.

SUTHERLAND

EDWARD IV, King of England, b. at Rouen, Apr. 28/9, 1441/2;
d. Apr. 9, 1483; m., May 4, 1464, Elizabeth Wydeville (Woodville), b. c 1437; d. June 7, 1492; widow of Sir John de Grey,
Lord Ferrers of Groby, and dau. of Richard, Lord Rivers,
afterwards Earl of Rivers, K.G., and his wife Jaquetta, Duchess of Bedford,

PRINCESS ELIZABETH (sister and heiress of King Edward V),
b. Feb. 11, 1464/5; d. Feb. 11, 1502/3; m., Jan. 18, 1485/6,
Henry VII, King of England, b. July 26, 1456; d. Apr. 21,
1509,

PRINCESS MARY TUDOR, b., Mar. 18, 1496; d. June 25, 1533;
widow of Louis XII, King of France; m., 2ndly, May 13, 1515,
(his third wife), Charles Brandon, Duke of Suffolk, K.G., d.
Aug. 24, 1545,

FRANCES BRANDON, eldest dau. and co-h. b. July 16, 1517; d.
Nov. 11, 1559; m. c 1534, Henry de Grey, Marquess of Dorset, Duke of Suffolk, K.G., beheaded Feb. 23, 1553/4,

CATHERINE DE GREY, b. c 1539; d. Jan. 26/7, 1567/8; m., 2ndly,
1560, Edward Seymour, Earl of Hertford, b. 1538; d. Apr. 6,
1621; son of Edward Seymour, Duke of Somerset, K.G., Lord
Protector of England,

EDWARD SEYMOUR, Lord Beauchamp, b. Sept. 21, 1561; d. *v.p.*
1612; m., 1585, Honora Rogers, dau. of Sir Richard Rogers,
Knt., of Brainston, co. Dorset, and his wife Cecilia, dau. of
Andrew Luttrell, Esq.,

WILLIAM SEYMOUR, Duke of Somerset, K.G., b. 1587/8; d. Oct.
24, 1660; m., 2ndly, Frances Devereux, eldest dau. of Robert
Devereux, Earl of Eu and Essex, K.G.,

MARY SEYMOUR, d. c 1673, m. Heneage Finch, Earl of Winchil-
sea, d. 1689,

FRANCES FINCH, d. c 1712, m. Thomas Thynne, 1st Viscount
Weymouth, b. c 1640; d. c 1714,

FRANCES THYNNE, m., c 1690, Sir Robert Worsley, Bart., of Appledorecombe, d. 1747,

FRANCES WORSLEY, only dau. and h., b. Mar. 6, 1693/4; d. June 20, 1743; m., Oct. 17, 1710, (his first wife), John Carteret, Earl Granville, Viscount Carteret, and Baron Carteret of Hawnes, K.G., b. Apr. 22, 1690; d. Jan. 2, 1763,

GEORGIANA CAROLINE CARTERET, d. Aug. 25, 1780; m.., first, John Spencer, of Wimbledon, Surrey, M.P., d. June 10, 1746,

JOHN SPENCER, 1st Earl Spencer, m. Margaret Georgiana Poyntz, dau. of Stephen Poyntz,

GEORGIANA SPENCER, b. June 7, 1757; d. Mar. 30, 1806, m., June 5, 1774, (his first wife), William Cavendish, Duke of Devonshire, Marquess of Hartington, Lord Clifford, K.G., b. Dec. 14, 1748; d. July 29, 1811,

GEORGIANA DOROTHY CAVENDISH, b. July 12, 1783; d. Aug. 8, 1858; m., Mar. 21, 1801, George Howard, 6th Earl of Carlisle, K.G., d. Oct. 7, 1848,

HARRIET ELIZABETH GEORGIANA HOWARD, b. May 21, 1806; d. Oct. 27, 1868; m., May 27, 1823, George Granville, 2nd Duke of Sutherland, K.G., b. Aug. 8, 1786; d. Feb. 28, 1861,

GEORGE GRANVILLE WILLIAM SUTHERLAND-LEVESON-GOWER, Marquess of Stafford, 3rd Duke of Sutherland, K.G., b. Dec. 19, 1828; d. Sept. 22, 1892; m., June 20/7, 1849, Anne Hay-MacKenzie, Countess of Cromartie, Viscountess Tarbat of Tarbat, Baroness Macleod of Castle Leod, Baroness Castlehaven of Castlehaven, b. Apr. 21, 1829; d. Nov. 25, 1888; only dau. and h. of John Hay-MacKenzie, of Newhall and Cromarty, and his wife Anne, 3rd dau. of Sir James Gibson-Craig, 1st Bart.,

CROMARTIE SUTHERLAND-LEVESON-GOWER, 4th Duke of Sutherland, 21st Earl of Sutherland, 5th Marquess of Stafford, Earl Gower, Viscount Trentham, Baron Gower, Baron of Strathnaver, K.G., b. July 20, 1851; d. June 27, 1913; m., Oct. 20, 1884, Millicent Fanny St. Claire-Erskin, b. Oct. 20, 1867, dau. of Robert Francis, 4th Earl of Rosslyn, and had,

    1.) GEORGE GRANVILLE SUTHERLAND-LEVESON-GOWER, 5th Duke of Sutherland, Marquess of Stafford, Earl of Sutherland, Earl Gower, Viscount Trentham, Baron Gower, Baron of Strathnaver, P.C., K.T., Lord-Lieutenant of Sutherland, Hon. Col. 5th Seaforth Highlanders, Commander R.N.R.; Under Secretary of State for Air, 1922-23; Paymaster-General to H.M.'s Government, 1925-28; Parliamentary Under Secretary of State for War, 1928-29; Lord Steward of H.M.'s Household, 1936-37; b. Aug. 29, 1888; m., Apr. 11, 1912, Eileen Gladys Butler, b. Nov. 3, 1891, eldest dau. of the late 7th Earl of Lanesborough;

2.) LORD ALASTAIR ST. CLAIRE LEVESON GOWER, b. Jan. 24, 1890; d. Apr. 28, 1921; m., Apr. 27, 1918, Elizabeth Helen Demarest, b. at New York, d. at Paris, Sept. 26, 1931, and had:

   a) LADY ELIZABETH MILLICENT SUTHERLAND-LEVESON-GOWER, b. Mar. 30, 1921.

3.) LADY ROSEMARY MILLICENT SUTHERLAND-LEVESON-GOWER, b. Aug. 9, 1893; d. 1930; m., 1919, William Humble Eric Ward, 3rd Earl of Dudley, Baron Ward, Viscount Ednam, T.D., D.L., J.P., Lord High Steward of Kidderminster, b. Jan. 30, 1894, and had, among others:

   a) WILLIAM HUMBLE DAVID WARD, Viscount Ednam, b. Jan. 5, 1920.

EDWARD IV, King of England,

See Page 227

GEORGIANA CAROLINE CARTERET, m., first John Spencer, of Wimbledon, Surrey, M.P.,

JOHN SPENCER, 1st Earl Spencer, m. Margaret Georgiana Poyntz, dau. of Stephen Poyntz,

HENRIETTA FRANCES SPENCER, d. Nov. 14, 1821; m., Nov. 27, 1780, Frederick, 3rd Earl of Bessborough, b. Jan. 24, 1758; d. Feb. 3, 1844,

JOHN WILLIAM, 4th Earl of Bessborough, Lord Lieutenant of Ireland, P.C., b. Aug. 31, 1781; d. May 16, 1847; m., Nov. 16, 1805, Maria Fane, d. Mar. 19, 1834, dau. of John, 10th Earl of Westmorland, K.G.,

WALTER WILLIAM BRABAZON, 7th Earl of Bessborough, Baron Ponsonby of Sysonby, 4th Baron Duncannon, b. Aug. 13,

1821; d. Feb. 24, 1906; m., Jan. 15, 1850, Louisa Susan Cornwallis Eliot, only dau. of Edward Granville, 3rd Earl of St. Germans, G.C.B.,

EDWARD PONSONBY, Viscount Duncannon, 8th Earl of Bessborough, Baron Bessborough, Baron Ponsonby, Baron Duncannon, C.B., C.V.O., J.P., High Sheriff of Carlow, b. Mar. 1, 1851; d. 1920; m., Apr. 22, 1875, Blanche Vere, d. 1919, dau. of Sir Josiah John Guest, Bart.,

VERE BRABAZON PONSONBY, 9th Earl of Bessborough, Baron Bessborough, Baron Ponsonby, Baron Duncannon, etc., B.A., P.C., J.P., M.P., G.C.M.G., C.M.G., D.L., LL.D., b. Oct. 27, 1850; Governor General of the Dominion of Canada, 1931-35; m., 1912, Roberte de Neuflize, dau. of Baron Jean de Neuflize, and have issue, among others:

1.) FREDERICK EDWARD NEUFLIZE PONSONBY, Viscount Duncannon, M.A., b. Mar. 29, 1913;

TECK

GEORGE III (William Frederick), King of Great Britain, France, and Ireland, King of Hanover, m. Princess Sophia Charlotte, dau. of Charles Louis Frederick, reigning Duke of Mecklenburg-Strelitz,

PRINCE ADOLPHUS FREDERICK of Great Britain and Ireland, Duke of Cambridge, Duke of Brunswick-Luneburg, Earl of Tipperary, Viceroy of Hanover, K.G., &c., b. Feb. 24, 1774; d. July 8, 1850; m., May 7, 1818, Augusta Wilhelmina Louisa, b. July 25, 1797; d. Apr. 6, 1889, dau. of Frederick, Land-grave of Hesse-Cassel-Rumpenheim, and his wife, Caroline Polyxena, dau. of Karl Wilhelm, Prince of Nassau Usingen,

PRINCESS MARY ADELAIDE WILHELMINA ELIZABETH, b. at Han-over, Nov. 22, 1833; d. Oct. 27, 1897; m., June 12, 1866, Francis Paul Charles Louis Alexander, Prince of Teck; cr. Duke of Teck, Sept. 16, 1871; b. Aug. 27, 1837; d. Jan. 20/1, 1900; only son of Alexander, Duke of Wurtemburg (nephew of Frederick I, King of Wurtemburg). Issue:

1.) VICTORIA MARY AUGUSTA LOUISA OLGA PAULINE CLAUD-INE AGNES, Dowager Queen of Great Britain, &c., née Princess of Teck, b. at Kensington Palace, May 26, 1867; m., July 6, 1893, His Imperial and Royal Ma-jesty George V, King of Great Britain and Ireland, Emperor of India, &c., d. Jan. 20, 1936;

2.) PRINCE ADOLPHUS CHARLES ALEXANDER ALBERT EDWARD GEORGE PHILIP LOUIS LADISLAUS of Teck, 2nd Duke of Teck, G.C.V.O., G.C.B., C.M.G., &c., Governor and Constable of Windsor Castle since May 21, 1914, b. in Kensington Palace, Aug. 13, 1868; m. Dec. 12, 1894, Margaret Evelyn Grosvenor, b. April 9, 1873, dau. of Hugh Lupus, 1st Duke of Westminster, K.G. Issue:

   a) PRINCE GEORGE FRANCIS HUGH of Teck, b. Oct. 1, 1895;

   b) PRINCESS VICTORIA CONSTANCE MARY of Teck, b. June 12, 1897;

c) PRINCESS HELENA FRANCES AUGUSTA of Teck, b.
Oct. 23, 1899;

d) PRINCE FREDERICK CHARLES EDWARD of Teck, b.
Sept. 23, 1907.

3.) PRINCE ALEXANDER AUGUSTUS FREDERICK WILLIAM AL-
BERT GEORGE of Teck, 1st Earl of Athlone, K.G., G.C.B.,
&c., Governor General of the Dominion of Canada,
whose marriage and issue are mentioned elsewhere
in this book.

CHARLEMAGNE

See Page 126

MARGARET DE AUDLEY, *de jure,* apparently *suo jure,* Baroness Audley, m. Ralph Lord Stafford, afterwards Earl of the County of Stafford, d. Aug. 31, 1372,

JOAN DE STAFFORD, m. John Cherleton, Lord Cherleton, feudal Lord of Powis, d. July 13, 1374, son and heir of John, Lord Cherleton, feudal Lord of Powis, and his wife Maud, dau. of Roger de Mortimer, 1st Earl of March, by Joan, dau. of Piers de Joinville,

SIR EDWARD CHERLETON, Lord Cherleton, Lord of Powis, K.G., d. March 14, 1420/1; m., first, 1399, Eleanor, d. Oct. 6/18, 1405, widow of Roger de Mortimer, 4th Earl of March, and dau. of Thomas de Holand, Earl of Kent, and his wife Alice, dau. of Richard FitzAlan, Earl of Arundel, by Eleanor, dau. of Henry, Earl of Lancaster,

JOYCE CHERLETON, m., (his second wife), Sir John de Tiptoft (or Tibetot), Baron Tibetot (or Tiptoft), Seneschal of Aquitaine in 1415; President of the Exchequer in Normandy; Chief Steward of the Castles and Lordships in Wales, 1425; d. Jan. 27, 1442/3; son and heir of Sir Pain de Tibetot,

JOYCE DE TIPTOFT, (sister of John de Tiptoft, Earl of Worcester), m., (his first wife), Sir Edmund Sutton *alias* Dudley, of Dudley Castle and of Gatcombe, d. *v.p.* about 1483,

SIR JOHN SUTTON, of Dudley, Lord of Aston-le-Walls, father of,

MARGARET SUTTON, heiress of Aston-leWalls, m. John Butler, son of Ralph Butler, of Sawbridgeworth, Herts.,

WILLIAM BUTLER, of Tighes, co. Sussex, father of,

MARGARET BUTLER, of Tighes, co. Sussex, m., Aug. 3, 1588, Lawrence Washington, of Sulgrave and Wicken, d. Dec. 13, 1616, son of Robert Washington, of Sulgrave, and his wife Elizabeth Lyte,

SIR JOHN WASHINGTON, Knt., of Thrapston, Northamptonshire, b. at Sulgrave Manor, about 1591; d. about 1668; m., about 1621, Mary Curtis, d. about 1625, dau. of Philip Curtis, of Islip,

JOHN WASHINGTON, b. about 1624, emigrated to Barbados about 1650, later in Surry County, Virginia; m. Mary (Flood) Blunt, dau. of Colonel John Flood,

RICHARD WASHINGTON, b. about 1660; d. about 1724; Landowner and Vestryman of Southwark Parish, Surry County, Va., m. Elizabeth, dau. of Arthur Jordan and his wife Elizabeth Bayinn,

JAMES WASHINGTON, b. about 1698; d. about 1766, settled in Northampton County, N. C., about 1745; Member of Colonial Assembly, New Berne, N. C.; m. Joyce, dau. of Robert Nicholson and his wife Joanna Joyce,

JOHN WASHINGTON, of Northampton County, N. C., d. about 1768; m. Sarah Inman, of Murfreesboro, N. C., dau. of John Inman and his wife Sarah Dawson,

JOHN WASHINGTON, b. about 1768; d. and buried in Cedar Grove Cemetery, New Berne, N. C., 1837; m. at Kinston, N. C., Elizabeth Herritage Cobb, b. at Kinston, N. C., 1780; d. there 1857; dau. of Jesse Cobb and his wife Elizabeth Herritage,

JOHN COBB WASHINGTON, b. at Kinston, N. C., Dec. 24, 1801; d. at Black Mountain, N. C., June 12, 1887; m. at Raleigh, 1827, Mary Bond,

MARY BOND WASHINGTON, b. at Kinston, 1829; d. at Washington, N. C., 1910; m. at Kinston, 1847, William Augustus Blount, b. at Washington, N. C., 1823; d. at Beaufort County, N. C., June 1900,

OLIVIA GRIMES BLOUNT, b. at Raleigh, April 1, 1860; m. there Oct. 14, 1880, Archibald C. Sanders, b. at Smithfield, N. C., Aug. 1, 1849; d. at Durham, N. C., Jan. 2, 1887,

OLIVIA BLOUNT SANDERS, b. at Raleigh, N. C., Nov. 1, 1882; Dame Companion of Order of the Crown of Charlemagne; Member of National Society of the Colonial Dames of America, &c., m. at Wilson, N. C., April 26, 1900, John Albert Long, of London and Ludlow, England, d. 1916,

JOHN BLOUNT LONG, m. Nancy Elizabeth Canady.

WINSTON SPENCER—CHURCHILL

EDWARD IV, King of England

See Page 224

CATHERINE COCHRANE

See Page 203

JOHN WINSTON SPENCER-CHURCHILL, 7th Duke of Marlborough, K.G., P.C., Lord Lieutenant of Oxon, Viceroy of Ireland, &c., b. June 2, 1822; d. July 5, 1883; m. July 12, 1843, Frances Anne Emily, dau. of Charles William Vane, 3rd Marquess of Londonderry,

RT. HON. LORD RANDOLPH SPENCER-CHURCHILL (brother of George Charles Spencer-Churchill, 8th Duke of Marlborough), b. Feb. 13, 1849; P.C., Chancellor of the Exchequer 1886; Secretary of State for India, 1885; M.P. for Woodstock, 1874-85, for So. Paddington, Dec. 1885; Leader of the House of Commons in 1886; m., Jan. 1874, Jenny, dau. of Leonard Jerome, Esq., of New York.

RT. HON. WINSTON LEONARD SPENCER-CHURCHILL, b. Nov. 30, 1874; P.C., C.H., M.P. (C.) for Oldham, 1900-06; M.P. (L.) for N.-W. Manchester, 1906-08, for Dundee, 1908-22, for Epping Div. of Essex since 1924; Under Secretary of State for the Colonies, 1906-08; President of Board of Trade, 1908-10; Home Secretary, 1910-11; First Lord of the Admiralty, 1911-15, and 1939; Chancellor of the Duchy of Lancaster, 1915; Lt.-Col. commanding 6th Royal Scots Fusiliers, France, 1916; Minister of Munitions, 1917; Secretary of State for War, 1918-21, and for Air, 1918-21; Secretary of State for the Colonies, 1921-22; Chancellor of the Exchequer, 1924-29; Prime Minister since 1940, &c., m., 1908, Clementine, C.B.E., dau. of the late Col. Sir Henry Montagu Hozier, C.B., 3rd Dragoon Guards, and his wife, Henrietta Blanche, dau. of David Graham Drummond, 7th Earl of Airlie, K.T., by his wife, Henrietta Blanche, dau. of Edward John, 2nd Lord Stanley of Alderley, and have issue one son and three daughters.

Woodhull—Berrien—Warner—Sayre

CHARLEMAGNE, King of the Franks and Emperor of the West,

Louis I, the Pious, *le Debonnaire*, King of the Franks and Emperor,

CHARLES II, *le Chauve*, King of the Franks and Emperor of the West, m., first, 842, Irmtrude (Ermintrude), dau. of Odo (Vodon), Count of Orleans,

PRINCESS JUDITH, b. about 843; m., 3rdly, about 862, Baldwin I, surnamed "Bras de Fer," Count of Flanders, d. about 879,

BALDWIN II, the Bald, Count of Flanders, b. about 865; d. Jan. 2, 918; m., about 884, Elstrude, d. June 7, 929, dau. of Alfred the Great, King of England,

ARNOLPH I, *Magnus*, (the Great), Count of Flanders and Artois, b. about 890; d. Mar. 27, 964/5; m., about 934, Adele (or Alix or Athele), dau. of Herbert II, Count of Vermandois,

BALDWIN III, Junior, Count of Flanders, and Artois, d. Nov. 1, 962; m. about 961, Mathilda, d. May 25, 1008, dau. of Hermann Billung, Duke of Saxony, and his wife, Hildegarde de Westerbourg,

ARNOLPH II, Junior, Count of Flanders and Artois, d. Mar. 30, 987; m., about 968, Susanne (often referred to as Rosela), d. 1003, dau. of Berengarius II, King of Italy, and his wife Willa, dau. of Boso, Count of Arles,

BALDWIN IV, Barbatus, Count of Flanders and Artois; cr. Count of Valenciennes, 1007; d. May 30, 1035; m., first, Ogive (Otgiva), d. Feb. 21, 1030, dau. of Frederick, Count of Luxemburg,

BALDWIN V, the Pious, Count of Flanders, d. Nov. 1, 1067; m., about 1028, Adele (Adelheid) d. Jan. 8, 1079, dau. of Robert II, King of France, and widow of Richard III, Duke of Normandy

MATHILDA OF FLANDERS, d. Nov. 3, 1083; m., 1053, William I, Duke of Normandy, the Conqueror, King of England, d. Sept. 9, 1087,

HENRY I, *Beauclerc,* King of England, m. Princess Mathilda, dau. of Malcolm III, *Canmore,* King of Soctland, by St.

Margaret, dau. of Prince Edward the Exile and his wife Agatha,

PRINCESS MATHILDA, b. 1104; d. Sept. 10, 1167; m., first, Jan. 7, 1114, Emperor Henry V, who d. May 23, 1125; m., 2ndly, April 3, 1127, Geoffrey Plantagenet, Count d'Anjou, d. Sept. 7, 1151,

HENRY II, King of England, b. 1133; d. July 6, 1189; m., May 18, 1152, Eleonore (Eleanor), dau. and co-h. of William V, Duke of Aquitaine, and the divorced wife of Louis VII, King of France,

JOHN, King of England, m., 2ndly, Isabel (Isabella), dau. and h. of Aymer, Count d'Angouleme,

HENRY III, King of England,, b. Oct. 1, 1206; m. Eleanor, dau. and h. of Raymond Berenger, Count of Provence,

EDWARD I, King of England, m., 2ndly, Princess Margaret, dau. of Philippe II, *le Hardi,* King of France, and his wife Marie de Brabant, dau. of Henry III, Duke of Brabant,

EDMUND PLANTAGENET, "of Woodstock," Lord Woodstock, Earl of Kent, &c., b. Aug. 5, 1301; executed Mar. 19, 1329/30; m., about 1325, Margaret, d. Sept. 29, 1349, widow of John Comyn, of Badenoch, dau. of Sir John Wake, Lord Wake, and sister and h. of Sir Thomas Wake, Lord Wake, of Liddel, Cumberland,

JOAN, styled "Fair Maid of Kent," d. about Aug. 8, 1385; m., about 1339, (her first husband), Sir Thomas de Holand, K.G., of Broughton, Bucks, Lord Holand, Earl of Kent, d. Dec. 26/8, 1360; son of Sir Robert de Holand, of Upholland, co. Lancaster.

SIR THOMAS DE HOLAND, Earl of Kent, Lord Woodstock, Holand and Wake, K.G., &c., d. April 25, 1397; m., 1364, Alice, d. March 17, 1415/6, dau. of Richard FitzAlan, Earl of Arundel, by Princess Eleanor, dau. of Henry, Earl of Lancaster,

ELEANOR DE HOLAND, m. Thomas de Montagu (Montacute), last Earl of Salisbury, K.G., cr. Count of Perche, in Normandy, April 26, 1419; d. about Nov. 3, 1428; son and heir of John, Lord Montagu (Montacute), Lord Monthermer, Earl of Salisbury, K.G., beheaded Jan. 7, 1399/1400,

ALICE, *suo jure* Countess of Salisbury, d. before Feb. 1462/3; m. Sir Richard de Neville, who was recognized as Earl of Salisbury, K.G., beheaded Dec. 31, 1460; son of Ralph de Neville, 1st Earl of Westmorland,

ALICE DE NEVILLE, (sister of Richard de Neville, Earl of Warwick and Earl of Salisbury, styled the "King Maker"), m. Henry, Lord FitzHugh, d. June 8, 1472, son and heir of William, Lord FitzHugh, and his wife Margery, dau. of Sir William de Willoughby, of Eresby, co. Lincoln, Lord Willoughby, by his first wife, Lucy, dau. of Sir Roger Lestraunge, Lord Lestraunge, of Knockin, Salop,

ELIZABETH FITZHUGH, m., (his second wife), Sir William Parr (Parre), of Kendal, d. 1483/4,

WILLIAM, Baron Parr of Horton, co. Northampton, chamberlain to his niece, Katharine Parr, the last Queen Consort of Henry VIII, 1543; Sheriff of co. Northampton; d. Sept. 10, 1546; m., 1505/6, Mary, d. July 10, 1555, dau. and co-h. of William Salisbury, of Horton,

ELIZABETH PARR, m., (his second wife), Sir Nicholas Woodhull, Lord of Woodhull, co. Bedford,

FULKE WOODHULL, of Thenford Manor, Northamptonshire, m. Alice, dau. of William Coles (or Colles), of Lye (or Leigh), co. Worcester,

LAWRENCE WOODHULL, younger son, father of,

RICHARD WOODHULL, b. at Thenford, Northamptonshire, England, Sept. 13, 1620; d. at Brookhaven, L. I., N. Y., Oct. 17, 1690; m. Deborah,

RUTH WOODHULL, b. at Setauket, L. I., N. Y.; d. at Newton, L. I., N. Y., before 1689; m., about 1678, Samuel Edsall, b. at Reading, Berkshire, England, about 1630; d. at Newton, L. I., N. Y., about 1706,

RUTH EDSALL, m. at Newton, L. I., N. Y., April 5, 1697, Lieut. John Berrien, d. April 1711, son of Cornelius Jansen Berrien and his wife Jeannetie, *née* Van Stryker,

CORNELIUS BERRIEN, b. at Flushing Bay, L. I., N. Y., Jan 8, 1698; d. at Berrien's Island, N. Y., March 30, 1767; m. at New York, Dec 29, 1719, Sarah Hallett, b. at Hallett's Cove,

L. I., N. Y., about 1704; d. at New York, Jan. 11, 1797; dau. of Major Samuel Hallett and his wife Bridget Blackwell,

PHEBE BERRIEN, b. at Berrien's Island, Jan. 30, 1735; d. at New York, July 17, 1810; m. at Newton, L. I., N. Y., Dec. 16, 1754, William Warner, b. at Yonkers, N. Y., Apr. 22, 1734; d. at New York, Jan. 1, 1815,

PHEBE BERRIEN WARNER, b. at New York, N. Y., Nov. 22, 1772; d. at Utica, N. Y., June 10, 1849; m. at New York, about 1793, Moses Sayre, b. at Westfield, N. J., May 3, 1769; d. at Rome, N. Y., Jan. 4, 1823; son of Benjamin Sayre and his wife Sarah Littell,

JAMES SAYRE, b. at Milton, N. Y., Jan. 25, 1799; d. at Utica, N. Y., Apr. 22, 1877; m. at New York, Aug. 11, 1824, Amelia Margaret Van Ranst, b. at New York, Sept. 25, 1797; d. at Utica, Mar. 17, 1892; dau. of Cornelius Willett Van Ranst and his wife Anna White,

CHARLES HENRY SAYRE, b. at Utica, Sept. 5, 1825; d. Apr. 27, 1894; m. at Utica, about 1854, Nora Flynn, b. at New York, Feb. 28, 1834; d. at Utica, May 16, 1919; dau. of John Flynn and his wife Elaice Foster,

CHARLES LANSING SAYRE, b. at Utica, Dec. 2, 1861; d. at Los Angeles, Calif., Dec. 17, 1912; m. at Cincinnati, Ohio, Feb. 23, 1887, Amanda Glenn Lytle, b. at Cincinnati, Feb. 8, 1865, dau. of James Paterson Lytle and his wife Louise Catherine Roll,

LANSING GLENN LYTLE SAYRE, b. at Cincinnati, Ohio July 24, 1901; Companion First Class (Officer) and one of the Deputy Priors of the Order of the Crown of Charlemagne; Former Governor General, General Court, Order of the Founders and Patriots of America; Secretary, Society of Colonial Wars in the State of Calif.; Secretary, Society of the Sons of the Revolution in the State of Calif.; Member of the Baronial Order of Runnemede, &c.

WOODHULL—THROCKMORTON

CHARLEMAGNE

See Page 237

LAWRENCE WOODHULL, of Thenford Manor, younger son, father of,

RICHARD WOODHULL, b. at Thenford, Northamptonshire, England, Sept. 13, 1620; d. at Brookhaven, L. I., N. Y., Oct. 17, 1690/1; m. Deborah,

RICHARD WOODHULL II, b. Oct. 9, 1649; d. Oct. 18, 1699; m., Aug. 19, 1680, Temperance, dau. of the Rev. Jonah Fordham, of Southampton, L. I., N. Y.,

RICHARD WOODHULL III, b. Nov. 2, 1691; d. Nov. 24, 1767; m. Mary Homan, b. about 1693; d. Dec. 27, 1768; dau of John Homan,

JOHN WOODHULL, b. Jan. 15, 1719; d. Jan. 3, 1794; m., Nov. 27, 1740, Elizabeth Smith, b. Nov. 12, 1718; d. Dec. 20, 1761; dau. of Major William Henry Smith, of the "Tangier Smith" family, L. I.,

JOHN WOODHULL, D.D., b. Jan. 26, 1744; d. Nov. 22, 1824; m., May 28, 1772, Sarah Spofford, b. Oct. 26, 1749; d. Oct. 14, 1827; only child of Capt. George Spofford, of the Royal Navy,

GILBERT SMITH WOODHULL, M.D., b. Jan. 11, 1794; d. Oct. 13, 1830; m., Nov. 25, 1817, Charlotte Wikoff, b. April 15, 1795; d. Jan. 11, 1862; 4th dau, of William Wikoff and his wife Hannah, dau. of Col. Nathaniel Scudder, M. D., of Monmouth County, N. J.,

SARAH SPOFFORD WOODHULL, b. Aug. 15, 1821; m., Nov. 25, 1846, Barbarie Throckmorton, b. March 11, 1813; d. Jan. 21, 1870; son of Judge Thomas Coffin Throckmorton, of Freehold, N. J., and his wife Elizabeth Craig,

HENRY WOODHULL THROCKMORTON, b. at Freehold, N. J., Sept. 26, 1847; d. at New York, Feb. 8, 1881/2; m., first, Dec. 14,

1871, Ella Klapp, b. at New York, Dec. 10, 1853; d. there Feb. 14, 1875,

HOWARD WOODHULL THROCKMORTON, b. at Jersey City, N. J., Nov. 12, 1873; Companion (Knight) of the Order of the Crown of Charlemagne; Member of the Naval and Military Order of the Spanish American War, United Spanish War Veterans, S.R., Society of Colonial Wars, &c., m., 3rdly, 1925, Ann Flower.

WYATT—ALLYN—NEWBERRY—CLARKE— GRAVES—McALPIN

ISABEL DE VERMANDOIS

See Page 106

MARGARET WYATT, m. Matthew Allyn,

MARY ALLYN, m. Capt. Benjamin Newberry,

REBECCA NEWBERRY, b. at Windsor, Conn., May 2, 1655; d. Oct. 17, 1718; m., June 22, 1675, Samuel Marshall, b. at Simsbury, Conn., May 27, 1653; d. at Northampton, Mass., Aug. 10, 1727,

ABIGAIL MARSHALL, b. at Northampton, Aug. 22, 1682; m. there Nov. 9/16, 1702, John Birge, b. at Windsor, Conn., Feb. 4, 1679/80,

JOHN BIRGE, b. at Northampton, Mass., about 1703; d. there Dec. 6, 1795; m. there, about 1726, Experience Stebbins, b. at Northampton, Mar. 18, 1703; d. there Nov. 12, 1748,

SIMEON BIRGE, b. at Northampton, Nov. 3, 1736; d. there June 18, 1816; m. there, about 1764, Lois Kentfield (Canfield),

LUCINDA BIRGE, b. at Northampton, Mass., Oct. 1764/5; d. there Jan. 25, 1840; m. there, about 1784, Thomas Clarke, b. at Northampton, Apr. 2, 1761; d. there Feb. 27, 1795,

PAMELIA CLARKE, b. at Northampton, Oct. 22, 1784; d. there Sept. 16, 1825; m. there Sept. 2, 1806, Kenaz Clark, b. at Southampton, Mass., May 29, 1784; d. at Lee, Mass., Apr. 20, 1866,

MARTHA CLARK, b. at Northampton, Mar. 13, 1817; d. at Lee, Mass., May 12, 1893; m. at Lee, Nov. 10, 1836, Milo A. Graves, b. at West Stockbridge, Mass., Feb. 6, 1813; d. at Lee, Sept. 15, 1898,

HARRIET P. GRAVES, b. at Lee, June 15, 1841; d. at New York City, Mar. 31, 1914; m. at Lee, Aug. 26, 1860, Robert McAlpin, b. Mar. 3, 1837; d. at South Bend, Ind., Mar. 2, 1911,

Captain Milo Frederick McAlpin, b. at Lee, co. Berkshire, Mass., Oct. 20, 1873; one of the founders of the American Legion; Secretary General, General Court, Order of the Founders and Patriots of America; Secretary General, General Society of the War of 1812; Member of Ancient and Honorable Artillery Company of Mass., Hereditary Order of Descendants of Colonial Governors, Huguenot Society, S.R., S.A.R., Society of Colonial Wars, St. Nicholas Society, &c.

APPENDIX

Barclay—Hoare

Edward III, King of England, m. Philippa of Hainault,

See Page 141

Joan Beaufort, m., first, James I, King of Scots,

James II, King of Scots, b. Oct. 16, 1430; killed at the siege of Roxburgh Castle, Aug. 3, 1460; m., July 3, 1449, Marie, d. Dec. 1, 1463, only dau. of Arnold (Arnolph), Duke of Gueldres, by his 2nd wife, Catharine, dau. of Adolph II, Duke of Cleves,

James III, King of Scots, b. July 10, 1451; murdered June 11, 1488; m., July 13, 1469, Princess Margaret, d. July 14, 1486, dau. of Christian I, King of Denmark, &c., by Dorothea, widow of Christopher III, King of Denmark, and dau. of Johann the Alchymist, Markgraf of Anspach-Bayreuth (eldest surviving son of Frederick, Markgraf of Brandenburg), and his wife, Barbara, only dau. and h. of Rudolph III, Elector of Saxony,

James IV, King of Scots, b. Mar. 17, 1472/3; killed at the battle of Flodden, Sept. 9, 1513; by his concubine, Margaret Drummond, dau. of John, 1st Lord Drummond, had,

Margaret Stewart, b. about 1497; m., first, Nov. 1512, John, Lord Gordon, Master of Huntly, d. Dec. 5, 1517, s. & h. of Alexander Gordon, 3rd Earl of Huntly,

Alexander Gordon, Bishop of the Isles 1553, Bishop of Galloway 1558, & titular Archbishop of Athens; P.C., Nov. 3, 1565; Extraordinary Senator of the College of Justice, Nov. 26, 1565; d. Nov. 11, 1575, father of,

John Gordon, D.D., Bishop of Galloway in Scotland, Dean of Salisbury in England; Laird of Glenluce in Scotland; d. about 1619; m. 2ndly, about 1594, Genevieve, dau. of Gideon Pétau (or Petaw), Lord de Maule (or Mauld) in France,

Louisa (or Lucy) Gordon, d. about 1680; m. at London, Feb. 16, 1613, Sir Robert Gordon of Gordonstown, Gentleman of

the bedchamber to Kings James VI and Charles I; Sheriff
Principal of Invernesshire, 1629; cr. Knight Banneret, becoming Premier Baronet of Nova Scotia, May 28, 1625; P.C.;
b. May 14, 1580; d. at Gordonstown, Mar. 1656; son of Alexander Gordon, 11th Earl of Sutherland, (who d. Dec. 6, 1594),
by his 2nd wife, Jane (or Janet), the divorced wife of James
Hepburn, Earl of Bothwell, and dau. of George Gordon, 4th
Earl of Huntly, by Elizabeth, sister of William, 4th Earl
Marischal, and dau. of Robert Keith, Lord Keith, and his
wife Elizabeth, dau. of John Douglas, 2nd Earl of Morton,

KATHARINE GORDON, b. Jan. 11, 1621; d. about 1663; m., Jan.
26, 1648, (marriage contract dated Dec. 24, 1647), Colonel
David Barclay, Laird of Urie, co. Kincardine, b. about 1610;
d. Oct. 12, 1686,

ROBERT BARCLAY, Laird of Urie, "The Apologist," Governor of
East New Jersey, b. Dec. 23, 1648; d. Oct. 3, 1690; m.,
Feb. 16, 1669, Christiana, d. Dec. or Feb. 14, 1722/5, dau.
of Gilbert Mollison (or Molleson), of Aberdeen,

DAVID BARCLAY, b. Sept. 17, 1682; d. May 18, 1769; m., first,
June 12, 1707, Anne Taylor, d. Dec. 3, 1720, dau. of James
Taylor, of London,

ALEXANDER BARCLAY, of Philadelphia, b. Nov. 10, 1711; d. Jan.
or Mar. 5, 1771; "Comptroller of the Customs of Philadelphia," m., 1st, Anne, d. June 18, 1753, dau. of Robert Hickman,

ROBERT BARCLAY, b. at Philadelphia, Penn., May 15, or Aug.
13, 1751; d. about 1839; m., 1st, 1775, Rachel Gurney, d.
Jan. 2, 1794, dau. of John Gurney, of Keswick Hall, Norwich,

CHARLES BARCLAY, b. Dec. 26, 1780; d. Dec. 5, 1855; High
Sheriff for Surrey, 1842; m., Aug. 1, 1804, Anna Maria, d.
Mar. 15, 1840, dau. of Thomas Kett, of Seething Hall, Nor-
folk, and had, among others,

CAROLINE BARCLAY, d. July 7, 1878; m., Mar. 18, 1837, John
Gurney Hoare, of the Hill, Hampstead Heath, Middlesex
& of Cliff House, Gromer, Norfolk, J. P. for Gromer, &c., b.
May 7, 1810; d. Feb. 16, 1875; son of Samuel Hoare and his
wife Louisa, dau. of John Gurney, of Earlham, Norfolk, and
had, among others,

Sir Samuel Hoare, 1st Bart., of Sidestrand Hall, Norfolk, &c., J.P. for Gromer, Norfolk; M.P. for Norwich, 1886-1906; b. Sept. 7, 1841; d. about 1915; m., Apr. 7, 1866, Katharine Louisa Hart, d. about 1931, dau. of Richard Vaughan Davis, Esq., of Frognal, and had, among others,

Rt. Hon. Sir Samuel John Guerney Hoare, 2nd Bart., of the Hill, Hampstead Heath, Middlesex, of Gromer, Norfolk, of Templewood, Northrepps, &c., P.C., G.C.S.I., G.B.E., C.M.G., D.L., J.P., &c., b. Feb. 24, 1880; M.P. for Chelsea since 1910; Secretary of State for Air, 1922-24, & Nov. 1924 - June 1929, & 1940; Secretary of State for India, 1931-35; Secretary of State for Foreign Affairs, 1935; First Lord of the Admiralty, 1936-37; Secretary of State for Home Affairs, 1937; Ambassador to Spain, 1940-   ; m., 1909, Maud Lygon, D.B.E., dau. of Frederick Lygon, 6th Earl of Beauchamp, P.C., D.C.L., M.P. &c.

Barclay—Forbes—Penn—Gaskell—Hall

ROBERT BARCLAY, "The Apologist," Laird of Urie, Governor of East New Jersey, m. Christiana Mollison (Molleson),

JANE (OR JOAN) BARCLAY, b. Dec. 27, 1683; m. at London, Apr. 12, 1707, Alexander Forbes, of London, son of John Forbes, of Aquorthes, near Aberdeen,

CHRISTIAN FORBES, d. Nov. 1, 1733; m., Dec. 7, 1732, William Penn III, b. at Worminghurst, Mar. 21, 1702/3; d. Feb. 6, 1746/7; son of William Penn, Jr., (and his wife Mary, dau. of Charles Jones, Jr.), and grandson of William Penn, the Founder of Pennsylvania, by his first wife, Gulielma Maria Springett, dau. of Col. Sir William Springett, Knt., of Sussex, by his wife Mary, dau. of Sir John Proude, Knt., and his wife Anne Fagge,

CHRISTIANA GULIELMA PENN, b. Oct. 22, 1733; d. Mar. 1803; m., about 1761, Peter Gaskell, of Bath, England, d. about 1785,

PETER PENN GASKELL, b. about 1763; d. July 16, 1831; came to America about 1785; m., about 1793, Elizabeth, d. July 19, 1834, dau. of Nathan Edwards, of Radnor, co. Del., Penn.,

CHRISTIANA GULIELMA PENN GASKELL, d. Mar. 29, 1830; m., Jan. 2, 1827, William Swabric Hall, b. about 1799; came to Philadelphia about 1825; d. Sept. 26, 1862, and had issue.

BULKELEY—OSBORN—SHERWOOD—SMITH—DEMAREST

CHARLEMAGNE

See Page 138

GRACE CHETWOOD m. the Rev. Peter Bulkeley,

PETER BULKELEY, b. at Concord, Mass., about Aug. 12, 1643; d. about 1691; m. Margaret,

DOROTHY BULKELEY, m. Sergt. David Osborn, d. about 1727,

SARAH OSBORN, bapt. about 1711; d. at Fairfield, Conn., after 1793; m. at Fairfield, about Feb. 17, 1731, Joseph Sherwood,

ELEAZER SHERWOOD, b. at Fairfield, about Oct. 18, 1733; served in the American Revolution; d. at Greenfield, Conn., Feb. 15, 1808; m. at Easton, Conn., Dec. 1770, Mary Squires, b. at Fairfield, Conn., Sept. 22, 1748; d. there July 18, 1828,

BETSEY SHERWOOD, b. at Fairfield, Jan. 28, 1786; d. at Greenfield, Conn., Apr. 9, 1845; m. at Fairfield, July 4, 1813, Daniel Smith, b. at Greenfield, Conn., Jan. 28, 1789; d. at Greenfield, Mar. 10, 1866,

HORACE SMITH, b. at Greenfield, Oct. 28, 1823; d. at Bridgeport, Conn., Aug. 20, 1900; m. at Westport, Conn., about 1850, Elizabeth Matilda Couch, b., Green Farms, Conn., Jan. 9, 1831; d. at Bridgeport, July 28, 1905,

ELI COUCH SMITH, b., Green Farms, Dec. 16, 1850; d. at Bridgeport, Jan. 9, 1901; m. at Westport, Oct. 21, 1874, Mary Elizabeth Wright, b. at New Milford, Conn., Aug. 26, 1851; d. at Bridgeport, July 28, 1921,

MARY ESTHER WRIGHT SMITH, b. at Bridgeport, July 28, 1875; Member of D.A.C. (Organizing Regent 1936-38 and Regent 1938-41 of Gov. Thomas Welles Chapter, Registrar since 1941), D.A.R. (Registrar, Chaplain, &c.), Daughters of Founders and Patriots of America (Director), U.S.D. of 1812 (Committee Chairman); Pres. C.A.C. in Conn.; m. at Bridgeport, Oct. 21, 1907, Richard Garret Demarest, b. at New York, N. Y., June 9, 1871; Member of S.A.R. Issue:

1.) RICHARD GARRET DEMAREST, b. at Bridgeport, Dec. 13, 1909; Member of S.A.R.; m. at Mt. Vernon, N. Y., May 16, 1936, Caryl Ruth Lee, b. at Naperville, Ill., Mar. 1, 1912. Issue:

    a) CARYL CARDER DEMAREST, b. at Bridgeport, Apr. 15, 1939;

    b) RICHARD GARRET DEMAREST III, b. at Bridgeport, Nov. 9, 1941.

2.) CHARY ESTHER DEMAREST, b. at Bridgeport, Nov. 13, 1911; Member of D.A.R.; m. at Bridgeport, Sept. 9, 1935, Harold Franklin Nash, b. at Westport, Conn., Nov. 7, 1907. Issue:

    a) HAROLD FRANKLIN NASH, b. at New Haven, Conn., Apr. 17, 1938.

BULKELEY—WELBY—FARWELL—HOLDEN—
BROWN—SNYDER—WHITE
CHARLEMAGNE

See Page 134

OLIVE WELBY (OR WELBIE), m. Henry Farwell, came from England to Concord, Mass., about 1635,

ENSIGN JOSEPH FARWELL, b. at Concord, Mass., Feb. 26, 1640/1; d. Dec. 31, 1722; m., Dec. 25, 1666, Hannah Learned, b. about Aug. 24, 1649,

JOSEPH FARWELL, b. July 24, 1670; d. at Groton, Mass., Aug. 20, 1740; m., Jan. 23, 1695/6, Hannah Colburn,

DANIEL FARWELL, b. at Groton, Mass., May 20, 1717; d. at Fitchburg, Mass., Jan. 15, 1808; m. at Andover, Mass., July 3, 1739, Mary Moon, b. July 10, 1718,

ISAAC FARWELL, b. at Groton, Mar. 28, 1744; d. about 1786; m., Dec. 6, 1770, Lucy Page, b. at Groton, about 1750,

EMMA FARWELL, b. at New Ipswich, N. H., Aug. 2, 1779; d. at Harford, N. Y., Apr. 30, 1859; m., Nov. 27, 1797, Benjamin Holden, b. Mar. 16, 1775; d. at Harford, Apr. 27, 1842,

MATILDA HOLDEN, b. Mar. 7, 1799; d. at Harford, N. Y., Nov. 9, 1890; m., 1819, Morris Brown, b. Sept. 6, 1799; d. at Harford, N. Y., Mar. 23, 1883,

JOSIAH H. BROWN, b. at Harford, Nov. 22, 1830; d. there Jan. 2, 1900; m. there Dec. 23, 1855, Elmina Hanchett, b. at Richford, N. Y., Apr. 12, 1833; d. at Holley, N. Y., Oct. 7, 1905,

LORA E. BROWN, b. at Hartford, Oct. 13, 1859; d. at Batavia, N. Y., May 29, 1932; m. at Hartford, May 1, 1884, Frederick C. Snyder, b. Apr. 5, 1857; d. at Stanton, Mich., Nov. 29, 1893,

GERTRUDE M. SNYDER, b. at Greenville, Mich., Mar. 11, 1885; m. at Batavia, N. Y., Nov. 8, 1917, Howard J. White, b. Jan. 2, 1884.

CASTELLANE [1]

CHARLEMAGNE

LOUIS I, the Pious, m., 1st, Ermengarde (Irmgard), d. about Oct. 3, 818,

LOTHARIUS I (Lothaire), King of Italy and Emperor of the West, b. about 795; d. about Sept. 29, 855; m., 1st, about Oct. 15, 821, Ermengarde (Irmgard), d. about Mar. 20, 851, dau. of Hugo II, Count of Tours (or of Alsace),

LOTHARIUS II, King of Lorraine, b. about 835; d. Aug. 8, 869; m., 2ndly, about 862, Waldrade,

PRINCESS BERTHA, b. about 863; d. Mar. 8, 925; m., 1st, about 879, Theobald (Thibaut), Count d'Arles,

BERTILLON D'ARLES, m. Hermengarde,

ENGILBERT D'ARLES, m. Emma de Rossillon,

PONS-ARBALD, assumed name of Castellane, m. Folcoava,

PONS-PULVEREL DE CASTELLANE, m. Walburge,

BONIFACE I, 1st Baron de Castellane, received the town, castle and rock of Castellane in Provence in 1089, father of,

LANGIER (or Leodogarius), Baron de Castellane, father of,

BONIFACE II, Baron de Castellane, father of,

BONIFACE III, Count de Castellane, m., about 1176, Adelaste de Monstiers,

BONIFACE-RUFUS, Count de Castellane, m. Orable,

BONIFACE IV, Count de Castellane, m. Agnes de Spata de Riez,

BONIFACE DE GALBERT, yongest son, m. Sibylle de Fos,

RAYMOND-GAUFFRIDY, m. Alixende de Voisins,

BONIFACE, m. Sibylle de Ventimille,

---

[1] NOTE: This pedigree is included as submitted by Count Bohdan Joseph Boniface de Castellane upon his assurance that he verified and found it correct. The compiler of this book did not check the Castellane pedigree.

BONIFACE, m. Laure d'Aube, widow of Bertrand de Grasse,

GEORGES, m. Marguerite de Villeneuve-Trans,

RAYMOND-GAUFFRIDY II, m. Alix d'Esparron et de St. Julien,

BONIFACE, m. about June 4, 1488, Honorée de Forbin de Janson, dau. of Palamede de Forbin de Janson, Governor of Provence,

GASPARD, Count de Castellane, m., about 1526, (her 3rd husband), Honorée de Lascaris de Tende,

PIERRE, Count de Castellane, m., 2ndly, Marguerite de Silve (or Silvy),

JEAN-FRANCOIS BERNARD, Count de Castellane, page to Henry, Duke d'Anjou (brother of Charles IX, King of France), m. Agnes de Junosza-Boyanowska,

JEAN II, Count de Castellane, m. Princess Marie Pronska, dau. of Prince Alexander Pronski,

BERNARD, Count de Castellane, m. Anna Maria, dau. of Heinrich von Promnitz, of Silesia,

CONSTANTIN AUGUSTUS, Count de Castellane, m. Catherine de Jonghe,

ERNEST ERIC, Count de Castellane, m. Christina-Joanna, dau. of Gustavus Adolphus de Wasaborg, by Angelica Catherine von Leiningen-Westerburg, his wife,

AUGUSTUS CHARLES, Count de Castellane, m. Sophia Haehlin von Storcksburg,

JOSEPH, Count de Castellane, m. Jadwiga de Dunin-Kamienomoyska,

LAURENT, Count de Castellane, m. Helena de Lubicz-Hrehorowicz,

CONSTANTIN, Count de Castellane, m. Hedwig von Schaermer,

LADISLAS (Wladyslaw), Count de Castellane, b. June 27, 1844; d. June 27, 1898; m. Josephine, d. Feb. 26, 1939, dau. of Joseph de Dombrowa-Kurmanowicz,

BOHDAN JOSEPH BONIFACE, Count de Castellane, b. at Matinsze, Province of Kiev, Russia, Sept. 13, 1878; m., 1st Jan. 17, 1928, Alix Forbes, of Scotland; m., 2ndly, at Genoa, Italy, Jan. 5, 1935; Alice Abercrombie Miller de Peyster. Issue by 1st wife:

    1.) ALIX-ROSSOLINE DE CASTELLANE, b. Mar. 31, 1929.

CLARKE—CORNELL—HALL—LAWTON— CARPENTER—BOWEN

EDWARD I, King of England

See Page 154

JEREMY CLARKE (Clerke), bapt. at East Farleigh, co. Kent, Dec. 1, 1605; d. at Newport, R. I., 1651; President Regent of R. I., &c; m., ca. 1637, Frances, widow of William Dungan, & dau. of Lewis Latham, gent.,

GOVERNOR WALTER CLARKE, b. ca. 1638; d. at Newport, R. I., May 23, 1714; m., 2ndly, Feb. 1667, Hannah Scott, b. ca. 1642; d. July 24, 1681; dau. of Richard Scott, of Glemsford, co. Suffolk, & of Boston, & of Providence, R. I., and Catherine Marbury, his wife,

DELIVERANCE CLARKE, b. July 4, 1678; d. at Portsmouth, R. I., Oct. 8, 1732; m. at Portsmouth, Jan. 18, 1699, (his 2nd wife), George Cornell, b. at Portsmouth, ca. 1676; d. at Newport, R. I., Apr. 11, 1752; son of Thomas and Susanne (Lawton) Cornell,

RICHARD CORNELL, b. at Portsmouth, Apr. 14, 1709; m. there Dec. 10, 1730, Mary Martin, dau. of Joseph and Mary (Albro) Martin,

DELIVERANCE CORNELL, b. at Portsmouth, R. I., June 18, 1733; m. there Aug. 10, 1749, Benjamin Hall, b. at Portsmouth, May 21, 1729; d. there 1805; son of Benjamin and Patience (Cory) Hall,

PATIENCE HALL, b. at Portsmouth, Apr. 5, 1753; d. at Assonet, Mass., Sept. 1825; m. at Portsmouth, Oct. 1, 1772/3, Job Lawton, b. at Portsmouth, June 22, 1753; d. Dec. 1777; son of George and Mary (Gould) Lawton,

CAPT. BENJAMIN HALL LAWTON, b. at Portsmouth, July 25, 1774; d. at Freetown, Mass., Nov. 1, 1838; m. at Freetown, Nov. 14, 1792, Betsey Paget, b. at Freetown, Dec. 12, 1773; d. there Sept. 7, 1801; dau. of George and Mary (Chase) Paget,

MARY PAGET (Lawton) Douglas, b. at Freetown, July 12, 1794; d. at Fall River, Mass., Dec. 8, 1871; m., 2ndly, Feb. 15, 1825, Stephen Carpenter, b. at Rehoboth, Mass., Sept. 9, 1793; d. there Sept. 28, 1841; son of Stephen and Hannah (Wilmarth) Carpenter,

WILLIAM MOULTON CARPENTER, b. at Fall River, Mass., May 30, 1827; d. at Seekonk, Mass., May 30, 1827; m. at Seekonk, May 20, 1851, Eunice Walker Bishop, b. at Rehoboth, Mass., Dec. 23, 1827; d. at East Providence, R. I., Nov. 3, 1889; dau. of John Jefferson and Sarah (Walker) Bishop,

CLARA FRANCES CARPENTER, b. at Seekonk, Mass., June 23, 1854; d. at Redlands, Calif., June 14, 1932; m. at Providence, Nov. 2, 1876, Thomas Le Baron Bowen, b. at Providence, Feb. 13, 1850; d. there June 15, 1897; son of William Bradford and Hannah Boyd (Miller) Bowen,

RICHARD LE BARON BOWEN, b. at East Providence, R. I., Apr. 4, 1878; Major, R. I. National Guard, retired; served in Spanish American War; former Representative to the R. I. Legislature; Member of Committee on Heraldry, New England Historic Genealogical Society, &c., m. at Providence, Apr. 9, 1917, Marjorie Champlin, b. at Providence, Mar. 15, 1890; d. at Rehoboth, Mass., Oct. 14, 1939; dau. of Irving and Julia (Doyle) Champlin. Issue:

    1.) RICHARD LE BARON BOWEN, JR., b. at Providence, Apr. 2, 1919; A.B., Princeton University, 1941;

    2.) PEGGY BOWEN, b. at Providence, Apr. 22, 1921.

Dudley—Wyllys—Woodbridge—Bradford— Du Pont—Ortiz

CHARLEMAGNE

See Page 133

ROGER DE QUINCY, 2nd Earl of Winchester, &c., m., 1st, Helen, dau. and co-h. of Alan, Lord of Galloway, Constable of Scotland,

ELENA (or Ela) de Quincy, m. Alan La Zouche, Baron Zouche of Ashby de la Zouche, Constable of the Tower of London,

EUDO LA ZOUCHE, m. Milicent, a widow, sister and co-h. of George de Cantelou (or Cantelupe), Baron Abergavenny (Bergavenny), and dau. of William de Cantelou (or Cantelupe), of Calne, Wilts, and Aston Cantlow, co. Warwick, Lord of Abergavenny (Bergavenny), by Eve de Briouze, dau. and co-h. of William de Briouze and his wife Eve, dau. of William Marshall, Earl of Pembroke and Strigul,

ELEANOR (Elena, Ela, Ellen) La Zouche, m., (his 1st wife), Sir John de Harcourt, of Stanton Harcourt, Oxfordshire, knighted about 1306, d. about 1330,

SIR WILLIAM DE HARCOURT, of Stanton Harcourt, d. about June 6, 1349; m., (her 1st husband), Jane, dau. of Richard, Lord Grey, of Codnor,

SIR THOMAS DE HARCOURT, of Stanton Harcourt, knighted about 1366; M.P. for co. Oxford 1376; d. about Apr. 12, 1417; m. Maud (or Alice or Eleanor), dau. of John, 2nd Lord Grey, of Rotherfield, and widow of Sir John Botetort, Lord Botetort,

SIR THOMAS HARCOURT, Knt., of Stanton Harcourt, m. Joan (or Jane), dau. of Sir Robert Francis (or Franceys), of Formark, co. Derby,

SIR RICHARD HARCOURT, Knt., of Wytham, Berks, m., 1st, Edith, dau. & co-h. of Thomas St. Claire, of Wethersfull, Suffolk,

ALICE HARCOURT, m. William Besilles (or Bessiles),

255

Elizabeth Besilles, m. Richard Fettiplace, of Basilsleigh, co. Bucks,

Anne Fettiplace, m. Edward Purefroy, of Shalstone, co. Bucks, b. about June 13, 1494; d. about June 1, 1558,

Mary Purefroy, m. Thomas Thorne, of Yardley, co. Northants,

Susanna Thorne, m. Capt. Roger Dudley,

Thomas Dudley, Governor of Massachusetts, &c., m., 1st, Dorothy Yorke,

Mercy Dudley, b. Sept. 29, 1621; d. July 1, 1691; m., about 1639, Rev. John Woodbridge, b. about 1613; d. Mar. 17, 1695,

Rev. Timothy Woodbridge, m., (her 3rd husband), Mehitable Wyllys, dau. of Samuel Wyllys (by Ruth, dau. of Governor John Haynes), and granddau. of George Wyllys (Willis or Willes or Willies), Governor of Conn., and great-granddau. of Richard Wyllys, of Fenny Compton, (the Wyllys line will appear in Vol. II in 1942-3),

Ruth Woodbridge, m. John Pierson,

Elizabeth Pierson, m., about 1757, Rev. Jacob Green,

Elizabeth Green, m., about 1776, Rev. Ebenezer Bradford,

Moses Bradford, m., about 1817, Phoebe George,

Judge Edward Green Bradford, b. 1818/9; d. 1844; m., 1852, Elizabeth Robert Canby,

Elizabeth Canby Bradford, m. Dr. Alexis Irénée du Pont,

Alice Eugenie du Pont, d. Nov. 5, 1940; m., Jan. 20, 1906, Julien Ortiz,

Marguerite du Pont Ortiz, b. July 20, 1907 (whose lineage appears elsewhere in this book); m., 2ndly, June 22, 1937, Harry Clark Boden (whose lineage also appears elsewhere in this book).

MARBURY—HUTCHINSON—DUNN—JONES—WASHBURN

EDWARD I, King of England, m., first, Eleanor, dau. of Ferdinand III, the Saint, King of Castile and Leon,

PRINCESS JOAN, b. at Acre in Palestine, c 1272; d. Apr. 23, 1307; m., first, 1290, (his second wife), Gilbert de Clare, Earl of Gloucester and Hertford, surnamed "the Red Earl," b. Sept. 2, 1243; d. Dec. 7, 1295,

ALIANORE DE CLARE, b. Oct. 1292; d. June 30, 1337; m., first, 1306, Sir Hugh Le Despenser, Lord Le Despenser, who was hanged on November 24, 1326,

ISABEL LE DESPENSER, m., Feb. 9, 1320/1, (his first wife), Richard FitzAlan, Earl of Arundel, surnamed "Copped Hat," Justiciar of North Wales, Governor of Carnarvon Castle, Admiral of the West, d. Jan. 24, 1375/6,

ISABEL FITZALAN, m. John, 4th Lord Strange de Blackmere, d. May 12, 1361,

ANKARET LE STRANGE, m. Richard Talbot, Lord Talbot de Blackmere, d. Sept. 7, 1396,

MARY TALBOT, d. Apr. 13, 1433; m. Sir Thomas Greene, Knt., of Greene's Norton, co. Northampton, d. Dec. 14, 1417,

SIR THOMAS GREENE (GRENE), of Greene's Norton, b. Feb. 10, 1399/1400; d. Jan. 18, 1461/2; m., first, Philippa de Ferrers, dau. of Sir Robert de Ferrers, Baron Ferrers, of Chartley, co. Stafford, by his second wife, Margaret, youngest dau. of Sir Edward Le Despenser, Lord Le Despenser, Lord of Glamorgan, by Elizabeth, dau. and h. of Sir Bartholomew de Burghersh, of Ewyas Lacy, co. Hereford, Stert and Colerne, Wilts, Lord Burghersh,

ELIZABETH GREENE (GRENE), m. William Raleigh, Esq., of Farnborough, Warwickshire, and Newbold, Northamptonshire,

SIR EDWARD RALEIGH, Knt., of Farnborough; Sheriff of Warwickshire and Leicestershire, 1467; J.P., 1461-1503; m. c 1467,

Margaret Verney, dau. of Sir Ralph Verney, Lord Mayor of London, etc.,

SIR EDWARD RALEIGH, Knt., of Farnborough, m. Anne Chamberlayne, of Sherbourne, Oxfordshire, dau. of Richard Chamberlayne,

BRIDGET RALEIGH, m. Sir John Cope, Knt., of Canons Ashby, Northamptonshire, Sheriff of Northamptonshire, M. P.,

ELIZABETH COPE, m. John Dryden, Esq., of Canons Ashby, d. Sept. 3, 1584,

BRIDGET DRYDEN, m., (his second wife), Rev. Francis Marbury, of Alford, Lincolnshire, and London, d. 1610/1,

ANNE MARBURY, bapt. in England, July 20, 1591; killed by Indians at Westchester, N. Y., Aug. 1643; (she was a sister of Katherine Marbury, b. about 1610; d. at Newport, R. I., about Mar 2, 1687; who m., about June 7, 1632, Richard Scott, and had issue) ; m. at London, England, Aug. 9, 1612, William Hutchinson, bapt. at Alford, England, Aug. 14, 1586; d. 1642,

CAPT. EDWARD HUTCHINSON, bapt. May 28, 1613; d. Aug. 19, 1675; m. at Ipswich, England, Oct. 13, 1636, Catherine Hamby,

ANN HUTCHINSON, b. Nov. 17, 1643; d. Jan. 10, 1717; m. Samuel Dyer, b. about 1635; d. at Newport, R. I., about 1678,

ANN DYER, m., Feb. 4, 1693, Carew Clarke, d. about 1670,

ANN CLARKE, b. Sept. 8, 1698; d. Nov. 9, 1746; m. Samuel Dunn,

SAMUEL DUNN, b. Feb. 11, 1724; m., Sept. 18, 1746, Esther Tourtellot,

ESTHER DUNN, m., Mar. 23, 1777, Thomas Jones,

FRANCES JONES, b. at Providence, R. I., Feb. 10, 1782; d. there Jan. 29, 1873; m. there Oct. 15, 1801, Elisha Dyer, b. at Providence, Jan. 5, 1772; d. there Feb. 11, 1854,

FRANCES JONES DYER, b. at Providence, Sept. 11, 1804; d. there Feb. 15, 1892; m. there Oct. 25, 1824, Amos Maine Vinton, b. at Providence, Oct. 30, 1798; d. there July 12, 1837,

ELIZABETH VINTON, b. at Providence, Oct. 23, 1832; d. there Apr. 14, 1880; m. there Oct. 5, 1858, Horation Nelson Slater,

Jr., b. at Webster, Mass., Mar. 20, 1835; d. at Providence, Aug. 12, 1899,

CAROLINE VINTON SLATER, b. at Providence, July 21, 1859; m. there Apr. 25, 1889, Charles Grenfill Washburn, b. Jan. 28, 1857; d. at Lenox, Mass., May 25, 1928,

MAJOR SLATER WASHBURN, b. at Princeton, Mass., Aug. 5, 1896; B. A.; Col., Mass. N.G., retired; Major, U.S.M.C.; Member of Worcester City Council, 1920-21; Member of Mass. House of Representatives, 1922-30; Dignitary (Commander) and Secretary General of the Order of the Crown of Charlemagne; Member of S.R., M.O.W.W., Society of Mayflower Descendants, Huguenot Society, American Legion, V.F.W., &c.; d. July 12, 1941; m., first, 1918, Beulah McClellan; m., 2ndly, Lylla Jardine.

MARBURY—SCOTT—REMINGTON—PECK—WILLIAMS

EDWARD I, King of England

See Page 258

BRIDGET DRYDEN, b. *ca.* 1563; d. *ca.* 1645; m., 1st, *ca.* 1587, (his 2nd wife), Rev. Francis Marbury, of Alford, Lincolnshire, & of London, d. *ca.* 1610/11,

CATHERINE MARBURY, b. *ca.* 1610; d. at Newport, R. I., May 2, 1687; m. at Berkhampstead, Herts, England, June 7, 1632, Richard Scott, b. at Glemsford, Suffolk, *ca.* 1607; d. at Providence, R. I., before Mar. 1681,

JOHN SCOTT, d. *ca.* 1677; m. Rebecca Browne,

MAJOR SILVANUS SCOTT, 1672-1742; m. Joanna Jencks, 1672-1756,

JEREMIAH SCOTT, 1709-95; m. Rebecca Jenkes,

BETSEY SCOTT, 1754-1823; m. Capt. John Short, 1752-1822,

PHEBE SHORT, m. Enoch Remington, 1792-1864,

LUCRETIA SHORT REMINGTON, b. at Barrington, R. I., Jan. 16, 1820; d. at Providence, R. I., Feb. 26, 1895; m., Mar. 24, 1839, Asa Peck, b. at Barrington, Apr. 7, 1812; d. there Feb. 26, 1890,

LEANDER REMINGTON PECK, b. at Barrington, Feb. 12, 1843; d. at Providence, Jan. 28, 1909; m. there Sept. 6, 1866, Sarah Gould Cannon, b. at New Bedford, Mass., Apr. 25, 1844; d. at Providence, Mar. 24, 1929; dau. of Charles and Mary Pease (Fisher) Cannon,

FREDERICK STANHOPE PECK, b. at Providence, Dec. 16, 1868; LL.D., *honoris causa,* Villanova College, 1930; Member of Barrington Town Council, 1909; Representative from Barrington in State Legislature of R. I., 1911 and 1913-26; State Commissioner of Finance of R. I., 1926-35; Member of Order of the Founders and Patriots of America, Society of Colonial Wars, S.A.R., Society of Mayflower Descendants, New England Historic Genealogical Society, R. I. Historical Society,

&c.; m. at Providence, June 6, 1894, Mary Rothwell Burlingame, b. at Williamsport, Pa., June 30, 1873, dau. of Edwin Harris and Eliza (Aylsworth) Burlingame,

HELEN PECK, b. 1895; m. Weir Williams, b. 1894; d. 1935. Issue:

    1.) MARCIA WILLIAMS, b. 1919;

    2.) WEIR PECK WILLIAMS, b. 1920;

    3.) MARY ELIZABETH WILLIAMS, b. 1922;

    4.) FREDERICK PECK WILLAMS, b. 1923.

LINEAGE VARIATIONS

CHARLEMAGNE, King of the Franks and Emperor of the West, m. Hildegard,

LOUIS I, the Pious, *le Debonnaire*, King of the Franks and Emperor of the West, m., 2ndly, Judith, dau. of Guelph I, Count of Altdorf (Altorff) and afterwards Duke of Bavaria,

CHARLES II, the Bald, b. June 13/23, 823; d. Oct. 6, 877; King of the Franks, 843; Emperor, 875; m., first, Dec. 842, Irmtrude (Ermintrude), d. Oct. 6, 869, dau. of Odo (Vodon), Count of Orleans,

LOUIS II, *le Begue*, b. about 846; d. Apr. 10, 879; King of the Franks, 877; Emperor, 878; m., 2ndly, Adelheid, d. about 901, presumably sister of Abbot Wulfard of Flavigny,

CHARLES III, *le Simple*, b. Nov. 17, 879; d. Oct. 7, 929; King of the Franks, 898-923; m., 2ndly, 918/9, Eadgifu (or Edgina or Ogina), dau. of Edward, the Elder, King of England, and granddau. of Alfred the Great, King of England,

LOUIS IV, *d'Outre Mer*, (Transmarinus), b. about 921; d. Sept. 10, 954; King of the Franks, 936; m., 939, Princess Gerberga, d. May 5, 984, widow of Gisilbert, Duke of Lorraine, and dau. of Henry I, the Fowler, Emperor of Germany, and his wife Mathilda, dau. of Dietrich, Count of Ringelheim,

PRINCESS MATHILDA (OR MAUD), m., about 964, (his 2nd wife), Conrad I, King of Burgundy, d. Oct. 19, 993, son of Rudolph II, King of Burgundy,

PRINCESS GERBERGA, b. about 965; d. about 1016; m. 2ndly, aobut 988, Hermann II, Duke of Swabia, d. May 4, 1003,

PRINCESS GISELE, b. about 999; d. Feb. 14, 1043; m., 3rdly, 1016/7, Conrad II, *le Salique*, Emperor of Germany, d. June 4, 1039; son of Henry, Duke of Franconia,

HENRY III, the Black, Emperor of Germany, b. Oct. 28, 1017; d. Oct. 5, 1056; m., 2ndly, Nov. 21, 1043, Agnes, d. Dec. 14, 1077, dau. of William, Count of Poitou and afterwards Duke of Aquitaine,

HENRY IV, Emperor of Germany, b. Nov. 11, 1050; d. Aug. 7, 1106; m., first, about 1066, Bertha, dau. of Otto, Count of Maurienne, and his wife Adelaide, presumably dau. of Ulric Manfred II, Count of Susa,

PRINCESS AGNES, d. about 1143; m., first, Frederick I de Buren, Seigneur of Hohenstauffen, Duke of Alsace and Swabia, b. about 1105, son of Frederick of Hohenstauffen, of the Palace of Buren, and his wife Hildegarde, widow of Conrad, Prefect of Nuremberg, and dau. of Hermann, founder of the House of Hohenzollern,

FREDERIC II of Hohenstauffen, Duke of Swabia, &c., b. about 1090; d. Apr. 6, 1147; m. Judith, dau. of Henry I, the Black, Duke of Bavaria, (d. Dec. 13, 1126), and his wife Wulfhild, dau. of Magnus, Duke of Saxony, and his wife, Sophia of Hungary, dau. of Bela I, King of Hungary,

FREDERICK III, *Barbarossa*, Duke of Alsace and Swabia, afterwards Emperor of Germany as Frederick I, d. June 10, 1190; m., 2ndly, about 1156, Beatrix de Macon, d. Nov. 15, 1184/5, dau. and h. of Renaud III (Reinald), Count of Macon and Burgundy,

PHILIP II, Emperor of Germany, Duke of Swabia, Marquis of Tuscany, assassinated June 23, 1208; m. about 1196, Irene Angela, widow of Roger, King of Sicily, and dau. of Isaac II, Emperor of Constantinople,

PRINCESS ETHISA (OR BEATRICE?), d. about 1234/5; m., (his first wife), St. Ferdinand III, King of Castile and Leon, d. May 30, 1252, son of Alphonso IX, King of Leon, and his 2nd wife, Princess Berengaria, dau. of Alphonso VIII, King of Castile, and his wife, Princess Eleanor, dau. of Henry II, King of England,

ALPHONSO X (IX?), King of Castile and Leon, b. Nov. 23, 1221; d. Apr. 21, 1284; m. Violante of Aragon, d. about 1264, dau. of James I (Jacques), King of Aragon, and his wife, Violante (or Yolande) of Hungary, dau. of Andrew II, King of Hungary,

SANCHO IV, King of Castile, d. Apr. 25, 1295; m., 2ndly, Maria la Granda, dau. of Alphonso, Count de Molino, and granddau. of Alphonso IX, King of Leon,

FERDINAND IV, King of Castile, d. about 1312; m. Constance of Portugal, d. about 1313,

ALPHONSO XI, King of Castile, d. about 1350; m. 1328, Maria of Portugal, dau. of Alphonso IV, King of Portugal,

Pedro I, *the Cruel,* King of Castile and Leon, d. about 1368; m. Maria di Padilla, dau. of Juan Garciez di Padilla,

Constance of Castile, b. about 1354; d. Mar. 24, 1394; m., 1369, (his 2nd wife), Prince John, "of Gaunt," Duke of Lancaster, titular King of Castile and Leon, K.G., &c., son of Edward III, King of England.

CHARLEMAGNE, King of the Franks and Emperor of the West,

LOUIS I, the Pious, le Debonnaire, King of the Franks and Emperor of the West; m., first, about 794/8, Irmgarde (Ermengarde), d. about Oct. 3, 818, dau. of Ingeramun, Count of Hasbaye,

LOUIS, le Germanique, King of Bavaria 817; b. about 806; d. Aug. 28, 876; m. Emma, d. Jan. 31, 876, (she was a sister of his stepmother, Judith, who m., as 2nd wife, Louis I), dau. of Guelph I, Count of Altdorf and Duke of Bavaria,

CARLOMAN, King of Bavaria 876; b. about 829; d. Sept. 29, 880, father of,

ARNOUL (ARNULPH), Emperor of Germany, d. Nov. 29, 899; m. Oda (or Utade) of Bavaria, dau. of Theudon, Count in Bavaria,

HEDWIGE OF GERMANY, m. Otto (Otho) I, the Illustrious, Duke of Saxony, d. Nov. 12/3, 912; son of Ludolph I, the Great, Duke of Saxony,

HENRY I, the Fowler, Emperor of Germany, Duke of Saxony, Brunswick and Zelle, d. July 2, 936; m., 2ndly, about 911, Mathilda, dau. of Dietrich, Count of Ringelheim, and sister of Siegfried, 1st Count (Markgraf) of Brandenburg,

PRINCESS HATWIDE (OR HAWISE OR HATWIN), m., (his 3rd wife), Hugh the Great, surnamed the White, Duke of France, Count of Paris, &c., son of Robert, King of France in 922,

HUGH CAPET, King of France, m. Adelaide,

ROBERT II, the Pious, King of France; m., 2ndly, Constance, dau. of William (de Taillefer), Count of Toulouse, by his wife, Blanche d'Anjou,

HENRY I, King of France, m. Anne of Kiev, dau. of Yaroslav I of Kiev, Grand Prince of Kiev, and his wife Ingegarde, dau. of Olave III, King of Sweden,

PHILIPPE I, King of France, m. Bertha, dau. of Florent I, Count of Holland,

CONSTANCE, m., 2ndly, Boemond I, Prince d'Antioche, d. about 1111,

BOEMOND II, Prince d'Antioche, b. about 1107; d. about 1131; m. Alix (or Alice), dau. of Baldwin II, King of Jerusalem,

Princess Constance d'Antioche, m., 2ndly, about 1152/3, (his 2nd wife), Renaud de Chatillon, Prince d'Antioche, d. about 1186, son of Henry I de Chatillon and his wife, Ermengarde, dau. of Alberic de Montjai (Montjay),

Agnes (often referred to as Anne), d. about 1184; m., about 1171, (his 1st wife), Bela III, King of Hungary, d. Apr. 18, 1196, son of Geza II, King of Hungary, who d. May 31, 1161, and grandson of Bela II, King of Hungary, who d. about Feb. 13, 1141,

Andrew II, King of Hungary, d. about Mar. 7, 1235; m., first, Gertrude of Meran, d. about 1213/4, dau. of Berthold IV, Duke of Meran,

Bela IV, King of Hungary, d. about 1270/75; m. Marie Lascaris, dau. of Emperor Theodore Lascaris I,

Stephen V, King of Hungary, d. about 1272, father of,

Princess Marie of Hungary, murdered Mar. 25, 1323; m. Charles II, le Boiteux, King of Naples, d. at Cassanova, near Naples, May 5/6, 1309, son of Charles I, King óf Sicily, Count d'Anjou, &c., (by his first wife, Beatrix, Countess of Provence, dau. of Raymond VII, Count of Provence), and grandson of Louis VIII, King of France, by his wife, Blanche of Castile,

Princess Margaret of Naples, m. Charles, Count of Valois, son of Philippe III, le Hardi, King of France,

Joanna (or Jane) of Valois, m. William III, le Bon, Count of Hainault and Holland, son of Jean I, Count of Hainault, by his wife, Philippa of Luxemburg, dau. of Henry, Count of Luxemburg,

Philippa of Hainault, d. Aug. 14/5, 1369; m., Jan. 24, 1327/8, Edward III, King of England.

PEPIN, b. Apr. 773; d. July 8, 810; he was named Carloman at birth, bapt. by Pope Adrian I, Apr. 12, 781, at which time he was christened Pepin, father of,

BERNARD, King of Italy, Sept. 813, abdicated Dec. 817; b. *ca.* 797; d. Apr. 17, 818; (according to Thegan and others he was *ex concubina natus*, but this statement cannot definitely be verified and seems improbable); m. Cunigunde, d. after 835,

PEPIN, b. *ca* 817/8; d. after 840, father of,

HERBERT I, Count of Vermandois, murdered *ca.* 900/8; m. Berthe, dau. of Guerri I, Count of Morvois, by Eve de Roussillon, dau. of Girard de Roussilon, Count of Paris and Metz, Regent of Provence, &c., d. 878/9,

HERBERT II, Count of Vermandois and Troyes, d. ca. 943; m. Liégard, dau. of Robert I, King of France,

ROBERT, Count of Troyes and of Meaux, b. *ca.* 920; d. *ca.* 967/8; m., first, Adelheid (or Wera), dau. of Gisilbert, Count de Bourgogne,

ADELHEID, b. *ca.* 950; d. *ca.* 975/8; (G. W. Watson and other authorities state that she was the dau. of Herbert II, Count of Vermandois and Troyes, above mentioned, and sister of Robert, Count of Troyes and Meaux, above mentioned, but the dates make this improbable); widow of Lambert, Count de Châlons-sur-Saône; m., 2ndly, Geoffrey, surnamed Grisegonelle (or Grisgonell), Count d'Anjou, d. July 21, 987, son of Fulke II, *le Bon*, Count d'Anjou,

ERMENGARDE (IRMGARD), m. *ca.* 980, (his 2nd wife), Conan I, *le Tort*, Count of Rennes, &c., d. *ca.* 992,

JUDITH, b. *ca.* 982; d. *ca.* 1017; m., *ca.* 1000, Richard II, Duke of Normandy, d. Aug. 23/8, 1027,

ROBERT I, surnamed *the Devil*, Duke of Normandy, d. July 22, 1035, had, by Harlotte (or Herleve or Arlette), dau. of Fulbert in Falaise:

    1.) WILLIAM I, Duke of Normandy, Conqueror of England, King of England; m. Mathilda of Flanders, dau. of Baldwin V, Count of Flanders;

PEPIN, b. Apr. 773; d. July 8, 810; he was named Carloman at birth, bapt. by Pope Adrian I, Apr. 12, 781, at which time he was christened Pepin, father of,

BERNARD, King of Italy, Sept. 813, abdicated Dec. 817; b. *ca.* 797; d. Apr. 17, 818; (according to Thegan and others he was *ex concubina natus*, but this statement cannot definitely be verified and seems improbable); m. Cunigunde, d. after 835,

PEPIN, b. *ca* 817/8; d. after 840, father of,

HERBERT I, Count of Vermandois, murdered *ca.* 900/8; m. Berthe, dau. of Guerri I, Count of Morvois, by Eve de Roussillon, dau. of Girard de Roussilon, Count of Paris and Metz, Regent of Provence, &c., d. 878/9,

HERBERT II, Count of Vermandois and Troyes, d. ca. 943; m. Liégard, dau. of Robert I, King of France,

ROBERT, Count of Troyes and of Meaux, b. *ca.* 920; d. *ca.* 967/8; m., first, Adelheid (or Wera), dau. of Gisilbert, Count de Bourgogne,

ADELHEID, b. *ca.* 950; d. *ca.* 975/8; (G. W. Watson and other authorities state that she was the dau. of Herbert II, Count of Vermandois and Troyes, above mentioned, and sister of Robert, Count of Troyes and Meaux, above mentioned, but the dates make this improbable); widow of Lambert, Count de Châlons-sur-Saône; m., 2ndly, Geoffrey, surnamed Grisegonelle (or Grisgonell), Count d'Anjou, d. July 21, 987, son of Fulke II, *le Bon,* Count d'Anjou,

ERMENGARDE (IRMGARD), m. *ca.* 980, (his 2nd wife), Conan I, *le Tort,* Count of Rennes, &c., d. *ca.* 992,

JUDITH, b. *ca.* 982; d. *ca.* 1017; m., *ca.* 1000, Richard II, Duke of Normandy, d. Aug. 23/8, 1027,

ROBERT I, surnamed *the Devil,* Duke of Normandy, d. July 22, 1035, had, by Harlotte (or Herleve or Arlette), dau. of Fulbert in Falaise:

    1.) WILLIAM I, Duke of Normandy, Conqueror of England, King of England; m. Mathilda of Flanders, dau. of Baldwin V, Count of Flanders;

CHARLEMAGNE, King of the Franks and Emperor of the West,

LOUIS I, the Pious, *le Debonnaire*, King of the Franks and Emperor of the West, by Judith, his 2nd wife,

PRINCESS GISELE, b. about 820; d. about 874; m., about 836/40, Eberhard, Count (Markgraf) of Frioul, d. about 864/6,

BERENGER I, King of Italy, Jan. 888; Emperor of the West, Dec. 915; Markgraf of Frioul; b. about 850; d. Apr. 7, 924; m., about 890, Bertila, d. Dec. 915, dau. of Suppo, Markgraf of Spoleto,

PRINCESS GISELE, d. about 910, m. Adalbert, Markgraf of Ivrea, d. about 923,

BERENGER II, King of Italy 950-61; d. Aug. 6, 966; m., about 936, Willa, dau. of Boso, Count of Arles, Markgraf of Tuscany, &c.,

PRINCESS SUSANNA (OR ROSELA) d. about 1003; m., first, about 968, Arnolph II, *le Jeune*, Count of Flanders, d. Mar. 30, 987, son of Baldwin III, Count of Flanders,

BALDWIN IV, *le Barbu*, Count of Flanders, b. about 980; d. May 30, 1035; m., first, about 1012, Ogive (or Otgive), d. Feb. 21, 1030, dau. of Frederick, Count of Luxemburg,

JUDITH OF FLANDERS, (also called Fausta) d. Mar. 4/5, 1094; m., first, Tostig (Toston), Earl of "all Northumbria," d. Sept. 25, 1066, younger son of Godwin, Earl of Wessex, and brother of Earl Harold; she m., 2ndly, about 1071, Guelph IV (Welf), Duke of Bavaria, d. Nov. 8, 1101,

HENRY I, the Black, Duke of Bavaria, b. about 1074; d. Dec. 13, 1126; m., about 1095/1100, Wulfhild, d. Dec. 29, 1126, dau. of Magnus, Duke of Saxony, and his wife, Sophia, dau. of Bela I, King of Hungary,

JUDITH, b. about 1100; d. about 1130; m. Frederick II of Hohenstauffen, Duke of Swabia, &c., b. about 1090; d. Apr. 6, 1147; son of Frederick I de Buren, Seigneur of Hohenstauffen, Duke of Alsace and of Swabia,

FREDERICK I, *Barbarossa*, Emperor of Germany, Duke of Alsace and of Swabia, b. about 1122; d. June 10, 1190.

Louis IV, *d'Outre Mer*, King of France, m. Princess Gerberga, widow of Gisilbert, Duke of Lorraine, and dau. of Henry I, the Fowler, Emperor of Germany, by Mathilda, dau. of Dietrich, Count of Ringelheim,

PRINCESS MATHILDA (OR MAUD), m. Conrad I, King of Burgundy (Arles),

PRINCESS GERBERGA, m., 2ndly, Hermann II, Duke of Swabia,

PRINCESS MATHILDA (OR MAUD), m. Frederick II, Count de Bar and Duke of Upper Lorraine,

SOPHIA, Countess de Bar-le-Duc, d. about 1092; m., about 1027, Louis, Count de Mouson et de Montbéliard, d. about 1067,

THIERRY II, Count de Mouson et de Montbéliard, Count de Bar-le-Duc, m., about 1076, Ermenson (or Ermentrude) de Bourgogne, dau. of William II (or I?), Count de Bourgogne,

RENAUD I, *le Borgne*, Count de Bar-le-Duc, d. about 1149/50; m., first, Gisele de Vaudemont, dau. of Gerard of Lorraine, Count de Vaudemont, by Hadoide (or Edith), Countess d'Egisheim, dau. of Gerard II, Count d'Egisheim,

RENAUD II, Count de Bar-le-Duc, d. Aug. 10, 1170; m. Agnes de Champagne, dau. of Thibault IV, Count de Champagne, by Maud, dau. of Engilbert II, Count of Ortenburg, and his wife, Edith, dau. of Henry II, Duke of Carinthia,

THIBAUT I, Count de Bar-le-Duc, d. Feb. 2, 1214; m., 2ndly, Isabelle de Bar-sur-Saône, dau. of Guy, Count de Bar-sur-Saône,

HENRY II, Count de Bar-le-Duc, d. about 1240; m., about 1219, Philippine de Dreux, dau. of Robert II, Count de Dreux, by his 2nd wife, Yolande, dau. of Raoul, Sire de Coucy,

THIBAUT II, Count de Bar-le-Duc, d. about 1296/7; m., 2ndly, Joanna de Toci, d. about 1317, dau. of Jean I, Vicomte de Toci (Toucy), by Emma, dau. of Guy VI de Laval,

ISABELLE DE BAR, d. about 1320; m. Guy of Flanders, d. about 1338, son of William of Flanders, and grandson of Guy II, Count of Flanders,

ALICE OF FLANDERS, m., about 1330, Jean of Luxemburg, d. about 1364, son of Waleran II of Luxemburg,

Guy of Luxemburg, Châtelain de Lille, d. about 1371; m., about 1354, Mahaut de Chatillon, Countess de St. Pol (St. Paul), d. about 1378, dau. of Jean de Chatillon, Count de St. Pol, by Joanna de Fiennes,

Jean of Luxemburg, Seigneur de Beaurevoir, d. about 1397; m., about 1380, Marguerite d'Enghien, dau. of Louis d'Enghien, Count de Brienne,

Pierre I of Luxemburg, Count de Conversan et de Brienne, Count de St. Pol, d. about 1433; m., about 1405, Marguerite de Baux, d. about 1469, dau. of Francis de Baux, Duke d'Andria, by Justine (Sueva) des Ursins, dau. of Nicholas des Ursins, Count de Nola, Senator of Rome,

Jaquetta (or Jacqueline) of Luxemburg, b. about 1415/6; d. May 30, 1472; widow of Prince John, Duke of Bedford, K.G., (son of Henry IV, King of England); m., 2ndly, about 1436, Sir Richard Wydeville (Woodville), Earl of Rivers, K.G., beheaded Aug. 12, 1469,

Elizabeth Wydeville (Woodville), b. about 1437; d. June 7, 1492; widow of John, Lord Ferrers of Groby; m., 2ndly, May 4, 1464, Edward IV, King of England, b. Apr. 28, 1442; d. Apr. 9, 1483.

Louis IV, *d'Outre Mer*, King of France, m. Princess Gerberga, widow of Gisilbert, Duke of Lorraine, and dau. of Henry I, *the Fowler*, Emperor of Germany,

Prince Charles of France, Duke of Lower Lorraine, b. about 953; d. about 992/5; m. Bonna d'Ardennes, dau. of Godefroy the Old, Count of Verdun and d'Ardennes,

Princess Adelheid (or Irmgarde), m. Albert I, Count of Namur, d. about 1011, son of Robert I, Count of Lomme,

Albert II, Count of Namur, m. Regilinde de Lorraine, dau. of Gothelon I, Duke of Upper and Lower Lorraine,

Albert III, Count of Namur, m. Ida (or Relinde) of Saxony, widow of Frederick, Duke of Lower Lorraine, and dau. of Bernard II, Duke of Saxony, by Bertrade, dau. of Harold II, King of Norway,

Ida of Namur, m. Godfrey I, Duke of Lower Lorraine, d. about 1140, son of Henry II, Count de Louvaine,

Godfrey II, Duke of Lower Lorraine, m. Luitgarde of Sultzbach, dau. of Berenger I, Count of Sultzbach, and granddau. of Gebhard I, Count of Sultzbach,

Godfrey III, Duke of Lower Lorraine, Count de Louvaine, m. Margaret de Limburg, dau. of Henry II, Count de Limburg, by his first wife, Mathilda, dau. of Adolph, Count of Saffenberg (Saphenberg) and Seigneur de Rolduc,

Henry I, Duke of Brabant, d. Sept. 5, 1235; m., first, Mathilda (or Maud), dau. of Matthew of Alsace, Count of Boulogne,

Henry II, Duke of Brabant, d. Feb. 1, 1247/8; m., first, Mary of Hohenstauffen, dau. of Philip II, Emperor of Germany, and granddau. of Frederick I, *Barbarossa*, Emperor of Germany, and had,

> 1.) Henry III, Duke of Brabant, d. Feb. 28, 1260/1; m. Alice de Bourgogne, d. Oct. 23, 1273, dau. of Hugh IV, Duke of Bourgogne, and his wife, Yolande, dau. of Robert, Count de Dreux, and had,
>
> > a) Marie de Brabant, m., (his 2nd wife), Philippe III, *le Hardi* and *Coeur de Lion*, King of France, and had,

i PRINCESS MARGARET, b. 1279; d. Feb. 14, 1317; m., Sept. 8, 1299, (his 2nd wife), Edward I, King of England, b. June 17, 1239; d. July 7, 1307.

2.) MATHILDA OF BRABANT, d. Sept. 29, 1288; m., first, about 1237, Robert, Count of Artois, son of Louis VIII, King of France; m., 2ndly, Guy de Chatillon, Count de St. Pol, who d. Mar. 12, 1289.

Louis IV, *d'Outre Mer,* King of France,

See Page 274

Albert III, Count de Namur, d. about 1105; m. Ida (or Relinde), widow of Frederick, Duke of Lower Lorraine, and dau. of Bernard II, Duke of Saxony, by Bertrade, dau. of Harold II, King of Norway,

Godfrey, Count de Namur, d. Aug. 19, 1139; m., 2ndly, Ermenson (or Ermensinde), d. June 24, 1143, widow of Albert, Count of Dagsburg, and dau. of Conrad I, Count of Luxemburg,

Henry, *l'Aveugle,* Count de Namur and de Luxemburg, d. about 1196; m., 2ndly, Agnes, dau. of Henry I, Count de Gueldres,

Ermensinde (or Eremansette) de Namur, m., 2ndly, Waleran IV, Marquis d'Arlon, afterwards Duke of Limburg, son of Henry III, Duke of Limburg,

Henry III (or I?) *le Grand* and *le Blond,* Count of Luxemburg et de la Roche, Marquis d'Arlon, d. Dec. 24, 1274; m., about 1240, Marguerite de Bar, d. Nov. 23, 1275, dau. of Henry II, Count de Bar-le-Duc, and his wife, Philippine de Dreux, dau. of Robert II, Count de Dreux,

Waleran I of Luxemburg, Sire de Ligni et de Roussi, d. about 1288; m. Joanna de Beaurevoir (Beaumez),

Waleran II of Luxemburg, m. Guiotte de Lille, dau. of Jean IV de Lille, and his wife, Beatrice, dau. of Simon II de Clermont,

Jean (John) of Luxemburg, d. about 1364; m., about 1330, Alice of Flanders, dau. of Guy of Flanders, and his wife, Isabelle, dau. of Thibaut II, Count de Bar-le-Duc,

Guy of Luxemburg, Châtellain de Lille, d. about 1371; m., about 1354, Mahaut (or Maud) de Chatillon, Countess de St. Pol, dau. of Jean de Chatillon, Count de St. Pol,

Jean (John) of Luxemburg, Seigneur de Beaurevoir, d. about 1397; m., about 1380/9, Marguerite d'Enghien, dau. of Louis d'Enghien, Count de Brienne.

Hugh Capet, King of France, m. Adelaide,

Princess Hedwige, m., first, Regnier IV, Count of Hainault, d. about 1013,

Regnier V, Count of Hainault, d. about 1030; m. Mathilda (or Maud) of Lorraine, dau. of Hermann, Vicomte de Verdun,

Richilde of Hainault, d. about 1086, widow of Hermann, Count of Hennegau; m., 2ndly, about 1055, Baldwin VI, Count of Flanders and Hainault, d. July 17, 1070, son of Baldwin V, Count of Flanders, and his wife Adele (Adelheid), widow of Richard III, Duke of Normandy, and dau. of Robert II, the Pious, King of France,

Baldwin II, Count of Hainault, d. about 1099; m., about 1084, Alix (or Ida) de Louvaine, d. about 1139, dau. of Henry II, Count of Louvaine,

Baldwin III, Count of Hainault, d. about 1120; m. Yolanda de Gueldre, dau. of Gerard I de Wassenberg, Count de Gueldre,

Baldwin IV, *le Bâtisseur*, Count of Hainault, d. Nov. 8, 1171; m. Ermessinde (or Alix), dau. of Godfrey, Count de Namur,

Baldwin V, *le Courageux*, Count of Hainault, d. Dec. 17, 1195; m., about 1169, Margaret I of Flanders, d. Nov. 15, 1194, dau. of Theodore, Count of Flanders, (by Sibyl d'Anjou, dau. of Fulk V, Count d'Anjou, by Ermengarde du Maine), and granddau. of Theodore I, Duke of Lorraine,

Baldwin VI, Count of Hainault and Flanders, afterwards Emperor of Constantinople as Baldwin IX, d. about 1206; m. Marie de Champagne, dau. of Henry, Count de Champagne, and his wife, Princess Maria, dau. of Louis VII, King of France, by his first wife, Eleanor of Aquitaine,

Margaret, Countess of Hainault and Flanders, d. about 1280; m., first, about 1212, Bouchard d'Avênes, Archidiacre de Laon et Chanorne de S. Pierre de Lille, d. about 1243/4, (marriage allegedly dissolved by divorce about 1221), son of Jacques d'Avênes,

Jean d'Avênes, Count of Holland, d. about 1256; m. Adelheid, d. about 1284, dau. of Florent IV, Count of Holland, and his wife, Mechtild, dau. of Henry I, Duke of Brabant,

JEAN I, Count of Hainault, d. about 1304; m. Phillippa, dau. of Henry II (or I?), Count of Luxemburg,

WILLIAM, *le Bon,* Count of Hainault and of Holland, d. about 1337; m., about 1305, Joanna (or Jane), d. about 1352, dau. of Charles, Count de Valois, and granddau. of Philippe III, *le Hardi,* King of France,

PHILIPPA OF HAINAULT, b. about 1312; d. Aug. 14/5, 1369; m., Jan. 24, 1327/8, Edward III, King of England, b. Nov. 13, 1312; d. June 21, 1377.

HENRY I, *the Fowler,* Emperor of Germany, d. July 2, 936; m., 2ndly, Mathilda, dau. of Dietrich, Count von Ringelheim,

PRINCESS GERBERGA, m., first, Gisilbert, Duke of Lorraine; she m., 2ndly, Louis IV, *d'Outre Mer,* King of France, (the question arises whether Princess Albreda, mentioned below, was the daughter by the first or second husband, authorities differ, however, whether by the first or second husband, the line as set down here is equally good),

PRINCESS ALBREDA, m. Renaud (or Ragenolde), Count de Rheims and de Roucy, d. about Mar. 15, 973,

GILBERT (OR GISILBERT), Count de Roucy, d. about 990, father of,

EBLES I, Count de Rheims and de Roucy, Archbishop of Rheims, d. about May 11, 1033; m. Beatrix (or Beatrice), dau. of Rainier (or Regnier) IV, Count of Hainault, and his wife, Princess Hedwige, dau. of Hugh Capet, King of France,

ALIX (OR ALICE OR ADELAIDE), h. of Roucy, m. Hildouin III, Count de Montdidier, Seigneur de Rameru, d'Arcis et de Breteuil, Count de Roucy,

HILDOUIN IV, Count de Montdidier, Count de Roucy, &c., d. about 1063; m. Adelaide, sister of Manasser, Archbishop of Rheims, and dau. of Manasser, Count de Rheims,

BEATRIX DE MONTDIDIER, m. Geoffrey II (or I?), Count du Perche,

MAHAUT (OR MATHILDA) DU PERCHE, m. Raymond I, Vicomte de Turenne, son of Boso I, Vicomte de Turenne,

MARGUERITE DE TURENNE, m., 3rdly, William IV, Count d'Angouleme, (his 2nd wife), d. about 1178, son of Wulgrin II, Count d'Angouleme,

AYMER DE VALENCE, Count d'Angouleme, d. about 1218; m. Alice de Courtenay, dau. of Pierre I de Courtenay, and granddau. of Louis VI, *le Gros,* King of France,

ISABELLE D'ANGOULEME, only dau. & h., d. May 31, 1246; m., Aug. 24, 1200, (his 2nd wife), John, King of England, b. Dec. 24, 1166; d. Oct. 19, 1216,

HENRY III, King of England, b. Oct. 1, 1207; d. Nov. 16, 1272; m., Jan. 14, 1236, Eleanor, dau. & co-h. of Raymond Berenger, Count of Provence.

BIBLIOGRAPHY

— A —

ABEL, S., & SIMSON, B.: Jahrbuecher des frankischen Reichs unter Karl dem Grossen. 2nd ed., 1888.

ALLAIS, VITON DE S.: Nobiliaire Universel de France. 1838.

ALLSTROM, C. M.: Dictionary of Royal Lineage in Europe. 1904. 2 vols.

AMERICAN GENEALOGIST, THE.

ANGLO-SAXON CHRONICLE, THE. Edited by Charles Plummer. 1892-99. 2 vols.

ANSELME, LE PÉRE: Histoire généalogique et chronologique de la Maison Royale de France, des Grands Officiers de la Couronne et de la Maison du Roy. 3rd ed., 1726-33.

ART, L': De Vérifier Les Dates des Faits historiques, des Chartres, des Chroniques, en autres anciens, 3rd ed., 1820-38. 8 vols.

ASSIGNY, D': Histoire des Comtes de Flandre. 1698.

— B —

BAINES, E.: History of the County Palatine of Lancaster. Edited by J. Croston. 1888-93. 5 vols.

BALUZE: Histoire de la Maison d'Auvergne.

BALZER, O.: Genealogia Piastow. 1895.

BANKS, T. C.: The Dormant and Extinct Baronage of England. 1807-09. 3 vols.

BAUER, H.: Abstammung der Würtembergischen Fürstenhäuser.

BEHR, K. VON: Genealogie der Fürstenhäuser. 1854.

BERRY, WILLIAM: Pedigrees of Berkshire, Buckinghamshire and Surrey Families. 1837.

Pedigrees of Essex Families. 1840.

Pedigrees of the Families in the County of Hants. 1833. 2 vols.

Pedigrees of the Families of the County of Kent. 1830.

Pedigrees of the Families in the County of Sussex. 1830.

Pedigrees of Hertfordshire Families. 1844.

BETHAM, REV. WILLIAM: Genealogical Tables of the Sovereigns of the World, 1795.

BETHANCOURT, D. FRANCISCO FERNANDEZ DE: Historia Genealógica y Heráldica de la Monarquía Española, Casa Real y Grandes de España. 10 vols.

BLAYDES, F. A.: Genealogia Bedfordiensis.

BRANDENBURG, PROF. DR. ERICH: Die Nachkommen Karl des Grossen. 1935.

BRENAN, G.: House of Percy. 1902.

BRESZLAU, H.: Jahrbuecher des Deutschen Reichs unter Konrad II. 1879-81.

BRIDGER, CHARLES: Index to Printed Pedigrees, Contained in County and Local Histories, etc. 1867.

BROWN, P. HUME: History of Scotland to the Present Time. 1911.

BURKE: A Genealogical and Heraldic Dictionary of the Landed Gentry of Great Britain and Ireland, 1849-50, 3 vols.; 8th ed., 1894, 2 vols.

A Genealogical and Heraldic History of the Commoners of Great Britain and Ireland. 1836-38. 4 vols.

Genealogical and Heraldic History of the Extinct and Dormant Baronetcies of England, Ireland, and Scotland. 1838.

A Genealogical and Heraldic History of the Landed Gentry of Great Britain, 12th ed., revised by Arthur C. Fox-Davies, 1914; 13th ed., edited by A. W. Thorpe, 1921.

A Genealogical and Heraldic History of the Landed Gentry of Ireland. Edited by Arthur C. Fox-Davies. 1912.

Genealogical History of the Dormant, Abeyant, Forfeited and Extinct Peerages of the British Empire, 1883.

A visitation of the Seats and Arms of the Noblemen and Gentlemen of Great Britain. 1852-55. 4 vols.

BURY, BARONESS DE: Life of the Princess Palatine.

— C —

CAMPBELL, JOHN A.: Royal Families of Scotland. 1863.

CAMPRESIS, DU: L'Estat de la Noblesse.

CARPENTIER, JEAN LE: Histoire généalogique des Païs Bas. 1664.

CHARLEMAGNE, ORDER OF THE CROWN OF: Publications.

CHENAY DES BOIS: Dictionnaire de la Noblesse. 1863.

CHESNE, ANDRE DU: Histoire généalogique des Maisons de Guines, d'Ardres, de Gand et de Coucy. 1631.
Histoire de la Maison de Chastillon-sur-Marne. 1621.

CHESNE, JEAN DU: Histoire de la Maison Royale de Courtenay. 1661.

CLAY, JOHN W.: Extinct and Dormant Peerage of the Northern Counties. 1913.

CLEVELAND, DUCHESS OF: The Battle Abbey Roll, with some account of the Norman Lineages. 1889. 3 vols.

COKAYNE, GEORGE EDWARD: The Complete Baronetage. 1900-1909. 6 vols.

COKAYNE, GEORGE EDWARD: The Complete Peerage. New Edition. Vols. I-IX. 1910-36.
The Complete Peerage, etc. 1887-98. 8 vols.

COLKET, JR., MEREDITH B.: The Marbury Ancestry. 1936.

COLLEGIO ARALDICO: Libro della Nobiltà Italiana. 1939. 2 vols.

COLLINS, ARTHUR: The Baronettage of England. 1720. 2 vols.
The Peerage of England. Edited by Sir Egerton Brydges. 5th edition. 9 vols.

COLONIAL DAMES OF AMERICA, NATIONAL SOCIETY OF: Publications.

COLONIAL DAMES OF THE SEVENTEETH CENTURY, SOCIETY OF:
Publications,

COLONIAL WARS, SOCIETY OF: Publications.

COLONIAL WARS, SOCIETY OF DAUGHTERS OF: Publications.

COURCELLES, DE: Dictionnaire Universel de la Noblesse de
France. 1820-22. 5 vols.

COURTHOPE, WILLIAM: Historic Peerage of England. 1857.

CRISP, FREDERICK ARTHUR, AND J. JACKSON HOWARD: Visitations of England and Wales. 1893-1921. 21 vols.

CROSSLEY, AARON: The Peerage of Ireland. 1725.

— D —

D. A. C.: Lineage Books.

D. A. R.: Lineage Books.

DAMBERGER, J. F.: Fürstentafel. 1831.

DEBRETT, J.: The Baronetage of England, etc. 1832. 2 vols.

DICTIONARY OF NATIONAL BIOGRAPHY.

DOUGLAS, ROBERT: The Baronage of Scotland. 1798.
THE PEERAGE OF SCOTLAND. 1864.

DOYLE, J. E.: The Official Baronage of England. 1886. 3 vols.

DUGDALE, SIR WILLIAM: The Baronage of England. 1675-76.
2 vols.

DUNBAR, A. H.: Scottish Kings. 1899. 2nd ed., 1906.

DUNCAN, JONATHAN: Dukes of Normandy. 1839.

DUNGERN, VON: Thronfolgerecht und Blutverwandtschaft der
deutschen Kaiser seit Karl den Grossen. 2nd ed. 1910.

— E —

EDMONDSON, JOSEPH: An Historical and Genealogical Account
of the Noble Family of Greville. 1766.

ELLENDORF, J.: Die Karolinger und die Hierarchie ihrer Zeit.
2 vols. 1868.

EYTON, R. W.: The Antiquities of Shropshire. 1854-60. 12 vols.

FAVYN, ANDRÉ: Le Théâtre d'Honneur et de Chevalerie, où Histoire des Ordres Militaires de Roys et Princes de la Chrestiente, et leurs Généalogie, etc. 1620. 2 vols. (English Translation. 1623.)

FEST, ALEXANDER: The Sons of Edmund Ironside at the Court of St. Stephen. 1938.

FINLAY, R. M.: Mainwaring Family. 1890.

FLETCHER: Leicestershire Pedigrees and Royal Descents.

FORDUN, JOHANNES DE: Chronica gentis Scotorum. Edited by W. F. Skene. 1871.

FORESTER: Memoirs of Sophia, Electress of Hanover.

FOSTER, JOSEPH: Noble and Gentle Families of Royal Descent. 1885-91. 3 vols. in 4 vols.
Pedigrees of the Leading Families of Lancashire. 1872.
Peerage, Baronetage, and Knightage of the British Empire. 1881.
Stemmata Britannica. 1877.

FOX-DAVIES, ARTHUR C.: Armorial Families. 7th edition. 1929. 2 vols.
Complete Guide to Heraldry. 1920.
Heraldry Explained. 1908.

FREEMAN, EDWARD A.: History of the Norman Conquest.
Western Europe in the Eighth Century and Onward. 1904.

GARNIER, E.: Tableaux généalogique des Souverains. 1863.

GARRAFFA, ALBERTO Y ARTURO GARCIA: Encicloppedia Heráldica y Genealógica Hispano-Americana. 57 vols.

GENEALOGICAL ADVERTISER, THE.

GENEALOGICAL MAGAZINE, THE.

GENEALOGISCHES TASCHENBUCH DER ADELIGEN HÄUSER. 1870-94. 19 vols.

GENEALOGIST, THE.

GENEALOGISTS' MAGAZINE, Organ of the Society of Genealogists, London.

GENEALOGY AND HISTORY.

GEORGEL, J. ALCIDE: Amorial Historique et Généalogique des Familles de Lorraine. 1882.

GOETHALS: Histoire généalogique de la Maison de Hornes. 1848.

GOTHA, ALMANACH DE.
Freiherrliches Taschenbuch.
Gräfliches Taschenbuch.

GOTHAISCHER GENEALOGISCHER HOFKALENDER.

GRANT, LORD LYON, SIR FRANCIS J.: Manual of Heraldry. 1924.

GREEN, MRS. EVERETT: Lives of the Princesses of England.

GROTE, H.: Stamm Tafeln. 1877.

— H —

HALL, MRS. MATTHEW: Royal Princesses of England.

HALL, SPENCER: Echyngham of Echyngham. 1850.

HANMER, CALVERT: Hanmers of Marton and Montford, Salop. 1916.

HARCOURT-BATH, WILLIAM: The Harcourt Families of England and France.

HARLEIAN SOCIETY, PUBLICATIONS OF.

HARRISON, H. G.: A Select Bibliography of English Genealogy. 1937.

HARTFORD TIMES, THE. Genealogical Section.

HAUTERIVE, BOREL D': Annuaire de la Pairie et de la Noblesse de France et des Maisons Souverains de l'Europe. 1843-72. 17 vols.

HAYDEN, HORACE E.: Virginia Genealogies. 1931.

HEITMAN, FRANCIS B.: Historical Register of Officers of the Continental Army During the War of the Revolution, April, 1775, to December, 1783. 1914.

HODGKIN, T.: Charlemagne.

HOEUTH, DR. CHRISTIAN: Genealogie des Erlauchten Stamm-hauses Wittelsbach. 1870.

HOFMEISTER, G. E.: Genealogie des Hauses Wettin. 1858.

HOLLAND, B. H.: The Lancashire Hollands. 1917.

HOPE, ASCOTT R.: Royal Youths.

HOPPIN, CHARLES ARTHUR: The Washington Ancestry, etc. 1932. 3 vols.

HOTTEN, JOHN CAMDEN: The Original List of Persons . . . who went from Great Britain to the American Plantations, 1600-1700. 1874.

HOZIERS, CHARLES D': Armorial Général de France.

HUEBNER, J.: Genealogische Tabellen. 1737.

HUGUENOT SOCIETY OF AMERICA, PUBLICATIONS OF.

HUGUENOT SOCIETY OF LONDON, PUBLICATIONS OF.

— J —

JACOBUS, DONALD LINES: The Bulkeley Genealogy. 1933. The Waterman Family. Vol. I. 1939.

— K —

KEITH, C. P.; The Ancestry of Benjamin Harrison, President of the United States. 1893.

KLEINCLAUCZ: L'Empire Carolingien, ses origines et ses trans-formations.

KNESCHKE, DR. ERNST HEINRICH: Neues allgemeines Deutsches Adels-Lexicon.

KNETSCH: Das Haus Brabant. 1917.

KOCH, C. G. DE: Tables généalogiques des Maisons Souverains du Nord, et de l'Est de l'Europe. 1815.

KREMER, J. M.: Genealogische Geschichte d. alten Ardennis-chen Geschlechtes. 1785.

KRUEGER, E.: Der Ursprung des Welfenhauses. 1899.

— L —

LANE, HENRY M.: The Royal Daughters of England. 1910. 2 vols.

LANG, ANDREW: A History of Scotland from the Roman Occupation. 1907.

LAPPENBERG, J. M.: Anglo-Norman Kings. 1857.

LATRIE: Trésor de Chronologie. 1889.

LAVOISME, PROF. C. V., AND C. GROS: Genealogical, Historical, and Chronological Atlas. 1807.

LEFORT, ALFRED: La Maison Souveraine de Luxembourg. 1902.

LEVILLAIN, L.: Recueil des actes de Pépin I et de Pépin II, rois d'Aquitaine.

LIEBERMANN, F.: Die Gesetze der Angelsachsen. 2 vols. 1898, 1906.
Ungedruckte Anglo- Normannische Geschichtsquellen. 1879.

LLOYD, J. Y.: Princes of Powys Vadoc. 1881.

LODGE: Peerage of Ireland. 1838.

LODGE, S.: Scrivelsby, the Home of the Champions, etc. 1893.

LOHMEIER, G.: Der Europaischen Kayser und Königlichen Häuser. 1730.

LOT, F.: Les Derniers Carolingiens (Bibliothèque de l'Ecole des Hautes Etudes, 87). 1891.

LYNCH: Feudal Baronies in Ireland. 1830.

— M —

MALMESBURY, WILLIAM OF: Chronicle of the Kings of England, from the earliest period to the Reign of King Stephen. Edited by J. A. Giles. 1911.

MARSHALL, GEORGE W.: The Genealogist's Guide to Printed Pedigrees. 1893.

MAYFLOWER DESCENDANTS, THE GENERAL SOCIETY OF: Publications.

MEARS, W.: The Lives of the Princes of the House of Orange. 1734.

MICHAUD, M.: Biographie Universelle Ancienne et Moderne . . . 1854-65. 45 vols.

MIGNE, J. P.: Patrologiae cursus completus, Series graeca. 161 vols. in 166.

MISCELLANEA GENEALOGICA ET HERALDICA. Five Series. Edited by A. W. Hughes Clarke et al.

MULHBACHER, E.: *Regesti Imperii I.* Regesten des Kaiserreichs unter den Karolingern. 2nd edition. 1899-1908. (Lechner).

— N —

NANTIGNY, CHASOT DE: Généalogies des Rois. 1736.

NATIONAL GENEALOGICAL SOCIETY QUARTERLY.

NEW ENGLAND HISTORICAL AND GENEALOGICAL REGISTER, THE. A Roll of Arms. 1928-40. 4 parts.

NEW YORK GENEALOGICAL AND BIOGRAPHICAL RECORD, THE.

NICHOLS, FRANCIS: The English Compendium. 10th edition. 1753. 3 vols.
The Scots Compendium. 1756.

NICHOLS, JOHN: Collectanea Topographica et Genealogica. 1834-43. 8 vols.

NICOLAS, SIR NICHOLAS HARRIS: Synopsis of the Peerage of England. 1825. 2 vols.

NOBLE, MARK: A Genealogical History of the Present Royal Families of Europe, etc. 1781.

NORTH CAROLINA HISTORICAL AND GENEALOGICAL REGISTER. Edited by J. R. B. Hathaway. 1900-03. 3 vols.

— O —

O'HART, JOHN: Irish Pedigrees. American Ed. 1915. 2 vols.

OMAN, CHARLES: England Before The Norman Conquest. 1910.

ORDER OF THE FOUNDERS AND PATRIOTS OF AMERICA, REGISTER OF. 1926.
Supplement. 1940.
Bulletin of.

ORDERICUS VITALIS: The Ecclesiastical History of England and
Normandy. English Translation by Thomas Forester.
1853-57. 4 vols.

ORMEROD, GEORGE: History of the County Palatine of Chester.
2nd ed. Edited by Thomas Helsby. 1882. 3 vols in 6.

— P —

PARISOT, ROBERT: Le Royaume de Lorraine sous les Carolingiens. 1899.

PAUL, SIR JAMES BALFOUR: Scots Peerage. 1904-14. 9 vols.

PENNSYLVANIA, GENEALOGICAL SOCIETY OF: Publications.

PERRY, W. C.: The Franks. 1857.

PHILLIPPS, SIR THOMAS: Glamorganshire Pedigrees.

PLANCHÉ, JAMES R.: The Conqueror and His Companions.

— R —

RAUSCHEN, G.: Die Legende Karls d. Gr. im 11. und 12.
Jahrhundert. 1890.

REVUE NOBILIAIRE. 1862-80. 17 vols.

RICHARD, A.: Histoire des comtes de Poitou. 1903. 2 vols.

RIETSTAP, J. B.: Armorial Général . . . Reprint, 1934. 2 vols.
(Original edition published at Gouda, 1884). Supplements
edited by V. H. Rolland, 1926-37. 4 vols.

ROBERTSON, GEORGE: A Genealogical Account of the Principal
Families of Ayrshire. 3 vols.

ROLLS SERIES: Rerum Britannicarum medii aevi scriptores.
London, 1858.

ROQUE, G. A. LA: Historie de la Maison de Harcourt. 1662.

ROUND, J. HORACE: Family Origins, and Other Studies. Ed-
ited by William Page. 1930.
Peerage and Pedigree. 1910. 2 vols.
Studies in Peerage and Family History. 1901.

RUVIGNY AND RAINEVAL, Marquis of: The Blood Royal of Britain. 1903.

The Plantagenet Roll of the Blood Royal. 1905. 1907. 1908. 1911. 4 vols.

Titled Nobility of Europe. 1914.

— S —

SANDFORD, FRANCIS: Genealogical History of the Kings of England and Monarchs of Great Britain, etc. 1707.

SEARLE, W. G.: Anglo-Saxon Bishops, Kings and Nobles. 1899.

SEGRAVE, CHARLES W.: The Segrave Family, 1066-1935. 1937.

SHARPE, THOMASIN E.: A Royal Descent. New Edition, 1904.

SHEPARD, CHARLES: The Lineage of the Counts of Anjou. 1923.

SHIRLEY, E. P.: The Noble and Gentle Men of England. 1859.

SIEBMACHER: Das erneuerte und vermehrte Deutsche Wappenbuch, etc. 1604-1806.

Grosses und Allgemeines Wappenbuch. 1854-1930.

SKELTON, JOHN: Mary Stuart. 1893.

SMITH, SHIRLEY: Genealogy of Queen Victoria from Adam and Eve. 1885.

SOUSA, A. C.: Historia de Casa Real Portuguesa. 1735.

SOUTH CAROLINA HISTORICAL AND GENEALOGICAL MAGAZINE.

STANARD, WILLIAM G., AND MARY N.: The Colonial Virginia Register. 1902.

STEINDORFF, E.: Jahrbuecher des Deutschen Reichs unter Heinrich III. 1874-81.

STEWART, ROBERT A.: Index to Printed Virginia Genealogies Including Key and Bibliography. 1930.

STOKVIS, A. M. H. J.: Manuel d'Histoire, de généalogie et de chronologie de tous les états du globe, etc. 1888-93. 3 vols.

STRICKLAND, AGNES: Lives of the Queens of Scotland from the Norman Conquest. 1871. 6 vols.

STUART, MARGARET: Scottish Family History. 1930.

SWALLOW, HENRY J.: De Nova Villa; or the House of Nevill in Sunshine and Shade. 1885.

SZENTPETERY, IMRE: Scriptores Rerum Hungaricarum Saeculi XI-XIII.

— T —

TAYLOR, DR. JAMES: The Great Historic Families of Scotland. 1887. 2 vols.

TAYLOR, W.: The Baronetage of England. 1720. 2 vols.

THROCKMORTON, COL. C. WICKLIFFE: A Genealogical and Historical Account of the Throckmorton Family. 1930.

TOPLIS, W.: A Genealogical History of the English Sovereigns, from William I to George III. 1814.

TOWNEND, WILLIAM: Descendants of the Stuarts. 2nd edition. 1858.

TUCKETT, J.: Devonshire Pedigrees, Recorded in the Herald's Visitation of 1620. 2 vols.

TURTON, LIEUT.-COL. W. H.: The Plantagenet Ancestry. 1928.

TURUL, Organ of the Hungarian Heraldic and Genealogical Society.

TYLER'S QUARTERLY HISTORICAL AND GENEALOGICAL MAGAZINE.

— V —

VALENTINE, EDWARD PLEASANTS: Papers. 1929. 4 vols.

VIRGINIA: The Virginia Magazine of History and Biography, Organ of the Virginia Historical Society, Richmond.
William and Mary College Quarterly Historical Magazine. 1892-1910. New Series, 1921——.

VIRKUS, FREDERICK ADAMS: The Compendium of American Genealogy. 1924-41. 7 vols.

— W —

WARNKOENIG, L. A., & GERARD, P. A. F.: Histoire des Carolingiens. 1862.

WATERS, HENRY F.: Genealogical Gleanings in England, 1901. 2 vols.

WEISS, S.: Tableaux généalogique de la Maison de Bar. 1910.

Westcote, Thomas: Devonshire Pedigrees. 1859.

William and Mary College Quarterly Historical Magazine.

Woegerer, H.: Geschichte Ungarns. 1866.

Woodhull, Mary Gould, and Francis Bowes Stevens: Wood-hull Genealogy. 1904.

Wotton, Thomas: The English Baronetage. 1741. 4 vols in 5.

Wree, Olivier de: La Généalogie des Comtes de Flandre depuis Bavdovin Bras de Fer Iusques à Philippe IV, roy d'Espagne. 1642.

— Y —

Yeatman, J. P.: The Early Genealogical History of the House of Arundel, being an account of the origin of the Families of Montgomery, Albini, FitzAlan, and Howard, from the time of the Conquest of Normandy by Rollo the Great. 1882.

ERRATA

Pages	Lines				
XIV	34	read : ANGOULÊME	instead of : ANGOULEME		
XVIII	1	" WARENNE	" " WARREN		
35	25	" DUKE OF BAVARIA	" " DUKE IN BAVARIA		
37	4	" GRAZ	" " GRATZ		
46	21	" THERESA	" " THERESIA		
47	4	" PRINCE CHARLES	" " PRINCESS CHARLES		
47	32	" FERDINAND I	" " FERDINAND IV		
54	6	" FERDINAND I	" " FERDINAND IV		
54	29	" FERDINAND I	" " FERDINAND IV		
66	33	" SAALFELD	" " SAALFIELD		
87	7	" MECKLENBURG	" " MECKLEMBURG		
89	1	" FREDERICK	" " FREDREICK		
09	6	" KNOKIN	" " KNOCKIN		
18	3	" FRANCIS II	" " FRANCES II		
26	7	" SAIER	" " SAIRE		
38	26	" MAINWARING	" " MANWARING		
63	13-14	" TAVISTOCK	" " TAVISSTOCK		
69	13	" LAYTON	" " LATON		
88	30	" JULIANA	" " JULIAN		
15	8	" JULIANA	" " JULIAN		
23	14	" TYLNEY	" " TILNEY		
30	4	" MECKLENBURG	" " MECKLEMBURG		
47	6	" CHRISTIANA	" " CHRISTIAN		
77	16	" GUELDERS	" " GUELDRE		
77	17	" GUELDERS	" " GUELDRE		
roughout book		" MUNICH	" " MÜNCHEN		
roughout book		" BRUNSWICK-LÜNEBURG	" " BRUNSWICK-LUNEBURG		

INDEX

Bavaria, Crown Princes of, 45, 79; Dukes and Duchesses of, 34, 35, 42, 45, 47, 48, 58, 63, 66, 82, 87, 90, 91, 92, 124, 132, 164, 264, 265, 267, 271; Electors of, 34, 42, 47, 58, 66, 92; Kings and Queens of, 35, 39, 41, 45, 46, 79, 92, 119, 124, 267; Princes and Princesses of, 35, 36, 45, 46, 58, 79, 103.

Bayeux, Vicomte de, 125.

Beare, Isabel, 178; Thomas, 178.

Beauchamp, Anne de, 158; Elizabeth de, 138, 220; Guy de, 121; Isabel de, xxvii, 105, 184, 219, Maud de, xxvii, 121, 189, 215; Richard de, 158, 220; Thomas de, 153, 189, 215; Walter de, xxvii, William de, xxvii, 121, 138, 160, 184, 219.

Beaufort, Edmund, 168; Joan, 141, 150, 168, 199, 220, 244; John, 141, 199.

Beaumont, Hawise, 125; Isabel de, xxvii, 105; Margaret de, xxvi, 129, 133, 137, 157, 188, 219; Robert de, xxvi, xxvii, 105, 125, 133; Robert II, xxvi, 125, 129, 133; Robert III, xxvi, 129, 133; Roger, 125, 133.

Beckett, Beatrice, 170; Gervase, 170.

Bedford, Dukes of, 163, 172, 203, 226, 273; Earls of, 200.

Beke, Elizabeth, 126, 130; Nicholas, 126, 130.

Belgium, Kings and Queens of, 36, 41, 48, 49, 50; Princes of, 36, 41, 48, 49, 50.

Bellomont, (see Beaumont.)

Benham, Paul, 214.

Bercher, Ludeweka, 113.

Bergavenny, (see Abergavenny.)

Berkeley, Humphrey, 108, 211; Isabel de, 188, 215; John, 158; Maurice de, 188, 215; Thomas de, 188.

Berners, Barons of 175, 179, 180.

Berrien, Cornelius, 237; Phebe, 238.

Berry, Dukes of, 52, 59.

Besilles, Elizabeth, 256; William, 255.

Bessborough, Earls of, 228, 229.

Bigod, Hugh le, xxvii, 121, 211; Isabel le, xxvii; Joan le, 211; Maud le, xxvii; Roger le, xxvii, 211.

Billung, Hermann, 183, 235.

Bindette, Elizabeth, 158; John, 158.

Bingham, Edith, 152.

Bird, Dighton, 158; John, 158.

Birdwell Family, 111.

Birge, John, 241; Lucinda, 241; Simeon, 241.

Bishop, Eunice, 254; John, 254.

Blackman, Sarah, 154.

Blandenburg, Duke of, 34.

Blois, Counts of, 56; Madamoiselle de, 47; Stephen of, 56.

Blount, Olivia, 233; William, 233.

Boden, Harry Clark, 131, 136, 256.

Boettiger, Adam, 144; John, 144.

Bohemia, Kings of, 34, 35, 39, 42, 47, 57, 66, 82, 90, 91; Princes of, 57.

Bohun, Alianore de, 179; Elizabeth de, xiv, 174, 220; Humphrey de, xiv, 179, 196; Margaret de, 196; William de, 146, 174, 220.

Clerke, Anne, 154; George, 154; James, 154; Jeremiah, 154; Jeremy, 154, 253; John, 154; Walter, 253; William, 154.

Cleveland, Josiah, 135; Mary, 135.

Cleves, Dukes of, 87, 98, 244.

Clifford, Catherine de, 169; Henry de, 168, 171, 223; Joan de, 189; John de, 189; Margaret de, 171, 223; Philippa de, 153; Robert de, 188, 215; Roger de, 153, 188, 215; Thomas de, 189.

Clinton, John, 121; Margaret de, 122.

Cobb, John, 212; Mildred, 212.

Cochrane, Catherine, 203, 224, 234; John, 224.

Cocke, Elizabeth Pleasants, 109; James, 109; Richard, 109; Thomas, 109.

Coe, Aaron, 127; Cornelia, 128; Sayres, 127.

Cokayne, Elizabeth, 147; John, 147.

Coleman, Ann, 198; John, 198.

Comyn, Alexander, 108, 211; Elizabeth, 108, 137, 211; John, 108, 137, 138, 236; William, 108, 211.

Condé, Prince of, 47.

Connaught, Duke of, 70; Prince Arthur of, 69, 71.

Conrad I, Emperor of Germany, 264; King of Burgundy, 264, 272.

Constable, Henry, 169; Joan, 109; John, 108, 109, 169; Katherine, 169.

Constantinople, Emperors of, 56, 265, 268, 277.

Conyers, John, 109.

Cooke, John, 209; Maria, 209; Mary, 149; Mildred, 148; Mordecai, 209; Robert, 148, 149.

Cope, Charles, 162; Diana, 162; Elizabeth, 258; John, 258; Rachel, 209; William, 209.

Corbet, Robert, 134; William, 121.

Cornell, Deliverance, 253; George, 253; Richard, 253; Thomas, 253.

Cornwall, Earls of, 105, 126.

Cotton, Joanna, 180; John, 138, 180; Roland, 180.

Courtenay, Agnes, 187; Alice de, xiv, 86, 184, 279; Elizabeth, 196; Henry, 186; Hugh, 196; Pierre de, xv, 86, 184, 279; William, 186.

Cracow, Grand Dukes of, 35, 39, 40.

Crane, Isaac, 123; Kate, 123; Matthew, 123.

Cray, Simon de, 165.

Criol, Ida, 165; John de, 165, 219; Nicholas de, xxii, 165.

Croes, Eleanor, 123.

Crowninshield, Fanny, 181.

Croy, 46, 119.

Culpepper, Joyce, 147; Richard, 147.

Cumberland, Earls of, 168, 171, 223.

Cummings, Cornelia, 128; Harry, 128; Philip, 128.

Cushing, Betsy, 144; Harvey, 144.

Cziráky, Countess Marguerite, 172.

303

304

305

Great Britain, Kings & Queens of, 42, 66, 67, 68, 77, 82, 88, 96, 98, 230; Princes and Princesses of, 42, 66, 67, 68, 69, 70, 71, 72, 73.

Greece, Princes of, 43, 55, 69, 72.

Green, Elizabeth, 256; Jacob, 256; Walter, 197.

Greene, Elizabeth, 135, 257; Thomas, 257.

Greenman, Amey, 154, 156; Jeremiah, 154; William, 154.

Gregory (Greogory), Elizabeth, 209; William, 209.

Greville, Margaret, 158; Robert, 200; William, 158.

Grey, Anne de, 199; Catherine de, 205, 226; Charles, 187; Edmund de, 199; Elizabeth, 200; Henry de, 226; John de, 199, 255; Reynold, 199; Richard, 255; Thomas de, 108, 205; William, 170.

Greystoke, Maud de, 216; Ralph de, 215; William de, 215.

Grosvenor, Elizabeth, 134; Randall, 134.

Guelders (Gueldres), Counts of, 276; Dukes of, 244.

Guelph I, 63, 124, 132, 164, 264, 267; IV, 271.

Guise, Dukes of, 54, 55, 65, 82, 119.

Gurdon, Brampton, 175, 180; John, 175, 180; Muriel, 175, 177, 180; Robert, 180.

Gurney, John, 245; Rachel, 245.

Gwynn, Nell, xiii.

— H —

Habsburg, Rudolph von, xiv, 90. (Also, see Austria.)

Hainault, Albert of, 57; Baldwin V of, 64; Margaret of, 57, 58; Philippa of, 64, 81, 141, 150, 168, 179, 199, 208, 244, 268, 278; Regnier III of, 164, 277; William of, 64, 81, 150, 179, 208, 268, 278.

Hales, Alice de, 174; Roger de, 174.

Halifax, Viscounts of, 187.

Hall, Alice, xxv; Benjamin, 253; Edmund, xxiv, xxv; Elizabeth, xxv, xxvi; John, 210; Martha, 210; Patience, 253; Richard, xxv, xxvi; Robert, 110; Sicily Ann, 110; William, 210, 247.

Halsnode, John, xxi, 166; Margaret, xxi, 166.

Hamilton, Archibald, 224; Charlotte, 224; Dukes of, 224; James, 203, 224; William, 224.

Hancock, Margaret, 166; Richard, 166.

Hanover, Electors & Kings of, 42, 66, 82, 92.

Harcourt, Agnes, 175, 180; Alice, 255; Bruno, 55; John, 121, 175, 180, 255; Orabella, xxvi; Richard, xxvi, 255; Thomas, 255; William, xxvi, 255.

Harewood, Earl of, xiii, 68.

Harfleet, Henry, 166; Margaret, xxi, xxii; Martha, 166; Thomas, 166.

Harrison, Ann, 221; Benjamin, 194; Elizabeth, 195; John, 194; Marthena, 195; Mary, 195; Russell, 194; William Henry, 194.

Hasbaye, Count of, 124, 183, 267.

Hastang, John, 126, 130, 157; Maud, 126, 130, 157.

Hooker, Edward, 107; Loua, 107; Margaret, 107; Roland, 107; Thomas, xxii.

Hooper, Marian, 182; Robert, 182.

Horn, Agnes, 142; James, 142.

Horsmanden, Daniel, 221; Maria, 221; Warham, 221.

Howard, Bernard, 206, 207; Charles, 186; Dorothy, 223; Edmund, 147; Edward, 207; Elizabeth, 186; Francis, 186; George, 227; Harriet, 227; Henry, 205, 206; John, 146, 174, 179, 185; Katherine, 147, 175, 179; Margaret, 147; Matthew, 186; Philip, 205; Robert, 146, 174, 185; Thomas, 146, 185, 186, 205, 223; William, 185.

Howell, John, 212.

Hozier, Clementine, 234; Henry, 234.

Hugh, Capet, King of France, xiv, xxv, 63, 124, 267, 277, 279.

Hugh, "of Kevelioc," 129, 157, 219; the Great, xiv, 63, 120, 121, 124, 125, 133, 267.

Hungary, Kings of, 35, 39, 40, 91, 147, 152, 265, 268, 271; Princes of, 39, 40, 41.

Hungerford, Katherine, 160; Robert, 160.

Huntingdon, Earls of, 165, 208, 270.

Huntly, Earls of, 244; Masters of, 244.

Hutchinson, Ann, 258; Edward, 258; William, 258.

Hyde, John, 148; Mary, 148.

— I —

Illyria, Kings of, 34, 35, 39.

India, Emperors & Empresses of, 88, 96, 98.

Inman, Annie, 213; John, 233.

Irby, John, 134; Olive, 134.

Ireland, 42, 82, 88, 96, 98, 121, 146, 148, 151, 174, 186, 188, 192, 199, 203, 208, 215.

Irvine, Ann, 142; Charles, 142; John, 142.

Irwin, Elizabeth, 194.

Isemburg, Counts of, 84, 85.

Italy, Crown Prince of, 50, 76; Kings & Queens of, 50, 53, 75, 120, 183, 235, 269, 271.

Ivrea, 183, 271.

— J —

Jackson, James, 213; Martha, 213; Thomas, 213; William, 213.

Jacobs, Eliza, 131; Melancthon, 131.

Jacobus, Donald Lines, xiv.

James I, King of Aragon, 64; King of England (& VI of Scotland), 34, 42, 44, 47, 82, 100, 147; King of Scots, 141, 244; II, King of Scots, 244; III, King of Scots, 65, 244; IV, King of Scots, 65, 81, 244; V, King of Scots, 65, 81.

Jeanmougin, Mary Alyce, 113; Henry, 113.

Jennings, Frank, 191; Minerva, 190.

Jerome, Jenny, 234; Leonard, 234.

Jersey, Earls of, 172.

Jerusalem, Kings of, 35, 39, 56, 267.

Luttrell, Andrew, 196, 226; Cecilia, 226; Elizabeth, 196; Hugh, 196.

Luxemburg, Charlotte, Grand Duchess of, 78; Counts of, 183, 235, 268, 271, 272, 273, 276, 278; Dukes of, 85; Grand Duchesses & Grand Dukes of, 45, 61, 77, 78, 79, 83; Princes of, xi, 45, 61, 78, 79, 80, 93.

Lygon, Elizabeth, 158; Frederick, 246; Henry, 158; Maud, 246; Richard, 158.

Lytle, Amanda, 238; James, 238.

— M —

Macomber, Emphraim, 159; Ruth, 159.

Mainwaring, Amicia, xxv; John, 138; Matilda, xxv; Ralph, xxv; Roger, xxv; Thomas, xxv; Warin, xxv; William, 134.

Malcolm III, King of Scotland, xxiv, 184, 236.

Mallet, Mabel, xxiv; William, xxiv.

Mallory, John, 109; Martha, 109; Thomas, 109; William, 109.

Manchester, Dukes of, 200, 201; Earls of, 200, 201.

Manners, Frances, 209; George, 209; Thomas, 209.

Marbury, Anne, 258; Catherine, 253, 258, 260; Francis, 258, 260.

Mareschal, Eve, 255; Isabel, xxvii; Maud, xxvii; William, xxvii, 126, 255.

March, Earls of, 65, 81, 168, 189, 199, 208, 215, 232.

Maria da Gloria II, Queen of Portugal, 118.

Marlborough, Dukes of, 172, 200, 203, 204, 234.

Marshall, Abigail, 241; Family, 112; Samuel, 241.

Martiau, Elizabeth, 212, 216; Nicholas, 212, 216.

Martin, Joseph, 253; Louise, 114; Mary, 253; Nancy, 213; William, 114.

Mather, John, 106; Julia, 107; Roland, 107; Samuel, 106.

Mathilda of Flanders, xv, 56, 57, 184, 235, 269.

Mauduit, Alice, xxvii; Isabel, xxvii, 121; William, xxvii, 121.

Maupassant, Lodoiska de, 110; Pierre de, 110.

Maurienne, Count of, 64.

Maximilian I, Emperor of Germany, 58; Emperor of Mexico, 41; King of Bavaria, 35; II, Emperor of Germany, 58.

McAlpin, Capt. Milo Frederick, 242; Robert, 241.

McAshan, Ann Watkins, 110, 115; Nehemiah, 110.

McKee, Benjamin, 195; James, 195; Mary, 195.

McKinley, 142.

McNally, Charles, 210; Douglas, 210; Susan, 210.

Meaux, Count of, 269.

Mecklenburg, Dukes of, 44, 54, 65, 66, 82, 83, 84, 87, 88, 230.

Meissen, Counts of, 86, 91, 93, 99.

Merrick, Dighton, 158; Isaac, 158.

Metsker, Lois, 112.

Meulan, Counts of, 105, 125, 133.

Mickle, Andrew, 178; George, 178.

Millard, David, 158.

Misnia, (see Meissen.)

Mitchell, Cora, 148; George, 148.

Modena, Dukes of, 40, 44, 47, 51.

Moleyns, William de, 146, 185.

Molyneux, Juliana, 206; William, 206.

Mons, Count of, 164.

Montagu, Alexander, 201; Charles, 200; Edward, 201; Ellen, 202; George, 200, 201; Robert, 200; Roderick, 202; Thomas, 236; William, 201.

Montault, Cicely, xxv; Leuca, xxv; Roger de, xxv.

Montdidier, Counts of, 279.

Montenegro, King of, 75; Princess Helen of, 75.

Montfort, 125, 129, 133; Amauri de, 105; Baldwin, 122; Katharine, 122, 127, 130; Robert, 122, 127; Simon de, xiii; William, 122, 127.

Montgomery, Ellen de, 127, 130; John de, 122, 127; Roger de, xxv, 127, 130; Sibyl de, xxv.

Montpensier, Duke of, 54.

Moon, Frances, 198; James, 198; Mary, 250.

Moore, Anne, 214; Nathaniel, 214.

Morgan, Charles, 181; Henry, 181; John, 181; John Pierpont, 181; Miles, 181

Moriarty, George Andrews, 151, 152; John, 151; Thomas, 151.

Morse, Marian, 182.

Mortimer, Anne de, 81, 208; Catherine, 189, 215; Edmund de, 126, 168, 189, 199, 208; Elizabeth de, 168, 199; Maud, 232; Ralph de, 270; Roger de, 81, 189, 208, 215; 232.

Morton, Earls of, 141, 245.

Moseley, Abigail, 151; David, 106; Grace, 106; John, 106; Joseph, 106.

Morvois, Berthe de, 120.

Mowbray, Alianore de, 160, 216; John de, 146, 160, 174, 185, 216; Margaret de, 146, 174, 185; Thomas de, 146, 174, 185.

Mules, Roger, 105.

Mullery, Helen, 149; Valentine, 149.

Murray, Anne, 224; Charles, 224; John, 223.

Musgrave, Edward de, 189; Eleanor, 189; John, 109; Richard, 189; Thomas, 189; William, 189.

— N —

Namur, Counts of, xxvi, 49, 274, 276, 277.

Naples, Kings of, 268.

Napoleon, Prince Victor, 50.

Nassau, Dukes of, 45, 77, 83, 85; Princes of, 45, 77, 83, 84, 93; William of, 223, 230.

Navarre, 44, 64, 160, 174, 184.

Needham, Dorothy, 138; Robert, 138; Thomas, 138.

Nemours, Dukes of, 48, 118.

Netherlands, Kings & Queens of, 83, Princes of, 84.

Neuerburg, Lords of, 84.

Neville, Alice de, 237; Cecily de, 65, 81; Edward de, 220; Eleanor, 199; George, 209, 220; Henry, 209; Jane, 150; John, 150; Katherine, 150; Mary, 209; Maud, 138; Philippa, 189; Ralph, 65, 81, 150, 168, 189, 199, 208, 220, 237; Richard, 237; Thomas, 138; Ursula, 220.

318